Defensible Programs for Cultural and Ethnic Minorities

Editorial Board

C. June Maker

Critical Issues in

Gifted

Education

Defensible Programs for Cultural and Ethnic Minorities

Editors
C. June Maker
Shirley W. Schiever

VOLUME II

Printed in the United States of America

Library of Congress Cataloging-in-Publication Data

Defensible programs for cultural and ethnic minorities / edited by C.
    June Maker and Shirley W. Schiever.
        p.   cm. — (Critical issues in gifted education)
    Bibliography: p.
    Includes index.
    ISBN 0-89079-184-8
    1. Children of minorities—Education—United States. 2. Gifted
    children—Education—United States. 3. Special education—United
    States. I. Maker, C. June. II. Schiever, Shirley, W. III. Series.
    LC3731.D44 1988
    371.95—dc19   88-992
                                                                                        CIP

8700 Shoal Creek Boulevard
Austin, Texas 78758

10 9 8 7 6 5 4 3 2 1   88 89 90 91 92

To

E. Paul Torrance

respected mentor and teacher
of many authors in this volume

who consistently, kindly, and tirelessly
has reminded all of us

"Differences are not deficits."

and

To

Darrell Anderson

self-taught artist and
"partner in life" of the series editor

who has demonstrated through
his art that

"Differences are not deficits,
but strengths."

Y-US by Darrell Anderson

TABLE OF CONTENTS

Preface   xi
Acknowledgements   xiii
Purpose and Organization of the Volume   xv

Part I: **Hispanics**   **1**

Chapter 1—Situational Identification of Gifted Hispanic Students   5
         Judd Perrine

Chapter 2—Identification of Gifted Hispanic Students: A   19
         Multidimensional View
         Irene Antonia Zappia

Chapter 3—Promoting Pluralism and Power   27
         Clarissa Banda

Chapter 4—"Pluralism and Power"—Dare We Reform Education of the   34
         Gifted Along These Lines?
         Ernesto M. Bernal

Chapter 5—Reaction to "Promoting Pluralism and Power"   37
         Lina S. Rodriguez

Chapter 6—Curriculum for Gifted Hispanic Students   41
         Anne J. Udall

Chapter 7—A Critique of "Curriculum for Gifted Hispanic Students"   57
         Barbara Clark

Chapter 8—Considerations in the Education of Gifted Hispanic Students 60
         Richard Ruiz

Chapter 9—Administrative Implications of a Program and Curriculum for 66
         Gifted Hispanic Students
         Alan M. Weiss

Chapter 10—Summary of Hispanic Section   69
      C. June Maker and Shirley W. Schiever

Part II: **American Indians**   **75**

Chapter 11—Identification of Giftedness Among American Indian People   79
      Diane Montgomery

Chapter 12—Identification of the Gifted and Talented American   91
      Indian Student
      Robert J. Kirschenbaum

Chapter 13—Purpose of Programs for Gifted and Talented and Highly   102
      Motivated American Indian Students
      Anita Bradley Pfeiffer

Chapter 14—Imagining and Defining Giftedness   107
      Karlene R. George

Chapter 15—It's About Time   113
      Stanley G. Throssell

Chapter 16—Programming for the Gifted American Indian Student   116
      Leslie Garrison

Chapter 17—Identifying and Nurturing Talent Among the   128
      American Indians
      Dorothy A. Sisk

Chapter 18—Give Me the Bow, I've Got the Arrow   133
      Charmaine Bradley

Chapter 19—Administrative Implications for Administering Programs for   138
      Gifted and Talented American Indian Students
      Deena Lyn Brooks

Chapter 20—Summary of American Indian Section   142
      C. June Maker and Shirley W. Schiever

Part III: **Asian-Americans**   **149**

Chapter 21—Identification of Gifted Asian-American Students   154
      Jocelyn Chen

Chapter 22—Critique of "Identification of Gifted   163
            Asian-American Students"
            Margie K. Kitano

Chapter 23—Are We Meeting the Needs of Gifted Asian-Americans?   169
            Rosina M. Gallagher

Chapter 24—A Response to "Are We Meeting the Needs of Gifted   174
            Asian-Americans?"
            Kazuko Tanaka

Chapter 25—Personal Reflections on the Purpose of Special Education for   179
            Gifted Asian-Americans
            Elaine Woo

Chapter 26—Teaching Strategies and Practices for the Education of Gifted   182
            Cantonese Students
            Sally Young Wong and Pauline Renee Wong

Chapter 27—The Gifted Asian-American Child: A General Response to a   189
            Specific Issue
            Sandra N. Kaplan

Chapter 28—The Unmentioned Minority   192
            Chris Hasegawa

Chapter 29—Administrative Implications in Developing Programs for   197
            Gifted Asian-American Students
            Paul D. Larson

Chapter 30—Summary of Asian-American Section   201
            C. June Maker and Shirley W. Schiever

Part IV: **Blacks**   **209**

Chapter 31—Identification of Gifted Black Students: Developing   213
            New Perspectives
            Mary M. Frasier

Chapter 32—Standardized Testing for Minority Students: Is It Fair?   226
            Leland Baska

Chapter 33—The Purpose of Education for Gifted Black Students   237
            Alexinia Y. Baldwin

Chapter 34—What the Children Taught Me: Comments on "The Purpose   246
        of Education for Gifted Black Students"
        Leonora M. Cohen

Chapter 35—Successful Adult Response to "The Purpose of Education for   255
        Gifted Black Students"
        Doris Jefferies Ford

Chapter 36—Gifted Black Students: Curriculum and Teaching Strategies   259
        Saundra Scott Sparling

Chapter 37—A Reaction to "Gifted Black Students: Curriculum and   270
        Teaching Strategies"
        E. Paul Torrance

Chapter 38—Black Students and Education: Points for Consideration   275
        Carl A. Grant

Chapter 39—Administrative Reactions to Chapters About Programs for   281
        Gifted Black Students
        Richard W. Ronvik

Chapter 40—Summary of Black Section   285
        C. June Maker and Shirley W. Schiever

Part V: **Volume Conclusion**   **293**

        Programs for Gifted Minority Students: A Synthesis
        of Perspectives
        C. June Maker

Bibliography   311

Index   329

PREFACE

T his book is the second volume in a series entitled *Critical Issues in Education of the Gifted*. The series was conceived and designed as an alternative to establishing a new journal since a book series could provide a forum for the consideration of issues in greater depth than could a journal.

The purpose of the series is to examine critically certain timely and controversial issues in the field of education of the gifted. This undertaking has as its goals the following:

- to rethink old issues
- to challenge the status quo
- to present conflicting opinions
- to generate a dialogue in print
- to analyze trends and directions
- to critique theory, practice, and research
- to provide not just a summary, but a true synthesis and transformation of ideas
- to develop awareness and understanding of new issues and new trends
- to provide new answers to old questions
- to ask new questions

The issues examined are related to all aspects of education of the gifted and include, but are not limited to, program development, curricula, teaching strategies, the nature of giftedness and talent, staff selection and training, sociological perspectives, psychological development, counseling approaches, parent education, research, affective needs, and various subgroups of gifted or talented children.

In each volume, the central issue is examined from a multidisciplinary, multifaceted point of view in an attempt to develop a comprehensive understanding of the various questions involved. Theories relating to the central issue, the research and evaluation data, and practical applications/educational implications are examined in each volume. The underlying philosophy is that comprehensive understanding requires that answers be given based on past experience and empirical data, but that unanswered questions and new perspectives accompany these answers.

Contributing authors are selected who represent a variety of disciplines and a variety of points of view, including theoreticians, researchers, and practitioners.

Most volumes in the series are designed by the series editor, with assistance in acquiring, reviewing, and editing from an advanced doctoral student. In some cases, however, a guest editor is responsible for these tasks. Finally, some volumes, like this one, have a co-editor who shares equally in the responsibilities of developing the plan for the volume and acquiring, reviewing, and editing the manuscripts submitted by chapter authors.

The task of the editor or editors is to reflect upon the different perspectives, identify areas of agreement among the authors, and call attention to other points of view not included in the articles. Finally, the editor's responsibility is to provide a synthesis of various perspectives and suggest possible new directions.

ACKNOWLEDGEMENTS

This book could not have been produced without the assistance and support of many people. In particular, the authors of chapters in this volume were patient, responsive, and dedicated. Many revised their chapters several times, responding to our constant question, "What are some *specific* examples of this idea?" Some even were prompt in meeting deadlines. All were patient as we struggled to produce a book with 38 authors, two editors, four sections, multiple (dependent) deadlines, and finally, two publishers.

Martha Sasser, assistant editor at Aspen, was always available and helpful. She listened to our complaints, helped us locate authors, and sympathized when each new problem arose. Martha was a good friend throughout the process, and we appreciate her help.

Thanks go to Mary Kord and Ann Ferraro for typing our correspondence and for keeping such good records of who had sent what to whom and when. Mary also helped "track down" June in Mexico and protected June from those who might have wanted too many pieces of her too often. Kathy Bolton was fast, accurate, and observant as she typed and revised the manuscript.

Students in the spring 1988 Issues and Research class provided critiques and insights that we were able to incorporate into the final versions of the manuscript. Their comments helped us avoid some miscommunication of ideas.

June wishes to recognize Tomas for his support and respect. Genuine respect for people and their differences characterize his life; his actions speak louder than others' words. Thank you, Tomas, for who you are and what you have taught me.

Shirley wants to recognize publicly what many know: Larry is not only kind, generous, and good-natured, but also unfailingly supportive. Thank you, Larry, for all that you give so willingly.

A final note . . . seldom does one author or editor acknowledge the contribution of co-author or co-editor. However, in this case, I wish to exercise my prerogative as senior author and editor of the series and say a public ''thanks'' to Shirley Schiever, junior editor and chief facilitator of the publication of this book. Every professor should have a student like Shirley Schiever at some time in his or her career, and Shirley was the first doctoral student to begin and end with me as a major advisor. She has set a high standard that few can reach. I cannot list even half of Shirley's assets, so I will not try. I simply will say, if I could choose only one person to give me a critique of something I write or do, I would choose Shirley Schiever.

PURPOSE AND ORGANIZATION OF THE VOLUME

PURPOSE

The title of Chapter 3, "Promoting Pluralism and Power," captures the spirit of this volume. Most, if not all, of the authors subscribe to the underlying philosophy that minority groups have two needs in common—pluralism and power. Pluralism is the means, power a needed result. Pluralism combines a need to preserve one's cultural heritage—one's "roots"—with a need to acquire the skills and knowledge necessary to succeed in the institutions of the majority culture. Power, both individual and collective, personal and cultural, is often lacking, for both social and economic reasons.

Emphasizing and developing true pluralism requires an attitudinal change on the part of educators who must first develop a respect for cultures, values, personal traits, and behaviors different from their own. Next, they must acquire knowledge of these traditions and values and how they can affect behavior, knowledge of the behavioral differences among students of differing backgrounds, and an understanding of the reasons for these differences. Educators must then understand what behaviors of minority students are indicative of giftedness,[1] which behaviors signal high and low motivation, and what behaviors show various other cognitive and affective needs or characteristics. Finally, educators, especially teachers, need to know how to modify their educational programs, curricula, and teaching strategies to enable minority stu-

---

[1] The editors' definition of giftedness includes intellectual abilities usually labeled "gifted" as well as artistic, musical, and other nonintellectual abilities often labeled "talent." Thus, when the word "gifted" is used alone, it is synonymous with the traditional concepts of giftedness and talent. However, some authors in this volume prefer to use both gifted and talented, and to make distinctions between the two terms.

xvi	CRITICAL ISSUES IN GIFTED EDUCATION

dents to be themselves and to be successful. The underlying key to success in these endeavors is the true belief and understanding of Paul Torrance's well-known statement, "Differences are not necessarily deficits," or, as Diane Montgomery so aptly states in Chapter 13, "[D]ifferences are not good or bad, or right or wrong, but are merely differences."

Much evidence exists to demonstrate the powerlessness felt by individuals of minority groups. Our society has changed and enabled more individuals to develop a sense of power than in the past, but the costs have been great and more changes are needed. Three examples are illustrative: (a) Children and youths of minority groups have lower self-concepts than those of "mainstream" American children and youths. (b) The economic status of most minority groups is much lower than that of mainstream Americans. (c) High-level governmental, institutional, and organizational positions are seldom held by individuals from minority groups.

Often, a vicious cycle of powerlessness exists. The adults in a family feel a lack of power, and this lack of power is communicated to their children. When children go to school feeling a sense of personal power, their failure to succeed in the system demonstrates that their sense of power was false. Eventually, entire communities develop a perception of themselves as having no chance to change their status.

What can educators do to break this cycle? First, they can recognize the causes of powerlessness:

- a sense of alienation from their own language and culture when children are not allowed to continue to develop their native language, or when parents can no longer communicate effectively with their children because their children speak a different language;
- the perception that success requires complete emulation of majority culture standards even when different from family standards;
- the lack of a sense of belonging when changes to achieve success in the majority culture result in lack of acceptance in either culture because the minority culture views the change as denial of one's heritage, and the majority culture continues to view the individual as physically and historically different;
- the perception that certain successes are unimportant or not valued in society and in school;
- the attribution of success to luck, and failure to personal inadequacy; and
- the perception that one's abilities are not valued and that people expect failure.

Next, educators can work to eliminate these causes and attempt to develop a sense of personal power in both students and their parents through

- increasing "ownership" of the school experience;
- building cultural "bridges;"
- maintaining and developing bilingualism;
- developing the student's sense of self-worth and potential through experiences with role models and mentors;

- involving families in the setting of educational goals and the design of educational programs for their children;
- developing the perception that teachers *really care* about children's success; and
- avoiding stereotypes, negative expectations, and the behaviors that imply they exist.

Readers now may be asking three common questions:

1. How are the principles you are advocating unique to gifted students from minority groups? Are they not important for all children?
2. What about standards? Are we not advocating a lowering of standards for excellence in education?
3. In what specific ways can the principles for developing power and pluralism be implemented?

In answer to the first question, the underlying principles are not unique, and they certainly are important for all children. However, personal experiences and research demonstrate repeatedly that certain principles are not being followed in the education of all children. Changing the education of gifted students to reflect the principles of pluralism and power is imperative. The gifted students of any minority group are those most likely to break the cycle of powerlessness that exists in our society and become successful not only by their own standards, but also by the standards of mainstream American culture.

The answer to the second question also is clear. The editors are not advocating a lowering of standards. However, we do advocate *changing* the indicators of quality to enable educators to recognize, accommodate, and encourage differences in values.

The answers to the third question are many and are available in this volume.

KEY QUESTIONS AND STRUCTURE OF VOLUME II

The purpose of this volume is to examine critical issues related to the provision of special services for gifted students from populations that are often underserved and that present problems not addressed adequately in most programs for the gifted. Provision of appropriate services for students from special populations is crucial to the survival of programs for gifted students in the 1990s and beyond.

Special populations include cultural and ethnic minorities that present unique problems for educators because of cultural and/or linguistic differences, students with disabilities, and other students who are so different from the gifted students usually served that they require special provisions. Obviously, many different populations could be included. The editors, however, have chosen those who present the greatest problems because of their numbers, their presence in many programs, or their differentness. Therefore, the Hispanic, American Indian, Asian, and Black populations are considered in this volume.

Certain key questions are addressed:

1. How can students from each population be identified?
2. What is the purpose of a special program for gifted students from each population?
3. Should the same type of program be provided for students from special populations that is provided for mainstream gifted students, or should the programs be differentiated?
4. If differentiated, how should the program be modified?
5. What special considerations should be addressed, and what are the administrative implications of proposed changes?

Each question is addressed in depth by individuals from diverse perspectives, experiences, and cultural groups.

The sections about each population are organized in the same manner, and similar issues are discussed. The series format emphasizing lead articles and reactions has been employed, but was modified to fit the critical issue being addressed. Brief descriptions of each section and key questions follow. These descriptions gave direction to authors and now provide an overview of the volume.

Overview and Introduction—description of the population and characteristics of gifted students in the population (by the editors).

Identification—lead article by an expert in providing programs for gifted students in the target population and critique by a school psychologist involved in testing students from the same population.

Key Questions: Who are the gifted students from this population, and how can they be identified?

Guiding Questions:

- What is a good working definition of a gifted student from this population?
- What screening procedures are appropriate?
- What standardized instruments are appropriate?
- What procedures other than standardized instruments would be useful?
- Should the same instruments or procedures be used with this population as those used with mainstream students?
- How should test scores be used?
- Should the same criteria for selection into a program used with mainstream students be used with these students?

Program Purpose—lead chapter and critique by experts in the area, and reaction by an adult from the focus group, preferably not an educator, who, judging from accomplishments, might be considered gifted.

Key Questions: What is the purpose of a special program for gifted students from this population? Should the same type of program be provided for students from special populations that is provided for mainstream gifted students, or should the programs be differentiated? If differentiated, how should the program be modified?

Guiding Questions (for Authors of Lead Chapter and Critique):

- Is the primary purpose of the program to develop abilities valued by the individual student, those valued by the majority culture, or those valued by the minority culture?
- Should the major concern of the program be to provide a bridge between the student's strengths and the requirements of the mainstream culture, or should it be to develop the individual's strengths?
- What role should bilingualism play in the program?

Guiding Questions (for Author of Reaction):

- Based on your experiences in school and as an adult, what is your perception of how the purposes outlined by the author of the lead chapter would have (a) met your needs as a student and (b) prepared you for life as a productive adult?

Curriculum and Teaching Strategies—lead chapter by a practicing teacher, and critique by an expert on curriculum for gifted students.

*Key Questions:*What specific learning experiences do you provide, and what need(s) of the population does each learning experience serve?

Guiding Questions:

- How should/does the curriculum you provide relate to the characteristics of the population and to the purpose of the program?
- What types of learning experiences and/or teaching/learning models are most appropriate for and successful with this population?
- What adaptations, if any, have you made in the particular teaching/learning models you use to make them more useful with this population?
- What materials have you used successfully?

Special Considerations—lead chapter by an educator from the focus population.

*Key Question:*In addition to identification and curriculum development/implementation, what special considerations should be addressed in other areas, such as service delivery (e.g., the manner in which special services are provided); social and emotional development; personal, academic, and career counseling; and role models?

Administrative Implications—reaction chapter by an administrator.

*Key Question:*What administrative implications are suggested by the concerns expressed in the previous chapters?

Section Summary—summary of the points and issues discussed in the section, related to the respective population of gifted students (by the editors).

DEFINING THE HISPANIC POPULATION

Hispanic is a term without precise meaning and, in fact, an extremely inclusive one. In the United States, Hispanic refers to Mexican-Americans or Chicanos, Puerto Ricans, Cubans, and others whose origin may be traced to a Spanish-speaking area. Thus, heritage, sometimes many generations removed, and not language proficiency defines Hispanic.

Other dimensions of Hispanic difference must be considered. Orange County Unified School District (1981), for example, identifies several groups of students within the Hispanic culture: (a) Assimilated students—those with Hispanic surnames whose background is otherwise similar to majority, middle-class students; (b) bilingual students— those who speak primarily Spanish at home, while learning English in school; and (c) Hispanic students new to this country, who may experience many of the same language difficulties of the second group as well as varying cultural expectations at home. Similarly, Ramirez and Castaneda (1974) discuss three types of Mexican-American communities: traditional, dualistic, and atraditional. Both sources outline distinctions among their three groups and discuss the subsequent differences that may be seen in educational settings.

Any Hispanic group also may be affected by the "culture of poverty" (Orange County Unified School District, 1981). Poverty, with its consequent physical deprivation and lack of enrichment, has a profound effect on the development of children.

The editors wish to thank Anne Udall for permitting us to include in this section much information about Hispanics that was originally included in her chapter. Some information also was taken from the chapter by Lina Rodriguez.

1

Hispanic women constitute a special group within the larger Hispanic population, as the dual pressures of being female and Hispanic create a unique set of needs. For the gifted Hispanic female, the additional demands of giftedness may contribute to profound stress.

Gifted Hispanic students who are in special programs are subject to yet another, and often overlooked, influencing factor—the ethnic composition of the special program. Behaviors of the Hispanic students in a program with a Hispanic majority may be remarkably different from those in a class with a non-Hispanic majority.

DEMOGRAPHICS

The Hispanic population is increasing rapidly, and by the year 2000, Hispanics will be the nation's largest ethnic group (Naisbitt, 1982). In the Tucson Unified School District in Tucson, Arizona, for example, of the school-age population, 43 percent of the students are Hispanic, with predictions of an increase to over 50 percent in the next ten years. In San Diego, California, minority students, including a large percentage of Hispanics, already make up 50 percent of the student population. In short, the minority in many school districts is soon to become the majority.

Educators must become more sensitive and responsive to students who are culturally different from the mainstream. Hispanic students, because of their growing numbers and subsequent impact on our schools, require immediate and special attention.

CHARACTERISTICS OF THE GIFTED HISPANIC STUDENT

Identification of gifted Hispanic students has received considerable attention (Argulewicz & Kush, 1984; Bernal, 1974, 1977; Chambers, Barron, & Spencer, 1986; Clarizo, 1982), but development of appropriate processes is needed. Characteristics of the students to be served should provide the foundation for a definition of giftedness, procedures for identification, and curriculum practices in a program for the gifted. What are the characteristics of the gifted Hispanic student? More importantly, how do these characteristics differ from those of gifted nonHispanic students? Answers to these questions are keys to the identification process.

One must, however, proceed with caution in answering these questions. Until more data are collected on the characteristics of gifted Hispanic students, care must be taken in generalizing from those few data that exist. Not all Hispanic students will exhibit the characteristics discussed here, nor will all respond to the strategies and techniques presented.

In short, one cannot assume that all Hispanic students are alike. As with all students, the cultural and social influences surrounding specific groups of Hispanics vary, and educators must identify these influences. Castaneda (1976) lists six factors to consider when working with a group of Mexican-American (Hispanic) students: (a) length of residence in the United States; (b) distance from the Mexican border; (c) degree of urbanization; (d) degree of economic and political strength of Mexican-Americans in the community; (e) identity with Mexican and/or Mexican-American history; and (f) degree of prejudice toward Mexican-Americans in the community. These six factors can be adapted to any situation.

All gifted students possess cognitive, affective, and social characteristics that distinguish them from students who are not considered gifted. A common assumption in the study of special populations is that these distinguishing characteristics vary among groups. For example, educators often assume that Hispanic students will have different cognitive, affective, and social characteristics from those of Anglo-American students. Others, however, believe that the characteristics that distinguish gifted students from students who are not gifted are the same, regardless of cultural or economic differences.

Leung (1981) provides a resolution of these opposing views by suggesting two categories of characteristics of giftedness: *absolute* aspects, or the underlying traits transcending historical time and cultural context, and *specific* aspects, or the behavioral manifestations of giftedness. Absolute traits are similar across cultural and economic groups, while specific traits vary.

Leung and others believe that absolute aspects of giftedness are "filtered" through a cultural context, and that this filtering results in particular clusters of traits labeled specific giftedness. Thus, the relationship is linear:

Absolute Traits $\longrightarrow$ Cultural Context $\longrightarrow$ Specific Behaviors

However, research and personal experience suggest that the relationship is not so simple.

Gardner (1983) states that for high levels of competence in any type of intelligence to develop, three conditions must be present: physiological capacity (or what some call "hard wiring"), motivation, and opportunities. Physiological capacity usually is determined by heredity, while motivation and opportunities are determined by social, economic, and cultural conditions.

Gardner's ideas thus can be combined with Leung's and, continuing to use a linear model, suggest that absolute traits correspond to physiological capacity; social, economic, and cultural influences constitute the cultural context; certain motivations and opportunities result from this context; and specific behaviors indicative of giftedness ultimately result from this cause-effect chain. The true spirit of Gardner's ideas, and certainly the philosophy of the editors and many authors in this volume, is that all these factors interact to produce behavioral differences in students.

To illustrate the process educators should follow, and to present a synthesis of ideas regarding the characteristics of giftedness in Hispanic students, Leung's concepts have been integrated with information from the chapters in this section and research on characteristics of gifted Hispanic students.

In Table I-1, absolute aspects of giftedness (Clark, 1983), the cultural values generally characteristic of Hispanics, and examples of the behavioral differences that can result from the interaction of these characteristics of giftedness with cultural values are listed.

As the reader peruses the following chapters, the complexity of educating gifted Hispanic students appropriately becomes increasingly apparent. However, the authors present insights and recommendations that make such an education more a possible achievement than an impossible dream.

Table I-1 Characteristics of Giftedness and Cultural Values of Hispanics, and the Behaviors Resulting from Their Interactive Influence

Absolute Aspects of Giftedness	Cultural Values Often Characteristic of Hispanics	Behavioral Differences
High level of verbal ability	Traditional language of family	Communicates fluently with peers and within community, even if using nonstandard English
Emotional depth and intensity	*Abrazo,* a physical or spiritual index of personal support	Requires touching, eye contact, feeling of support to achieve maximum academic productivity
Unusual sensitivity to feelings and expectations of others	Family structure and dynamic-male dominance	Personal initiative, independent thought, and verbal aggressiveness often inhibited in females
Conceptualize solutions to social and environmental problems	Nuclear and extended family closeness valued	Often assumes responsibility for family and/or younger siblings
Unusual retentiveness; unusual capacity for processing information	Traditional culture	Adapts to successful functioning in two cultures
Leadership	Collaborative rather than competitive dynamic	Accomplishes more, works better in small groups than individually

Situational Identification of Gifted Hispanic Students

Judd Perrine, M.A.
Los Angeles Unified School District

Why are Hispanic students lagging behind in the numbers identified as gifted in Los Angeles, in California, and in the nation as a whole? The 1987 figures for total school enrollment in the Los Angeles Unified School District indicate 56 percent of the students are Hispanic, whereas only 29 percent of the students identified as gifted are Hispanic. Is underrepresentation due to Hispanic students being ill-prepared to demonstrate their intellectual abilities in Anglo-American terms on traditional testing instruments? Or, is underrepresentation due to factors within the Hispanic culture and the interference of bilingualism? Whatever the explanation, a need exists for schools with Hispanic students to define giftedness within the context of culture and language; to cluster students for appropriate instructional nurturance, reflective of that culture and language; and to monitor students' academic progress as a prelude to identification.

In 1985, such a method was developed in the Los Angeles Unified School District Gifted/Talented Programs: *Screening and Instructional Program for Able Under-achieving Students from Diverse Backgrounds*.

In East Los Angeles, the *Screening and Instructional Program* was adapted to reflect how culture and language impact on the expression of giftedness in Hispanic students, and to reflect the learning strategies that best capitalize on the Hispanic culture in developing learning potential.

EAST LOS ANGELES—AN HISTORICAL PERSPECTIVE

For perhaps 60 years the suburb of East Los Angeles has been described as a barrio. Because of its cultural homogeneity, essentially Hispanic, and the presence of certain economic factors, a stereotype of the Hispanic Angelino from East Los Angeles as impoverished and ill educated has developed.

From the perceived homogeneity of need, as projected from test scores and other indicators, a certain homogeneity of student expectation developed—that is, that all or most Hispanic students of East Los Angeles were deficient in basic skills and that the following planned, systematic approach to the basics was necessary: (1) divide reading, mathematics, and language into small instructional components that can be tested; and (2) keep the students "on task" at all costs. From there perhaps some day students will be able to think, to solve problems, and, in effect, to apply basic knowledge to develop higher level thinking. A highly structured classroom evolved.

DEFINING, NURTURING, AND MONITORING POTENTIALLY GIFTED HISPANIC STUDENTS—WHAT COMES FIRST?

In 1984, and subsequently with the introduction of the *Screening and Instructional Program,* descriptions of the intellectual, linguistic, and social characteristics of gifted students were disseminated widely in the school community. School staffs, parents, and even playground workers and education aides were trained to search for evidence of giftedness. Much observation and discussion were required, and, finally, a written analysis was developed based on checklists submitted by teacher, parent, and student. (See Exhibits 1-1, 1-2, and 1-3.)

The tactic used was to cluster students who might later be identified as gifted within regular classrooms and to give special instruction or nurturance within these clusters. The result, educators hoped, would be a situation leading to the "flowering" of each candidate's capabilities so that identification based on a standard intelligence instrument or high achievement would follow. The concept of situational identification would be reflective of the cultural learning characteristics of the student, predominantly Hispanic in the case of East Los Angeles.

What comes first, then, is the process of defining and clustering the students who may be gifted; subsequent recommendations (called nurturance imperatives) follow.

METHODOLOGY

The *Screening and Instructional Program* consists of three phases: search, instruction, and evaluation. Each phase must be completed before the student moves to the next.

Phase I: Search

Each candidate referred for the screening and instructional program is reviewed by the local school personnel to determine whether participation is appropriate. To assist in the identification, a program handbook describes the intellectual, linguistic, and social characteristics (behaviors) of giftedness that are observable in children in the educational setting; indicators of underachievement in classroom performance also are

Exhibit 1-1 Checklist of the Characteristics of Able Underachieving Students from Diverse Backgrounds

LOS ANGELES UNIFIED SCHOOL DISTRICT
Student Guidance Services Division
Psychological Services

Name _____ Date of Birth _____ Today's Date _____

School _____ Region _____ Grade _____

Teacher _____ Subject _____

Listed below are some of the characteristics that may be exhibited by capable but underachieving students from diverse backgrounds. Since there is a considerable amount of individual difference among these students, *not all students will exhibit the same characteristics.*

Read each statement and indicate in the column to the right the degree to which the student exhibits each characteristic. Please rate the student on all items.

Intellectual Characteristics	Low 1	2	3	High 4	*N.O.
Demonstrates ability to absorb information rapidly					
Exhibits rapid insight into cause-effect relationships					
Tries to discover the how and why of things					
Demonstrates alertness in observational skills					
Sustains interest span in selected topics Specify:					
Has skill in spatial visualization and analysis					
Is creative and productive in small groups					
Applies previously learned information to new situations					

continues

Exhibit 1-1 continued

Linguistic Characteristics

Exhibits verbal fluency in native language					
Shows rapid acquisition of (oral) English language skills (although written skills may lag behind)					
Communicates effectively (with fluency) with peers and within community (although non-standard English may be used)					

Social Characteristics

Assumes adult responsibilities at home and in the community					
Is looked to by peers for leadership					
Demonstrates ability to evaluate and control social situations					
Exhibits a sense of humor					
Has ability to relate well with peers and adults					

Listed below are indicators and background factors that may contribute to a student's underachievement. Check and describe briefly those indicators and factors that have influenced the student's academic performance.

Indicators of Underachievement	*N.O.*
Achieves below grade level	
Work is frequently incomplete or not turned in	

Exhibit 1-1 continued

Dislikes routine work or memorization for mastery

Skill levels scattered (demonstrates proficiency in certain skill areas but displays gaps in mastery of subject)

Does not participate willingly in class projects or discussions

Background Factors Contributing to Underachievement

School changes

School attendance

State to what degree the student has had exposure to educational, social, and/or cultural resources at home and in the community and explain the effect on the student's achievement.

Explain how family disorganization (due to divorce, death, unemployment, or other factors) has affected the student's achievement.

Cite family social conditions that may be affecting the student's achievement.

continues

Exhibit 1-1 continued

Cite language factors that may be affecting student's achievement.

_____

_____

_____

_____

*N.O.—No opportunity to observe.

Source: Developed by staff members of the Los Angeles Unified School District in 1985 for the experimental publication *Screening and Instructional Program for Able Underachieving Students from Diverse Backgrounds*.

Exhibit 1-2 Screening and Instructional Program for Able Underachieving Students from Diverse Backgrounds

LOS ANGELES UNIFIED SCHOOL DISTRICT
Student Guidance Services Division
Psychological Services

Student Self-inventory

Student Name _____ Date of Birth _____

School _____ Grade _____ Date _____

Please read each statement carefully and show how often you have observed the behavior in yourself by placing an *X* in the appropriate place according to this scale:

1. Seldom/Never   2. Occasionally   3. To a Considerable Degree   4. Almost Always

	1	2	3	4
I like organizing things, people, and events.				
Students in my class(es) ask for my help and ideas.				
I can get other students to follow my example.				
I need to know the reasons why before I do something asked of me.				
I like to know how and why things work the way they do.				
I like to watch/observe how other people do things.				

I learn quickly by observing/watching and listening.				
I like to think of new ways of doing things.				
When I find something interesting, I like to learn all I can about it.				
I have trouble completing school work that requires memorization or repetition.				

Comments regarding educational goals, special interests, future plans.

_____

_____

_____

Source: Developed by staff members of the Los Angeles Unified School District in 1985 for the experimental publication *Screening and Instructional Program for Able Underachieving Students from Diverse Backgrounds*.

Exhibit 1-3 Screening and Instructional Program for Able Underachieving Students from Diverse Backgrounds

LOS ANGELES UNIFIED SCHOOL DISTRICT
Student Guidance Services Division
Psychological Services

Parent Inventory

Student Name _____   Date of Birth _____

School _____ Grade _____ Date _____

Please read each statement carefully and indicate how often you have observed the behavior in your child by placing an *X* in the appropriate place according to this scale:

1. Seldom/Never   2. Occasionally   3. To a Considerable Degree   4. Almost Always

	1	*2*	*3*	*4*
Organizes things, people and events.				
Friends look to him/her for leadership.				

continues

Exhibit 1-3 continued

Is able to influence others.					
Does not accept what someone says without questioning it.					
Is able to find new solutions to problems.					
Shows curiosity about how and why things work the way they do.					
Learns quickly through observation and listening.					
Enjoys observing how others solve problems or create things.					
Becomes very involved in projects he/she finds interesting.					

Comments (Optional)

_____

_____

_____

_____

Parent's Signature   Date

Source: Developed by staff members of the Los Angeles Unified School District in 1985 for the experimental publication *Screening and Instructional Program for Able Underachieving Students from Diverse Backgrounds*.

outlined. Checklists of observable characteristics (Exhibit 1-1) as well as a list of indicators of underachievement are given to the referring teacher. A student self-inventory (Exhibit 1-2) and parent inventory (Exhibit 1-3) also are completed. Selection for admission to a nurturance cluster is based on the analysis of these checklists and a review of the cumulative record by designated school personnel.

Phase II: Instruction

Selected students are grouped together for a minimum of one semester. Teachers implement an instructional program specially designed to enhance and to nurture the students' possible giftedness or talents. Progress (growth) in the program is documented through administration of pretests and posttests, and through informal recording of other data deemed important by the teacher.

Phase III: Evaluation

Teachers complete a brief evaluation of each student in the screening and instructional program, based on the student's development and performance. Following the evaluation, one of three recommendations is made: continue in the screening and instructional program; return to the regular program; or, refer to the Psychological Services Office for possible identification as gifted and/or talented.

GUIDELINES FOR NURTURANCE

Once students are selected, three imperatives or commands are used to guide teachers in planning instructional nurturance for Hispanics who may be gifted. Here is where the marriage of culture and language meets the daily lesson plan and the student's home environment.

> **Nurturance Imperative No. 1:**   Teachers of Hispanic students must first discover the knowledge base of those students, and then use that knowledge to design the classroom experience, to develop the students' capabilities to the highest possible level.

One of the verities of accepted educational practice is, "Take the students from where they are." What base of knowledge do Hispanic students bring to the classroom (i.e., where is the student) that teachers must understand, appreciate, and employ in the delivery of instructional services to create the optimal situation (i.e., where can the student be) for nurturing and thus identifying students who may be gifted?

Some educators believe that the Hispanic child in East Los Angeles is deficient in cognitive experiences that must precede instruction in higher order thinking skills. However, this is a myth. The reality is that gifted Hispanic students do observe, do ask insightful questions, and can function at high cognitive levels based on familiar experiences *if* the teacher knows what those experiences are and builds on them. The following case study illustrates this principle.

> **CASE STUDY**
>
> Elizabeth Mendoza was a gifted bilingual student in the author's sixth grade class. Quiet and compliant, she seldom shared her experiences or observations through oral or written expression. After a class discussion on the concept of heroes and a comparison of various views of Pancho Villa in English and Mexican textbooks, Elizabeth volunteered that her grandfather, who lived with her

family and whom she loved dearly, had known personally and fought with Pancho Villa. The class was fascinated: Pancho Villa, hero or renegade? The textbooks could not provide a clear answer. What about Elizabeth's grandfather—a first person account!

The students in the bilingual gifted cluster, including students who might be gifted, wrote to Sr. Mendoza and invited him to visit the class. Such questions! Such thinking as they prepared to interview him! Would time alter Sr. Mendoza's perceptions, they wondered? Would his rank have any effect on his perceptions of the events surrounding Pancho Villa's forays across the border? What about nationalism and allegiances then, and now?

The day of the visit arrived and Sr. Mendoza appeared in uniform, with photographs, stories, and opinions. For Elizabeth, who translated for her grandfather, it was the public debut of her Spanish-speaking ability! It was a new experience in self-expression and self-possession.

History related orally was a natural progression for the students' burgeoning interest in history and served as a check on validity of textbook statements about historical events. High cognitive functioning was a natural outcome, motivated by commonly held experiences.

The teacher's task is to learn what knowledge is common and to use it appropriately. Teachers who provide optimal learning experiences for gifted students or students who may be gifted need to be aware that students come to the learning situation with knowledge in the affective (feeling) mode as well as the cognitive (thinking) mode. Teachers need to consider those characteristics that are affectively unique to Hispanic students and employ them to capitalize on the culture. The following example illustrates how one teacher uses this knowledge of the affective mode to enhance the learning situation.

CASE STUDY

The Spanish word *abrazo* ("embrace") is an essential factor of the affective mode in teaching Hispanic students. Simply put, a closeness, sometimes physical, but moreover spiritual—is an index of personal support. Dr. Jaime Escalante, a teacher of mathematics and calculus at Garfield High School in East Los Angeles, understands the dynamic and employs it every day. He understands the attitudes, the will to achieve, and the communication required to invite his Hispanic students to learn.

When students enter and leave his classroom, he is there, shaking a hand, touching a shoulder, speaking to them on a first-name basis, and making personal remarks. Eyes meet eyes, hands clasp, and the result is a manifestation of the closeness that is endemic to the Hispanic culture.

Dr. Escalante is available to his students. He is popular and respected, not feared. His students speak of his commitment to his discipline, and to them. Dr. Escalante has the habit of repeating the phrase, "It's easy." Calculus is not easy, but the constant support, coupled with his availability, allows no excuse for lack of effort on the part of his students. Jaime Escalante says it all comes down to *ganas* ("the will to succeed, to pursue the challenge") and he is there for them. He is well prepared in his discipline, and his students know of his preparation.

Nurturance Imperative No. 2: Teachers of Hispanic students who are or may be gifted must include the parents of students in planning, evaluating, and enriching the instructional program.

The dynamic of families in the Hispanic culture is a vital force and must be considered in planning the daily classroom experience of the gifted Hispanic student. This same dynamic needs to be inclusive of parents themselves. Parental support is a critical factor in determining whether or not children's capabilities are esteemed and nurtured, particularly in the elementary school years.

Several factors, characteristic of the dynamic of family in the Hispanic culture, have the potential to mitigate against the nurturance of giftedness at school. They include family structure, parental view of the educational process, and family view of the general value of education and school success.

The structure of the Hispanic family is critical with respect to role modeling. Male dominance in the family setting does not encourage a gifted student's tendency for independent thought and behavior. A gifted girl may find little or no opportunity to exercise personal initiative, independent thought, or verbal aggressiveness within the context of the home. Children are embraced and cared for, but infrequently included in family decisions.

Based on limited experience, parents of children in East Los Angeles initially do not perceive participation in "school life" as their domain. Many Hispanic families, whether they have lived in the United States for generations, or recently arrived, reflect a different view of parental association with the school and the duties of the teacher than do Anglo-American families. In Mexico and Central America, teachers garner enormous respect, and parents do not feel they, as nonexperts in education, should make educational decisions. Many parents also feel uncomfortable visiting the classroom to observe a lesson and to evaluate the instructional delivery.

The factor of education is not a dynamic force in socioeconomic mobility in Mexico and Central America. Often a child is needed at home or in the workplace, and education must be interrupted or deferred until a later time. This ethic often carries over to the Hispanic culture in the United States. Parental support for consistent school attendance frequently is a problem, as is the provision of a time and place for a child to study at home.

An additional complicating factor is that sometimes a communication schism develops in the parent-child relationship when parents conduct their lives predominantly in Spanish and their sons and daughters develop a predominant facility in English. As a child grows older, less conferring and sharing can occur about the issues and decisions a young person faces. The family support system, previously so important, becomes rudimentary.

Thus, parental awareness of behaviors that foster academic excellence and high self-esteem through opportunities at home must become the focus of parent participation activities at school. Strategies to entice parents to the school in order to involve them become a science. Many educators in East Los Angeles elementary schools have had outstanding success by providing communication in Spanish and English, simultaneous interpretation at meetings, and a sophisticated system of mailings and telephone contacts. At some schools, computerized telephone messages remind parents the night before an upcoming meeting. Special conferences with psychologists, parent leaders, instructional specialists, and college admission officers provide special knowledge and incentives for parents. College-bound gifted high school students often are included in a forum setting to reflect personally in English, and in Spanish, on the impact of home influences on their motivation to continue their education, and on career choices. The dignity of the parent as a leader in the school community is crucial, regardless of education or economic circumstances.

Parental involvement is essential to the identification process. Parents may be aware of factors related to potential capabilities evidenced at home, in the context of family, that are not displayed in the school setting because students may lack those experiences to be discussed in Nurturance Imperative No. 3. A pervasive and continuing parent training program will alert parents to characteristics of gifted children.

A good training program for Hispanic parents can underscore the value of maintaining the closeness of the family, while recognizing the necessity of enforcing certain parenting strategies that facilitate greater school success. For example, cultural anthropologists describe Hispanic culture as having an elastic or subjective sense of time. Parents can modify this tendency by maintaining time-certain tasks at home and coordinating homework and school projects to build appropriate planning and task completion skills, which are vital to success in school. Another characteristic of Hispanic cultures noted by anthropologists is the view of recreation and work as equally important, nonmutually exclusive endeavors. Parents can assist gifted students in completing required schoolwork before pursuing personal interests not viewed as valuable in the educational setting.

All in all, the Hispanic parents' understanding of *lo bueno* ("it is good") and *lo necesario* ("it is necessary") for nurturing the potential for giftedness in the family setting is critical.

Nurturance Imperative No. 3:   Teachers of Hispanic students who may be gifted must plan each day of classroom instruction to include the proactive use of oral language in a variety of cooperative learning situations.

Teachers talk too much. The tendency to soliloquize is so strong that a teacher designing an optimal learning classroom to nurture giftedness always must be on guard. Before a child, especially one who is gifted, starts school, questioning is the predominant way of learning about the world. Many children alert us to their unique intellectual capabilities through the questions they ask. In school, however, questioning seems to belong to the teachers. Suddenly, the game plan doesn't permit students to ask. The Hispanic child in East Los Angeles who may be gifted, dealing with varying language facility and depth of language experience (English and Spanish), needs a classroom environment that encourages and nurtures native inquisitiveness.

Proactive language orientation requires that the teacher employ an inquiry mode that esteems the asking of pertinent evaluative questions more than answering recall questions. Simulation, debates, and small committees provide the student with a diversity of language roles. Especially vital for the Hispanic child, whether bilingual or monolingual, is to use both English and Spanish in original thinking. Hispanic students tend to be very self-critical. Proactive language experiences enhance self-esteem through a critical examination of issues and viewpoints, and of those who hold those viewpoints.

Hispanic students are accustomed to structure in the family, community, and religious practice. Such familiarity with structure may explain their comfort with consistency in learning. Cooperative learning strategies are productive, as they capitalize on the less competitive and more collaborative dynamic within the Hispanic culture. Working in small groups that develop partnering and blur the lines drawn by competitiveness is sound practice. The following two examples illustrate the use of proactive language orientation to enhance learning.

CASE STUDIES

John Bennett uses a cooperative learning technique to great advantage in his Advanced Placement history classes at Garfield High School. Students sit in a circle and routinely follow a design that focuses on training members of the group to listen with purpose and to contribute their ideas on a subject in a criticism-free experience. Contributions are entirely voluntary. The discussion is focused on issues determined by the students rather than the teacher. The strategy capitalizes on the Hispanic communal ethic. After several months of almost daily practice, the students are able to conduct an issue-oriented forum that builds an academic competitiveness that is cohesive rather than divisive.

Several miles west of Hammel Street Elementary, Hilary de Rocco is sitting on the floor among a group of her gifted and potentially gifted fourth graders. This is one of the several study groups de Rocco creates to explore new ideas. During this particular visit the subject is a survey of architecture and history; books and pictures are passed about, and a question-generating dialogue ensues. Vocabulary is presented; questions are raised, rephrased, and repeated; but there is no worksheet, no follow-up. Pictures, books, and other resources are pointed out in the classroom. The dialogue will continue tomorrow and the concepts will build gradually with partners or triads developing out of similar interest, and differentiated products will emerge.

Hispanic students, no matter how disparate their facility with either English or Spanish, must see their native language, Spanish, in something other than a skill-building dimension. An example of how this can be accomplished follows.

CASE STUDY

Some years ago in the author's sixth grade class of gifted students, most of whom were bilingual, the subject of discussion was heroes in Mexican history, as described in an English language text entitled, *The People of Mexico*. Students were curious about Marina, the Indian princess who, with her knowledge of many Indian dialects and Spanish, was able to ease the entry of the Conquistadores into Mexico. They were curious because she was a woman in a role that generally was viewed as a male occupation—adventuring, laying waste, and general conquering. The importance of women in history was intriguing. The following day, a student brought to the discussion a Mexican history book, printed in Mexico, with quite a different point of view of Marina. The boy had discussed the issue with his mother, who made a very different observation on Marina, whom she called "Malinche." She led him to her history book and he read in Spanish that Malinche was a traitor to the

Indian people of pre-Hispanic Mexico. He understandably was full of questions. Spurred on by this contribution, his peers asked to read the volume and a bilingual investigation ensued. The teacher was delighted with one remark, "But, Mr. Perrine, I thought that books contained the whole truth!" Bilingual ability was seen in a new light, not just a skill or ability to be maintained in the classroom, nor something vague to be celebrated periodically, but rather an academic asset in the world of thinking and knowing.

In summary, teachers of Hispanic students must give maximum attention to the impact of language as a tool for developing giftedness. As children learn the rules and principles that govern language, they apply them to the development of thinking processes as well. Spanish is a synthetic language that produces a deductive mind set, wherein the question, "Why?" is the most important word. Generally, people whose dominant language is Spanish attend more to global meanings than details of a subject. Therefore, collaborative, oral language experiences will capitalize on the linguistic deductive predisposition, give needed inductive experience, and develop the competitive language competencies valued in school success.

IN CONCLUSION

A community dynamic is requisite to the fostering of a consciousness of giftedness that allows nurturance imperatives to live and breathe in local school classrooms. This community dynamic is an intangible that used to be described by the phrase, *Sal si puedes* ("Get out if you can"): the barrio was not the place where dreams were realized. Today, however, in the East Los Angeles schools a consciousness exists that recognizes the presence of gifted students in Hispanic communities. *Si, se puede* ("Yes, it can be done") is the feeling one gets at teacher inservice training classes and at parent meetings.

Should traditional tests to identify giftedness continue to be used with Hispanic students? Should testing procedures be altered, criteria revised, or new tests designed that accommodate the current understanding of cultural diversity? Are cultural elements present in a child's life that have an impact on the measurability of that child's academic potential? Moreover, what implications do cultural elements have for educators responsible for the quality of everyday classroom experience for Hispanics? Does that classroom experience capitalize on their culture and provide for optimum development of their capabilities? The answers to these questions should be in the affirmative, if the experience in East Los Angeles is used as an index to measure movement toward equitable and appropriate identification of gifted Hispanic students. Identify Hispanic students who may be gifted, cluster and nurture them, capitalize on their culture, and thus maximize the likelihood of their progress commensurate with expectancies for gifted students.

2

Identification of Gifted Hispanic Students: A Multidimensional View

Irene Antonia Zappia, Ph.D.
Tucson Unified School District

In Judd Perrine's chapter on nurturance imperatives for Hispanic students in East Los Angeles who may be gifted (see Chapter 1), the crucial question of *how* to identify gifted Hispanic students has been left unanswered. How Perrine proposes to identify this population is not clear, nor does he state clearly how the checklists (see Exhibits 1-1, 1-2, and 1-3) used for student selection into a nurturance cluster are interpreted.

How to identify gifted Hispanic students is a complex question, with no easy answer. I believe that a search for the answer requires a holistic view that incorporates the work and research of educators, psychologists, anthropologists, sociologists, and linguists. I propose to look at some crucial questions and research that may point in the right direction.

In responding to Perrine's chapter, I have addressed some very important issues that were omitted. Some are pertinent to Hispanics, some to students in general who may be gifted. To gain a better appreciation of the problem of identification, background information relevant to Hispanics, intelligence, and gifted Hispanics is presented. Because many Hispanic children are bilingual, or enter the school system with only Spanish language facility, I have examined issues of second language acquisition. Also, since I believe the low representation of Hispanics in programs for the gifted is a product of the use of traditional methods of identification and lower than average academic achievement, I have addressed briefly both factors. Finally, recommendations are made for identification and selection procedures that are less biased than traditional ones.

BACKGROUND INFORMATION

Hispanics constitute America's youngest and fastest growing minority, and the school dropout rate of Hispanic students is alarming. Applebome (Machado, 1987) estimates that 45 to 66 percent of Hispanics will drop out before graduating from high school. In contrast, 17 to 27 percent of Anglo-Americans will drop out. According to the U.S. Census Bureau, of Hispanics over age 25, 13.5 percent have completed less than five years of school, compared to 6.1 percent of Blacks and 2.2 percent of Anglo-Americans.

According to Webb (1982), approximately 3 percent of all children, regardless of race or ethnic background, qualify as gifted. In Table 2-1 are shown various ethnic groups; their representation (i.e., percentage of enrollment) in programs for the gifted is compared to their representation in the public schools. The underenrollment of Hispanics in programs for the gifted is clearly illustrated when the data in Table 2-2 are examined.

In 1972, the U.S. Office of Education promoted a definition of giftedness that included the areas of general intellectual ability, specific academic aptitude, creative or productive thinking, leadership ability, visual and performing arts ability, and psychomotor ability. In 1981, Public Law 95-561 removed psychomotor ability from the definition.

Later, Renzulli (1977) defined giftedness as "an interaction among three basic clusters of human traits—these being above-average general abilities, high levels of task commitment, and high levels of creativity" (p. 261).

SECOND LANGUAGE ACQUISITION

When discussing the selection of students for special programs, a basic theoretical understanding of the child who enters a school system with a primary language other than English is needed. Often, erroneous judgments are made regarding the language proficiencies exhibited by children with two linguistic codes. Because a bilingual child

Table 2-1 Representation of Various Ethnic Groups in Public Schools Compared to Their Representation in Programs for the Gifted

Ethnic Group	Public School Enrollment (% Enrolled)	Programs for the Gifted Enrollment (% Enrolled)
Anglo-Americans	71.2	81.4
Blacks	16.2	8.4
Hispanics	9.1	4.7
Asians	2.5	5.0

Source: From "Gifted Hispanics Underidentified in Classrooms" by M. Machado, 1987, *Hispanic Link Weekly Report,* 5(7), p. 1. Copyright February 1987 by Hispanic Link News Service. Adapted by permission.

Table 2-2 Percentage of Hispanics in States Having the Highest Hispanic Populations, and Their Respective Representation in Programs for the Gifted by State

States with Highest Hispanic Populations	Hispanic Population (% of State Population)	Programs for the Gifted (% Hispanic Enrollment)
Arizona	21.5	9.2
California	29.2	11.1
Florida	8.1	1.9
Illinois	8.0	2.7
New Mexico	43.4	19.7
New York	13.6	9.4
Texas	27.9	15.0

Source: From "Gifted Hispanics Underidentified in Classrooms" by M. Machado, 1987, *Hispanic Link Weekly Report*, 5(7), p. 1. Copyright February 1987 by Hispanic Link News Service. Adapted by permission.

speaks English, educators assume that the child can be evaluated fairly and adequately in English. Let us consider why this may not be an accurate assumption, and how it can affect identification of the gifted Hispanic student. Cummins (1980, 1984) integrated the work of Skutknabb-Kangas and Toukomaa (1976) and Shuy (1978, 1981) with his own ideas and research to develop the hypothesis that when learning a language, whether our first or second, we first must develop basic interpersonal communication skills (BICS). These are the surface features of language (e.g., pronunciation, vocabulary, and grammar) seen at the top of the "iceberg" in Figure 2-1. These surface features take about two years to develop, and rely heavily on the visual cues received from others. As a language is used and practiced, cognitive academic language proficiency skills (CALPS) are developed. These deeper cognitive functions (e.g., semantic and functional meaning), which are measured by intelligence tests, take five to seven years to develop.

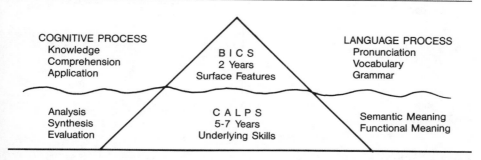

Figure 2-1 Adaptation of Cummins's Interdependence Model. *Source:* From *Bilingualism and Special Education: Issues in Assessment and Pedagogy* (p. 138) by J. Cummins, 1984, San Diego, Calif.: College-Hill Press, Inc. Copyright 1984 by College-Hill Press, Inc. Adapted by permission.

Cummins elaborated on this hypothesis by proposing that language can be placed along two intersecting continua (see Fig. 2-2): (a) context-embedded to context-reduced communication, and (b) cognitively demanding to cognitively undemanding communication. In context-embedded communication the participants can provide feedback to interpret meaning, and language is supported by a wide range of paralinguistic situational cues requiring only a BICS level of communication. Context-reduced communication, on the other hand, relies on language exclusively to interpret the meaning, and requires a CALPS level of communication. Cognitively undemanding communication requires the cognitive processes of knowledge, comprehension, and application; and the language processes of pronunciation, vocabulary, and grammar. Cognitively demanding communication, on the other hand, requires the cognitive processes of analysis, synthesis, and evaluation, and the language processes of semantic meaning and functional meaning.

In standardized tests, meaning is context reduced and, by its very nature, cognitively demanding. Thus, because of potential bias in testing, the score obtained by the limited English proficient (LEP) student is not a true measure of his or her intellectual potential.

Understanding the process of second language acquisition provides educators with an appreciation of why a child who appears to be proficient in his or her second language may, in fact, not be so, and may explain why bilingual children may experience more difficulty than monolingual children in reaching the cutoff points used to determine giftedness when using traditional intellectual assessment. This understanding also may provide information about causes for the lower than average academic achievement of Hispanics.

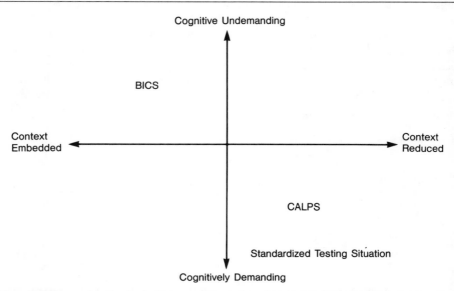

Figure 2-2 Intersecting Continua of Language Processes and Their Relationship to Assessment. *Source: From Bilingualism and Special Education: Issues in Assessment and Pedagogy* (p. 139) by J. Cummins, 1984, San Diego, Calif.: College-Hill Press, Inc. Copyright 1984 by College-Hill Press, Inc. Adapted by permission.

The lower than average academic achievement of Hispanics and their underrepresentation in classes for the gifted are interrelated.

Cummins (1986) addressed the causes for low academic achievement of minority students. He believes that a redefinition of the roles of educators and education with respect to minority students and communities is necessary. Cummins assigns a central role to three inclusive sets of interactions, or power relations: (a) classroom interactions between teachers and students; (b) relationships between schools and minority communities; and (c) intergroup power relations within the society as a whole.

The theoretical framework proposed by Cummins is based on the belief that students from dominated societal groups are either empowered or disabled as a direct result of their interactions with educators in the schools. He believes that these interactions are mediated by the implicit or explicit role definitions that educators assume in relation to the following four institutional characteristics of schools; that is, the extent to which (a) minority students' language and culture are incorporated into the school program; (b) minority community participation is encouraged as an integral component of children's education; (c) pedagogy promotes intrinsic motivation on the part of students to use language actively to generate their own knowledge; and (d) professionals involved in assessment become advocates for minority students rather than making legitimate the location of the "problem" in the students. These four structural elements in the organization of education contribute to the empowerment or disability of minority students.

When students are empowered by their school experiences they develop the ability, confidence, and motivation to succeed academically (Cummins, 1986). Rather than Perrine's term "nurturance," I prefer Cummins's word "empowerment." The first step in the identification of gifted Hispanic students, as described in depth by Perrine in his nurturance imperatives, is to provide an educational experience that empowers them to succeed academically.

The model proposed by Cummins (1983a) provides a research-based theoretical framework from which to view the nurturance imperatives proposed by Perrine. A thorough review of Cummins's model is not possible in this chapter, but a listing of research demonstrating support for the components and assumptions of his model may be helpful as references for the reader.

1. The addition, rather than subtraction, of culture and language in a school program correlates positively with academic success of minority students (Campos & Keatings, 1984; Cummins, 1983a; Rosier & Holm, 1980).
2. Community-school collaboration empowers minority students (Tizard, Schofield, & Hewison, 1982).
3. The use of instructional pedagogy in which students (a) assume control over their own learning goals, (b) collaborate actively with each other in achieving goals, and (c) interact in a reciprocal manner with teachers and other students enables minority students to learn English and other language skills and to achieve academically (Cummins, 1983a; Wong-Fillmore, 1983).

Cummins believes that historically, assessment, the fourth element in his model, has played the role of legitimizing the disabling of minority students. The assessment procedure certainly has played a role in keeping Hispanic students out of classes for the gifted. With minimal regard given to environmental, cultural, and language variables that could affect test performance, Hispanic students have been evaluated in their nondominant language with instruments standardized on an Anglo-American, middle class population. These traditional assessment practices have resulted in inappropriate labeling, misplacement of many minority students into special education classes, and an underrepresentation of students in classes for the gifted (Mercer, 1973).

The vast majority of referrals for assessment or placement in a special program for the gifted are from teachers. Extensive reliance on teacher nomination has come under attack because researchers have discovered that teacher nominations alone are insufficient to create an adequate referral pool (High & Udall, 1983; Sullivan, 1973). Gear (1976) and others (Clark, 1983; Jacobs, 1971; Pegnato & Birch, 1959) found that teachers failed to identify gifted students because their perception of a gifted student often was limited to high achievers. Marland (1972) stated that if teachers are the only source of referrals, 50 percent of all gifted students will remain undiscovered. High and Udall (1983) found that teachers nominate a disproportionate number of Anglo-American students even in schools with a high minority population.

Bernal (1981) concluded that traditional notions of giftedness produce restrictive, highly inaccurate identification procedures that, especially when combined, identify too few as gifted. If the use of standardized tests is questionable for mainstream students, on whom they were standardized, the problems of their use with minority students are even greater.

CURRENT IDENTIFICATION PRACTICES

Kitano and Kirby (1986) describe four ways that students usually are identified. In the first and most common approach, set criteria, one or two tests are used to rank order the students to determine their placement. Achievement and intelligence tests are used most frequently. The problems associated with this method already have been discussed.

In the second approach, the matrix method, several classes of ratings and test results are incorporated, providing several combinations of scores that can allow a student entry into a program for the gifted. Because many scores are used and more students are likely to be discovered using this method, it is superior to the set criteria approach. Even though the matrix method is better, this method relies too heavily on test results and equates dissimilar measures.

A third approach, the revolving door model, was developed by Renzulli (1978). Using this approach, one starts with the selection of a large number (20 to 25 percent of a school population) of students, the "talent pool." Usually developed through testing and observation, the pool is above average in intelligence, ranks relatively high in creative ability, and demonstrates what Renzulli calls "task commitment." During the school year, students in the talent pool experience various enrichment activities. Although this method offers the potential of recognizing more gifted students than other schemes, the concept of task commitment is not clearly defined and may be culturally based.

The fourth approach, the case study, involves the review of a variety of screening information by appropriate school personnel. In some cases, study teams perform different functions. For example, one team might collect and organize identification information, while another might study the data to make final placement decisions. A case study method is promising for Hispanic students, because many sources reflecting student performance or ability potential can be considered, rather than depending exclusively on numbers or rating summaries. The case study method may be the best approach for identifying gifted Hispanic students and, according to Renzulli and Smith (1977), more sensitive in locating students from all minority groups who are gifted.

RECOMMENDATIONS

How Perrine proposes to select students to nurture is unclear, as are criteria for analysis of the checklists used in preplacement. Whether the purpose of the checklists is to determine who is nurtured, or who is actually selected, also is not clear. The concept of nurturance for all students is commendable, and in keeping with Cummins's philosophy of empowerment. Hispanics as a group are diverse; questions of how we nurture and what criteria we use to identify and select Hispanic students for programs for the gifted should be equally diverse.

I propose that the identification and selection of gifted Hispanic students be conducted by an interdisciplinary team of professionals, committed to including greater numbers of minorities and accepting a multidimensional definition of giftedness. This team should include members who are knowledgeable in the areas of second language acquisition, bilingual education, cultural differences, and issues related to minority assessment. A case study approach that makes use of the following five variables is recommended.

1. *Observations*. Observations can be obtained informally through the use of objective checklists, and with formal time samples of frequency, rate, and duration of behaviors. The child should be observed in as many situations as possible to determine language preference, proficiency, and use patterns (in both languages) in school, home, and community. Sociocultural background, level of acculturation, degree to which the child maintains traditional cultural values, and socioeconomic status and composition of the child's family also are important variables to examine. Observers must compare the child to other children of the same language and cultural background.

2. *Interviews*. Interviews should be conducted with persons knowledgeable about the student—parents, teachers, peers, and the students themselves. Rating scales appropriate for the child, neighborhood, and school can be incorporated into the interviews. Emotional adjustment, curriculum, and teacher and student variables, also can be examined through the use of interviews. This information can be used to support or to question test results.

3. *Formal Tests*. A wide variety of formal tests should be available from which to choose. The tests should be culture free and culture fair,[1] and be designated to assess,

---

[1]Chapter 11 by Montgomery contains a complete discussion of the term "culture fair." "Culture neutral," in Montgomery's discussion, is synonymous with "culture free."

for example, how much learning takes place in the test-teach-test situation (Feuerstein, 1979) or how a child solves problems. The test(s) and examiner should be matched to the child, considering the language of the test as well as the ethnicity of the examiner. The abilities of minority students are unlikely to be measured accurately by the use of formal tests, so results must be interpreted cautiously and substantiated with other measures.

4. *Informal Tests*. Informal tests, those that are nonstandardized or norm-referenced, as well as examiner-made informal probes can be used to examine how well a child solves problems. Interpretation of informal tests is based on examiner judgment, so these tests also have a potential for bias.

5. *Review of Cumulative Records*. Examining the child's educational history can add crucial information to the evaluation procedure. Because of the fundamental role of primary language in the development of second language, the following are only a few of the questions to be considered. Did the child enter the school system as monolingual in Spanish and receive instruction in English? Has the child been transferred from monolingual English to bilingual classes, or vice versa? If the child was in a bilingual educational program, what type of program was it? Bilingual educational programs differ in the amount of primary language instruction, and in goals related to the primary language. Some educators strive to maintain the primary language, while others strive to use it only as a transition to English.

IN CONCLUSION

We need to subscribe to a philosophy of inclusion (Bernal, 1976), wherein children who manifest one or more indicators are candidates for selection to programs for the gifted. The selection process must reflect current research and a variety of methods, and make an optimal match between program and student characteristics. Programs for the gifted and talented should nurture as many students as possible that have the potential of being identified as gifted (Bernal, 1984b).

Hispanic students who are gifted, or who may be identified as gifted, are being disabled by our school system. Discussing assessment instruments is absurd when the problem of underrepresentation of minorities in programs for the gifted actually stems from our schools, our attitudes, and our values. The problem is much greater than merely the choice of appropriate instruments, and the solution is complex. As a culturally diverse society, we need to use cultural indicators of giftedness; to find more valid, more widely applicable alternatives to standardized tests; and to train teachers to recognize creative behavior among Hispanic and other minority students.

Bias is not limited to tests themselves and, therefore, specific tests intentionally have not been mentioned. Bias permeates the entire decision-making process—referral, testing, interpretation of test results, determination of eligibility, and recommendation for placement. State and local policies continue to require cutoff scores on tests of intelligence as indicators of giftedness. This author offers advice on the selection, supplementation, and interpretation of instruments so that such cutoff scores will not exclude Hispanics and other non-mainstream students from programs for the gifted.

3

Promoting Pluralism and Power

Clarissa Banda, M.A.
Montebello Unified School District,
California

The educational needs of gifted Hispanic students vary widely, and depend on national origins and degree of acculturation, family socioeconomic levels, educational aspirations, facility in English, and, most importantly, the form that giftedness takes in these individuals. As the educational community develops broader and less culture-bound methods of identification, the number of identified gifted Hispanic children is increasing. Most of these students are of Mexican- or Central-American descent, and many of them are economically disadvantaged. Some are identified for abilities that are valued by the majority culture; but some have been identified for academic potential, or for those abilities valued by the Hispanic culture, such as very early bilingual ability, divergent thinking, and leadership skills (Bernal, 1974; Clark, 1981; Cox, Daniel, & Boston, 1985). An educational program designed to serve gifted Hispanics must provide for and nurture this diversity.

A strong program for gifted Hispanic students should focus on individual abilities, assisting students in developing at their own pace abilities they value, while introducing and developing other abilities that will aid their success as gifted persons of two cultures.

TRADITIONAL PROGRAM FOCUS

One reason for low school success among gifted Hispanic students is that they are usually placed in programs that focus on developing abilities valued by the majority culture. In this type of program, Hispanic students must work twice as hard to succeed, overcoming obstacles of differing value systems, behavioral patterns, inadequate academic preparation, and differing language (Leung, 1981; Passow, 1972).

HISPANIC CULTURE FOCUS

An alternative to traditional programs is to focus on abilities valued by the Hispanic culture. Abilities valued by the Hispanic culture should be recognized and developed in a program for gifted Hispanic students. Staff should be provided with information on, and educational approaches to, the Hispanic community's conception of giftedness and valued abilities, to aid in the implementation of such a program. However, this focus should not neglect other areas of talent, nor the building of cultural bridges for these students.

Bilingual/bicultural programs for gifted students, which are rare and have not been mandated, would be excellent experiences for some Hispanic students (Davis & Rimm, 1985; National Advisory and Coordinating Council of Bilingual Education, 1985). However, if such programs segregated Hispanics from other gifted students, and if such programs could not be adapted to meet a wide range of abilities and interests, they would not provide a comprehensive educational answer for gifted Hispanics.

INDIVIDUALLY VALUED ABILITIES FOCUS

The best focus of a program for gifted Hispanic students is to develop individually valued abilities—such as areas of traditional academics, leadership and organizational skills, and divergent thinking—and other varied abilities that occur in bicultural individuals. A program with an individualized focus should include some of the goals and methods of traditional and pluralistic models, but with primary emphasis on the students' unique and varied strengths.

Individual Student Education Plan

Individual student profile. To ensure the best possible programming and services, individual student profiles should be developed, summarizing (a) area(s) of giftedness or talent, and the ways talents are expressed; (b) general intelligence (IQ), creativity, and other academic abilities (Baldwin, Gear, & Lucito, 1978); (c) process skills that require strengthening for effective participation in challenging courses; (d) affective and social development; and (e) socioeconomic status, family organization, home and work responsibilities, time and space constraints that may impact on educational progress, and family attitudes toward the children's giftedness (Frasier, 1979).

Individual plan conference. Using student profiles, staff should meet with identified students and their families to define and clarify abilities, and to formulate individual educational goals and expectations. Parents, children, and staff also could use this conference to clarify expectations and responsibilities, such as projected study time and special needs, and any logistical arrangements needed for the study program. All program information and conferencing should be available in Spanish and English.

Differentiated Program Goals

In addition to individualized goals for students, a program should have general goals that are designed to meet the specific needs of gifted Hispanics. Goals can be grouped under the following seven dimensions.

1. Academic Development Dimension

GOAL: Provide acceleration and challenge in all areas of giftedness and potential, emphasizing individual pace and diversity.

GOAL: Develop students' appreciation of their majority culture-valued abilities and their nontraditional abilities, providing ways for them to continue developing these talents.

GOAL: Provide a quality academic program that equips students for success in school and community leadership, and that has high standards of academic credibility, challenge, and performance.

These academic goals include traditional forms of challenge and acceleration, but with an emphasis on individual pacing and nurturance of diverse abilities. Acceleration and teaching strategies should be adapted to diverse learning styles (Gallegos & Flores, 1982), and should provide for optimum development of nontraditional forms of giftedness.

GOAL: Provide an early and accelerated Spanish language and literature program, and provide bilingual students with optimal language learning experiences through a differentiated foreign language program.

If encouraged and supported from the start of their education, many Hispanic students could far surpass the challenge of high school and Advanced Placement Spanish courses, and they might profit from opportunities to study Spanish on college campuses or abroad. Use of the primary language and development of higher level cognitive abilities in Spanish would enrich the curriculum, and provide academic and cognitive advantages to minority group children such as cognitive flexibility and metalinguistic awareness (Barik & Swain, 1974; Bernal, 1974; Davis & Rimm, 1985; DeAvila & Duncan, 1979; Lambert, 1977). Finally, respect for achievement in Spanish would effect increased ethnic pride and individual self-esteem among Hispanics.

GOAL: Enhance students' sense of the interconnectedness of knowledge and reduce alienation and culture conflict through a humanities and interdisciplinary approach (Kravetz, 1986).

This approach would integrate multicultural curricula into the program and have the flexibility to allow students of diverse talents and interests to learn in unique ways.

A characteristic of most gifted individuals is their ability to understand the relationship(s) between different concepts, and the connections among ideas (Clark, 1981). Culturally diverse, bilingual gifted individuals have even more possibilities for making connections and for integrating experience with theory.

GOAL: Foster involvement in learning and critical thinking through problem solving.

Researchers have recommended the use of creative problem-solving strategies, group inquiry techniques, and simulations to increase student involvement and to make full use of relevant life skills, gradually leading to inductive activities (Sato, 1974; Thompson, 1984). For some students these practices would provide stimulation, relevancy, and enrichment; for others, the strategies would more closely approach their learning styles, and would be effective ways to introduce new lessons.

2. Affective Development Dimension

Affective development is important for all children, and is frequently ignored in programs for gifted students. Gifted Hispanic students particularly would benefit from emphasis on affective development because of cultural stress, unique learning styles, and the need for support from significant adults and peers (Clark, 1983; Frasier, 1979; Leung, 1981; Roedell, 1984).

GOAL: Foster in all participants an appreciation for the uniqueness, difficulty, and responsibility of being a gifted Hispanic individual.

GOAL: Strengthen students' sense of inner locus of control and self-direction (Henderson, 1980).

Opportunities for students to choose and control their educational activities would be provided, and independent thinking and valuing would be recognized and encouraged in the program. Student responsibility would be developed through classroom strategies, such as those described in the Shared Responsibility Model (Sparling, 1986).

GOAL: Develop a supportive family atmosphere that promotes cooperative, not competitive, learning; values individual differences and contributions; increases student self-esteem and power; and encourages risk taking.

GOAL: Provide a "shelter" for gifted students where they may turn for emotional support and understanding (Davis & Rimm, 1985).

GOAL: Provide a comprehensive guidance program that includes individual, group, and family counseling (Frasier, 1979; Gallegos & Flores, 1982).

GOAL: Provide career education and counseling in students' high ability areas in order to give direction, motivation, and relevance in the educational aspect of their lives (Cox, Daniel, & Boston, 1985; Davis & Rimm, 1985).

3. Hispanic and Multicultural Education Dimension

GOAL: Increase students' knowledge and appreciation of their own and others' value systems, including that of the majority culture, through both direct instruction and indirect attitudinal modeling and activities.

GOAL: Develop students' sense of their individual and ethnic identities, and their potential contributions to society.

GOAL: Educate students who are confidently bicultural and ultimately multicultural, who have a sense of the oneness of all people (Clark, 1979).

Ethnic self-awareness would be a cornerstone to this approach. Instruments, such as Banks's levels of ethnic development, and values clarification activities, simulations, and role playing would be invaluable (Banks, 1979; Simon, Howe, & Kirschenbaum, 1972). Gallegos and Flores (1982) suggest that multicultural programs should include the following subject areas: cultural ideologies; sociology of culture; attitudes in and about culture; and technological and artistic aspects of cultures. Quality guest performances and Hispanic mentors and role models would contribute to this component.

4. Compensatory Education Dimension

GOAL: Develop English communication skills, particularly public speaking and vocabulary.

GOAL: Remediate and develop abilities in areas in which Hispanic students as a group have not had success in school, such as high level mathematics and science.

GOAL: Assist each student in developing an individualized plan for academic remediation and self-evaluation.

GOAL: Assist students in acquiring process skills necessary for success in challenging classes (e.g., research, independent study, computer use, listening, note taking, and class discussion).

When educational gaps are addressed on a timely and individual basis, gifted students develop at a faster rate than otherwise possible, and become skilled in areas that may have resulted in underachievement (Frasier, 1979; Passow, 1972). Academic areas in which students are deficient cannot be ignored, or those areas will become even greater limitations as individual strengths are accelerated.

5. Coping Skills Dimension

Coping skills are defined as those social and psychological skills participants need to cope with new and conflicting cultural experiences and expectations. Coping skills addressed would be individualized to students.

GOAL: Develop in students a strong system of coping skills that will aid them as citizens of two cultures.

GOAL: Relieve culture conflict through understanding and practical intervention (Jaramillo, 1974).

GOAL: Expose students to majority culture experiences they may not have encountered because of economic disadvantage or cultural restrictions.

6. Family Support Dimension

GOAL: Increase family support for the gifted Hispanic child through a parent education program.

As participants develop their unique abilities and avail themselves of more unusual educational opportunities, an increased risk is that problems will arise at home over issues, such as family expectations, home responsibilities, and lack of adequate communication about the educational program. As the gifted child grows, so must the child's family grow and shift in its attitudes (Gallegos & Flores, 1982; Leung, 1981).

Career planning and preparation sessions would help families to support students' long-range goals and to see the value of the educational program. Of course, all family services and information should be provided in Spanish and English.

GOAL: Increase family support of the special program through parent participation in all phases.

Parents should participate on all levels possible, particularly in the classroom. The result of such participation would be the support of individual learners, the development of a community spirit, and a richer program of committed participants (Gallegos & Flores, 1982).

7. Differentiated Staff Dimension

GOAL: Hire staff who are pluralistic in attitude, and who can serve as models for students (Clark, 1983).

GOAL: Hire staff knowledgeable in their own subject matter, and in the areas of education of the gifted, individualization, Hispanic culture, and multicultural education.

GOAL: Secure a commitment from the entire staff to participate in ongoing staff-development programs in the areas of education for the gifted, multicultural and individualization methodologies, Hispanic culture, and curricula (Passow, 1972).

GOAL: Maintain a staff comfortable in sharing decisionmaking with students and their families, and willing to take the time necessary for community-based education.

GOAL: Hire guidance personnel who are bilingual and skilled in areas of culture conflict and family counseling, and in working with gifted students (Frasier, 1979).

IN CONCLUSION

Although the purpose of this chapter has been to suggest a program and differentiated goals for gifted Hispanic students, such a program would have the flexibility to serve a diverse and dynamic group, and would be effective and appropriate for all gifted children. Indeed, the effects of the goals outlined here would be enhanced if students of different cultures learned side by side.

When we design and implement programs that are truly student centered, culturally valid, and supportive of the particular needs of Hispanic students, we will see an increase in this group's academic and personal successes. All the difficulties and joys of differentiating for the highly able learner are compounded by the inclusion of culturally diverse learners. Those who plan programs for the gifted need the wisdom and flexibility to provide for culturally diverse learners. Ultimately, quality programs for culturally diverse gifted students will expand opportunities for all gifted children and assist our schools in meeting the challenge of a pluralistic society.

4

"Pluralism and Power"—Dare We Reform Education of the Gifted Along These Lines?

Ernesto M. Bernal, Ph.D.
Northern Arizona University

In my experience, a simple explanation exists for why so many authors, in discussing education of the gifted, perpetuate its image of elitism. Educators of the gifted do not perceive the need to reform their own business with a view to accommodate—to find and educate—the gifted adults of tomorrow, most of whom will not be from the upper-middle and upper socioeconomic classes, and many of whom will be from nondominant ethnic groups. The educational practices these authors essentially would maintain are insensitive to the realities that poor children and their parents must face. In traditional programs, educators expect that those people, not our programs, should do the accommodating, since selection standards and familiar curricular and extracurricular practices should never be compromised. Banda's chapter is a notable exception to this literature, as I shall try to demonstrate.

To begin, Banda is not an acculturationist, one who would encourage minority children to become Anglo-American, no matter what the cost. The first paragraphs of her chapter prepare us for what is to follow. Educational programs for gifted Hispanic students must not merely recognize diversity, but honor it. While some Hispanic students should be selected because they meet the traditional profile for gifted Anglo-American students, others should be selected for having met criteria valued by Hispanic communities. Educators should help develop bicultural, indeed, multicultural competencies, and reduce the at-risk status of Hispanic students by focusing on self-valued strengths and instilling a sense of participatory control based on individualization and self-pacing.

Banda's approach seems very sensitively Hispanic. She combines personalism and the demands of objective reality with a recognition that one need not slavishly follow a highly structured, traditional curriculum to be prepared to take a place among the excellent in later life. Her approach also reflects a profound and patient faith that the best foundations for human development and personal unfolding are seldom laid in a hurry, but build on individual readiness at different points or stages in life and on support networks of significant others, including parents and teachers. Such an option for the education of gifted minorities might be viable for the best and brightest of all our children.

At times Banda's suggestions are too general, at times very specific. How to implement a whole program like the one she envisions requires more space than was allocated to her, yet many of her recommendations ring true to those of us who have managed multi-ethnic programs for bright, minority youngsters. My own experience with the Migrant and Gifted Impact Center (MAGIC) in Fresno, California, suggests that the individual student profile and the individual plan conference she recommends could be important, specific aspects of a successful program. Her seven program dimensions, while discussed in broader terms, also make sense as presented.

One of the few areas of contention might be with the dimension of compensatory education. Actually, Banda's plan is not nearly as compensatory as what this term connotes to the profession, but rather focuses on important process skills, such as taking notes efficiently and engaging effectively in class discussions. The problem I have with compensatory education is that bright students should be taught, not compensated. Remediation approaches tend to be direct, and aimed at changing behavior or instilling new skills through head-on methods that, experience and research show (Cummins, 1983b), are often self-defeating and counterproductive. For example, older English-as-a-Second-Language (ESL) methods, which stressed repetition and drill, have no place in education for gifted students. Modern ESL techniques, such as *comprehensible input,* in which English is acquired as a byproduct of learning something else (content), are better because students use language when they have something to say rather than when they are required to practice (Krashen, 1982).

Highly structured experiences have their place, but only when they are attuned to the diverse needs and learning styles of the minority students and these students volunteer to participate. The Saturday school and summer school enrichment classes provided by MAGIC in central California, the Future Leaders of America projects in southern California, and the Summer Career Institute directed by the Center for Excellence in Education at Northern Arizona University are but three examples of successful, short-term programs. Organized, intellectually stimulating activities that capitalize on the interests of the participating gifted minority students and broaden their options before they are assigned to non-college-bound tracks in high school are provided in these programs.

I also would like to underscore the importance of continuing to develop the native language skills of bilingual students in integrated programs for gifted students. First, certain cognitive advantages seem to accrue to individuals who become proficient bilinguals (Llanes, 1980), especially in the areas of cognitive flexibility (Hakuta, 1985), originality, and elaboration (Torrance, Gowan, Wu, & Aliotti, 1970). Second, while the development of bilingualism often has not been a priority in public school programs for the gifted in the United States, it has been emphasized in the *gymnasia* (college preparatory schools) in Europe, in many of the public schools of Canada, and in the more prestigious private schools in the United States, Mexico, and Central and South America. The non-English language abilities of Hispanics, American Indians, Asians, and other minority groups in the United States should not be wasted. These individuals could enjoy many advantages and contribute valuable perceptions to dominant ethnic students through the deliberate and systematic cultivation of their linguistic abilities.

Banda could be criticized for not having discussed at greater length the issues surrounding identification of Hispanic students, but her category of able learner should suffice. In the last analysis we really do not identify many gifted individuals while they are children; what we do, or should do, is select youngsters who, by any of a variety of indicators, seem to possess the potential to become gifted adults (Bernal, 1984b). The challenge for schools, then, is to provide for maximum development of able learners, which implies that a program must be designed around the learners. Instead of devoting great efforts to designing special identification strategies for minorities, all that is needed is to recognize any one of several legitimate indicators of high potential. For language-minority children, this includes first and second language proficiency levels and achievements.

As with majority children, selection criteria should be set and modified in light of experience, not based on the prestige value of certain tests or, worse yet, based on the number of students who can be serviced. The arbitrary and restrictive use of screening tests has checked the enrollments of Hispanic and other minority students in classes for the gifted, just as monocultural, traditional programs for the gifted have discouraged minority students' participation and limited their successful adaptation and their contribution to the curriculum. I agree with Banda that a culturally pluralistic alternative could solve the problems of access and success.

In case some readers are still doubtful about the feasibility of designing and implementing such pluralistic programs, I would like to emphasize that recent events have made me again hopeful. In the last few years educators in a number of states have undertaken major efforts to accommodate minorities into programs for the gifted. In Nebraska and Kansas, for instance, different departments within the state educational agencies have pooled resources and executed statewide conferences and workshops to teach educators to design and implement ways to meet the educational needs of all bright students. Arizona law and educational regulations for programs for the gifted now provide explicitly for the selection and equitable treatment of minorities.

Programs designed to accommodate gifted students from nondominant ethnic groups are risky, since educators have little research and educational precedent on which to rely. Yet the need to respond intelligently to the challenge of finding, attracting, and educating able learners from the whole of our society cannot be denied. Perhaps now is the time for educators of the gifted to take on this prodigious task and model the kinds of real-life intelligence, commitment, and creativity we would have our students exhibit.

5

Reaction to "Promoting Pluralism and Power"

Lina S. Rodriguez, J.D.
Arizona State Superior Court

As I understand it, the primary purpose of Banda's proposed program for gifted Hispanics is to teach those skills necessary not only to survive, but also to succeed in the majority culture without sacrificing cultural values and talents. To achieve this, Banda proposes an individually valued abilities focus. Educators would seek out all gifted Hispanic students, not just those who are academically gifted; involve actively the family and community role models; educate students in career development; enhance those talents recognized by the majority culture, including advanced English skills; and increase effectively ethnic pride and individual self-esteem among Hispanics. The development of Spanish language skills also would be included.

Based on my personal experiences, I will respond to the question of how Banda's proposed program would have met my needs as an Hispanic child, and would have prepared me for life as a productive adult. The following personal account provides information for an appropriate comparison of what was, and what might have been.

I am a second generation Hispanic; that is, my mother and father were born in the United States, and my grandparents were from Mexico. Until I was about five years old, Spanish was my and my parents' primary language. Through the years, English became our primary language.

Although my mother and father spoke and understood English, they experienced extreme discrimination during their school years, and as adults. They were disciplined in school for speaking any language but English. Separate schools, restrooms, drinking fountains, and public facilities were provided for Hispanics, and they were excluded from many public eating establishments. My perceptions are heavily clouded by the discrimination suffered by both of my parents.

Because of their experiences, my parents wanted to protect me from the same hurt. Although not as extreme as my parents', I have experienced discrimination throughout my life. As I was growing up, I had a sense that it was not good to be a Mexican. I wore only long-sleeved clothing and long socks to school so that I wouldn't get "dark."

My mother discouraged speaking Spanish and admonished repeatedly that we learn to speak English well, and then learn to speak Spanish well.

I clearly recall one school incident that exemplifies my experiences of growing up Hispanic, and a typical perception of Hispanics at the time. When I was in fifth grade, a classmate, having heard my last name for the first time, exclaimed, "Gosh, I didn't know you were Mexican. I thought you were Italian." I was so pleased she thought I was Italian instead of Mexican that I replied, "Oh, thank you." I also recall in sixth grade, when my mother enrolled me in a different school, the school administrator commented, "Oh, her last name is Rodriguez; put her in the 'slow class'."

My mother vigorously fought this placement and managed to get me into the "smart class." Through strong encouragement from my family, I excelled in academic courses and became a "success." However, this success was attained at the expense of much self-esteem and pride in who I was, and at a great sacrifice to my Mexican heritage and my ability to speak Spanish as fluently as I would have liked.

Ironically, when I entered law school I felt alienated from both cultures. My Anglo-American classmates greeted me with statements such as, "So you're the super minority; no wonder you got into law school. I could too if my last name were Hispanic." This was during the era of affirmative action programs, but, in fact, I had been selected for law school based on my academic record. Most of my Hispanic classmates had a very tight Hispanic cultural assimilation; they came from the same community and spoke Spanish fluently. They viewed me as a *coconut* (brown on the outside, white on the inside, or Hispanic and trying not to be) because I was so anglicized, and they resented me for their perception that I was putting on airs and wasn't proud to be a Chicana. In fact, I was very proud of both my American and my Mexican heritage.

Obviously, I didn't fit in with either culture. I was not an Anglo-American, and I was not a Chicana. I was, culturally, somewhere between. I felt left out and developed a "chip on my shoulder."

These personal experiences demonstrate that Banda's proposed program, which would promote pluralism and focus on individual abilities, would have addressed many, if not most, of my needs as a child, and would have prepared me more for life as a productive adult. Also, because such a program recognizes the reality that in order to succeed in our society, you have to excel in those abilities traditionally valued by the majority culture, it certainly would have met my needs as a child and as a judge, in that it encourages and enhances the development of proficient communication skills in English, and the development of public speaking abilities.

Banda's affective development dimension, in which career education is encouraged through role models and mentor programs, would have been of great value to me. I came from a small mining community, and my only role models, other than my parents, were teachers and physicians who worked in the mine hospital. Prior to law school, I never had met a lawyer, much less a judge, and never had been to a courthouse. Consequently, my sole education about a law career was gained by watching "Perry Mason" every week on television. Indeed, I became a lawyer because of a chance comment by one of my high school teachers, who suggested that I might make a good one.

A program with Banda's Hispanic and multicultural education dimension would have been of tremendous benefit to me. My primary language (Spanish) was sacrificed so that I might better fit the majority culture and its primary language (English). I realize now this was, and is, a fallacy. Clearly, my abilities have been enhanced by my bilingualism.

Fortunately, I improved my Spanish-speaking skills by obtaining a minor in Spanish in college. However, many, especially among second and third generation Hispanics, have lost the ability to speak Spanish; this is not uncommon, yet, this loss is not necessarily accompanied by enhancement of English-speaking skills. My observation has been that Hispanics tend to speak "Spanglish;" that is, they speak neither Spanish nor English well. Consequently, they don't excel. Banda's academic, affective, Hispanic and multicultural, and compensatory dimensions would all address this deficit.

I find the coping skills dimension to be of real personal value, based on the experiences I have outlined above. My self-esteem would have been enhanced greatly had I been told that being a Mexican was OK, or even a source of pride.

Likewise, the proposed program addresses many of the sociological deficiencies found in Hispanic children due to social and economic restrictions, and would have impacted on my personal experiences. As examples, I did not eat in a public restaurant or travel out of the state of Arizona (except to go to Disneyland once) until I was an adult. I did not travel in an airplane until I was in my late twenties.

A program to assimilate Hispanic students would have been of great value to me. Twice the work is necessary for success when one has to learn basic social concepts and expend unnecessary energy worrying about committing a social faux pas. Yet, my peers, with whom I was competing, had for the most part assimilated totally into the majority culture, and not only did not need to concern themselves with such basics, but had to have a working knowledge of careers they intended to pursue.

An example of the difficulties that were brought on by my lack of legal socialization follows. My first year of law school was torture and excessively difficult because I had never been exposed to legal language. I spent hours reading a case and a full year learning the foreign language of "legalese." Banda's proposed program would address some of these problems and, thus, would have assisted me.

I strongly endorse the proposed family support dimension. While I was very fortunate to have my family's encouragement of academic excellence, I was woefully ignorant of possibilities after graduation. The major goal of our family was that each child graduate from high school; my father did not want me to go to college; my mother very much wanted me to do so. Fortunately, my mother's wishes prevailed. Banda's program involving the family and educating them in career models and educational expectations would go a long way toward helping Hispanics achieve higher education.

Finally, of all Banda's suggestions, the one of most value is that traditional academic goals, especially the use of English, not only must be taught, but also actively encouraged. The reality is that English is the prevailing language in this country, and one must speak it well in order to succeed.

Unfortunately, discrimination still exists. All one has to do is read the newspapers to see how many states are attempting to establish English as the official language of the country. Numerous states have statutorily mandated English as their official language, and the Arizona Legislature presently has various English Only bills pending in the House and Senate. The proposed legislation, unfortunately, not only designates English as the official language in Arizona, but includes *enforcement* provisions that have sanctions imposed if the statute is violated.

A strong movement against teaching any language other than English exists in this country. Indeed, a "luxury" program for gifted Hispanics may not be encouraged in the present social and political xenophobic atmosphere where even bilingual programs are about to meet their demise.

Thus, Banda's proposed program, with its individual flexibility and emphasis on English skills, would work on a practical level both for gifted Hispanic and other gifted students. Such a program has a much greater chance of meeting approval from legislators and the public who are endorsing English only and encouraging the demise of cultural diversity.

I must add that I can't help wondering how I would have turned out if I had had such a program as Banda proposes for gifted students. Perhaps I have been successful because of the chip on my shoulder and my need to prove myself. Then, again, perhaps I would have been more successful had I had Banda's school program. I guess it all depends on how you define success. Nevertheless, such a program would have patched a gaping hole in the process of my education and my feelings of self-worth as a child and as a young adult, and would have prepared me better for life as a productive and happy adult and eliminated many of the obstacles over which I had to stumble.

6

Curriculum for Gifted Hispanic Students

Anne J. Udall, Ph.D.
Tucson Unified School District

In the past, minority students in general, and Hispanic students in particular, have been underrepresented in programs for gifted students (Deleon, 1983; High & Udall, 1983; McKenzie, 1986). To continue to disregard gifted minority students not only will dangerously undermine the continued success of our society, but also could irreparably damage the credibility of educational programs for the gifted.

In this chapter, curriculum for gifted Hispanic students is addressed and the following questions are answered: (a) How are the issues of definition and identification related to curriculum? (b) What are the characteristics of gifted Hispanic students? (c) How do these characteristics relate to the curriculum needs of gifted Hispanic students? (d) What teaching strategies are effective with gifted Hispanic students? (e) What teaching/ learning models provide the most appropriate framework for implementing the curriculum? (f) What is the role of the teacher? In a final section are presented questions about curriculum for gifted Hispanic students that need to be answered.

RELATIONSHIP OF DEFINITION AND IDENTIFICATION TO CURRICULUM

Curriculum for gifted Hispanic students cannot be discussed in isolation from the issues of definition and identification. As Maker (1982a, 1986) has so aptly pointed out, curriculum is intricately interwoven with both the definition of giftedness employed and the identification procedures used. Once students are identified, program curriculum should reflect program goals.

I wish to express my deepest thanks to Mari Helen High for the ideas and collected information expressed in her unpublished manuscript, *Closing the Gap for the Disadvantaged Gifted.* Her willingness to share these ideas made this chapter much easier to write.

The relationship of definition and identification to curriculum is particularly important when discussing gifted minority students. In an effort to correct past mistakes, we have resorted to a wide variety of nontraditional identification measures to identify gifted Hispanic students (e.g., Bernal & Reyna, 1974; DeAvila & Havassy, 1975; Hilliard, 1976; Tidwell, 1979). Consequently, Hispanic students often are placed in programs for the gifted based on high scores on instruments that have little relationship to the program goals. Minority students are set up to fail if we identify them using one set of theoretical assumptions and serve them using another.

CHARACTERISTICS OF GIFTED HISPANIC STUDENTS

Many of the factors that must be considered when defining the characteristics of gifted Hispanic students have already been discussed in the introduction to Section I. For brevity, the reader is referred to the introduction to Section I for an elaboration of these points, particularly those addressed by Castenada (1976), Leung (1981), Orange County Unified School District (1981), and Ramirez and Castaneda (1974). This and others' (described below) research can be synthesized to provide a framework to design a curriculum specific to gifted Hispanic students. The following six major points summarize the characteristics of gifted Hispanic students, and form that framework.

1. No one profile of a gifted Hispanic child exists. The Hispanic culture in this country is composed of numerous groups with differences in history, language, and customs. In addition, length of residence in the United States, amount of urbanization, and political and social strengths are important factors, as is poverty.
2. All gifted students, both Hispanic and non-Hispanic, share similar cognitive, affective, and social characteristics; behavioral expressions of giftedness, however, vary from culture to culture. Table I-1 (in the introduction to Section I) is a summary of characteristics differentiating gifted Hispanics from other students. In the first column are listed the cognitive, affective, and social characteristics of all gifted students (defined by Clark [1983]; further defined as characteristics of *absolute* giftedness—the underlying aspects of giftedness transcending historical time and cultural context—by Leung [1981]). In the second column are listed the cultural values generally characteristic of Hispanics, and in the third column are listed the behavioral manifestations (defined as *specific* aspects of giftedness by Leung [1981]) of the absolute cognitive, affective, and social characteristics in Hispanics. An appreciation of the shared characteristics of giftedness, but the differentness of expression, is a key concept.
3. Manifestations of giftedness are affected by behavioral styles (Hilliard, 1976; Ramirez & Castaneda, 1974) and cultural values. Anglo-American and Hispanic cultures value differently home, school, the role of the individual, work, and religion. These differing values influence how each culture manifests behaviors indicating giftedness. In Table 6-1 contrasting values held by Anglo-American

Table 6-1 Comparison of Hispanic and Anglo-American Values

Hispanic Values	*Anglo-American Values*
Being rather than doing	Doing rather than being
Limited stress on material possessions	Material well-being
Present time orientation	Future orientation
Simple patterns of work organization and group cooperation	Individual action and reaction
Central importance of the family, personal relations	Impersonal relations
Fatalism, accommodation to problems	Man's mastery over the universe
Tradition	Change

Source: From *Culturally Diverse Exceptional Children in School* (p. 32) by J. Nazzaro (Ed.), 1981, Reston, Va.: Council for Exceptional Children. Copyright 1981 by Council for Exceptional Children. Reprinted by permission.

and Hispanic cultures are listed and how they differ in key areas is shown. These cultural differences affect a child's behavior in school, and must be considered by teachers in their interactions with Hispanic children.

4. The way Hispanic students express their giftedness may be valued less by the dominant culture than by Hispanics. As a result, the gifted Hispanic student is likely to be overlooked in the identification process.
5. The gifted Hispanic student may or may not display certain characteristics, depending on ethnic composition of a classroom.
6. Two key areas distinguish the Hispanic student from the Anglo-American student: (a) language skills and proficiency, particularly for bilingual or monolingual Spanish students; and (b) complex demands resulting from living in two cultures. Movement between two cultures creates tremendous pressure on the Hispanic student, and affects achievement, self-concept, and behavior patterns. The ability to adapt successfully to such demands is a key distinction between the gifted and the nongifted Hispanic student. In fact, Hilliard (1976) and Bernal (1974), among others, view giftedness as the ability of an individual from a minority culture to balance successfully the demands of both cultures.

CURRICULUM NEEDS OF GIFTED HISPANIC STUDENTS

Standards of good curriculum for the gifted apply to all students, regardless of social, economic, or cultural backgrounds. A curriculum for gifted Hispanic students should meet already established standards for a qualitatively different curriculum.

The first key to serving gifted Hispanic students successfully is to follow established guidelines for creating a qualitatively different curriculum for the gifted; the second is to individualize. The process of individualization involves two steps: (a) assessment of students' strengths and weaknesses; and (b) development of a curriculum based on this initial assessment (Baldwin, 1978). Hispanic students, particularly those who are bilingual or monolingual Spanish and who come from low socioeconomic backgrounds, may have weaknesses in language and may lack experiences that facilitate academic success. Strengths can be found in creativity, problem solving, leadership, and adaptability.

Given these strengths and weaknesses, various methods can be designed to individualize for gifted Hispanic students and build on an already established qualitatively different curriculum. For example, teachers can individualize so that students show mastery of learning through the use of tape recorders, computers, and other technological devices rather than through writing. Creating products that involve building or fixing things is another strength of Hispanic students. Teachers need to recognize and develop this product development strength by assigning or permitting products, such as oral presentations, drawings, or models, to be substituted for written reports.

TEACHING STRATEGIES

Eight teaching strategies, commonly found in the literature on the curriculum needs of gifted minority students, are based on the characteristics of gifted minority students, and the rationale for incorporating each, are now discussed. Each teaching strategy builds on principles of a differentiated curriculum; furthermore, each strategy provides ample opportunity for individualization. Materials and resources for each strategy are listed at the end of this chapter (see Appendix 6-A).

1. *Use concrete materials to teach abstract concepts.*

Minority students, particularly from impoverished homes, lack much of the stimulation and exposure needed to develop abstract academic concepts, and, as a result, need concrete materials to manipulate. Gradually the teacher can move from concrete to abstract examples. For instance, when teaching the concept of classification, one might begin by using known objects (e.g., people pieces, tangrams, geoboards, balance scales, puzzles, Cuisenaire rods, geoblocks) and later introduce words, concepts, or ideas.

A note of caution is in order when using concrete examples and material to teach higher level concepts: One must clearly understand the higher level concept being taught and how the manipulative used can develop a child's understanding of the concept. Otherwise, students do little more than play with materials, and do not generalize to the underlying concept.

2. *Use examples that are relevant to culture and experience.*

When teaching students about revolutions the Mexican Revolution is equally as relevant as the French Revolution; in teaching poetry one can study Pablo Neruda as well as Robert Browning.

Gifted Hispanic students, because of an alienating history in the public schools, are less likely than Anglo-American students to be motivated to learn. Relevancy is the cornerstone of motivation. Using concrete examples from students' experiences, from topics about which they are knowledgeable, and from areas of intrinsic interest will make the curriculum relevant.

A relevant curriculum could include: (a) studying the legal, political, social, and/ or economic history of the community where the program is located; (b) doing a unit on genealogy and studying family folklore; (c) researching a current issue in the local Hispanic community and producing an original solution for the problem; (d) studying local Hispanic writers as part of a unit in literature or poetry; (e) learning about the local municipality and Hispanic political leaders as an example of government; or (f) investigating significant environmental issues in the neighborhood. Any abstract concept can be taught using immediate, understandable, culturally relevant examples.

3. *Involve the community in the program.*

Parents form the backbone of any school environment and their involvement is the most important component of any plan to engage the local community. However, many parents of gifted Hispanic students will not be familiar with the inner workings of the public school and will be uncomfortable within the school environment because of lack of communication, inaccessibility of the meeting sites, lack of child care, and lack of follow-up. The teacher's efforts can make an alien system more comprehensible.

Maker, Morris, and James (1981) describe a parent component in their program for potentially gifted, inner-city kindergarten children in a school with 60 percent Hispanic students. Participation by parents was encouraged on several levels, ranging from minimum communication concerning goals of the program and individual student growth to participation in class activities and field trips. In addition, parents were encouraged to participate in the following activities in the school environment: (a) a materials center in the classroom, with books for both children and parents to take home; (b) special nonthreatening activities, such as cooking; and (c) an open house with student entertainment.

Nazzaro and Portuondo (1981) suggest that parents can be involved if (a) meetings are scheduled at times and in places that are accessible; (b) interpreters are available; (c) a warm and caring environment is created; (d) ample information is provided; and (e) meetings are held in places other than school. When involving the community, one must be careful to communicate in culturally appropriate ways as well. Sometimes a visit will be more appropriate than a letter, and letters should be in Spanish when that is the family's primary language.

In addition to parent involvement, community involvement should include various groups (e.g., public welfare programs, local museums, social service agencies, hospitals, and universities). The contributions of the Hispanic individuals in the community should be noted by teachers and known by Hispanic students (Gear, 1978).

4. *Include leadership training as an important part of the curriculum.*

Minority students need training in leadership skills (Baldwin, 1978; Gallagher, 1975) for the following three reasons (Fuchigami 1978): (a) Leaders are needed in all aspects of our society. (b) Minority children need to see minority leaders as role models. (c) We must develop our leadership talent from all sources.

Fuchigami (1978) briefly outlines the necessary components for a leadership curriculum: (a) learning the skills of reading, writing, oral communication, critical and analytical thinking, and problem-solving techniques; (b) developing the personality traits of leaders; (c) learning about the social, economic, and political system; and (d) gaining information about the process of enacting change.

In response to unusually high apathy among students, Cantu, Trevino, and Walther (1982) developed a high school program in which Hispanic students who demonstrated leadership ability participated in two components: a double period of civics and economics, and community activities. Community activities included attending school board and city commission meetings, attending voter registration drives, performing internships in city government, and organizing candidate forums.

5. *Incorporate mentors into the curriculum.*

Mentors provide positive role models, exemplify possible career options, and offer much-needed personal and academic support needed by gifted minority students (Baldwin, 1978; Fitzgerald, 1973). Using mentors is particularly relevant to gifted Hispanic females, who face dual pressures. A mentor program can be set up as either an informal or formal experience; part of an internship experience in a professional setting; or a series of informal contacts over a period of time.

Mentor programs are valuable for both leadership training (see previous section) and career education. Career education can provide the gifted Hispanic student with a focus on future goals and plans. Hispanic students, particularly those who are poor, monolingual in Spanish, or female, need to be exposed to a wide variety of career options.

6. *Incorporate basic skills training if necessary.*

Frequently, nonacculturated Hispanic students, particularly those who are bilingual or monolingual Spanish speakers with language-related difficulties, will enter programs for the gifted with fewer basic skills than their Anglo-American counterparts. Melesky (1984) notes that one key difference in programs for gifted Hispanic students is the inclusion of basic skill development in reading and language, often provided before formal entrance into the program. A preprogram is one option, or communication and language skills can be incorporated into existing programs for the gifted.

Students also may need to acquire "school" skills—time mangement, organization, independent learning, and studying. A growing body of curriculum material is available. (Refer to Appendix 6-A.)

7. *Use creative and problem-solving strengths.*

In addition to remediating basic skills deficits, teachers must acknowledge the strengths and abilities of their Hispanic students. Strengths in leadership and multicultural experiences already have been noted; creativity and problem solving are two additional strengths that can be developed effectively in the classroom.

One method of incorporating creativity and problem solving is through the use of the Creative Problem Solving (CPS) model (Parnes, 1966). Students can be taught the five steps of the CPS model (see Maker [1982a] and the section on Curriculum Implementation in this chapter), and then it can be applied in a variety of content, social, and leadership areas. Other materials are listed at the end of this chapter.

Some writers, notably Bernal (1976), have cautioned against overemphasizing creative strengths, if such emphasis overshadows intellectual strengths. Hispanic students have equally strong cognitive abilities and must not be given a "watered down" version of the curriculum because of a misguided interpretation of the literature. One should use the creative strengths of Hispanic students to encourage cognitive growth and intellectual pursuits by integrating creativity development with the teaching of curriculum content.

8. *Concentration on affective needs.*

The affective needs of gifted Hispanic students, particularly the development of a positive self-concept, are great and require tremendous attention (Taba & Elkins, 1964). The research is clear: minority students have lower self-concepts than nonminority students (Dabney, 1980). Gifted Hispanic students, because of a heightened sensitivity to the world, will be affected strongly by discrimination, racist attitudes, and conflicting values at home and school. In short, a curriculum for gifted Hispanic students should include a special emphasis on self-concept development.

High self-esteem will occur when students (a) learn to handle the conflicts caused by the demands of two cultures; and (b) establish a strong self-identity while maintaining a cultural identity. Having a strong multicultural component in the curriculum can lead to a greater understanding of both differences and similarities in cultures and, in turn, will encourage a strong sense of pride and identity.

Lack of motivation is related to a poor self-concept. An external locus of control is often responsible, in part, for low motivation. Addison (1982) discusses developing an internal locus of control through activities, such as values clarification, goal setting techniques, time management, and creative problem solving.

The eight teaching strategies listed in this section can be used in programs for all gifted Hispanic students. However, special consideration should be given to females, a population whose needs have been overlooked. They face dual pressures of being a female in a culture where sex roles are rigidly defined and being a minority in the context of the larger society. Earlier sections of this chapter have included discussions of the latter pressure of being a minority in the society; the problem of being a female in the Hispanic culture deserves additional attention.

Traditionally, the status of women in the Hispanic culture is lower than the status of men, and this fact carries with it some important implications. First, Hispanic females might hide their intellectual ability, since it is not highly valued. Education for Hispanic females may be less valued than education for Hispanic males and, therefore, females may not be given the same opportunities as their male counterparts. A gifted Hispanic female may be reluctant to pursue nontraditional educational careers because of the cultural emphasis on traditional roles. Finally, the Hispanic female may be reluctant to challenge her family's decisions or opinions about her education because of the high value placed on authority and, therefore, acquiesce to a family decision she violently opposes.

Given these facts, several strategies are of particular importance when teaching gifted Hispanic females. These girls and women need strong role models, and using mentors is one method of providing this source. Career education for the student and her family needs to be incorporated early. The affective needs of gifted Hispanic females should be a priority; they need to have a realistic sense of their abilities and to be taught strategies for coping with the dual pressures noted above. Finally, teachers must be sensitive to the special needs of the gifted Hispanic girl, and individualize accordingly.

In conclusion, no quick and easy "cookbook" is available for teaching any gifted student. Curriculum needs should be based on the goals of the program; the goals of the program, in turn, should be based on the characteristics of the learner and the definition of giftedness chosen. In addition to principles of curriculum development, the eight teaching strategies described are important components of an appropriate curriculum for gifted Hispanic students at both elementary and secondary levels.

CURRICULUM IMPLEMENTATION

When a curriculum is implemented within a logical framework it can enhance greatly the success of a program for gifted Hispanic students. Both the type of program and the student to be served will determine the best teaching and learning program model(s) to implement.

For brevity, in Table 6-2 the components necessary to implement a successful curriculum for gifted Hispanic students are summarized; that is, the teaching strategies (first column) and differentiated curriculum principle(s) on which they are built (second column), and appropriate teaching/learning models (third column) that can form the framework for curriculum implementation. Models are listed only if the teaching strategy (e.g., mentors) is an essential element of the model's design.

ROLE OF THE TEACHER

Although no research is available to substantiate this statement, I believe many gifted Hispanic students fail in programs, not because of a deficit in cognitive or academic skills, but because the social environment is alien, and/or hostile. When students from impoverished and/or culturally different homes enter programs with Anglo-American students from wealthier homes, the discrepancy between their home environments can cause a discomfort level that eventually may lead the Hispanic student to drop out of the program. Differences in values and cognitive styles (Ramirez & Castaneda, 1974) also will lead to subtle classroom conflict. The creation of a nurturing, accepting environment is of particular importance if such conflict and alienation are to be minimized.

In Table 6-1, *supra,* some basic values of the Hispanic culture were noted. The teacher must understand these values and translate such understanding into classroom practice. In Table 6-3, key values related to education and held by rural Mexican-American parents are contrasted with key values of Anglo-American parents. These contrasting values can be thought of as extreme points on a continuum, and can be useful in interpreting behavior of Hispanic students. Factors that can influence a family's position on the continuum include degree of acculturation, length of residence in the U.S., primary language, SES, country of origin, and geographic location.

Table 6-2 Components for the Implementation of a Successful Curriculum for Gifted Hispanic Students

Teaching Strategies	Curriculum Principles	Appropriate Teaching/Learning Models
1. Move from concrete to abstract	Accelerated or advanced content; interdisciplinary content; high level of abstractness in content; higher levels of thinking	Bloom; Taba; Renzulli
2. Use relevant teaching experiences	Interdisciplinary content; higher levels of thinking; emphasis on real problems	Renzulli
3. Involve community	Emphasis on real problems; development of research/ methodological skills; independent study; open-endedness	Renzulli
4. Include leadership training	Interdisciplinary content; generation of new information or products; development of personal growth	Betts
5. Use mentors	Advanced content; generation of new information or products; development of personal growth; independent study skills; development of research/ methodological skills; open-endedness	Betts; Feldhusen & Robinson
6. Incorporate basic skills if needed	Development of personal growth; development of research/ methodological skills	Renzulli; Betts; Feldhusen & Kolloff; Taylor
7. Employ problem solving and creative strengths	Interdisciplinary content; higher levels of thinking; generation of new information and/or products; open-endedness	Parnes; Treffinger; Feldhusen & Kolloff; Williams
8. Concentrate on affective needs	Development of personal growth; open-endedness	Clark; Betts

---

Table 6-3 Key Values Regarding Education Held by Anglo-Americans and Mexican-Americans in Rural Areas

Anglo-American Culture	Hispanic Culture
Education	*Education*
Focus: Child-centered	*Focus*: Family-centered
Function: Socialization (both education and instruction) (family-school roles coincide)	*Function*: Socialization (instruction only; the family "educates;" school as extension of family)
Goal: Develop child's highest potential (achieve what he or she can do)	*Goal*: Develop child's personality (be what he or she can be)
Objectives: Teach good health, good character, good citizenship Teach how to compete and initiate change Teach basic academic skills	*Objectives*: Teach respect of self and others Learn how to cooperate and cope with change Teach basic academic skills
Teaching style: Stresses active, two-way discussions and problem solving	*Teaching style*: Stresses lectures, one-way presentations and memory exercises
Discipline: Persuasive, based on explanation	*Discipline*: Affective, based on scolding and shaming
Class behavior: Active interaction with teachers and peers	*Class Behavior*: Refrain from interaction unless called upon to answer
School policies: Acceptance of "reasonable" rules (students and parents willing to challenge teachers)	*School policies*: Acceptance of authority and educational expertise
Teacher role: mediator of knowledge	*Teacher role*: Authority figure
Student role: Active participant in learning process	*Student role*: Passive recipient of knowledge
Motivation: Competition	*Motivation*: Family honor and respect
Use of language: Direct, objective, concise (language—tool of communication)	*Use of language*: Indirect, subjective, digressive (Language—aesthetic experience)
Reasoning: Inductive (principles elicited from concrete examples)	*Reasoning*: Intuitive (principles applied to examples)
Tests: Primary means of assessing student potential and achievement	*Tests*: Only *one* means of assessing student potential and achievement
Extracurricular activities: An integral part of school education	*Extracurricular activities*: *Not* a part of school education

Source: From "Identifying First Generation Rural Mexican-American Gifted" by J. Laudenslager and A. Valdez, a paper presented at National Association for Gifted Children, Las Vegas, Nevada, November 1986.

Suggestions for classroom practice have been made in previous sections, but other methods of creating a safe psychological environment are needed, and are described below.

1. Cooperative learning methods should be used, including small group problem-solving exercises. (See Appendix 6-A, Burns [1984], for sample cooperative

learning rules; and Flugelman [1976], for other material that stresses cooperative learning.)

2. Regular classroom meetings and discussions should occur. (See Appendix 6-A, Bushman and Jones [1977], and Stanford and Stanford [1969], for ways to develop discussion skills and positive group dynamics.)

3. Multicultural activities are needed in the classroom (e.g., note birthdays of significant individuals, holidays such as Cinco de Mayo, and cultural traditions for holidays such as Christmas and Easter).

4. Fairness and impartiality should be maintained in all situations. A teacher must be consistent in all proceedings, and make expectations clear for assignments and grades. Finally, teachers should be aware of any financial demands they may unknowingly place on students.

5. Nonverbal and verbal activities should be emphasized equally, and opportunities should be provided for students to excel.

6. Teachers should take a student-centered, rather than task-centered, approach in the classroom, with frequent expressions of physical warmth and caring, and overt concern for the student's well-being.

7. Reinforcement for students does not have to be material but, instead, can include such rewards as a note sent home to the parents or a chance to work with the teacher.

8. Teachers should be particularly aware of the traditional sex roles of males and females in the Hispanic culture and of any demands placed on students that are culturally embarassing. At the same time, however, the teacher must work to assure that gifted Hispanic females are offered the same opportunities to learn as gifted Hispanic males.

The role of the teacher may vary depending on the ethnic composition of the classroom. Although no research can be cited to substantiate this statement, personal experience has shown that Hispanic students, when in the majority, are more gregarious and assertive. When in the minority they are less likely to show this behavior. Therefore, teachers must be especially careful to follow suggested guidelines when Hispanic students are outnumbered in the classroom.

In summary, the role of the teacher is crucial in the education of gifted Hispanic students. Teachers not only need to be familiar with the standards of a qualitatively different curriculum for gifted students and other strategies to meet the needs of Hispanic students, but also must create a safe and nurturing learning environment that minimizes cultural conflict and miscommunication, and encourages genuine acceptance of others.

IN CONCLUSION

Curriculum for gifted Hispanic students cannot simply be taken from a template and applied to any situation. Educators interested in providing quality programs for gifted Hispanic students must be willing to assess students' needs and plan accordingly.

The following thirteen questions—modifications and expansions of Schulkind's (1982) ten questions to address when developing programs for the gifted, culturally different child—are presented here as guidelines for curriculum development.

1. Are the program goals and identification measures consistent with each other?
2. Have I assessed the strengths and weaknesses of the learners in my classroom or program?
3. Have I assessed the particular social, cultural, and economic influences that surround and influence my students?
4. Have I assessed my own attitudes toward my students, and my expectations for their learning?
5. Can I expect, and to what extent, community cooperation in this effort?
6. Will the program increase the child's self-concept, while increasing cognitive skills as well?
7. Did I set concrete, product-oriented, touchable, displayable results that serve as a reminder that success can be achieved?
8. Did I carefully research local customs and history before designing the program?
9. Did I consider cultural values before proceeding with the plan? Does the program threaten these values?
10. Is the curriculum qualitatively different, as defined by the experts in curriculum for gifted students?
11. Can the program be streamlined so that it is cost effective, realistic, and viable within the given physical environment?
12. Do I have an evaluation component to assess the success of my program?
13. Is the community informed and/or actively involved?

One should be willing to try new ideas, and to change if necessary. The challenge is immense; yet, when we successfully meet the needs of gifted Hispanic students, all students stand to gain. As Cordova (1985) states: "The survival of America as a strong, respected nation and world leader depends on if and how rapidly a multilingual, multicultural, pluralistic education system can be established in the public schools" (p. 91). Ours is a multicultural society, and programs for the gifted must offer multicultural, pluralistic education to all students. Cordova (1985) continues: "Educational and political powers-that-be must take the farsighted, visionary, bold first step to begin the process of changing the structure, scope and thrust of public education from fantasy to reality, from old to new, from monoculturalism to multiculturism and, most important, from inequity to equity" (p. 91).

Appendix 6-A

Materials and Resource List

Teaching Strategies

1. Use concrete materials to teach abstract concepts.

Brooks, P.R. (1984). *A teacher's guide for Project Step: Strategies for targeting early potential.* (ERIC Document Reproduction Service No. ED 254 015)

Cobb, V. (1972). *Science experiments you can eat.* New York: J.B. Lippincott.

Cobb, V. (1979). *More science experiments you can eat.* New York: J.B. Lippincott.

Creative Publications, 5005 West 110 St., Oak Lawn, IL 60453

ESS: Elementary Science Study, McGraw Hill Publications, 1221 Avenue of the Americas, New York, NY 10020

Taba, H., & Elkins, D. (1964). *Teaching strategies for the culturally disadvantaged.* Chicago: Rand McNally.

2. Use examples that are relevant to experience.

Taba, H., & Elkins, D. (1964). *Teaching strategies for the culturally disadvataged.* Chicago: Rand McNally.

3. Involve the community in the program.

Gear, G.H. (1978). Within the community and its schools. In A.Y. Baldwin, G.H. Gear, & L.J. Lucito (Eds.), *Educational planning for the gifted: Overcoming cultural, geographic, and socioeconomic barriers.* Reston, VA: The Council for Exceptional Children.

Golden, J. (1980). *Como ser apdres de ninos superdotados y talentosos: Manual para los padres (Parenting the gifted and talented: A handbook for parents).* New York: New York City Board of Education. (Available from Community School District Ten, Board of Education of the City of New York, P.S. 95, 3961 Hillman Ave., Bronx, NY 10463).

Maker, C.J., Morris, E., & James, J. (1981). The Eugene Field Project: A program for potentially gifted young children. In *Balancing the scale for the disadvantaged gifted: Presentations from the Fourth Biennial National Conference on Disadvantaged Gifted/Talented.* Ventura, CA: Ventura County Superintendent of Schools Office.

Nazzaro, J., & Portuondo, M. (1981). Understanding where the students are coming from. In J. Nazzaro (Ed.), *Culturally diverse exceptional children in school.* Reston, VA: The Council for Exceptional Children.

Roeper Review, 1982, *5,* 2–16; contains special section on involving the community.

San Bernandino City Schools. (1964). *A minority of one. The story of the Franklin Junior High School Training Natural Talent Project, 1959–1963.* San Bernandino, CA: Author. (ERIC Document Reproduction Service No. ED 032 350)

4. Include leadership training as an important part of the curriculum.

Cantu, R., Trevino, D., & Walther, K.P. (1982). Meeting the needs of the Hispanic gifted. In *Identifying and educating the disadvantaged gifted/talented: Selected Proceedings from the Fifth National Conference on Disadvantaged Gifted/Talented*. Ventura, CA: Ventura County Superintendent of Schools.

Ellis, A.S., & Ratner, R. (1976). *Decision making manual*. St. Charles, IL: Aron Communications.

Feldhusen, J., & Richardson, W.B. (1984). *Leadership education: Developing skills for youth*. New York: Trillium Press.

Fuchigami, R.Y. (1978). Summary, analysis, and future directions. In A.Y. Baldwin, G.H. Gear, & L.J. Lucito (Eds.), *Educational planning for the gifted: Overcoming cultural, geographic, and socioeconomic barriers*. Reston, VA.: The Council for Exceptional Children.

Gallagher, J. (1975). *Teaching the gifted child* (2nd ed.). Boston: Allyn & Bacon.

Gallagher, J. (1982). *The use of teacher–scholar teams to develop units for the gifted*. New York: Trillium Press.

Lamb, R.A., & Busse, C.A. (1983). Leadership beyond lip service. *Roeper Review, 5*, 18–21.

Los Angeles City Unified School District, Instructional Planning Division, Programs for Gifted. (1976). *Leadership: A survey of literature*. Los Angeles, CA: Author.

National/State Leadership Training Institute on the Gifted and Talented. (1977). *A new generation of leadership*. Ventura, CA: Author.

Sisk, D. (1986). Social studies for the future: The use of video for developing leadership. *Gifted Child Quarterly, 30*, 182–185.

Whitmore, J.R. (1973). *Student leadership: Guidelines for developing programs in distressed low income elementary schools* (Research and Development Memorandum No. 113). Stanford: Stanford University, Stanford Center for Research and Development in Teaching.

5. Incorporate mentors into the curriculum.

Booth, L. (1980). An apprentice-mentor program for gifted students. *Roeper Review, 3*, 11–13.

Dunham, G., & Russo, T. (1983). Career education for the disadvantaged: Some thoughts for educators. *Roeper Review, 5*, 26–28.

Feldhusen, J., & Kolloff, P.B. (1986). The Purdue three stage enrichment model for gifted education at the elementary level. In J.S. Renzulli (Ed.), *Systems and models for developing programs for the gifted and talented*. Mansfield Center, CT: Creative Learning Press.

Feldhusen, J., & Robinson, A. The Purdue secondary model for gifted and talented youth. In J.S. Renzulli (Ed.), *Systems and models for developing programs for the gifted and talented*. Mansfield Center, CT: Creative Learning Press.

Middlebrooks, M.W., & Strong, J.H. (1982). Project career, *Roeper Review, 5*, 36–38.

Moore, B.A. (1979). A model career education program for gifted disadvantaged students. *Roeper Review, 2*, 20–23.

Nash, D., & Treffinger, D. (1986). *The mentor*. Buffalo, NY: DOK Publishers.

Noller, R.B. (1982). *Mentoring: A voiced scarf*. Buffalo, NY: Bearly, Ltd.

Noller, R.B., & Frey, B.R. (1983). *Mentoring: An annotated bibliography*. Buffalo, NY: Bearly, Ltd.

OrRico, M.J., & Feldhusen, J.F. (1979). Career education for the gifted, creative and talented. *G/C/T, 6*, 38–40.

6. Incorporate basic skills training, if necessary.

Chase, L. (1975). *The other side of the report card: A how-to-do-it program for affective education*. Santa Monica, CA: Goodyear Publishing.

Doherty, E.J.S., & Evans, L.C. (1980). *Self-starter kit for independent study*. East Windsor Hill, CT: Synergetics.

Ellis, D.B. (1984). *Becoming a master student* (5th ed.). Rapid City, SD: College Survival.

McElmurry, M.A. (1981). *Caring: Learning to value yourself, family, friends and school*. Carthage, IL: Good Apple.

Nearine, R.J., & Freedman, A.I. *Developing programs for the gifted limited English speaker*. (ERIC Document Reproduction Service No. ED 188 365)

7. Use creative and problem-solving strengths.

Allen, J. (1977). *The other side of the elephant*. Buffalo, NY: DOK Publishers.

Allison, L., & Katz, D. (1983). *Gee whiz: How to mix art and science or the act of thinking scientifically*. New York: Little, Brown.

Eberle, B., & Stanish, B. (1980). *CPS for kids: A resource book for teaching creative problem solving to children*. Buffalo, NY: DOK Publishers.

Frank, M. (1979). *If you're trying to teach kids how to write, you've gotta have this book!* Nashville: Incentive Publications.

Maker, C.J. (1979a). Developing multiple talents in exceptional children. *Teaching Exceptional Children, 11*, 120–124.

Stevenson, G., Seghini, J.B., Timothy, K., Brown, K., Lloyd, B.C., Zimmerman, M.A., Maxfield, S., & Buchanan, J. *Project implode: Igniting creative potential*. Salt Lake City, UT: Bella-Vista-Institute for Behavioral Research in Creativity.

Taylor, C.W. (1968). The multiple talent approach. *The Instructor, 77*, 27;142;144;146.

Torrance, E.P. (1977). *Discovery and nurturance of giftedness in the culturally different*. Reston, VA: The Council for Exceptional Children.

Williams, F.E. (1970). *Classroom ideas for encouraging thinking and feeling* (2nd ed.). Buffalo, NY: DOK Publishers.

8. Concentrate on affective needs.

Addison, L. (1982). Strengthening the minority and disadvantaged gifted student: Curricula to develop locus of control. In *Identifying and educating the disadvantaged gifted/talented*. Ventura, CA: Ventura County Superintendent of Schools Office.

Bauer, M.P., Bock, S., Kennedy, K., Lowe, O., Machotka, M., Moore, E., Scott, R., & Cummings, M.A. (1975). *A supplement to individual differences: An experience in human relations for children*. Madison, WI: Madison Public Schools.

Canfield, J., & Wells, H.C. (1976). *100 ways to enhance self-concept in the classroom*. Englewood Cliffs, NY: Prentice-Hall.

Chase, L. (1975). *The other side of the report card: A how-to-do-it program for affective education*. Santa Monica, CA: Goodyear Publishing.

Frasier, M.M. (1982). Bibliotherapy: Educational and counseling implications for the gifted disadvantaged. In *Identifying and educating the disadvantaged gifted/talented*. Ventura, CA: Ventura County Superintendent of Schools Office.

Programs for Gifted Hispanic Students

AIM High for Bilingual Students, Austin Independent Schools District, Austin, TX.

Brooks, P.R. (1984). *A teacher's guide for Project Step: Strategies for targeting early potential* (ERIC Document Reproduction Service No. ED 254 015).

Encendiendo Una Llama, Bilingual Gifted and Talented Program, Webster School, 5 Cone Street, Hartford, CT 06105 (ERIC Document Reproduction Service No. ED 196 197)

Ferguson, L. (1986). A fair share: Opening doors for the gifted bilingual students. *Equity and Choice, 2*, 5–13.

Orange County Unified School District. (1981). *GATE-way to success: Hispanic gifted program. Identification packet and instructional guide.* Orange County, CA.: Author. (ERIC Document Reproduction Service No. ED 239 438)

Prince George's County Public School District, 7801 Laurel Spring Rd, Prince George's County, VA 23875.

Project Focus, Omaha Public Schools, Omaha, NE.

Project SABER, Edgewood Independent School District, 5358 W. Commerce, San Antonio, TX 78237.

Curriculum Implementation

Maker, C.J. (1982). *Teaching models in the education of the gifted.* Rockville, MD: Aspen Publishers.

Renzulli, J.S. (Ed.). (1986). *Systems and models for developing programs for the gifted and talented.* Mansfield Center, CT: Creative Learning Press.

Role of the Teacher

Anaya, R.A. (1976). *Bless me, ultima.* Berkeley, CA.: Tonatiuh-Quinto Sol.

Burns, M. (1984). *The math solution: Teaching for mastery through problem solving.* Sausalito, CA: Marilyn Burns Education Associates.

Bushman, J.H., & Jones, S.K. (1977). *Effective communication: A handbook of discussion skills.* Buffalo, NY: DOK Publications.

Clark, B. (1983). *Growing up gifted: Developing the potential of children at home and at school.* Columbus, OH: Charles E. Merrill.

Flugelman, A. (Ed.). (1976). *The new games book.* Garden City, NJ: Doubleday.

Hendrick, G., & Wills, R. (1975). *The centering book.* Englewood Cliffs, NY: Prentice-Hall.

Ramirez, M., III., & Castaneda, A. (1974). *Cultural democracy, bicognitive development, and education.* New York: Academic Press.

Riding, A. (1985). *Distant neighbors: A portrait of the Mexicans.* New York: Alfred A. Knopf.

Rodriguez, R. (1982). *Hunger of memory: The education of Richard Rodriguez.* New York: Bantam Books.

Stanford, G., & Stanford, B.D. (1969). *Learning discussion skills through games.* New York: Citation Press.

7

A Critique of "Curriculum for Gifted Hispanic Students"

Barbara Clark, Ed.D.
California State University

Udall implies that certain lessons we must learn to allow us as a people to benefit from cultural differences are still before us. The vision of a country unified by bonds of respect and esteem, gaining strength from the diversity of all its citizens, is still unrealized. The noted shift in cultural composition affects education; how it affects education for the gifted is the thrust of Udall's inquiry.

In exploring the fit between definition, identification, and curriculum—as it applies to Hispanic students—Udall discusses the unfortunate practice of identifying culturally diverse students by different criteria from those used to identify other students, and then not addressing the different criteria in the programs provided. As noted, too often failure is the outcome for the culturally diverse student when such practices occur. Solving this problem by identifying students only by preset program goals has inherent problems and limitations. Needs of all students must be assessed and, as much as possible, curriculum must be designed to meet these needs. Of course, limitations will result from lack of available resources and professional talents; but within these constraints the needs of all students, including those of the culturally diverse, should be addressed.

Udall appropriately cautions us not to assume that all Hispanic students are alike. She alludes to the impact of poverty and its resulting toll on the development of human potential. How ethnic, assimilation, and language differences affect the expression, or even the development, of giftedness is not clear.

Udall presents an interesting summary of the differences that might be expected between an Anglo-American and a Hispanic view of education. We are to assume that this contrast holds true for all the differing ethnic populations of Hispanics as well as those who are deeply involved in the culture of poverty. According to the data presented, this contrast should be true for the Hispanic in Florida, in Arizona, in California, or in Colorado. Does such a generalized overview create the stereotype that Udall would have us avoid? Enculturation data set a base for understanding the Hispanic child, but do not necessarily provide accurate information about any individual child. Udall's caution of remembering individual differences must apply here as well.

Because of the human tendency to generalize, Hilliard's (1976) label of synthetic-personal as a style of behavior that differentiates ethnic groups seems overly generalized and highly misleading. A focus on behaviors rather than categories of behavior seems a far better approach. The risk of misinterpretation is still present, but to a lesser degree. How would the Hispanic value of scolding and shaming affect the development of independence in the learning setting? How would the implied value of authority and passive resistance affect the initiative required for creativity and independent study? Such questions seem far more productive of useful solutions than further categorization or overgeneralization.

The discussion of the need for Hispanic students to relate effectively in two cultures is quite thought provoking. This concern, however, is not unique to the Hispanic student and can be found with all culturally diverse students, especially those caught in the culture of poverty.

After a discussion of individualization and the principles of differentiation that are necessary to all good curriculum planning, Udall sets forth eight teaching strategies thought to be important in planning for gifted minority students. The strategies are useful. However, the author is unclear about whether these strategies are directed toward the needs created by poverty, or by enculturation. Unfortunately the data used in the rationale sections seem to confuse the concepts of poverty and enculturation. Even more troubling is the focus on deficits in these strategies. Are strengths a result of the values of the Hispanic culture? Again the focus on uniqueness is missing.

The involvement of the community as a support for learning is needed by both the gifted Hispanic and gifted non-Hispanic student. Perhaps the values of the Hispanic family make family involvement in school-related events less likely, but the need for such involvement is critical for all families and all learners.

A second strategy suggested for use with Hispanic learners is leadership training. In what way is the need and the curricular planning for leadership different for gifted Hispanic students? The same question must be asked for the use of mentors, basic skills, creativity, problem-solving skills, and an affective focus. Consideration of these strategies makes the needs of the gifted Hispanic and gifted non-Hispanic more identical than dissimilar. Most of the rationale for using these strategies could be applicable equally as rationale with any gifted student. One can conclude only that implementation of a program that (a) is individualized, (b) follows the principles of differentiation, (c) incorporates leadership skills and mentors, and (d) balances affective and cognitive needs would provide appropriately for both the gifted Hispanic and gifted non-Hispanic student. While some cautions one must use in working with the Hispanic learner are identified, the curricular plan and delivery do not seem to be affected by these cautions.

Udall introduces the person who must translate these enculturated differences—the teacher. The teacher must bridge between cultures and not allow stereotypes and the resulting bias to affect the learning experience. The teacher must understand the needs of the child and use all the educational resources possible to meet those needs. The teacher's understanding of the effect of any culture's values must be reflected in strategies used and in the development of solutions to problems. I believe that the enculturated differences are not addressed in the content, the skills taught, or the curricular plan (as Udall contends), but in the attitude, the interpersonal interactions, and the very heart of the teacher.

The chapter ends with thirteen questions to be used in classrooms serving the gifted Hispanic student. We also are asked to consider Fuchigami's (1978) question as to whether we would educate gifted minority learners for the betterment of humanity and the human condition, or for their own personal development. This is a false dichotomy, for we must do both. As all learners' unique needs are addressed, as curriculum is truly differentiated, and as all are allowed to grow to the fullest extent possible, both the children and the society benefit. Indeed, Udall's thirteen questions should be asked by all teachers, in all classrooms, with all learners. While the author fails to justify or model the creation of a different curriculum for gifted Hispanic students, she gives us a better understanding of such students and of good educational practices that can benefit all gifted students.

8

Considerations in the Education of Gifted Hispanic Students

Richard Ruiz, Ph.D.
University of Arizona

Addressing the issues that impact on the education of gifted Hispanic students requires a clarification and definition of what is meant by "Hispanic"—a term others (Rivera-Martinez, 1985) and I have found unclear. The introduction to Part I includes a detailed discussion of the diversity of this term and the populations it includes, and provides a working definition from which this chapter can draw to suggest special considerations in the education of gifted Hispanic students. (The reader is referred to the introduction to Part I for an elaboration of the definition of Hispanic.)

I propose four areas of concern: (a) problems of service delivery; (b) questions of social and emotional development; (c) nature of role models; and (d) effects of teacher expectation on student self-esteem and achievement. The points made can be found in the literature on the education of Hispanics; but I have chosen, instead, to derive them for the most part from my experiences as a student in, and of, the schools.

SERVICE DELIVERY

No one should be surprised that Hispanics generally do not make use of the social services for which they are eligible (Rivera-Martinez, 1985). Even less surprising is the underrepresentation of Hispanics in "high status" programs such as those designed for gifted students. This underrepresentation is due to a variety of factors, including the nature of the social service delivery system and the characteristics of Hispanic communities.

Any system of service delivery treats problems of access and communication. *Access* implies that the services and their respective agency providers are known to the client, and that the service providers respond to needs perceived by the clients in ways that encourage, or at least do not discourage, their participation. *Communication* implies that the service providers find adequate strategies for overcoming whatever language barriers and cultural differences exist and that hinder an understanding of the system of services. These two aspects of service delivery are particularly relevant to the provision of special education for gifted Hispanic students.

For any service aimed primarily at children, the principal clients are not the children, but parents and guardians. This is as it should be, from both a social and educational point of view. Parents not only have ultimate responsibility for their children's education, but also their interest and direct participation in classroom activities enhance student achievement (Cummins, 1986). Excluding Hispanic parents from school can be an important factor in the underutilization of education by gifted Hispanic students, even after eligible children have been identified.

Frequently, parents in Hispanic communities do not have a school tradition; not only are they reluctant to involve themselves in school matters (conceiving of involvement as an intrusion), but also they often know little of school bureaucracy and institutional behavior. This lack of involvement may obscure the fact that these parents are vitally interested in the education of their children; instead, their reluctance may be traced to a history of tension and alienation between them and the schools. If my own experience is any indication of the general state of affairs, the only direct contact minority families have with school officials is when the student has done something wrong. This results in frustration; ultimately, it develops into what might be called a lack of ecosystem trust. Consequently, if parents can no longer be sure that the members of society in general, and the staff of schools in particular, have their interests in mind, they tend to be suspicious of school programs of any sort, including positive programs such as those for gifted students.

The burden is on the school—that is, its administrators and teachers—to restore trust and communicate the benefits to Hispanic families. Such a restoration entails accommodating Hispanic culture and language in service delivery and communication strategies. For example, use of Spanish media and translators may be necessary to advertise programs of education for gifted students. Taking advantage of the "natural support networks"—multigenerational extended families, churches, neighborhood groups, clubs, and others—that already exist in Hispanic communities also may be wise (Rivera-Martinez, 1985; Escobar & Randolph, 1982).

Two points are relevant here: (a) For many Hispanics, social services are provided not so much by detached professionals as by attached familiars. Parish priests, aunts and uncles, neighbors, community service workers, and others known in the community may be much more effective than school officials in helping parents and students understand the benefits of a program for gifted students. (b) Motivation levels of Hispanic students may be appreciably enhanced if the family is included in whatever recognition and awards the students receive (Ramirez & Castaneda, 1974). Perhaps more for Hispanics, than for other groups, "giftedness" is not strictly an individuated concept.

As a more general point, the problems surrounding service delivery do not begin when we try to involve parents in a program for gifted students. Rather, the problems are endemic to society; many of the conditions that lead to problems are merely reinforced in the schools. The general state of society and its members can be only mentioned here. On the part of schools, its officials must understand that, to the extent they generally exclude and create tension in Hispanic communities, they reduce the likelihood that Hispanic children will be represented appropriately in any of the special programs. In other words, without greater accommodation of Hispanics and their general needs by school officials, Hispanic children will continue to be overrepresented in special education and underrepresented in programs for gifted students.

SOCIAL AND EMOTIONAL DEVELOPMENT

Most Hispanics in the United States can be considered "subordinated" minority groups (Ogbu, 1978). Hispanics are not merely subcultural in status; they tend to be viewed as an underclass by the dominant society. This perceived status has a significant impact on identity formation and values development.

Perrone and Aleman (1983) contend that children who grow up in minority sub-cultures have an achievement orientation different from that of children of dominant groups. They further contend that minority children attribute any success to luck, and failure to personal inadequacy, and therefore tend to disbelieve people who try to convince them of their abilities. Again, my own case serves as an appropriate illustration. I still attribute the fact that I was admitted to college to a series of accidents. People are puzzled when I explain to them that I went to college because I forgot to set my alarm clock one Saturday morning. I have such explanations for other achievements, as well. I can imagine that for many students, some of their anxiety in life comes from the anticipation that, some day, their luck will run out.

Living and growing in subordinated subcultures also means that one's successes may not be those valued in the larger society and in schools. "Gifted children from minority cultures possess talents valued and nurtured within their own culture, but these talents frequently go unrecognized in school" (Perrone & Aleman, 1983, p. 273). Let me discuss two examples.

As one example, Hispanics conceive of, and define the term, "education" much more broadly than do most who speak English in this society. To be *educado* goes far beyond school, or may not involve school at all; it means to be well mannered, respectful, considerate, and knowledgeable about practical things. In schools these may be recognized as admirable qualities, but not as talents. For their part, Hispanics may resist school programs that are merely cognitive in orientation—programs, in their terms, that may add to one's "schooling" but not to one's "education."

Another example involves language behavior. A source of great concern (and with a long history) is that many Hispanics are identified as "semilingual" or even "alingual." These diagnoses of course may have something to do with the adequacy of test instruments or with differential language behavior between school and non-school contexts, but also they must have something to do with differential social evaluations of language. Many Hispanics speak a nonstandard variety of Spanish; many also engage in code-switching—moving easily between English and Spanish even within utterances. These two aspects of language behavior, generally misunderstood, also are generally devalued. No amount of academic research on the nature of language and the benefits of bilingualism has convinced many of us of the value of these sorts of behavior; yet, it is clear to me, as it is to many researchers, that the cultural adaptations and innovations entailed in nonstandard varieties and code-switching require great linguistic sophistication. Furthermore, the aesthetic richness and communicative effectiveness of these language strategies should be evident to anyone who has seen them in operation. Nevertheless, because of our social biases, we may be assigning students to special programs designed to address these "problems," rather than to programs for the gifted that may help students build on these important "talents."

These two examples suggest the need for those who design programs for the gifted to take special account of cultural knowledge. These educators might then not only attract deserving students, but also may begin to recognize talent where once they saw deficiency.

ROLE MODELS

In *The Plum Plum Pickers,* Barrio's (1969) novel about the life of a farmworker family, Manuelito is asked by one of the *guero* kids: "Hey, Manuelito, you got Mexican brains?" The question is an occasion for some outward hostilities, but both Manuelito and the reader understand what is being said. The idea of "Mexican brains" has developed a social meaning generally accepted by *guero* and Mexican alike. The kids fight because these are fighting words, but not because anyone disputes their meaning. The clear message for Manuelito is that his low social position is to be explained by his culture and history; in terms more personally relevant to Manuelito, his social disadvantage is to be found in his family and everyone else close to him. While he may fight against this idea, he nevertheless comes to understand it as a terrible social fact. He faces a cruel choice: To reject his family, friends, culture, language, and identity, or to remain as he is—with little chance of economic well-being or social acceptance.

This is the choice of the Hispanic in the United States, a choice faced in one way or another, every day, in all contexts. The school environment is sometimes in contradistinction to minority families. The alienation of family and school is sometimes explained by terms, such as "home-school disarticulation" (by educational anthropologists), or "cultural reproduction" (by critical social theorists). However defined, the child experiences it much more immediately and personally: Two sets of role models, represented most obviously by teachers and parents, have very attractive qualities; to embrace one is to reject the other.

A great shock to many in this society is that some minority group members choose their families over school. This choice is seen as irrational, even suicidal, since many feel to live without hope of economic and social mobility is to live barely at all. Yet, alarming evidence exists that this choice continues to be made. Where is the evidence? Perhaps the easiest place to look is in the schools. Recent studies in New York, California, Illinois, and Texas show that the dropout rate for Hispanics is higher than for any other group in the United States, in some cases as high as 62 percent by the ninth grade. Dropping out is one way of making the choice between family and school;

another way is to tune out, and tuning out occurs about as often as anything else in school. While the dropout rate is not completely explained by the home-school choice Hispanics feel forced to make, its magnitude eventually will force us to look toward such explanations as correctives to the formerly predominant (though much stranger) theories of cultural and cognitive disadvantages.

School programs for the gifted do not exist in a social vacuum. They are embedded in an institution that has not served Hispanics well. This history of disservice will no doubt handicap educators who try to attract Hispanic children for special programs. But if change is to come to the school, it may as well come in programs for gifted students. The key is to understand a central attitude among many Hispanics: They want their children to succeed, but also they want them to grow up as Hispanics (McCready, 1985). The childrens' traditional role models—parents, aunts and uncles, religious figures, historical personalities—may not be "schooled," but they have been important in shaping the young person's identity. Forced to make a choice, many students will prefer to remain what they are.

TEACHER EXPECTATIONS AND STUDENT ACHIEVEMENT

I will not recount here the many general studies documenting the importance of teacher expectations as an influence on student self-esteem and achievement. Teacher expectations and attitudes are important factors in programs for gifted students, as well (Rodriguez, Prieto, & Rueda, 1984). I will make only a general point here, by way of conclusion.

Hispanic students, along with their associated antecedents—language and culture, families, neighborhoods, and academic training—have up to this time been treated in the framework of a problem orientation. The social function of schools with respect to Hispanics and other minority groups has been to eradicate the deficiencies their children inherit and bring with them to school. For most minority groups, including Hispanics, their non-English language has been seen as an important aspect of those deficiencies. This "problem orientation" is in direct contrast to the "resource orientation" associated with children of the dominant Anglo-American groups, since they represent the ideal fostered in schools.

How will educators of the gifted deal with this basic orientation in U.S. society? Consider the matter of language. A non-English mother tongue virtually defines educational and social disadvantage; evidence of this is that bilingual programs in this society are designed not for bilingualization, but for creating English language dominance in speakers of other languages. The U.S. Department of Education considers English language proficiency to be the single most important criterion for a successful bilingual program, even if it means the total eradication of the first language. Now I consider part of the giftedness of Hispanics to be their (actual or potential) bilingualism. How will educators of the gifted deal with the society's skepticism about the value of "ethnic" bilingualism? Will these educators try to overcome such bilingualism by replacing it with advanced English monolingualism or another, more "academic," form of bilingualism? Or will they consider the child's first language an important asset to be preserved and developed? Beyond that, since language is only one antecedent involved here (and not in every case), how will educators view parents and other family members, cultural tradition, religious background, and so on?

DuBois (1961) begins his most famous book by considering what he calls the "unasked question": "How does it feel to be a problem?" The Black man, he says, is forever confronted with it. This question faces all minority groups. It is a question that is never answered adequately, because the particular markedness of subordinate status, however much it is analyzed, only can be felt. The success of programs for gifted students in attracting Hispanics rests ultimately on whether these programs are conceived as another way of treating the Hispanic "problem," or as a way of demonstrating that the society has all along been asking of them the wrong question.

9

Administrative Implications of a Program and Curriculum for Gifted Hispanic Students

Alan M. Weiss, M.S.
New World School of the Arts

The administration of a program for the gifted in today's multipluralistic society forces district administrators to face the reality that many Black and Hispanic students have been excluded from these programs. If one accepts the theory that intellectual ability within a population occurs regardless of ethnicity, and if one accepts the fact that approximately 2 percent of the population falls into the gifted range of intellectual ability, approximately 2 percent of all populations, including Blacks and Hispanics, should be gifted. In those school districts in which a minority group comprises a significant portion of the student population, many times political pressure has been exerted to equalize the disparity between majority and minority representation within a program for gifted students.

As with other ethnic minority groups, environmental deprivation within the Hispanic population is not to be ignored. However, language is the major barrier to identifying gifted Hispanic students.

Training bilingual teachers, with facility in English and Spanish, to look for students demonstrating characteristics of giftedness in English as a second language (ESL) classes will result in a small pool of students who may be gifted. Using the Spanish version of the *Wechsler Intelligence Scale for Children—Revised (WISC–R)* administered by bilingual school psychologists will increase the identification rate from this pool of students who may be gifted. Unfortunately, many gifted Hispanic students are not referred for psychological evaluation because of prejudice on the part of teachers, guidance personnel, and administrators. These individuals believe that a student with limited proficiency in English could not possibly be gifted or function in a program for the gifted.

The Dade County Public School system is the fourth largest school district in the nation and is made up of 33 percent Black, 41.7 percent Hispanic, and 25.3 percent Anglo-American and other students. To increase the Black and Hispanic representation within the program for the gifted, extensive use of the System of Multicultural Pluralistic Assessment (SOMPA) (Mercer & Lewis, 1978) and the Spanish version of the *WISC–R* were incorporated into the identification process.

As the population of Hispanic students recommended for psychological evaluation was examined, a fact that became very apparent was that the percentage of students qualifying for the program was higher than anticipated. Approximately 50 percent of the students referred for the program for the gifted were identified as gifted. Generally, less than 40 percent of all students referred for the program for the gifted actually qualify for it. To capitalize on this phenomenon, the district began to develop programs in which thinking skills could be taught through the student's dominant language to large numbers of students in predominantly Hispanic schools. All of the Hispanic students involved in these programs were not identified as gifted. By teaching critical and creative thinking skills to these students, the ability to score above the 130 level on the *WISC–R* (Spanish version) was increased and, additionally, students increased their proficiency in their second language (English).

The most efficient way to increase the number of Hispanic students within the identified gifted population may be to focus on developing a pool of potentially gifted students who are taught thinking skills in concert with ESL instruction. In this way, students who may be gifted do not have to wait to be assimilated into English-speaking classes to receive instruction in strategies useful for the gifted.

The programs to develop thinking skills in identified and non-identified gifted students in the Los Angeles Unified School District are similar to those used in the Dade County Public Schools. Unfortunately, Dade County is unable to adjust the entrance requirements for programs for the gifted since the state of Florida has rigid IQ requirements that cannot be ignored.

Administratively, several problems develop after these Hispanic students are placed in the program for gifted students. The type of delivery system used to provide instruction often creates more problems for the gifted Hispanic student than does the identification process.

In Dade County, two delivery models have been used at the elementary school level. A pull-out model or magnet program was established originally in which centers for the gifted were organized and students from surrounding schools were bused to the centers two days a week. A second delivery model was implemented, in which a school with 30 or more identified gifted students attending could offer instruction for gifted students on a daily basis. These home-based programs became very popular because students did not have to leave their home schools for special instruction.

Many parents were hesitant to allow their children to board a bus at their home school and go to a center for gifted students two days a week. This hesitance was manifested by Hispanic parents withdrawing their children from the program, thus denying these children special instruction.

In an effort to counteract the problem of nonparticipation, parent support groups within the center and the individual feeder schools were organized. Meetings were held with parents to discuss the problems of the gifted child, the role of the parent in supporting the development of the gifted child, and the critical importance of sustained enrollment in the program for gifted students. Meeting with parent groups creates a major demand on the administrator's time; however, the benefits of such meetings outweigh the time commitment. Many of the issues cited by Ruiz and Udall indicate a universality of problems associated with the delivery of services to gifted Hispanic children. If one understands that most Hispanic parents want their children to succeed, the administrator of the program for the gifted must involve the individual parent and the entire Hispanic community in solving the problems of "home-school disarticulation."

Another issue relating to program delivery is cost. For the instructional format of a program for gifted students to be effective, the student/teacher ratio must be low. When the student/teacher ratio climbs, the effectiveness of the program begins to diminish. When parents realize that their children are not getting the individualized attention they require, parent support begins to fall as well.

From a fiscal point of view, service delivery in a home school is much more cost effective because no ancillary transporation costs are present. The cost of the teaching unit is the same in center and home-based programs because the allocation of teaching units is based on a fixed student/teacher ratio. The decision to establish home-based programs is administratively sound, providing the school has sufficient enrollment to support the teacher unit.

The current trend within the state of Florida and in the Dade County Public Schools is toward a full-time program for the gifted. From an instructional point of view, a full-time delivery system is the most effective means of providing special teaching strategies and maximizing the learning of gifted children. Since the students participating in this model remain in the school they normally attend, no additional transportation costs exist.

Like the home-based delivery model, the full-time model can be effective only if the number of students enrolled in the program justifies the allocation of teacher units. When enrollment in home-based schools is not sufficiently high, magnet schools with full-time programs can be established. This, however, is a major problem for many Hispanic parents, because they are often unwilling to transport their children away from the neighborhood. To increase effectively Hispanic participation in any program for gifted students, the administrator must be an aggressive protagonist in creating a pool of children who may be gifted and finding appropriate identification measures. Community agencies, community leaders, and political groups must be educated regarding the needs of gifted children and the importance of reaching all segments of the community. Only by gaining the support of individuals in the community can an administrator institute programs that will benefit our gifted minority students.

10

Summary of
Hispanic Section

C. June Maker, Ph.D.
Shirley W. Schiever, Ph.D.
University of Arizona

GENERAL STATEMENTS

Based on the writing of authors in this section, certain general statements can be made about the education of gifted Hispanic students. These statements, along with supporting information and a few examples, are presented below.

1. *Because Hispanics are viewed as an underclass or subordinated, they tend also to be viewed from a remedial or deficit perspective.*

Banda and Udall discuss this phenomenon by noting that student weaknesses are often the focus of programs. Bernal notes that compensatory education is often discussed, but that gifted students should be taught rather than compensated. Rodriguez and Ruiz describe personal experiences in which they were viewed as "dumb" or not very smart simply because they were Hispanic. Perrine describes a structured remedial education approach in the East Los Angeles Public Schools that resulted from the perception of east-side Hispanics (even by themselves) as underachieving, underprivileged, and in need of remediation. Zappia discusses underachievement as a phenomenon that interferes with the identification of giftedness. Ruiz further describes how Hispanics have been treated in the framework of a "problem orientation," rather than the "resource orientation" with which children from dominant, Anglo-American groups are treated.

2. *Before beginning a program or considering ways to identify students, educators must believe that Hispanic students have strengths and talents that can be identified and that should be nurtured.*

Ruiz and Udall call our attention to the extensive research demonstrating the important effects of teacher expectations on student accomplishment, while Perrine includes as an "instructional imperative" finding out what the children *know* and *can do*. Banda emphasizes self-identification of strengths as well as recognition of strengths by others. Bernal supports Banda's position and indicates that in schools diversity should be not only *recognized,* but also *honored.* Clark admonishes Udall (and all of us) to identify the educational strengths Hispanic children have as a result of their cultural values.

3. *Placing total emphasis on standardized tests, using tests in traditional ways, and focusing totally on characteristics valued by the mainstream culture are not effective ways to identify gifted Hispanic students.*

Perrine describes an innovative, classroom-based identification process currently being used successfully in the East Los Angeles schools. Using this approach, students who may be gifted are placed in classrooms in which they are encouraged to develop and display their abilities. Progress in this program is documented, and students' abilities are judged on the basis of participation in activities over a long period of time rather than during a test. Bernal cautions us against the arbitrary and restrictive use of tests because minority children are excluded from programs, and suggests that we only need legitimate indicators of high potential, such as assessment of first and second language proficiency, to place students in programs. He would like us to select those who will become gifted adults rather than those who are gifted as children. Zappia recommends the use of a case study approach incorporating many methods for documenting abilities. Udall suggests that we become aware of Hispanic children's differing behavioral styles and how differing cultural values may influence their behavior.

4. *Once identified, gifted Hispanic students should be encouraged to develop individually valued abilities, abilities valued by their cultures, and abilities needed to be successful in a mainstream culture.*

Banda is the leader in suggesting ways to accomplish this balance between cultural values since the focus of her chapter was on program purpose. Both she and Bernal would have us begin with individually valued abilities, and introduce other skills as the need for them is recognized. Rodriguez comments that the program proposed by Banda would have "patched up a gaping hole" in her education and strengthened feelings of self-worth. Both Rodriguez and Ruiz recount personal experiences illustrating that abilities valued by individuals, Hispanic cultures, and mainstream American schools are different. Rodriguez recalls painful experiences in which she was not accepted by other Hispanics because she was "anglicized," could not speak Spanish fluently, and was perceived as not being proud of her heritage. To be successful in school, she had sacrificed her pride in "who she was."

5. *Bilingualism is a strength, and the development of true bilingualism should be a focus of programs for gifted students.*

Perrine reminds us that students who are learning two languages can learn easily the rules of language, and can apply these rules to thinking. Bernal, Ruiz, and Banda cite research showing that bilingual students show strengths in cognitive flexibility and metalinguistic awareness.

Banda and Rodriguez remind us of a fact many of us encounter every day: Many children who come to school speaking Spanish must stop learning their first language and begin learning a second. After several years of concentration on English, these students may be given an opportunity to develop their Spanish in a formal context, or they may simply continue learning Spanish informally from family and friends. Often, because of this situation, Hispanic children do not speak either language well. Zappia reminds us that if neither language is spoken well, intelligence and achievement tests designed to identify abilities will fail because students have no language sophisticated enough to express high level cognitive abilities. Thus, Bernal's suggestion of assessing development in both languages would not be likely to result in identification of many gifted students.

Ruiz advocates a different role of language in the identification process. He suggests that we observe carefully children's "code-switching" and use of nonstandard varieties of Spanish because they require a great deal of linguistic sophistication, and can be indicators of giftedness. Similarly, Perrine notes that Spanish is a deductive language, and that native Spanish speakers tend to attend to global meanings rather than details; native English speakers tend to have opposite characteristics. When attempting to identify giftedness, the cognitive results of these different characteristics of languages should be considered seriously.

All authors discuss the positive effects of bilingualism on students' development in affective as well as cognitive areas. If students' families speak only Spanish, a communication gap does not result from the students' education; they, in fact, can become interpreters for families when necessary. In addition, an emphasis on bilingual development demonstrates that at least one aspect of the students' home background is valued in school, thereby eliminating at least one source of alienation of students from the school.

Finally, Bernal notes that even though bilingualism has not been promoted in the United States, it has been a focus of quality educational programs all over the world. As the world becomes "smaller" and more interdependent, monolingualism will become obsolete and multilingualism necessary.

6. *Because the Hispanic culture places a high value on family and personal relationships, and because academic programs for gifted students often make necessary a choice between family and school, strong and continued involvement of the family in the educational process is imperative.*

Ruiz expresses this conflict very poignantly when he notes that Hispanic students often have two sets of role models—teachers and parents—and "to embrace one is to reject the other." How many children, who have grown up respecting their parents and who have defined themselves using their parents' values, would want to reject their heritage to choose an institution that does not value that heritage? On the other hand, how many children with the potential for a high level of success would want to reject what the school has to offer, or limit their chance for success in a career of interest by dropping out of school? A final statement made by Ruiz sums up the problem. Hispanics want their children to succeed, but they want them to grow up as Hispanics.

The authors in this section provide many specific ways Hispanic families can become more involved in educational programs. Ruiz notes that parents and guardians are the actual clients for our special programs rather than the children. If parents and guardians do not have a "school" orientation and, in the past, direct contact with the school has occurred only when something was wrong, school officials must restore trust and communicate the benefits of a special program. To accomplish this Ruiz suggests that we make use of "attached familiars" (e.g., parish priests, aunts and uncles, neighbors, community service workers, and others known and respected in the community) in helping parents and students see the benefits of education. He also recommends including the family when giving awards and recognition for academic success. Perrine lists three successful aspects of the parent involvement component in the East Los Angeles program. Banda recommends having (a) conferences with the family to determine educational goals for students; and (b) a program to help parents learn about giftedness, ways to support the child at home, and career possibilities. Zappia would involve parents in the identification process. Udall lists involving the community in the program as a teaching strategy, and suggests that teachers gather information about the contributions of citizens and agencies so these can be included in the program.

7. *The starting point for curriculum design in any program should be to identify and plan for development of student strengths.*

In addition to bilingualism, Hispanic students bring to the educational process strengths in such areas as seeing connections between ideas (Banda), creativity, problem solving (Banda, Udall, and Perrine), and leadership. Perrine also suggests capitalizing on Hispanic students' knowledge and experiences, which may be very different from other students in the class. Udall suggests building upon creative strengths through use of the creative problem-solving process, then applying this process to both academic and nonacademic situations. Banda also suggests that involvement in problem solving can enhance critical thinking skills. Udall describes several programs for the development of leadership skills, many of which also can involve practicing language skills in a social context.

8. *Even though educators should begin with development of strengths of gifted Hispanic students, they must not ignore the students' weaknesses.*

All authors discuss this idea, and make specific recommendations. Banda recommends a "compensatory" dimension for programs, but Bernal cautions against use of the word "compensate" because it implies the use of a "deficit" approach directly aimed at changing behavior or instilling new skills through "head-on" methods that may be counterproductive. Rather, he states, we should develop skills in a meaningful context. A teaching technique such as *comprehensible input*—the more modern method for teaching English as a second language—is much better to use with gifted students because necessary skills (in this case, language) are acquired as a byproduct of learning something else. Many of Perrine's suggestions for proactive learning of language fall into this category. Udall recommends that we incorporate "basic skills" training, and names many of the same skills as Banda as needs of gifted Hispanic students. Rodriguez applauds this focus, and notes that the "coping skills" dimension would have been very helpful to her. A lack of certain kinds of experiences, due to social and economic conditions, was the cause of her discomfort. She also suggests that development of coping skills could have helped her deal with the rejection she felt from both the Hispanic and Anglo-American cultures.

9. *Role models and mentors should be incorporated into the program because they can serve as a source of motivation, a vehicle for career exploration, and a way to involve the community (including parents) in a meaningful, positive way.*

Banda notes that teachers can be role models while Ruiz and Bernal remind us that they *are* role models for students and that they should take this responsibility seriously. Rodriguez tells us that having a mentor, or at least knowing someone who was a lawyer, would have helped her tremendously. Udall provides useful guidelines for the incorporation of mentorship programs into the curriculum, and gives examples. She recommends, and Rodriguez's experiences would support, that role models and mentors are particularly important for gifted Hispanic girls. Mentorship and internship programs can be informal or formal parts of the total school experience.

10. *Gifted Hispanic girls present a special problem, and should receive appropriate support and attention.*

Because of male dominance in Hispanic families (Ruiz, Perrine, Udall, Rodriguez, and Banda), girls often are not encouraged to excel in academic areas or pursue careers outside the home. Girls may hide their intellectual abilities, making them difficult to identify (Udall, Perrine) and, when identified, may receive less support than boys from their families for participating in a special program. According to Perrine, gifted girls also have little or no opportunity to exercise personal initiative, independent thought, or verbal aggressiveness in the home. Knowing gifted Hispanic women through association with teachers, mentors, and others in the community can help gifted Hispanic girls to make academic and career decisions based on knowledge of the challenges and satisfactions they may face.

11. *Cooperative learning and other noncompetitive learning strategies should be incorporated into a program to build on the collaborative dynamics of the Hispanic culture.*

Perrine suggests that we incorporate the "proactive" use of language into situations where students are role playing, serving on committees, holding debates, and participating in discussions. His suggestions in this area are very similar to Bernal's recommendation that English skills be developed as a byproduct of learning something else, Zappia's discussion of research on academic achievement of Hispanic students, and Udall's suggestion that teaching examples be relevant to experience. When discussing methods for creating a safe and positive classroom learning environment, Udall provides suggestions and resources for using cooperative learning, holding regular classroom meetings and discussions, and developing a child-centered classroom.

12. *A strong counseling and affective development component should be included in a program.*

Ruiz reminds us that the concept of *educado* ("to be educated") goes far beyond what is usually taught in schools and that a strictly cognitive orientation in a program will not be valued. Inclusion of an affective component would address these abilities as well as assist in developing the coping skills Rodriguez indicates are important to help students deal effectively with their need to participate and succeed in two different cultures. Banda recommends the use of Banks's (1979) levels of ethnic development to help students analyze their values and experiences, as well as the use of value clarification exercises.

OTHER IMPORTANT IDEAS

Certain ideas discussed by only two authors in this section have significance for educators.

1. General statements about Hispanic students can help us to understand patterns of behavior, but such statements do not yield information about individual students. Assessments of individuals are necessary to obtain specific data for counseling and teaching (Clark).
2. The behavior of Hispanic students may vary according to the ethnic composition of a classroom. When in the majority, for example, Hispanic students are more assertive and gregarious than when they are in the minority (Udall).

IN CONCLUSION

The authors in this section showed high levels of agreement in basic philosophies and principles related to the education of gifted Hispanic students. In many cases, the philosophy was the same, but the perspective was different. However, many specific techniques were advocated by all these authors.

One final area of agreement is that the teaching strategies and principles advocated for these students can be helpful for and important in the education of all gifted students. Nonetheless, many of these principles are not incorporated into all programs for gifted students, and they are essential if the program is to be successful with gifted Hispanic students.

Part II

AMERICAN INDIANS

DEFINING AMERICAN INDIANS

The American Indian population is diverse and composed of many subgroups. The U.S. government recognizes 177 different tribes, each with its own culture, varying degrees of traditionalism and acculturation, and educational levels. This diverse population, while embracing many differences, shares basic concerns, such as (a) protection of lands and treaty rights, (b) economic development, (c) retention of tribal culture, (d) continuation of social welfare services for members, and (e) provision of educational services (Tonemah, 1987).

According to a Bureau of Indian Affairs report (1986), approximately 1.4 million American Indians, Eskimos, and Aleuts in the United States were recorded in the 1980 census. Additionally, the American Indian population is increasing more rapidly than any other ethnic group in the country, and has a median age of 18 (Bureau of Indian Affairs, 1984). Over 50 percent of American Indians live on or adjacent to about 300 federal reservations. More than 75 percent of the school-aged children go to public schools, on and off the reservations, and over 26,000 students are enrolled in college. In fact, in 1980–81, a larger percentage of the American Indian population was either enrolled in two- and four-year colleges or had received a baccalaureate degree, than the percentage of Hispanic and Black populations (0.25% versus 0.20% and 0.23%, respectively, who had earned a baccalaureate degree) (Plisko & Stern, 1985).

The editors wish to thank Anita Pfeiffer and Robert Kirschenbaum for permitting us to use much information about American Indians that was originally included in their chapters.

Often, the term "Native American" is used to refer to this population. However, the editors surveyed numerous groups, and found that "American Indian" is the preferred term because of its precise reference to Indian groups in this country.

HISTORICAL CONTEXT

Among minority populations, American Indians are unique due to their trust relationship with the U.S. government. This trust relationship permeates all facets of Indian life—health, education, business, transportation, mineral extraction, fishing and water rights, land boundaries, and law enforcement.

American Indian education has a history of varied administration. Before 1824, it was administered through the War Department, and after 1824 through the Bureau of Indian Affairs, various mission schools, and various state public school systems. Historically and currently, educational policies lack relevance to American Indian students, due to the wholesale importation of foreign thinking. This lack of relevance is perceived through the content of curricular materials used in the schools that American Indian students attend (Fuchs & Havighurst, 1973; Schierbeck, 1982; Szasz, 1977).

Until 1966 when the first contract school was initiated at Rough Rock, Arizona, American Indian parents had not had the opportunity to voice their concerns about education in a policy-making body or to participate in the formal education of their children. Johnson (1968) states that the Rough Rock school is controlled and directed by the Navajo people; and the supremely important aspect of this local control is to prove that the American Indian has the interest, desire, and capacity to provide real leadership, direction, and self-determination in education. The year 1986 marked the twentieth anniversary of the Rough Rock Demonstration School and the contract school movement, which numbers 64 institutions nationally. Twelve of these contract schools are located on the Navajo reservation, and the remaining 52 schools are scattered throughout American Indian country. Two hundred government schools exist for American Indians in the United States, serving 50,000 students or about 15 percent of the total number of students. The other 250,000 American Indians attend public schools, predominantly schools that are on or near a reservation (Chavers, 1982).

The federal government has always maintained a strong hand in setting policies for American Indians. These policies have fluctuated from genocide, removal, termination, relocation, and assimilation to the present "self-determination" stance. Self-determination is expressed in the Indian Self-Determination and Education Assistance Act of 1975, which legislates that direction and leadership should come from American Indians. Federal policies affect the daily operation of the schools American Indian students attend. Contract schools, although governed by locally elected school boards that have the responsibility for making policy and hiring and firing personnel, are still largely constrained in their daily operation. This constraint results from following state-adopted minimum standards required for the school's curricula or being preoccupied with teaching the knowledge required to pass district-wide or reservation-wide testing programs adopted by the Bureau of Indian Affairs.

SPECIAL EDUCATION FOR THE GIFTED AND TALENTED AMERICAN INDIAN STUDENT ON THE RESERVATION

Formidable obstacles to the development of effective educational programming for gifted and talented American Indian students, as well as to the identification of those students for programs, exist in public schools on or near reservations.

First, a serious alcohol abuse problem occurs among American Indians, which undoubtedly is a major reason why an American Indian is twice as likely to die by accidental death, in a car or otherwise, as a person in the general population (Bureau of Indian Affairs, 1986). American Indian children, especially adolescents, are severely affected by the problem of alcohol abuse. American Indian students are almost twice as likely to get into serious trouble with the law than are other minority students (Plisko & Stern, 1985). Alcoholism is partly a reflection of the poverty and unemployment on reservations; unemployment on the reservations is between 39 percent and 49 percent overall, and reaches 80 percent among certain small tribes. Only 23 percent of employable American Indian adults earn $7000 or more annually (Bureau of Indian Affairs, 1985).

A second obstacle is the high turnover of instructional staff in many public and Bureau of Indian Affairs schools. For example, the turnover rate is over 50 percent in some school districts on the Navajo reservation. New, and often young, teachers may not notice and nominate students during the process of screening to locate gifted and talented students. Identification and programming for such students is directly hampered by a turnover in the staff responsible for these activities.

The most serious obstacle that limits the number of American Indian students selected to participate in programs for gifted students is the perception that few American Indian students are gifted and that most require a remedial education approach because of low reading ability and limited English proficiency. A higher percentage of American Indians is included in programs for the learning disabled than are students in any other ethnic group (Plisko & Stern, 1985). The suggestion that American Indian students are talented in areas of art or athletics arouses less resistance than the assertion that they are gifted intellectually. Tonemah and Brittan (1985) surveyed school districts in Oklahoma and found that of their American Indian students identified as gifted and talented, 68 percent had less than one-fourth American Indian blood, while about 9 percent were listed as three-fourths American Indian or full blooded. If the degree of American Indian blood is related to the degree of assimilation into the Anglo-American culture, one could surmise that the more American Indian students are assimilated, the more likely they are to be identified as gifted and talented.

The identification of gifted and talented American Indian students hinges on defining those specific behaviors that may result when the absolute aspects of giftedness interact

Table II-1 Characteristics of Giftedness and Cultural Values of American Indians, and the Behaviors Resulting from Their Interactive Influence

Absolute Aspects of Giftedness	Cultural Values Often Characteristic of American Indians	Behavioral Differences
Unusual sensitivity to expectations and feelings of others	Collective self—the Tribe	Is a good mediator
Ability to generate original ideas and solutions		Figures out strategies to help group or team project
High level of language development		Communicates effectively collective idea of tribe
Idealism, a sense of justice, and advanced levels of moral judgment		Has personal and religious integrity
Leadership; strongly motivated by self-actualization needs		Accepts responsibility and discipline of leadership
High expectations of self and others		Encourages others to explore and develop abilities while developing own abilities
Creativity in endeavors	Traditions, heritage, beliefs	Makes up stories or poems
Extraordinary quantity of information, unusual retentiveness		Recalls old legends about landmarks, etc.
Creativity in various areas of endeavor		Reproduces traditional designs or symbols in a variety of media

with cultural values and influences. In Table II-1 the possible manifestation of certain absolute aspects of giftedness by American Indian students is illustrated. In column one are listed selected absolute aspects of giftedness; in column two, American Indian cultural values; and in column three, resulting behavioral differences.

The authors in the American Indian section of this volume offer a clear and insightful view of the selected issues and their relationship to this population. The reader will undoubtedly conclude that existing problems are indeed complex, but the proposed solutions reflect common sense and sound educational practice.

11

Identification of Giftedness Among American Indian People

Diane Montgomery, Ph.D.
Elmhurst School

"It is not necessary to deny another's reality in order to affirm my own."
—Anne Wilson Schaef, *Women's Reality*

Discovering who among American Indian students would benefit from a specialized educational program to develop exceptional ability is a complex problem. The purposes of this chapter are to examine some of the reasons identification of gifted American Indian students is difficult, and to propose a methodology that would have maximum effectiveness and efficiency in identification. The chapter is divided into four sections: (a) the reasons why a differential identification procedure for American Indian students is needed; (b) the philosophical concerns encountered in attempting to identify gifted minority students; (c) the potential identification strategies to be used with American Indian students; and (d) the areas that require further investigation before answers to the identification question will become apparent.

American Indian students typically have been underrepresented in programs for the gifted in public schools because of distinction between public, contract, tribal, and Bureau of Indian Affairs schools. (Tonemah & Brittan, 1985). The talents of Buffy St. Marie, Sequoya, Jim Thorpe, or Will Rogers are recognized as outstanding in any culture, and they all have one thing in common; that is, they are American Indians who have excelled in those areas that are represented in almost all cultures and are measurable on a scale from ordinary to outstanding—music, leadership, athletics, and storytelling. Yet, a concern is that such identification is made only by the dominant cross-cultural norm, which may reflect none of the characteristics that give a cultural group its individual identity.

The richness of any single culture lies in its inherent differences from other cultures. Along with these natural differences comes the implication that different groups will view the world with unique perspectives. This variety of cultural perspectives or world views on giftedness provides the basis for the approach to identification outlined here.

THE NEED FOR DIFFERENTIAL IDENTIFICATION

Before standards can be developed to identify gifted American Indian students, several essential questions must be asked.

Why must educators identify American Indian students who are in the "top" categories of performance, skills, or abilities? Who will benefit from a system that promotes gifted American Indian children? These questions must be answered not only in terms of benefit for the individual gifted American Indian child, but also in terms of impact on the individual tribe, and American Indians in general. Second, in addition to considering who will benefit, addressing the problem of who will decide what standards are appropriate for judging American Indian giftedness is essential. Are the decision makers to be the tribes, the school systems, the parents, the children themselves, educational theorists, or some other outside parties?

To discuss effectively issues surrounding the identification process, certain assumptions must be made about potential answers to these questions. We must first assume that the need to identify gifted American Indian students exists; and this need exists because parents, the tribal community, and the schools place inherent value in the identification process and will support and participate in the identification procedures (Tonemah, 1986). Closely tied to the assumption that the tribe values the identification process is the belief that accommodating basic cultural concerns, such as the meaning some tribes may place on equality within the group, is possible within the identification process. Finally, the assumption is made that an educational program will be designed to develop each individual's potential.

Purpose for Identification

American Indians want their gifted students to be served with appropriate educational programs. When 172 school personnel, American Indian parents, and American Indian students in Oklahoma were surveyed, they overwhelmingly reported that a critical need for American Indian-specific gifted and talented educational programming exists, and that sufficient numbers of gifted and talented students are present to justify this unique programming (Tonemah, 1986). Tribes recognize a need to develop tribal leadership among people who possess the skills of creative and analytic thought, organizational management, and a futuristic perspective to be able to meet the demands of their resources in the future (Tonemah, 1986).

The U.S. Department of Education statistic for determining the prevalence of giftedness (Marland, 1972) can be applied to estimate the number of gifted American Indian students. Using 45,000 as the total number of students and a gifted and talented prevalence rate of 3 to 5 percent, as many as 1,350 to 2,250 gifted and talented students who are not currently receiving specialized instruction to develop their giftedness could be attending Bureau of Indian Affairs schools.

More and more, tribes are recognizing that enhancing and using individual tribal members' special talents can promote the general welfare of the tribe. Gifted and talented children, appropriately educated and encouraged, grow up to become gifted and talented adults whose contributions to their tribe, culture, and future generations can serve to ensure the perpetuation of each individual tribe.

Differential Characteristics

To understand and appreciate fully cultural differences, one must first embrace the concept that differences are not good or bad, or right or wrong, but are merely differences. This is especially true when attempting to understand the "Indianness" of American Indians. Attempting to answer the question, "Who is an American Indian?" is beyond the scope of this discussion. However, to substantiate that certain differences exist and that they are important to the process of identifying gifted minority students, comparative continua of characteristics are presented in Table 11-1.

This list is a stereotypical generalization of cultural differences; each pair of traits represents a continuum with the extreme characterization on either pole. As with any list of characteristics, seldom does one person possess all traits at one side of the continuum.

An attempt has been made to delineate those special characteristics that discriminate the gifted and talented students from among the general American Indian student population. Tonemah (1985) surveyed 266 parents and educators (American Indian and non-American Indian teachers of American Indians) from across the nation to determine their tribal/cultural perspectives of gifted and talented American Indian students. The results of this study are shown in Exhibit 11-1.

In a study in which Advisory Board members of American Indian Research and Development, Inc. (who represent tribes from all of Oklahoma) were surveyed, Montgomery (1986) found factors that describe three types of gifted American Indian students. The factors become descriptions of the types of people who define the category as it emerges naturalistically from the data. In this study, the first type of gifted student, constituting the "family ties" factor, is loyal to the tribe, displays respect for elders, and places value on tribal culture and tradition. The second type, constituting the "dominant culture" factor, scores well on achievement tests, does well in school, and receives good grades. The third type, constituting the "leadership" factor, has (a) influence over others in any number of situations; (b) the ability to think of ways to solve group problems; and (c) respect from peers.

Crawford and George (1980) reported that certain behaviors of gifted students may not be exhibited in the classroom. These authors also have noted that gifted and talented American Indian students withdraw from active participation in classroom activities from grades 4 through 9. Because of this withdrawal, the characteristics noted above often are difficult to observe. The development of an "all-purpose" instrument for identifying gifted American Indian students is impossible. However, to be effective, an identification methodology must accommodate the cultural diversity that exists.

Table 11-1 Comparative Continua of Differential Characteristics of American Indian and Dominant American Groups

American Indian Perspective   *Dominant American Perspective*

Right brain	Left brain
Spatial	Verbal
Cooperative	Competitive
Feminine	Masculine
Rural	Urban
Family	Individual
Large social orientation	Small social orientation
Communal living space	Individual living space
No facial feedback	Facial expressive
Stoic	Dramatic
Tribal/family	Individual/family
Tribal identity	Self-identity
Naturalistic	Mechanistic
Magical/linguistic	Scientific/probabilistic
Auditory, storytelling	Visual, reading books
Custom	Convention
Readiness orientation	Clock-time orientation
Wisdom of life experiences	Wisdom of education
Physical, psychomotor	Mental, cognitive
Concern for accuracy	Concern for speed
Multilingual	Unilingual

PHILOSOPHICAL APPROACHES TO IDENTIFICATION OF MINORITIES

Two dramatically different approaches to identifying the gifted minority student exist. One focuses on the idea that use of multiple psychometric measures will be more inclusive than use of a single measure. The other approach centers on the assumption that giftedness is defined by the culture (Bernal, 1974a,b; Bruch, 1971; Passow, 1972; Renzulli, 1974).

Psychometric Approach

The use of a psychometric approach to the identification of gifted students of any cultural group has been debated in the schools and in the courts. Much of the publicity for this debate was provided initially through the legal assessment of bias in competency testing in schools. The term "bias," when used in testing situations, has a specific and unique meaning, defined as a systematic error in the measurement process. It affects and changes all measurements in the same way. Bias, then, is a technical term

Exhibit 11-1 Categories of Characteristics for Identifying Gifted American Indian Students

Acquired Skills	***Personal/Human Qualities***
Learning skills	High intelligence
Language/communication skills	Visionary/inquisitive/intuitive
Technological skills	Creative
Tribal/Cultural Understanding	Individualistic—self-disciplined
Knowledge of ceremonies	Leader
Knowledge of tribal traditions	Athletic prowess/coordinated/dexterous
Knowledge of tribes	Respectful of elders
Aesthetic Qualities	
Demonstrated visual art talent	
Demonstrated performing art talent	
Creative expression	
Indian art(s) talent	

Source: American Indian Research and Development, Inc., Norman, Oklahoma.

and denotes nothing more or less than the consistent distortion of a statistic (Osterlind, 1983).

Cultural bias, on the other hand, is a concept subject to many definitions and interpretations. Some would define bias to encompass any situation in which a systematic difference in test scores exists among groups, whereas others would limit the term to situations in which items within a test are substantially more difficult for one group than another relative to other items (Lynn, 1976).

While the development of a ''culture-fair'' test may be an impossible goal, one possible solution to this problem is to design a test that reflects all aspects of our pluralistic society, or at least the extent of diversity reflected by the student population. This would have the effect of equalizing the test by placing students at an equal advantage or disadvantage. Such an approach also has the advantage of being a more accurate measure of the skills needed to function effectively in a pluralistic society. A functional competency test given in Miami or San Antonio should include a number of Hispanic skills and content items, as one can argue reasonably that some cross-cultural competence is necessary to successful functioning in those cities.

The technical difficulties involved in designing a fair pluralistic test lead some to favor the goal of culturally neutral tests. The problem, of course, is that development of a culturally neutral test is a more evasive goal than construction of a pluralistic test. Tests usually perceived as culturally neutral in our society are almost inevitably tests that favor the predominantly Anglo-American, middle-class culture. Other ways exist to approach the concept of giftedness.

Ethnographic Approach

Charlesworth (1976, 1979) has proposed a methodology to study intelligence by defining intelligent behavior as it occurs in everyday life in an individual's natural environment. Labeling the approach ethnological, he advocates naturalistic observation of behavioral responses to environmental demands. This problem-solving perspective would eliminate any advantages given to the dominant culture and would yield greater understanding of the above-average use of cognitive processes that cross cultural boundaries. Comparisons of individuals are based on an individual's adaptation to the native environment and not on individual differences with group to group comparisons.

Faas (1982) identified three groups of American Indians based on the opinions of tribal members and teachers of American Indian students. One group is characterized by its rejection of American Indian tradition and motivation to be similar to the dominant culture. A second group is interpreted to be bicultural, continuing the maintenance of American Indian traditions combined with the life style of the dominant culture (particularly employment and entertainment). The third group is seen as holding on to a conservatively traditional Indian culture as a standard way of life. Faas and others believe that the bicultural group has the largest membership with greatest diversity within the group.

A strictly ethnographic approach has difficulties. For example, certain questions arise: What are the implications for programming? How will the great differences between tribal opinions be accommodated? After gaining understanding of one tribe, how will individual variances be accommodated? Thinking of Faas's (1982) three groups, how might each of these groups define giftedness? All three groups could have children in the same school. What would be the likely methodology to employ so that the American Indians' beliefs about giftedness would be implemented in the school? These are not simple questions to answer. For example, if one uses native language facility as a criterion for identification, each group would react differently. The first group may believe this strategy is inappropriate and that it discriminates against its children. Members of the second or third group usually have traditional language, so they would probably view such techniques as appropriate.

Both identification approaches discussed have been described as the extreme. Using the psychometric, one seeks strictly to test and measure based on predetermined norms and to use cutoff scores in predetermined, but legally fair, ways. Using the ethnographic, one seeks to ignore the time-honored approaches and to describe individuals strictly on the basis of norm-free concepts. The goal of this discussion is to prescribe an approach that combines these two extremes, that is, a methodology or set of procedures for identifying American Indian giftedness flexible enough to allow the blending of ethnographic criteria or factors with the traditional psychometric concept.

IDENTIFICATION: DEVELOPING A DEFINITION, SCREENING, AND DIAGNOSIS

Three fundamental steps are necessary in identifying gifted children: (a) developing a definition; (b) screening; and (c) diagnosis. One must develop a definition of giftedness to provide the direction needed for screening and diagnosis. The purpose of screening is to find children who may need a specialized educational program, and the purpose of diagnosis is to discover the uniqueness of the students' talents in an effort to outline the programming requirement.

Developing a Definition

The necessary first step in identification and programming is to develop a definition of giftedness. Many states have adopted the federal definition commonly in use (Karnes & Koch, 1985); however, a number of other methods can be employed to develop a workable, culturally meaningful definition of giftedness. Thinking more psychometrically, one could employ a tribal survey measuring reactions about behavioral characteristics or one could administer an assessment of what the tribal people perceive to be educational needs for students. Then, one can use both dominant and minority culture beliefs by averaging the responses and at least accommodating most of the people who answered the survey or questionnaire.

Defining giftedness using an ethnographic approach, Williams (1983) experimented with a semantic differential process to test its effectiveness as a method to derive a culturally relevant definition. She was able to generate a list of descriptors on opposite or polar continua within several semantic scales, each scale related to areas of potential excellence. The method is based on the concept that words could be used as building blocks for an instrument to determine what abilities are considered to be gifts in any particular culture. Although empirical evidence supporting her methodology is necessary before it can be standardized for application, the procedure appears to have great potential for defining giftedness because the data are derived from the opinions of members of the particular culture.

Faas (1982) interviewed American Indians and non-American Indians from three groups, designated traditionality groups (similar to dominant culture, bicultural, traditional), and discovered that his population of Navajos defined giftedness to include "wisdom" and a wide range of specific talents.

Another successful way to discover the perceptions, opinions, and beliefs considered to be essential is through the implementation of a Q-study (Brown, S.R., 1980; Stephenson, 1953). Because of its focus on self-referent discoveries, Q-methodology would allow personal meanings of giftedness to be identified. Montgomery (1983) identified four types of giftedness based on the self-perceptions of a group of gifted students and recommends Q-methodology for identifying types of giftedness among culturally different populations.

The first step in a Q-study to understand giftedness would be to collect a large number of statements about the meaning of exceptional ability from within the culture. The statements may emerge from ideas stated in focus groups, interpersonal interviews, or cultural literature. A representative sample of the "population" of statements (universe or concourse) would serve as items to be sorted in modified rank order according to a related variable. The variable is the condition of instruction or question for the subject, or sorter. Great care and consideration must be given to stating the condition of instruction in a way to obtain the beliefs needed. Perhaps the meaning of excellence, the qualities of leadership, or the tradition of the tribe would exemplify the tacit knowledge of the culture toward "giftedness." A possibility exists that if the question is What is gifted? the answers may be what the majority culture teaches is the quality of giftedness. The Q-sorts can be factor analyzed to produce general types. The pattern of opinions that emerges as the data are interpreted offers direction to school personnel for constructing culturally relevant measures.

Screening

Some of the data that can be categorically and numerically arranged into a screening matrix as suggested by Baldwin (1977) and Maker (1979b) are presented below. In an effort to resist the psychometric paradigm's orientation to strict categorization (inclusion/exclusion; gifted/nongifted; further testing required/no testing required; special needs/regular program) I have resisted providing suggested cutoff scores for the diagnosis of "giftedness."

Referral System

Some appropriate strategies to screen a population with large numbers of American Indians must include tribal and family-related opinions. A referral system that includes the opinions of parent(s), tribal leaders, and students referring self and/or peers can be developed out of the data that emerge from the definition research. For example, some items that are culturally relevant to American Indians in Oklahoma (Tonemah, 1986) are shown in Exhibit 11-2.

Naturalistic Observation

Maker, Morris, and James (1981) report success with employing diagnostic observation of group activities using predetermined criteria as a screening strategy for

Exhibit 11-2 Sample Referral Items Culturally Relevant to American Indians in Oklahoma

---

Parent Referral
- is alert beyond years
- has "wisdom of life"
- finds and corrects own mistakes
- is able to laugh at self

School Referral
- interest level in classes
- social adjustment
- test scores and grades

Community Referral
- leadership potential
- tribal understanding
- area of outstanding ability

Self Referral
- strengths in singing, dancing, music, running
- interests in experimenting, problem solving, inventing
- like for magic and mystery
- knowledge of tribal government, customs, history

Source: From "Indian Student Biographical Data Questionnaire," American Indian Research and Development, Inc., Norman, Oklahoma, 1986.

---

culturally different gifted students. Their approach included using an adaptation of the Torrance Checklist of Creative Positives (Torrance, 1973) as criteria for making judgments about the individual abilities observed during a lesson using the Peabody Language Development Kit (PLDK).

To conduct an observational screening effectively, the criteria for making judgments must emerge from the culture, the observer must be trained in detecting behavior that is indicative of the criteria (asking many or different questions is easier to score than asking or answering "wisdom of life" questions), and the students must be comfortable with the activity. Understanding what is done in the classroom under normal conditions will facilitate the use of an observation strategy.

Naturalistic observation is a strategy that can be used to detect exceptional ability, and any number of special talent areas can be observed. Torrance (1977) has worked extensively with culturally different gifted children and has generalized some of the talent areas and potential exceptional characteristics as found in Exhibit 11-3.

Specific Talent Recognition

Although the initial definition research will more adequately guide decisions about which talent areas to screen, some of the probable common tribal values (from Exhibit 11-3) may focus on the areas of problem solving, dance or creative movement, visual arts, and storytelling. A strategy for screening for storytelling ability, for example, may be begun by setting up the cultural criteria as discovered from the ethnographic research. For instance, a group of children might be asked to tell a story and observers would rate the story according to the criteria as displayed in Exhibit 11-4.

One can reason that the ability to solve problems, employ strategic thinking, or use other cross-cultural cognitive processes could be evaluated during a controlled-environment completion of a task. Success at Pente, chess, Master Mind, or other strategical

Exhibit 11-3 Torrance Creative Positives

General Categories

Ability to express feelings and emotions	Enjoyment of and ability in group problem solving
Ability to improvise with commonplace materials	Responsiveness to the concrete
Articulateness in role playing and storytelling	Responsiveness to the kinesthetic
Enjoyment of and ability in visual arts	Expressiveness of gestures and body language
Enjoyment of and ability in creative movement and dance	Humor
Enjoyment of and ability in music and rhythm	Richness of imagery
Use of expressive speech	Originality and inventiveness
Figural fluency and flexibility	Problem centeredness
	Emotional responsiveness
	Quickness of warm-up

Source: From *Discovery and Nurturance of Giftedness in the Culturally Different* (p. 26) by E.P. Torrance, 1977, Reston, Va.: Council for Exceptional Children.

Exhibit 11-4 Storytelling Criteria

Child Name	STORYTELLING							
	Creativity				Tribal Values			
	Fluency	Flexibility	Originality	Elaboration	History	Elders	Family	Fantasy

thinking games could be evaluated. Threats to cross-cultural interpretation of the results of such an evaluation would be a subject's past experience with the actual task, familiarity with similar tasks or objects, and the understanding of the directions for completing the task (Maker, 1980).

Diagnosis

After screening, diagnostic testing can be used to develop an individual education plan. Using parents, tribal leaders, school personnel, and the students to make recommendations for programs may lead to the placement of American Indian students in special programs for gifted, mentorships or preceptorships (an apprenticeship in medicine), college classes, art shows, and so forth.

NEEDED RESEARCH

Current literature has limited numbers of empirical studies and discussions that relate directly to gifted American Indian students. More empirical evidence for assistance in making the necessary identification and programming decisions is greatly needed.

A major decision to make is whether the approach to identification and measurement of the gifted student should be to include the cultural context as an interpretive factor (ethnographic) or to use a statistical demarcation based upon a "standardization" process using cultural norms (psychometric). The problem of deriving meaning from the data gathered in a way that can be interpreted with the smallest degree of error remains.

Several questions need to be addressed empirically prior to the development of final protocols. A key question is, What thought processes, perhaps related to solving problems or adapting to environment, might be universal factors among students? In addition, discovering the ways that personality (emotional, motivational) factors and environmental factors influence the development of exceptional ability is important (Patel, 1977).

Research is needed to provide the structure for the design of different protocols for identification of various groups of students. For example, characteristics of a gifted child may be widely divergent across groups. The possibility also exists that the lists of characteristics will contain factors that to one group may identify the gifted student but, when considered or interpreted in the context of a second group, are either neutrally or negatively related to giftedness and talent.

Research is needed to determine how an individual's self-perception of "Indianness" is related to the identification procedure. For example, students or families could rate themselves according to their own perception of which of Faas's (1982) three groups they may fit. The result of the rating would help determine which procedure for identification works best for each of the groupings. A semantic differential using the continua from Table 11-1 would help to discover which techniques and items work best to discriminate levels of "Indianness." These items could then be correlated to successful procedures.

A great deal of effort has been expended to identify gifted students through content analysis and psychometric systems, but such methods have typically focused only on the mechanical structure of the measurement items under consideration (question order, alternative choices, and so forth). The focus has been on tests and test items that discriminate against, or for, one group of students at the expense of another, and "explaining" the discrimination. Researchers have typically relied only on psychometric analysis and have not, for example, included analysis of linguistic understanding and interpretation of the deep structure of the items (Chomsky, 1968). How a respondent interprets the meaning of a sentence is dependent upon his or her own language facility and on cultural contexts. This understanding is especially critical for bilingual groups or for groups for whom English is a second language.

The cultural meaning of receiving a specialized education for gifted American Indian students also must be understood. If a compelling need exists to develop and nurture these students as a future resource, one must identify clearly factors related to the culture of the particular tribal group which preclude students from reaching their full potential. If students, in spite of the "home" culture, are supported by the school in the development of and participation in programs for the gifted, what then is the impact of that experience on the students' ability to return to their home group without penalty?

IN CONCLUSION

When identifying giftedness among American Indian students, we must examine (a) the collective beliefs, (b) the thinking and perspective of the school district, and (c) the particular tribe(s) involved. The first step is to develop an understanding of what it means to be an American Indian, to be gifted, and to employ testing instruments to discover giftedness. This author has reviewed the issues involved in this difficult first step to establish the importance of a mutual understanding of the use of tests with suggested cutoff scores. While identification processes may be similar, the procedures of identification need to be individualized for each population.

The diversity of culture between tribes influences the identification process, but defining American Indian culture is as difficult as defining European culture. Understanding the values of any culture leads to finding its strengths or gifts; additionally the characteristics of giftedness that are common across cultures must be considered. Skillfully and appropriately blending ethnographics and psychometric procedures to reflect the beliefs of the people involved is a promising approach to the identification of gifted American Indian students.

12

Identification of the Gifted and Talented American Indian Student

Robert J. Kirschenbaum, Ph.D.
Tolleson Union High School

Montgomery has ably reviewed the strengths and weaknesses of the various methodological options available to those seeking to identify gifted and talented American Indian students. In this chapter, I will try to fill the gaps I see in her treatment of individual identification methods by describing how available instruments can be used, describing instruments being developed especially for American Indian students, and recommending an identification procedure for locating gifted and talented students of various ethnic backgrounds.

I agree with Montgomery on several points. Identifying American Indian students (hereafter referred to as Indian students) who can benefit from a program for the gifted and talented is problematic, partly because so little has been done in this area. Exclusive reliance on testing is inappropriate because (a) few tests have included Indian students in their norm samples; (b) many Indian students have limited English proficiency and are lacking in cultural and social experiences tapped by standardized tests; and (c) Indian students tend to have a nonanalytic cognitive style that puts them at a disadvantage on tests that emphasize analytic thinking. Only a few nontest instruments exist that are based on the cultural values of individual American Indian tribal groups.

Many agree that a program for gifted and talented Indian students is desirable, and therefore identification methods that are valid and reliable for this population are necessary. Montgomery recommends a battery of identification methods for this purpose. In this chapter, I will specify types of instruments that should be included in this battery and in what order they should be used in the overall identification procedure.

I disagree with Montgomery on three points. First, definitions of giftedness and talent should not be contingent on the cultural characteristics of any ethnic group. The manifestations of giftedness and talent in students, however, do depend on the ethnic and environmental background of students.

Second, identification requires at least three phases—screening, selection, and diagnosis. Selection is more than just a final screening phase and involves a consideration of the flexibility and specificity of an identification procedure, which will be explained in this chapter.

Finally, Montgomery recognizes that few empirical studies of gifted and talented Indian students, and of education for the gifted, have been conducted on reservations. I disagree with her suggestion that a decision has to be made about whether to rely on either ethnographic or psychometric sources of information. With available programming options always in mind, *both* psychometric and ethnographic information need to be considered in making selection decisions that are based on comprehensive, diagnostic assessments of students.

The final question voiced by Montgomery underscores the paradox of special education for the Indian student: What is the impact of the identification of and programming for gifted and talented Indian students on their families and tribal societies? A survey of Indian parents and educators in Oklahoma shows overwhelming support for education for the gifted (Tonemah, 1986); but the fact that the question is raised implies that special education for the gifted and talented Indian student is a new, and potentially controversial, phenomenon.

OBSTACLES TO EDUCATION OF THE GIFTED AND TALENTED AMERICAN INDIAN STUDENT

Major obstacles to identifying, and providing an effective educational program for, gifted and talented Indian students in public schools on or near American Indian reservations include the effect of (a) alcohol abuse among American Indians, (b) school staff turnover rate, and (c) bias in the perception of giftedness. (The reader is referred to the introduction to Section II for an elaboration of these obstacles.)

In addition, intertribal and interclan rivalries have a detrimental effect on program development. School board members and administrators may oppose new ideas for personal and political reasons. Most serious, the prevalence of rivalries restricts the networking of people from various school districts on the reservation, resulting in a lack of cooperation and sharing of information. Finally, personal conflicts between Anglo-American administrators and teachers usually occur at reservation schools that are located in isolated areas. The high turnover rate of teachers results in administrators having a great deal of unchecked power, and resentments tend to develop when people of various backgrounds live and work in a small area with few opportunities to interact with people outside the community.

A few examples from my personal experiences can be used to illustrate the obstacles to programming. In one case, a Navajo fifth grader, wearing torn and dirty clothing, was referred to me for discipline problems. The student lived in an impoverished setting without running water, and perhaps without electricity, with just his father, who spoke only Navajo. Yet, he was able to speak to me in articulate English about himself and his problems with the classroom teacher. Tonemah and Brittan (1985) show that fluent bilingual ability is considered a characteristic of the gifted and talented Indian student. When I informed the student's teacher of my assessment of his ability, she realized that his behavior problems in class may have stemmed from being unchallenged. Her first reaction, however, was to consider him emotionally handicapped and in need of remedial help.

In another situation, the principal of a school for Maricopa and Pima Indian students told me no gifted students were in his school of about 60 students in grades kindergarten through eight. He would not even consider the possibility that one of his students might enter a program for the gifted at an integrated high school in the near or distant future.

As a final example, a Navajo special education teacher in a middle school had been employed for many years, and was widely recognized as being very capable. Teachers referred students to her for counseling and discipline, and she also taught groups of special education students. When special education for gifted and talented students was mandated in the state, she was given the added responsibility of establishing and coordinating a program for gifted and talented students in her school, even though she had no training in this area.

The preceding anecdotes from reservation schools illustrate (a) the problem of identifying gifted and talented Indian students from impoverished backgrounds; (b) how administrative perceptions and decisions are often to the detriment of gifted and talented students; and (c) how, because of high staff turnover, a few, longtime teachers can be given so many responsibilities over the years that they are unable to handle adequately the added responsibility of coordinating the identification and special education of gifted and talented students.

My personal experiences with teaching, testing, and observing Indian students in the Southwest, as well as in interacting with American Indian administrators, school board members, parents, teachers, and tribal leaders (mostly Navajo), have shown me that the American Indian nations are at an embryonic stage in terms of their political development as a cohesive, ethnic force in this country. Just as the early, colonial Americans had to choose between allegiance to a monarchy or to the new concept of democracy, American Indians who have completed a high school education must decide to what degree their way of thinking is to be determined by cultural traditions and myths, and how much their lives are to be influenced by new associates, professional training, and bureaucratic job responsibilities. How are the old ways to be synthesized with the new, technological, and economic realities? Education must play a key role.

DEFINITIONS OF GIFTEDNESS AND TALENT

Against the sociological backdrop that has been painted, the plight of the gifted and talented student can be considered. Montgomery asks, Who will benefit from a system that promotes gifted and talented Indian children? The answer is the children, primarily, and the American Indian society, secondarily. How? By exercising their abilities for the benefit of themselves and their society, gifted and talented children can make valuable contributions.

Giftedness is evident when a child's awareness of patterns and relationships in the environment is superior to that of others'. The gifted child has a greater consciousness of the world. (Consciousness, as it is used here, refers to (a) the speed and depth of thought; (b) the ability to think abstractly, use cognitive strategies, and draw meaning from events; and (c) the facility with which symbols are manipulated by reasoning.)

Talent is demonstrated when a child shows facility for manipulating the physical environment in a purposeful manner. Once exposed to a medium of expression and productivity, the talented child will have a natural tendency to become involved in repeated use of the medium, and will seek a level of mastery for its own sake. The talented individual develops skills in the use of tools in the chosen medium at a faster rate than other students; shows greater interest in learning about the use of these tools; and is able to integrate various skills in the field of expression to produce a result that is superior to the results obtained by other students of similar backgrounds.

Based on her research into the Navajo conception of giftedness, Abbott reveals that gifted persons know how to act because they practice "good thought." The gifted Navajo child demonstrates good thought, not only by being a very fast learner but also by speaking, acting, and approaching life according to the precepts of Navajo teachings and philosophy that comprise the "Navajo way." The Navajo conception of giftedness incorporates talent for working in the crafts or performing in cultural rituals. Being gifted and talented for a Navajo means doing things that are constructive and responsible, helping one's family, learning quickly how to do things, and doing these things well.

While many have acknowledged for some time that gifted students are brighter than other students and therefore are expected to score higher on tests of cognitive abilities, cognitive psychologists such as Sternberg (Davidson & Sternberg, 1984; Sternberg, 1981) and Scruggs (Scruggs, 1986; Scruggs & Mastropieri, 1985), report that gifted students process information more deliberately and consciously. No psychometric instruments are available at this time to measure directly insightful problem solving and the degree to which strategies are used in information processing, but high problem-solving ability is considered a primary characteristic of gifted and talented Indian students (Tonemah & Brittan, 1985).

A review of research by Rogers (1986) supports the claim that gifted students use strategies more effectively than nongifted students to acquire and store complex information, which means they have larger vocabularies and a more extensive knowledge of how to solve problems. Using this information-processing definition of giftedness in the context of the traditional American Indian culture suggests that to identify gifted Indian students, one should attempt to determine the degree to which a student is intelligent, resourceful, attentive, a quick learner, self-sufficient and dependable, knowledgeable, insightful, and able to handle new situations, solve problems, and distinguish underlying meaning.

THE GIFTED AND TALENTED INDIAN STUDENT IN THE SOCIAL CONTEXT

Gifted and talented students, regardless of ethnic background, need to associate with each other to share their ideas and experiences. Galbraith's (1985) interviews with gifted students reveal that their chief cause of anxiety is feeling alone and different from other children because of different interests, higher ethical standards, and different concerns. This is very likely the case with gifted Navajo students, according to statements made by parents (Abbott, n.d.). Gifted students tend to search for each other to alleviate this sense of aloneness, so identified students might be helpful in locating unidentified students. In addition, teachers can be asked to look for students who express concern about issues or events that peers tend to ignore or who do not seem to fit in with the group.

Without encouragement to express their ideas through constructive projects at school, students may choose to keep their gifts and talents hidden. Social pressures among some American Indian groups are directed at minimizing outward differences. Obviously, these social pressures hinder identification efforts. I am aware of students in an art class in a nonreservation high school who display evidence of artistic talent but will not finish their assignments and turn them in for credit. They prefer to rip up their drawings rather than display their talents and compete with their peers.

Indian students who are talented in traditional modes of expression for a particular American Indian society, such as in the areas of art, dance, or even athletics, probably will be supported in the development of their talents by parents and relatives. Those students who come from families adhering to a conservatively traditional American Indian culture as a way of life, however, may experience difficulties if they attempt to express themselves more creatively than usual. Torrance (1969d) has concluded from his cross-cultural studies that the more closely a culture attempts to adhere to traditions, the less it encourages creative thinking. Since the role of women in societies that are very tradition-minded is usually very narrowly defined as mother and housekeeper, creativity in young girls in these groups would be least encouraged. This phenomenon portends some real problems in identifying gifted and talented American Indian girls.

SPECIFICITY AND FLEXIBILITY OF IDENTIFICATION PROCEDURES

Specificity and flexibility are two important aspects of an identification procedure (Kirschenbaum, 1983). Specificity refers to the definition of giftedness used, and whether it has a broad or narrow conception. To evaluate this aspect one needs to determine how homogeneous are the abilities and interests of selected gifted students. If a program is designed only for those students who demonstrate superior ability in mathematical reasoning or drawing, the identification procedure must be high in specificity. A program that offers gifted students the chance to learn about various advanced topics through mini-course units could have an identification procedure that is low in specificity.

Flexibility is related to specificity, but is determined not by the focus of an identification procedure related to program design, but by the extent to which students who do not meet prerequisite criteria are selected into the program on the basis of demonstrated strengths. If the selection of a student for a special program is totally dependent on whether the student reaches a cutoff score on a single test, then flexibility is very low. If a student has weaknesses—such as underachievement, behavioral problems, a learning disability, or weak basic skills—but is selected to be part of a program for gifted and talented students on the basis of definite, recorded strengths in performance, leadership, or creativity, then the identification procedure is very flexible. Because Montgomery is reluctant to propose a cutoff score for diagnosing giftedness, I assume that she would opt for a procedure having a moderate amount of flexibility.

An identification procedure can be only as specific and flexible as the program design will allow. A program must accommodate students with a broad range of strengths and weaknesses if minimum specificity and maximum flexibility are to be achieved. Since special education for gifted and talented students is a new phenomenon on American Indian reservations, I recommend that identification be fairly specific and moderately flexible, especially for elementary school programs. With insufficient specificity, the teacher of the gifted will be unable to interest a majority of the students in any particular topic and unable to provide a curriculum suited to many of the students. A procedure with too much flexibility might result in some underachieving students being intimidated by other students with superior academic skills.

A MULTI-OPTION PROCEDURE FOR IDENTIFYING GIFTED AND TALENTED INDIAN STUDENTS

Montgomery recommends that, after screening, diagnostic testing can be used to develop an individual education plan (IEP). While presenting a potpourri of methods to screen students for a program for gifted, she neglects to explain how the gifted students finally are identified and selected. How are tests integrated into the total identification procedure besides being used to develop an IEP? Should other collected information be used to develop the IEP? Montgomery's chapter raises many interesting questions but offers little in the way of practical guidance in developing an identification procedure.

I recommend that a "funnel approach" be used in the identification of gifted and talented Indian students who will be placed in enrichment programs, because this approach allows for moderate specificity and flexibility. The funnel approach allows many students to be screened, and multiple sources of information on students to be tapped, before final selection decisions are made.

To begin the screening, all students who have above-average scores on subtests (of the achievement test used in the school district) or who were on the most recent honor roll listing go into the wide mouth of the funnel. At the same time, nominations of students who may be gifted and talented are solicited from parents and teachers. Nomination categories should include culturally valued behavioral characteristics and abilities—such as respect for elders, capable of taking care of livestock, and knowledge about clan rituals (Tonemah & Brittan, 1985). These characteristics address what Montgomery calls the "family ties" factor. A peer nomination procedure may be employed to assess the "leadership" factor.

Tonemah and Brittan (1985) have developed the Indian Student Biographical Data Questionnaire for use in nominating students for a special program for gifted and talented students. (See also discussion in Chapter 11, and Exhibit 11-2.) It has separate parts to be completed by parents, school personnel, a community member, and students.

Students who have been identified using the above methods are considered to be in the ''screening pool.'' They are given a group-administered test of nonverbal reasoning. This type of test has the least possible amount of cultural bias. The *Ravens Progressive Matrices* (Raven, Court, & Raven, 1985) provides one of the best assessments of the ''g'' factor of intelligence, a theoretical general factor that cuts across specific areas of cognitive ability such as verbal or spatial reasoning. The tests do not require any use of language in choosing answers, and instructions are very simple.

The names of all students who are referred, or who are in the top third or so with respect to their scores on achievement or nonverbal reasoning tests, are now compiled in a matrix, with all scores recorded and checks given for teacher, parent, and peer nominations. Very strong nominations may be starred or otherwise marked. The list now may be reviewed by a panel of persons who collectively know all or most of the children, and it can be reduced to include only those who are likely to be gifted or talented, based on the panel's extensive knowledge of individual students. If anyone questions whether a student should be removed, he or she should remain on the list. Any student who has been nominated also should remain in the screening pool, since someone believes the student has superior ability.

In grades four and above, students listed in the matrix now may be informed by letter that they can apply formally for the program by filling out an autobiographical application form. Learning, productive, and leadership activities are listed on this form, and students check those in which they have engaged. Open-ended questions are included to ascertain values, productive interests, and academic attitudes.

Information can be obtained by having students complete an autobiographical application form, not the least of which is whether the student is interested enough in the program to complete the form and submit it. Unless a program for the gifted is designed to help the underachieving, poorly motivated student, the identification procedure should be designed to find the student who is motivated to participate in the special program being offered.

All students who return completed application forms next may be scheduled for special testing in the selection phase. If the *Wechsler Intelligence Scale for Children— Revised* (*WISC-R*) (Wechsler, 1974) is used, the tester should recognize that Indian students generally perform differently from other ethnic groups. Reynolds (1983) states that Indian students generally score higher on the subtests that assess perceptual organization (Picture Completion, Picture Arrangement, Block Design, Object Assembly), and lower on those that assess verbal conceptualization (Vocabulary, Similarities, Comprehension), than the norm group. In particular, I have found that Indian students tend to score high on the Picture Completion and low on the Information subtests. This information on the testing pattern of Indian students on the *WISC-R* should be considered if the scores of Indian students are to be compared to the scores of Anglo-American students.

The use of behavior rating forms is often a part of the identification procedure used in this country. I recommend that students be allowed to ask a teacher of their choice to complete these forms.

Another option of this recommended identification procedure is to assess creativity, which was ranked the second most important characteristic by those surveyed by Tonemah and Brittan (1985). Creativity can be assessed by administering divergent thinking activities to students, or by having them complete creativity self-report forms. The *Torrance Tests of Creative Thinking* (Torrance, 1974b) are available in both figural and verbal forms and can be used to make a normative assessment of a student's originality, fluency, flexibility, elaboration, and creative strengths. Given that Indian students do better on tests of perceptual organization, one might expect that they would perform more creatively on the figural, than on the verbal, forms.

The creativity self-report form is used to assess self-perceptions students have about their behavioral characteristics. Students check whether the listed behavioral characteristics and attitudes that are associated with the creative personality describe them. The self-report forms developed by Rimm (1986)—the *PRIDE, GIFT* and *GIFFI,* each designed for a different age range—have been tested cross-culturally with Indian students. Scores on these instruments have demonstrated high correlations with assessments of creativity in writing and art. Another creativity self-report form is the *How Do You Really Feel about Yourself?* Inventory (Williams, 1972).

Abbott's (1983) *Gifted Attitudes Inventory for Navajos (GAIN)* is a self-report instrument based on the values of the Navajo people. Abbott conducted ethnographic research to extract a multidimensional Navajo conception of giftedness, a term not easily translated into the Navajo language, from interviews with members of the Navajo tribe. The *GAIN* records student attitudes toward attributes of a Navajo definition of giftedness. Students must choose which statement in each of 66 pairs best represents their own feelings, attitudes, or opinions. The statements on the form require at least a seventh grade reading level. The *GAIN* shows little correlation with measures of intelligence or achievement, but does correlate significantly with some measures of creativity. It may tap leadership traits specific to the Navajo people.

In the elementary school, screened students can be asked to make something out of clay or other construction material. The final product can be assessed for imagination (unusual viewpoint), elaboration (detail), persistence (total time spent), orginality (uniqueness of subject), and quality (overall impression). If possible, a professional artist should be included among the raters, thereby increasing the credibility of the evaluation.

Once all the screening information from tests, nominations and recommendations, application forms, and ratings has been collected and compiled in a data matrix, the final selection phase begins. The program teachers and coordinator interview the students who have submitted the application form. Short problem-solving situations are presented and students are expected to offer alternative solutions. The interest inventory serves as a source of many questions about outside activities, accomplishments, topics students would like to investigate in a program for the gifted, how they can cooperate and work with others, and reading preferences. During the interview students have the opportunity to show enthusiasm, depth and breadth of knowledge, imagination, ingenuity, and social skills such as poise under fire. Students are asked why they want to be in the program and if they will be able to find the time for research and project work. After all the interviews are conducted, the teachers and coordinator make the final selection decisions.

No substitute can be offered for examining the results of an assessment battery to determine the profile of strengths and weaknesses of individual students. The procedure described above is certainly lengthy, but does not have to be repeated every year. Most students initially in the screening pool will not be reconsidered. Students who were strongly considered but not selected should be reexamined within two or three years. The special program for gifted and talented students should be publicized and self-nomination sought, with the application form made available to new students and, at the end of the school year, to all students. An underused source of information is the gifted and talented students presently in the program who may have friends they feel belong in the program.

A multi-option identification procedure is appropriate for schools with extensive minority student populations, such as an American Indian reservation school, because it brings together numerous sources of nonacademic information about students. In reservation schools, generally over 99 percent of the students are American Indians. Even under these conditions, I have found that many of the students in programs for the gifted are non-American Indian children of school teachers and administrators.

The basic assumption of those who use a multi-option identification procedure is that any source of information about a student's abilities is valuable. I have attempted to show through my description of a multi-option identification procedure that Montgomery is wrong in suggesting that a decision has to be made whether to use one source of information or the other. Psychometric measures provide information about students' background knowledge, ability to reason, ability to read in English or to do mathematical computation, which are important for competing in the American society. Ethnographic information tells us something about students' abilities with respect to their ethnic background and native culture.

IDENTIFYING INDIAN STUDENTS IN NONRESERVATION PUBLIC SCHOOLS

Many Indian students go to public school off the reservation with students from other ethnic groups. As Montgomery states, these Indian students are rarely selected to participate in a program for gifted students.

Two primary circumstances can be identified under which Indian students can be selected to participate in a special program for the gifted and talented in a predominantly non-American Indian public school. Each is discussed below.

1. *Indian students may meet the necessary criteria for being selected.*

In the Zuni Elementary School, 0.6 percent of the student body met the state criteria for intellectual giftedness. At least 0.6 percent of full-blooded Indian students in nonreservation schools also can meet the same test criteria and be considered intellectually gifted.

The multi-option identification procedure was designed as a basic approach to the identification of gifted and talented students of all ethnic backgrounds in any setting. The design of the procedure allows for flexibility in the selection process. Built into the procedure is the opportunity to identify those students who score very high on any particular measure.

Special programs for students talented in the arts usually emphasize auditions, review of portfolios, and the assessment of creative thinking ability. Many Indian students display artistic talent and should be encouraged to apply to these programs even if their academic achievement is less than exemplary.

2. *Indian students may be selected by being identified as the most gifted relative to their ethnic peers.*

Those Indian students who show the highest scores on the measures of ability used in the identification procedure enter a program for the gifted. Federal legislation and court decisions have long mandated that all peoples in the United States deserve an equal opportunity to be educated and employed. Since the purpose of special education for the gifted and talented is to provide special programs for the ablest, a special effort needs to be made to identify the ablest among the American Indian subpopulation.

Gowan (1975) notes that a successful enrichment program for the gifted needs to be comprised of students from different backgrounds. If sufficient flexibility is incorporated into an identification procedure, students with strengths in nonacademic areas will be allowed to participate in a program for gifted and talented students. Gordon (1961) has remarked that a creative problem-solving group is most effective when it is comprised of individuals with backgrounds in different areas. The identification procedure described in detail in this critique can be effective in identifying a heterogenous group of gifted, talented, and creative youngsters who can work together successfully.

IN CONCLUSION

Special educational programming for the gifted and talented has been officially supported at the national, state, and tribal level. Education of the gifted and talented can be used to help these students develop their abilities to a greater degree than is generally possible in a regular program. It also can improve the attitude students have toward school.

Montgomery describes various categories of assessment methods for identifying gifted and talented students, as well as some individual instruments, but fails to integrate them into a coherent procedure. In this critique, a concerted attempt has been made to suggest how different methods for assessment can be ordered sequentially to funnel students through the screening phase into the selection phase, with sufficient information obtained through this process for diagnostic assessment.

In this critique, I claim that the single most important and unifying characteristic of all gifted students is their ability to comprehend and cognitively manipulate information of some sort—that is, students are gifted because they are excellent information processors. Talent is exhibited when students are able to demonstrate their understanding of patterns and relationships through artistic performance that is creative and expressive in a manner that cannot be trained. Students' cultural and experiential backgrounds determine the medium in which their gifts and talents will mature and develop. Personality characteristics and a combination of training, emotional support, and career guidance determine what use the students eventually make of their gifts and talents.

In programs for the gifted and talented, we must teach students (and provide the circumstances for them to learn) when and how to use their exceptional information processing and expressive abilities for the mutual benefit of themselves and society. But before we can provide special educational programming in whatever form will benefit these students the most, we must first identify the gifted and talented Indian students.

13

Purpose of Programs for Gifted and Talented and Highly Motivated American Indian Students

Anita Bradley Pfeiffer, M.Ed.
University of New Mexico

HISTORICAL BACKGROUND

When writing about the purpose of programs for gifted and talented and highly motivated American Indian students (hereafter referred to as gifted American Indian students) in the United States, my immediate focus is on how educational policies and delivery of general education have occurred historically. The introduction to this section provides a discussion of the historical background surrounding education of the American Indian, and for brevity the reader is referred there for an elaboration of this subject.

Of particular significance is the unique relationship between American Indians and the federal government, and the impact of that relationship not only on decisions centering around the composition and delivery of education, but also on all areas of American Indian life. Federally mandated versus self-determined direction in that relationship, as it relates to education, is a key factor.

Within the history of imposed educational policymaking, I have discussed the purpose of programs for gifted American Indian students. Issues specifically addressed include (a) meeting individual students' needs and abilities within the context of their culture; and (b) bridging individual strengths to the requirements of the mainstream culture.

PROGRAM PURPOSE

The primary purpose for instituting appropriate education for gifted American Indian students is to strengthen the quality of life of various American Indian tribes. Improved health, excellence in education, language maintenance, cultural maintenance, and economic security would improve the quality of life for American Indians. Informed leadership must be developed to deal with retention of fishing and water rights; juris-dictional problems of the federal and state governments; development of mineral leases; protection of human rights; retention of land; and development of a strong and viable tribal government. The ultimate goal of all tribal groups is to acquire an economic stability and spiritual tranquility for tribal members' lives.

American Indian tribes are complex and diverse in their economic, linguistic, cul-tural, social, political, and religious concerns. Although diversity is apparent, American Indians also are similar in areas such as kinship orientation, reservation status, unique trust relationships with state and federal governments, traditions of child-rearing prac-tices, customary law, and tribal government. American Indian tribes believe they are unique and sovereign, and that they contribute to the character of the nation and the world.

Meeting Students' Needs within Their Culture

The resolution of critical tribal, national, and international problems requires the thinking of gifted American Indian students. These students need the strength and support of their own tribal groups and that of the non-American Indian population to reach their potential. A desperate need exists to look beyond ethnicity, to plan for resolving critical issues that are of concern to the world population. However, because ethnicity (Banks, 1975) is part of our social system, an essential component of education is that students master the facts, and develop the concepts, generalizations, and theories needed to understand and interpret events related to intergroup and intragroup inter-actions and tensions.

Helping students master interpersonal skills and nurturing academic growth must begin by capitalizing on students' strengths (e.g., culture, language, extended family support system). This type of education can be accomplished by organizing the school curricula to include the language and culture of the students through an appropriately differentiated scope and sequence of courses.

Tonkin and Edwards (1983) assert that the single most important task now facing education may be the cultivation of an understanding of other people's motives and the social, psychological, and historical settings that cause people to think and act as they do. A crucial component of the purpose of the education of gifted American Indian students is curricula addressing tribal history and historical settings of non-American Indian groups.

A program for gifted American Indian students should be designed to nurture the students' abilities, skills, and intellectual power by systematically exposing them to the conditions, changes, and possibilities of tribal policies affecting all areas of life. In addition, these students need to know the function, responsibilities, and importance of the extended family and clan relationships.

Using Cultural Strength as a Bridge

A strong component of the program purpose should be to teach students to become problem solvers and critical thinkers. Using real-life situations to prepare students for similar and dissimilar situations facing mankind will help them to gain insight into factors impinging on tribal affairs; and, from this process of deliberate introspection and critical thinking, students will be prepared better to address issues for the resolution of problems facing the world at large.

Examples of how other countries plan and develop their domestic and foreign affairs can be very useful to compare and contrast with an analysis of the affairs of tribal governments. The goal of maximum economic growth is a central one for many tribes struggling to attain economic gain and stability. Therefore, in studying economic development, students should become familiar with countries such as Japan for models.

According to Coleman (1985), several premises are necessary to plan an educational program:

1. The students' strengths are to be encouraged and developed.
2. The learning environment should provide opportunities for expanding students' knowledge and building more effective cognitive, affective, and creative abilities.
3. Arrangements must be made to accommodate individual differences—such as interest, abilities, learning rates, and learning styles.
4. Contact with other gifted children promotes socioemotional development, and must be incorporated.
5. A program should be responsive to the community it serves and involve families of the students included.
6. Evaluation is an indispensable part of effective programming.

In addition, three other areas seem especially important to include when programming for gifted American Indian students.

7. An understanding and in-depth knowledge of the inter- and intrapersonal relations of the extended and clan relationships should be an integral part of a program.
8. The philosophy and goals of the program for gifted students should support clearly an appropriate differentiated curriculum that will provide for maximum development of the students' potential within a culturally pluralistic context.
9. The polarity of the rich and poor in global relations should be explored.

Social and Educational Influences

I am suggesting that those who plan programs create curricula to harmonize with the social forces that influence the lives of gifted American Indian students. Cultures are always in a state of change, and therefore the purpose of a special program must undergo constant revisions and change to reflect forward-thinking goals that emphasize future trends at home and abroad.

The program for gifted American Indian students should include a study of how cultures function. An important part of understanding a culture is learning how things are organized and how one goes about learning them in that culture. For example, Bergman (personal communication, 1969) states that one of the most significant differences between Navajo family structure and that of middle-class Americans is the relationship of the child to a number of caring people. In general, the relationship to aunts and uncles is much more important to the Navajo family than it is to the middle-class American family. A great deal more nurturing responsibility is given to various members of the extended family, and the child is attached closely to the entire group.

In an extended family each member has a functional role for daily existence. Strong support exists in child rearing, care of the elderly, moral support, maintenance of health, economic survival and sustenance, emotional stability, and political partici-pation. Strengthening the extended family unit might result in the strengthening of the tribal body.

Education should touch the soul and emotions of students. Education should be joyous, but also rigorous, meaningful, differentiated, and of the highest order of excellence. In Table 13-1, I present a dichotomy of prevailing versus preferred practices that exemplify my mindset.

Table 13-1 Prevailing versus Preferred Practices of Education

Prevailing Practice	*Preferred Practice*
1. Students who have a first language other than English as a strength are placed in a program that uses English only.	1. Students who have a first language other than English as a strength are instructed in their first language.
2. Scheduling dominates and is rigidly set; therefore, students' needs are not often met.	2. Students' needs determine flexibility and periodic changes in scheduling.
3. Education is immersion in the dominant culture's curricula.	3. Education is relevant to the lives of American Indian students.
4. Very few educational programs for gifted American Indian students exist, except the Navajo Academy in Farmington, New Mexico.	4. Schools provide differentiated curricula for gifted students.
5. A compensatory, remedial educational model prevails.	5. Strengths of students (e.g., language, culture, history, music) are used in instruction.
6. Learning difficulties are ascribed to students.	6. Students' needs are met through diagnosis of academic needs, properly trained teachers, and differentiated educational programs.
7. Institutional needs are priorities.	7. Students' varying needs are the focus of concern.
8. Parents are excluded from participation in the formal education of their children.	8. Parents work in partnership with school personnel.
9. Community resources are not tapped.	9. Community resources are an integral part of students' education through mentorships, apprenticeships, and work-study.

Each tribal group, regardless of the cultural changes, wants to maintain its culture, language, and land. Parson (1967) maintains that certain fundamental requisites must be met in every social system, large or small, if it is to endure.

The first is pattern maintenance: The system must be preserved in its essential patterns; that is, the patterns must be reproduced time and again so as to preserve them over a succession of persons, groups, or generations.

Second, for a society to endure, it must adapt: Every organization and every society must adapt itself to its environment, derive its sustenance from it, and adjust to its changes. According to Parson (1967), in every country the chief task of adaptation is performed by the economic sector and its institutions and activities.

The third is goal attainment: Every organization and society has one or several goals it is trying to approach or attain, or which its members wish to attain. The behavior of societies is modified beyond the simple requirements of pattern maintenance and adaptation toward this goal attainment.

In like fashion, tribal governments, through their elected councils, maintain tribal life, adapt to changes, and develop policies for tribal goal attainment pursuant to federal treaty commitments.

IN CONCLUSION

A relevant program for gifted American Indian youths must include these factors: (a) a review and analysis of policy implications in light of more than a century of federal, church, and/or state educational program delivery; (b) educational policies that incorporate the values and goals of the respective tribes in a systematic, comprehensive manner; (c) the early identification of preschool American Indian children who are gifted and talented; and (d) the provision of appropriate tutelage—a progression from culturally relevant experiences to national and global concerns.

Nothing in the attempt to provide for the needs of gifted American Indian students precludes the continued interaction and contribution to tribal society, American mainstream life, or the world community. Gifted American Indian students must develop self-understanding; that is, knowing one's roots (history, culture, language); recognizing one's intellectual abilities and talents; accepting one's responsibilities within the extended family structure; and pursuing self-actualization. A psychological imperative is that self-worth be nurtured first within the cultural context of the individual. This self-worth may then serve as the foundation for bridging tribal, national, and global issues. To denigrate the former is most assuredly to doom the latter.

14

Imagining and Defining Giftedness

Karlene R. George, M.Ed.
Port Madison Reservation

INTRODUCTION

Human beings define themselves in some way; they believe in, and become, that definition. Momaday (1982) offers this Kiowa perspective:

> From the time the Indian first set foot upon this continent, he has centered his life in the natural world. He is deeply invested in the earth, committed to it both in his consciousness and in his instinct. In him the sense of place is paramount. Only in reference to the earth can he persist in his true identity. . . , for the Indian conceives of himself in terms of the land. His imagination of himself is also and at once an imagination of the physical world from which he proceeds and to which he returns in the journey of his life. (p. 13)

Non-American Indian educators often have difficulty in accepting and appreciating fully the American Indian person's concern for "the land" as synonymous with concern for "self." The American Indian collective self—the tribe—may be even less understood.

Without a frame of reference, non-American Indian educators often discuss a tribe as if it were a club; that is, fraternal, exclusive, politically powerful, but still an external framework encompassing people, but having neither spirit, will, nor life of its own. This has been a grave mistake, and we have only to look at the littered bones of educational programs that attempted to serve American Indian students (on or near tribal reservations) to realize that, however meritorious, these programs were planned and developed without considering the collective American Indian self—the tribe or tribes involved.

In the previous chapter, Pfeiffer presented background for understanding the tribe as a cultural and legal entity. I must reiterate that American Indian tribes are, and historically have been, regarded by the U.S. government as separate nations.

The process of defining and maintaining "self" is the challenge that American Indians have faced in all the political, economic, social, and cultural realities of the last two centuries. As Pfeiffer points out, they will continue in this process because self-knowledge, self-actualization, and self-worth also are the foundation for the survival of a people. Understanding that the choice and pursuit of knowledge is inextricably bound with a sense of self, place, and one's people is basic to understanding Pfeiffer's contention: The unique strengths and needs of gifted American Indian students should be examined within the context of their particular tribe or cultural community.

In an effort to build on that understanding, I have described how two tribal communities in the Pacific Northwest developed an instructional program for their highly capable students. This description is included here to provide additional insight into the practicality of the ideas that Pfeiffer has offered.

THE TWO TRIBES PROJECT

Assumptions

The school district's American Indian education specialist and an education of the gifted specialist joined forces to form the Gifted Program Planning Committee (GPPC). In addition to the specialists, the GPPC was comprised of representatives from the Tribal Education Committee of both tribes, a district psychologist, a media technician, director of the Indian Education Program, and American Indian education classroom aides.

After much study and discussion, the GPPC developed a set of assumptions (listed below) that reflected their thinking on education for the gifted and talented. In so doing, they were able to provide a relevant goal for the gifted program—the development of special abilities by and for service to the community.

1. The tribal community is the focal point for all economic, social, and emotional interactions with the "important others" in a Gifted/Talented Native American's (G/T NA) circle. (The term Native American was used in the official funding documents of this program in 1977 rather than American Indian, which is more commonly used today. This term and its respective acronyms will be used in this chapter when referring to the two tribes program.)
2. The tribal community defines "self" and "important others" in terms of traditions, heritage, beliefs, values, and other aspects of culture.
3. What the tribe values collectively, the parents, G/T NA students, and their important others will value.

4. G/T programs will be successful when G/T NA students participate with joy, vigor, and commitment.
5. G/T NA students will participate in a G/T program with joy, vigor, and commitment if its goals, objectives, and activities are consistent (or do not conflict) with the goals, objectives, and activities of the tribal community.
6. The more the goals, objectives, and activities of the G/T program are seen to be consistent and relevant to those of the tribal community, the greater the Native American parent and G/T student cooperation. Thus, opportunity for growth of special abilities is more likely to occur within the program.
7. G/T NA students must find personal satisfaction, pertinent interest, and commitment to tasks in the program in order to avail themselves of the opportunities provided by participation.

Definition

The committee needed a sound definition that would describe clearly the target student for the new program. Any definition that was to be put in place needed to cover a range of specialties and still contain solid statements on which all the committee could agree. Consensus was necessary to the operations of the committee.

The following definition from the Program was the first culturally adapted definition to be accepted by the U.S. Office of Education, Title III, Innovative Programs section:

Gifted children shall be defined as those children who consistently excel, or consistently show potential to excel, beyond their age and the expectations of their cultural community in the following areas:

1. Cognitive and higher level thinking skills
2. Creative and performing skills
3. Social helping and leadership skills
4. Those skills the cultural community may deem important to the well-being of its members

to the extent that they need and can benefit from specially planned and developed educational services presented by qualified staff (George, 1980).

To be gifted by this definition, a child was consistent in possessing either actual or potential excellence, which provided for a range of productive behavior. The word consistent was chosen carefully by the originators to convey persistence—a sustained and steady performance of excellence beyond the expectations of the cultural community.

What does "consistently show potential to excel" mean? An acknowledgment is made by the cultural community that children exist who show consistently that they are capable; but for social, emotional, financial or whatever reasons, never quite excel beyond that capability. These are the children who might especially need and benefit from the differentiated methods and activities of a program for gifted students.

Gifted Profile

Observable behaviors were ascribed to the four skill areas by means of a Q-sort process (Stephenson, 1953). In this way, the cultural community not only set specific expectations for each skill area, but determined the focus of program activities that were to enhance these qualities and develop others.

The measure of giftedness in each skill area of the definition was an exceeding of expectation. Of course, each of the two cultural communities had expectations for its youths. By stating the expectations in written form, the GPPC became aware that community expectations often were not communicated to its youth. To determine if students were meeting, exceeding, or falling short of community expectations, the expectations had to be shared with the young people and parents in a systematic manner.

In addition to the profile of giftedness, other indexes to assess the ability to excel consistently or consistently show potential to excel were used in a multicriterion identification process:

- nominations from parents, students, teachers, and others;
- metropolitan (school district use) test scores;
- *Structure of Intellect Learning Abilities* Test scores, focus on Divergent Production and Memory;
- analyses of student writing, art or special projects, and taped storytelling;
- school participation in learned-skill activity;
- community participation in learned-skill activities; and
- student interview for commitment.

Over 300 American Indian students within Kitsap County were tested or screened using the suggested identification process, and thirty students were identified for the program.

Curriculum

In her chapter, Pfeiffer clearly supports a curricular concept that draws on real-life experiences and needs as the basis for problem solving, critical thinking, and innovation. The curricular design that was adapted and developed in the NAG program actualized this concept by assuring that students were given opportunities (a) to determine the needs of their community; (b) to determine the talents and abilities within the group that might be applied to the problems or needs in creative ways; (c) to participate in shared decisionmaking; and (d) to polish and practice skills that could be used to benefit self and society.

Guidance

In the two tribes project, the students were encouraged to create within the context of their culture and, thus, to move toward self-actualization. Students were given opportunities to understand the dimensions of their special abilities and to assign them a value.

To form a realistic identity, students' skills were identified, discussed, practiced, and then applied to a project of their choice that benefited the community in some manner. In Exhibit 14-1 an example is presented from the curriculum that illustrates how guidance was combined with elements of the curriculum.

Teachers of Gifted Students

Although Pfeiffer has not addressed directly the role of the teacher in programming for gifted American Indian students, she supports development of a positive learning environment in which members of the extended family, in partnership with school personnel, nurture academic growth. In the program this partnership was provided by qualified staff and community craftspersons and other mentors.

IN CONCLUSION

In her chapter, Pfeiffer presents a perspective of education for the gifted American Indian child that is rooted in cultural reality and in vision. I support totally her contention that gifted American Indian students must develop a self-understanding that relates not only to their own intellectual abilities and talents, but also to the history, culture, and language of their community, or tribe as well. I see development of this self-understanding as the first critical issue when developing a program for gifted American Indian students.

Exhibit 14-1 An Example of Guidance, Combined with Content, Process, and Product, To Form Identity

Student Skill	Practice	Use It
High divergent production or the ability to produce a variety of creative responses from given information; verbal, kinesthetic, artistic	Students: (a) Study models of intelligence and learn the terms; (b) give examples of divergency and look for them; (c) write cartoon captions, make up scenarios for hilarious problem solving; and (d) invent and create by applying divergency to convergent production	Students: (a) share legends, then elaborate on them; (b) choose one legend and add dialogue, scenes, and other details; and (c) present the legend in theater form to the community (fourth to sixth grade project)

I see the establishment of a vehicle or delivery system to actualize a culturally based curriculum in the classroom as the second critical issue. Such a curriculum brings empowerment and self-determination, which develop confidence. Confidence becomes willingness, and willingness becomes self-directed choice.

I would submit that self-directed choice bridges gifted American Indian students' needs and abilities to the requirements of the mainstream culture, and back again. The bridge makes possible free passage between cultures without toll on self-worth or self-identity.

Are American Indian communities shaping the educational futures of their ablest children? To me this is the third critical issue and one that we have not addressed adequately; only nine programs nationwide have been developed specifically to identify and meet the needs of gifted and talented American Indian children.

As educators examine the American Indian culture, we find that, as Pfeiffer has said, our society is a complex and pluralistic weave of cultures within a culture. The patterns of learning that apply to one group of gifted children in our society do not always apply to American Indian children.

I believe that the first step toward sorting out sound curricular practices begins when American Indians—the least and the ablest—insist on their right to define themselves. Such a definition holds the key to what we value and aspire to become, and all people have the right to develop their potential to that end.

Sanborn (1981), drawing from 20 years of experience at the Research and Guidance Laboratory for Superior Students, University of Wisconsin, said it best:

> Gifted and talented children are whoever we say they are. . . . Methods of assessment may have logical or empirical histories, but the criteria themselves are arbitrary. Even when multiple criteria are used they do not cover the developmental possibilities that children have. Further, regardless of a child's potentialities, he or she will not be identified unless somehow those potentialities are expressed in ways that we value. (p. 43)

Gifted and talented American Indian students are who we say they are. We must be sensitive in saying who they are and selective in choosing curriculum to determine what they will become.

15

It's About Time

Stanley G. Throssell, B.A.
The Quijotoa Company

Well, it's about time.

That is my initial statement about the creation of a program to identify, encourage, and promote gifted and talented and highly motivated American Indian children.

HOW WOULD SUCH A PROGRAM HAVE MET MY NEEDS AS A CHILD?

Looking back to my years in a reservation elementary school, I feel my involvement in a program like this would have accomplished several things: First, it would have changed the way my family was involved in my education. Second, it would have shown me that individual gifts and talents are just as important as "book learning." Finally, it would have given me the opportunity early on to recognize in what areas I probably would perform best as an adult.

The involvement of my family, as best I can recall, was limited to my mother's activity in the Parent-Teacher Association; her never-ending help to make sure my at-home, out-of-classroom activities were safe ones; and generally being at all the social activities that surround a youngster in grade school. Her support beyond that was intermittent and mostly verbal: "School is important. Study hard. Get your work done." To her way of thinking, which unavoidably became my way of thinking, school was limited to books, reading, and arithmetic. Only much later in life did I discover my strength and joy in creativity, art, and writing.

I think if she had realized early that creating art, writing creatively, and even thinking creatively could be just as important and meaningful as memorizing books and successfully writing examinations, she could have better enjoyed my creative strength, and more important, have offered encouragement and support at an early age. Had I known early that textbooks and being able to perform in the classroom, though important, were just one part of education, I think the abilities and talents I have would be much more mature and polished—for art and writing skills only improve slowly and with effort.

I believe a program such as Pfeiffer describes would have helped me discover at an early age the good and useful parts of my character and talent, and it would have made me feel good about being able to do those things I do well.

In giving my opinion about how such a program might have helped meet my needs as a child, I refer to my family because now, as a parent, I can see how very important it is for children not only to have support, but also genuine adult interest in what they are doing. I had only limited doses of those things, mainly because no one, not even I, knew what I did best.

HOW WOULD THIS PROGRAM HAVE PREPARED ME FOR LIFE AS A PRODUCTIVE ADULT?

I feel the longer people do something and the more experience they gain, the more inventive and innovative they will be with this skill. And very likely, they will be able to perform this skill better than others. If so, they will be successful, at least in the area of their choice.

In my case, setting a direction early would have been useful, because art and writing are very individual and creative, built on experiences, mistakes, and successes.

About ten years ago I walked into the office of a man I know and noticed a framed painting of a desert landscape. I thought it was good, so I asked him the artist's name. He said he had painted it. A year later he took me to his home to show me his very first painting done many years earlier. When I saw it, it was all I could do to keep my surprise to myself. It was of a stick-figure man walking near a shed, and the colors looked to be straight from the tubes.

As time passed he became more polished at his craft. One could see in his paintings that he viewed his subject matter with a more critical eye, saw the subtle colors in shadows, saw that nature is made up of shapes and soft edges. His strokes became more sure; but his gains were made painstakingly over many years. The man now appears to be approaching 60, and I wonder if at times he speculates, "If only I had started 15 years earlier."

I started learning about art and writing when I was 25, discovering just how much joy I derived from them, looking forward each day to being creative at both. Writing has stayed with me. I became impatient with art, however, and have not touched a brush, pencil, or piece of charcoal in 12 years. Once, several years ago, I felt a stirring about art, so I dragged wrinkled tubes of paint and some stiff brushes from the back of a closet. I arranged everything, ready to follow that stirring, but nothing happened. I had even forgotten how to combine the paints properly. At times I too muse, "If only I had started ten years earlier."

Beyond allowing an early start on talents, I feel a special program offers the chance to make choices early. I recognized art would likely be a slow and deliberate process, writing perhaps not. I did not give art a chance, thus eliminating one of my choices before finding out how good I could be.

Beyond my speculations of what such a program might have done for me, I want to respond to one of Pfeiffer's ideas. One statement in the final paragraph of the chapter jumps from the page: ''A psychological imperative is that self-worth be nurtured.'' I pull the statement out of context on purpose, because I wonder if self-worth needs to be tied to a cultural context, as suggested by Pfeiffer. In my opinion self-worth—that sense of confidence and satisfaction with oneself—is derived not from those around, but from within. Of course, those around can contribute to a sense of self-worth, but they also can be effective in tearing it down.

I am not sure how to build self-worth or self-esteem; but I do know that if it is lacking, no matter how gifted a person is, he or she will succeed only to a certain level, and then will sit and wait for failure to catch up. If indeed self-worth can be built and nurtured, then this most certainly should be done. I say this from first-hand knowledge, because too often I find myself looking over my shoulder, slowing my pace, and giving failure a chance to catch up.

16

Programming for the Gifted American Indian Student

Leslie Garrison, M.S.
Anchorage Public Schools

As programs for the gifted and talented have been established across the nation, many have become aware that the needs of certain populations have not been addressed. The number of minority students identified as gifted in most school districts falls far short of their percentage in the total school population. This discrepancy is especially critical among American Indians.

In many districts across the nation an awareness of the problem of underidentified populations is apparent, and tools and procedures are being developed to find gifted minority students. Identification alone is not enough, however, as identification, philosophy, and curriculum are inextricably bound together. The needs of special population students must be written into the program philosophy, addressed in the identification procedures, and met in the program curriculum. Only through an aggressive and deliberate approach can underserved populations be educated appropriately.

PROGRAM PHILOSOPHY

Two major types of multicultural programs for the gifted exist; each with a distinct philosophy, selection procedure, curriculum, and outcome. The goal of the first is to ensure the perpetuation of students' native culture. This type of program builds cultural identity and pride, develops cultural leaders, and ensures the survival of cultural values, language, and arts.

The goal of the second type of program is to provide for maximum development of high-ability students' educational and career opportunities. Many gifted American Indian students lack the academic and cultural skills needed to be successful in mainstream institutions of higher learning. The goal of such a program is not to make American Indian students "Anglo-American," but to make them bicultural by giving them the skills, pride, and self-confidence to enable them to move between cultures.

CULTURAL CHARACTERISTICS

The Context

A discussion of common cultural characteristics of American Indians is valuable to teachers because it provides a context in which to interpret the behavior of American Indian students in the classroom. Poor educational programming results when teachers incorrectly interpret the behaviors of American Indian students by mainstream standards.

The two cultures can be put at opposite ends of a continuum, followed by continua of characteristics that describe each culture. (See also Table 11-1.)

American Indian Culture   *Mainstream Culture*

less dependent on language ————————————— more dependent on language
learn by observation ————————————————— learn by questioning
instruct by modeling ————————————————— instruct by language
cooperative in nature ————————————————— competitive by nature
group most important ————————————————— individual most important
cyclical view of time ————————————————— linear view of time

The teacher's job is not to move students from one culture to another, or from one end of the cultural scale to the other, but to determine the cultural range within which students can move comfortably and then provide educational programming that will increase that range. To do this, teachers need to have the skills to determine where students are culturally, and give validity and value to the students' present position on the scale.

A list of general characteristics should not be used to stereotype or limit an individual student. If generalizations that apply to a group are assumed to apply to an individual within the group, the individual has been stereotyped. While the characteristics discussed in the following sections are frequently found in American Indian populations, one should never assume they describe the behavior of an individual student. Students must be evaluated on their own personal characteristics. The generalizations should be used as a guide for the teacher, providing a chance to gain insight into student behaviors that might otherwise be confusing or misinterpreted.

Use of Language

Studies of gifted students show they are very verbal (Welch, 1967). However, numerous studies of American Indian students show they are less verbal in classroom situations than are other students (Darnell, 1979; Harrison, 1981; Kleinfeld, 1975; Philips, 1972). When less verbal American Indian students enter a highly verbal class, they feel overwhelmed and intimidated. They are often reluctant to join in the activities and may distance themselves from the rest of the group (Scollon & Scollon, 1980).

I had what I imagine to be a similar experience in college after I met my new neighbors from the East Coast. I had learned my social conversational etiquette from a rural section of the West Coast where I grew up. I knew how far away to stand when conversing. I knew it was impolite to talk at the same time as someone else, and I knew that a full second courtesy should elapse between speakers. What I did not know was that my new neighbors had apparently never heard of any of these rules. As we conversed, it seemed they were both standing in my face, talking at twice the normal rate. Frequently, they would both be talking to me at the same time, and I could not decide which one to look at, let alone what to say. When I did manage to scratch up a thought or two, there was never an opening long enough to interject my thought before the conversation was whisked off in another direction. To give myself an opening, I designed a plan of action. I was poised on the edge of the conversation, waiting and ready to spring. Just as soon as there was the tiniest break in the conversation I dove in and started talking as fast as I could. I know I fired at least two clear words into the breach before anyone else could reload. I was sure this would give me the floor and I could finish my sentence uninterrupted. Boy, was I ever wrong! By midsentence both had joined me, and in the confusion I forgot what I was going to say, but no one seemed to notice. I felt very frustrated and overwhelmed, and withdrew into the observer mode as I watched them rattle on. One of them, after noticing my withdrawal from the conversation, advised me not to wait for them to stop talking, but just to jump in and talk with them!

I went away from the conversation feeling these people were very intrusive, rude, and self-centered. I can imagine what they thought of me: Low level intelligence, passive, unsociable, and unwilling to adopt any reasonable values, attitudes, and ways of doing things.

Low verbal interaction and similar characteristics such as laziness, uninvolvement, inattention, and a lack of ability have been cited as characteristics that describe American Indian populations (Calfee et al., 1981). I cannot help but wonder if the reasons for these behaviors of American Indian students were not the same as for mine.

What I understand now is that my neighbors were communicating completely within the norms of their geographic and cultural backgrounds. They were conversing according to their rules of social etiquette, but not according to mine. Our failure to communicate came when each tried to interpret the actions and messages of the other by his or her own cultural guidelines. The actions of my neighbors, according to my standards, implied they were aggressive and insensitive; the message they were trying to convey was one of openness and friendliness. I was sending a message of respect and consideration, but they were receiving a message of disinterest and slowness.

A similar type of miscommunication takes place between American Indians and mainstream Americans on a regular basis. In this gap of communication styles, many American Indian students are lost. A long time was needed to enable me to communicate with my neighbors with any degree of comfort, as I had to learn to do things I had previously considered rude. This same verbal aggressiveness or rude behavior is what may be expected of American Indian students at school. To learn a new communication style takes understanding, patience, and time.

Home and School Teaching Styles

In American Indian cultures teachers, or elders, perform (model) a skill to be learned while students watch quietly, observe carefully, and mentally retain each move elders make. Verbal explanations are minimal and questions almost nonexistent. After students observe for what they determine to be a sufficient amount of time, they try to duplicate the skill. If elders observe a mistake by the students, they do not interfere with the learning process to correct it, but allow students to discover and correct the error on their own (Calfee et al., 1981; Kleinfeld, 1975). If students are not aware of the error, elders will model the skill with special emphasis on the problem area. Thus, in traditional American Indian education, the main mode of instruction is through modeling, and the "guided practice" phase of the lesson is guided by the student, not by the teacher (Darnell, 1979).

In schools, American Indian students traditionally are not comfortable with asking or being asked direct questions (Darnell, 1979; Philips, 1972); both are considered impolite as they not only put the burden of answering on the other person, but also may interfere with the thought processes of that person. Silence in response to a direct question is an appropriate response in American Indian culture. When American Indian students refrain from responding to questions in the classroom, they are acting in a culturally appropriate manner, but their silence is often interpreted out of context as hostile or passive aggressive behavior.

Verbal language does play an important role in American Indian culture when storytelling or visiting (Darnell, 1979). Many abstract concepts such as love, fairness, and truth are taught through stories. In this situation, many students gather around the elder (or storyteller) and listen quietly, never asking questions as the story unfolds. The children are expected to listen, remember the story, interpret its meaning, and apply the meaning in their lives. Each child is to act individually. Thus, comprehension quizzes or analyses after the story, a mainstay of mainstream education, are inappropriate in American Indian culture.

Competition versus Cooperation

Competition and cooperation have different roles in most American Indian societies from mainstream Anglo-American culture. Within the living group or clan, cooperation is of utmost importance while competition is reserved for one's enemies.

In most American mainstream schools competition has a place both within the classroom and between schools. Interschool competition parallels traditional competitions between tribes, making it easily understood by most American Indian students. Competition within the classroom has no cultural counterpart in traditional American Indian society and so can be more difficult for American Indian students to comprehend.

American Indian students also may be reluctant to compete in classroom activities because of the loss of face that accompanies defeat. Not competing is often easier than risking shame for oneself or one's classmates. Therefore, American Indian students may voluntarily withdraw from classroom competitions by noncompliance. Quiet noncompliance when asked to engage in a disagreeable task, like silence when asked a question, is an appropriate response in the American Indian culture.

Group versus Individual

American Indian and mainstream American cultures each view differently the role of the individual. Mainstream American culture places a high value on the individual. However, individualism is not the American Indian way. In American Indian culture, the group is what is of value (Harrison, 1981; Philips, 1972). To separate from the group and try to rise above others is only to bring shame on oneself. In American Indian culture, tasks are given to and accomplished by a group, and when the task is fully completed and credit is given, it is given to the whole group.

American education, as a product of the mainstream culture, stands in sharp contrast to this characteristic of American Indian culture. Most of the work done in school is assigned to and completed by individuals. When praise or admonishment is given, it usually is given to individuals. This cultural difference can cause miscommunication in the classroom and can affect significantly the school performance of American Indian students.

As an example, imagine that an American Indian girl has just entered a class of gifted students. This student is observing the dynamics of the class and trying to ascertain the price of membership. She wants to know how much she will have to act "out of character" in order to be part of the group, and if membership is worth that price.

The teacher, aware of the strains of assimilating into a new group, is looking for ways to make the new student feel welcome. The class is working on an assignment of drawing buildings to scale, and the new student's work is exemplary. The teacher jumps at this opportunity to demonstrate the new student's value and ability to the rest of the group, and to show the student how glad he is to have her in class. The teacher picks up the drawing, gets the attention of all the other students, and points out the quality of her work. When he sees that she's hanging her head and not making eye contact, he realizes how shy she must be and decides he will help her get over it by bringing attention to her work more often.

The message that an American Indian student receives is entirely different from that intended by the teacher. The student's work has been used to raise her above the others of the group of which she wants to be a part. This is very upsetting because of the value the American Indian student places on group membership. The teacher has further humiliated her by pointing out her lack of membership to the whole class. The student then determines not to let the quality of her work separate her from the group in the future.

Loss of Cultural Identity

Culturally different students' ethnic identity may be jeopardized when they enter a program for the gifted. Frequently, an American Indian student must adopt a mainstream interaction and communication style in order to be successful. While this might be seen as a significant achievement by the teacher, it can be seen as putting on airs by other members of the American Indian culture.

I am reminded of an incident that took place at the Sheldon Jackson Boarding School, a school serving large numbers of rural Alaska, American Indian students from villages without schools. Many of the students at the school spoke English with a native dialect and seemed unable to utter certain essential sounds in the English language. A new group of speech teachers was sent in to correct the problem. The teachers worked consistently with the students in an attempt to improve speech patterns and intonation, but found that their efforts were in vain.

One night, the boys in the dormitory were seeming to have too much fun, and peals of laughter were rolling out from under the door. An investigating counselor approached cautiously, and listened quietly outside the door to see if he could discover the source of the laughter. From behind the door he heard a voice, speaking in perfect English, giving instructions to the rest of the crowd. The others were finding the situation very amusing. When the counselor entered the room he found that one of the students was speaking. "Joseph," he said, "You've been cured! Your English is perfect." "No," said Joseph returning to his familiar dialect, "I was just doing an imitation of you." "But if you can speak in standard English, why don't you do it all of the time?" the counselor queried. "I can," responded Joseph, "but it sounds funny, and I feel dumb doing it."

We have all experienced how Joseph felt. Who has not entertained friends by carrying on elaborate conversations with a British, French, or Southern accent? It is great fun and can have hilarious results. If, however, we were expected to carry these charades out in public, trying to pass off the dialect as our own, we would feel artificial to ourselves and appear ridiculous to our peers. This type of "fake" behavior is often expected from minority students in both language and behavioral areas. If students fail to exhibit the appropriate behavior, they are ridiculed or remediated.

Time

Another difference between mainstream and American Indian cultures is how each considers time. From a mainstream perspective, time is linear and sequential, starting at one point and continuing forever onward in one direction. In contrast, from an American Indian perspective, time is circular. At the end of each year, one has not traveled 365 days away from the beginning, but has completed a cycle and returned to a beginning. In the American Indian culture one travels around the circle with time, not ahead of it or behind it, as it flows.

Differing concepts of time can cause problems in the classroom as a teacher, who has one eye on the clock figuring the time until library class, and the other on the amount of work to be completed before the students leave, encounters the American Indian student who has a broad and cyclical view of time. Based on their study, Mohatt and Erickson (1981) indicate that mainstream teachers think in blocks of time and have a clear delineation of the tasks to be completed within each block.

American Indian teachers flow with students in tasks and activities. They synchronize the students to themselves and the rest of the class instead of the clock. Synchronization is established with each student by a personal touch or a few, soft words with individual students. Once the group is synchronized, it flows through the day's activities with pacing determined more by the accomplishments of the group than by the clock. Classes managed in this flowing concept make progress discernible, but make difficult seeing where one task ends and another begins (Barnhardt, 1982; Mohatt & Erickson, 1981). American Indian people see no need to control time or to let it control them. What does not get done now can easily be accomplished tomorrow when the cycle starts anew. The goal is not to limit the time, but to experience and enjoy time as it passes.

TEACHING STRATEGIES FOR AMERICAN INDIAN STUDENTS

In an informal poll taken among my colleagues who work with American Indian students, an understanding of American Indian interactional characteristics was seen as far more crucial to student success than either the program model or a specific curriculum. This idea is reinforced by Crawford and George (1980), in their investigation of programs for gifted American Indian students, when they state: "The program planning of curriculum should *not* take precedence over student-teacher rapport—a factor which we consider to be the most important element in any program for G/T students" (p. 25).

Selection of the Teacher

The most important aspect of instruction of American Indian students is the selection of an appropriate teacher. Teachers who state that, because American Indians live in this country, they should do things our way fail to understand the American Indian culture and are poor role models for their students. Successfully combining cultures within a classroom takes a tremendous amount of flexibility on the part of teachers and students. Teachers who demand more flexibility on the part of their students than they are willing to exercise themselves are modeling intolerance, as they are not willing to tolerate, let alone accommodate, individual cultural differences in the classroom.

Within the American Indian culture, what people do or model speaks louder than what they say (Darnell, 1979). Thus, teachers who model intolerance are likely to instill the same quality in their students.

Establishment of a Cultural Comfort Zone

Teachers must first determine a student's cultural comfort zone. This comfort zone may be indistinguishable from that of the rest of the class, or it may be radically different.

A useful method to establish this zone is initially to remove obstacles in the environment that may alienate the student. These would include direct questions and spotlighting. Potential obstacles are added one by one as the teacher checks for student discomfort after each addition.

For example, I welcome new students in a quiet and personal way when they first enter the classroom, frequently assigning a student guide from the group to help explain procedures and protocol in the new classroom and school. The selection of a student guide is the first key decision of the day. I try to match the personality of the guide to that of the new student. I have found most effective the matching of a new student with another recent enrollee who is likewise without an established group feeling, rather than with established group members whose need for membership has already been satisfied.

My introduction of students to the group is short and clear. Name, school, grade, and perhaps one other pertinent fact is given before continuing with the day's activities. I avoid having students introduce themselves, asking new students to share information about themselves, or providing prolonged introductions because all these activities spotlight newcomers and can make them feel removed from the group instead of part of it. Meanwhile, I carefully gauge new students' reactions to try and determine a comfort zone. If, for instance, new students maintain eye contact with the group while being introduced, then I can reasonably assume they consider themselves in the limelight, not the spotlight, and may disregard the above strategies.

Expansion of Cultural Range

Teachers must follow certain procedures to help students increase the range of cultures in which they can move comfortably. First, they must be able to determine students' current position on the cultural scale. Students must never feel their present position or cultural behaviors are being judged as wrong. Their behaviors may be different, or may be more appropriate in another setting, but they are not wrong. Second, teachers must be flexible enough to find common ground with their students as the concept of expanding cultural ranges does not, and should not, apply only to students. Finally, cultural instruction must take place in small attainable steps with sufficient time allowed for mastery and assimilation before a new level is introduced.

Techniques for Less Verbal Students

I avoid calling on students unless they have their hands raised. Allowing students to indicate when they feel comfortable volunteering information to the group is a courtesy to them. Student attention during discussions is required, but verbal interaction is generally optional.

Eye contact is not required, especially when talking personally to American Indian students. Looking down while being addressed is a sign of respect in many American Indian cultures, especially when being addressed by someone in authority. The nod of a head is a more culturally valid cue than eye contact for gauging attention.

Students in my classroom are allowed to assume the role of observer if they are giving cues that they are not ready to be full group participants. The cues may be in the form of extreme reticence to answer questions or reluctance to start work on an assigned task. If personal instruction or modeling of the task does not seem to alleviate the problem, then I usually interpret the message to be that the student needs more time and space to adjust.

Introducing the less verbal student into the classroom presents the challenge of being less verbal in instruction, and it provides opportunities for all students to increase their observational skills. One nonverbal technique of gaining student attention is in beginning to write instructions, cartoons, or a dialogue on the board. Soon, everyone is focused, reading, and trying to anticipate what will come next. Another strategy is to teach a lesson by demonstration and modeling with no verbal interaction by the teacher or the students. Some students seem compelled to talk and to try and gain a verbal signal that their work is correct. In time and with practice they gain the confidence to learn by observation.

Nonverbal instruction often creates a role reversal in which the more verbal students are struggling while the less verbal students are excelling. This situation can be advantageous for both groups as it brings self-esteem and a sense of accomplishment to the less verbal student and gives the more verbal student, who may be accustomed to picking up ideas very quickly, the chance to experience a learning situation common to most school children. The experience can offer a wonderful opportunity to discuss feelings and develop understanding and empathy for others.

Multisensory Approach

A multisensory or multiple modality approach is effective in instruction of American Indian students. Traditional and home learning modalities of the American Indian have a heavy visual component, making it the modality of choice for many of these students. Many mainstream students are excellent auditory learners, and good kinesthetic learners can be found in both cultures. The use of a multiple modality approach is a good teaching practice, but is even more important with the diversity of a multicultural classroom.

Cooperation and Competition

Classroom competition is always difficult to handle because it is dreaded and culturally inappropriate for some groups, while motivating and very appropriate for others. To allow each group to have the opportunity to receive instruction in its preferred style, classroom competition can be handled in one of two ways: (a) If it is individual, make it optional. (b) If it is an all-class competition, divide the students into small groups and have the groups compete with one another.

Small group cooperative learning activities are good strategies to use with gifted American Indian students (Harrison, 1981). This delivery format not only helps to establish a group feeling, but also puts students in a peer teaching situation, one that is consistent with traditional American Indian instruction (Calfee et al., 1981; Harrison, 1981; Philips, 1972).

Cultural Sharing

American Indian students are outstanding resources for classes, but how their input is solicited is important.

First, students should be allowed time to become comfortable with the group and then to initiate conversation. Initially students will volunteer only the information they hold in common with the group, and when their comfort level increases they will start to share more personal information that differentiates them from the others. Second, asking questions that are too general should be avoided because they are difficult to answer. Third, because the students are American Indian, do not assume that they are experts on American Indian history or culture. Students can be very uncomfortable if they are expected to know things beyond their experience.

Time

Accepting cultural differences in relation to time can be very difficult in a classroom. One strategy to deal with the problem is to adopt the mind-set that having a linear view of time and being able to meet a schedule are not synonymous with intellectual giftedness. Whether students enter the program with the ability to follow a timetable is not an indicator of whether they belong in the program.

Punctuality, like the multiplication tables, is a skill that can and should be taught to gifted students who do not already possess it, especially if its absence is impeding learning. An acceptable instructional sequence for punctuality would look remarkably like that for any other skill: (a) Assess the student's present level of functioning (How long a task can the student complete on time?); (b) add gradually to the length of task the student is asked to perform; (c) make the steps small and attainable; and (d) use positive rather than negative reinforcement.

Flex time also can be used to allow for differences in the production rate of students. Before or after school, or during lunch, students can be given time to work on projects. American Indian students frequently find this quieter, more personal time to be highly productive.

ATTRIBUTES OF A MODEL FOR AMERICAN INDIAN STUDENTS

Below is a brief discussion of desirable criteria for a program for gifted American Indian students and the ways several of the recognized teaching models meet these criteria. Each model is referred to by name; but, because of space constraints, the reader is referred to *Teaching Models in Education of the Gifted* (Maker, 1982b), for full descriptions of each model.

Conceptual Approach

An appropriate model for gifted American Indian students should deal with information from a conceptual approach. Many of the teaching models recommended start with a fact-gathering stage, and build on it to help students learn to make inferences, determine cause and effect relationships, draw conclusions, evaluate outcomes, and/or determine general principles or concepts underlying their study. The Taba social studies curriculum is particularly outstanding as an example of curriculum based on a conceptual approach. In addition, the concepts are based on examples from many different cultures. This curriculum is designed to help students determine some of the principles that guide the actions of all humankind, and in so doing points out the commonalities, not the differences, among people.

Student Knowledge As an Information Base

Programs in which student knowledge is used to establish the information base for the course of study are particularly appropriate for American Indian students. Students who are culturally different frequently have a knowledge base that differs from that of mainstream students and can be tapped effectively when a model begins with a fact-gathering session. The Parnes Creative Problem Solving model and the Hilda Taba Teaching Strategies both initiate studies by having students pool facts and ideas. This approach ensures an expanded awareness and a common working knowledge for all the students in the class.

Entry Skills Assessment

The model used in teaching must include assessment of students' present skill levels, and include a method to teach the desired thinking strategies. Reasoning strategies may differ from culture to culture, so using a model that does not assume students are familiar with a particular style of reasoning that, in fact, may be foreign to them is best. Meeker's work, which is based on Guilford's Structure of the Intellect model, has a strong assessment instrument with complementary exercises to develop student reasoning skills. Treffinger's Self-Directed Learning model also has an evaluation procedure and a hierarchy of skills for teaching students how to direct their own learning.

Multiple Modalities

American Indian students perform best when taught through multiple modalities. A heavy reliance on the verbal modality can inhibit their performance; thus, a variety of interaction and response modes should be included in the program design. The models of Renzulli, Treffinger, and Meeker have a great deal of response latitude built in, making accommodation of individual differences easy. However, the Taba and Parnes models are both highly verbal in design and would have to undergo major modifications to satisfy this criterion.

Learning from Peers

Situations should be designed for American Indian students to learn from their peers. This teaching design correlates with traditional American Indian learning styles and has been shown to be effective with American Indian students (Harrison, 1981; Philips, 1972). The Taba and Parnes models make extensive use of learning from peers during the questioning and brainstorming sessions.

Open-Ended Approaches

An open-ended approach is desirable for American Indian students, who tend to work better and more willingly if the curriculum allows for latitude in responses, rather than restricting students to a single right answer response. The requirement of open-endedness is easily met in programs for gifted students, as most major teaching/learning models encourage open-ended questioning strategies.

In summary, all models advocated for gifted students have aspects that make them suitable for American Indian students. However, no single model would meet all the criteria desirable for gifted students without modifications.

IN CONCLUSION

Not until American Indians are in positions of power and influence within the government and community will the needs of American Indian people be translated to the mainstream population and the actions of the mainstream population be interpreted adequately to American Indian people. Cross-cultural communication is the challenge that faces gifted American Indian students, and providing students with the confidence and skills to communicate cross-culturally is the challenge that faces teachers of the gifted.

17

Identifying and Nurturing Talent Among American Indians

Dorothy A. Sisk, Ed.D.
University of South Florida

> "If a man does not keep pace with his companions, perhaps it is because
> he hears a different drummer. Let him keep step to the music he hears,
> however measured or far away."
> —Henry David Thoreau

A general concern in education of the gifted is the special populations who demonstrate superior ability or potential in spite of, or in addition to, special needs and characteristics that can cause motivational, learning, or behavior problems. In her chapter on the American Indian, Garrison addresses this problem in a practical manner, and I am in agreement. The profile of the American Indian child as presented by Garrison is accurate and timely.

I particularly liked Garrison's emphasis on open-ended, "doing"-centered, process-centered education for American Indian children. This approach complements the profile of the gifted American Indian student as one of strong visual spatial skills, and having strengths in observation, problem solving, and memory (Sisk, 1987).

CHARACTERISTICS OF GIFTED AMERICAN INDIAN STUDENTS

As director of the federal Office of Gifted and Talented from 1976 to 1979, my responsibility was to implement a broad charge of identifying and serving gifted and talented children and youths throughout the United States. This charge included the American Indian. While working with leaders from American Indian groups, I became convinced that gifted students from these groups were different from gifted students from the majority culture.

At a conference in Red Lake, Minnesota, in 1979, a list of characteristic differences between the minority and majority cultures was identified by a joint study team of educators from the Office of Gifted and Talented (OGT) and the Office of Indian Education (OIE), and includes those listed in Table 17-1.

Because of the above differences, the primary purpose identified by the OGT/OIE study team was to plan programs for gifted American Indian students to develop the

Table 17-1 Differential Characteristics of American Indian and Anglo-American Cultures

American Indian Values	*Anglo-American Values*
Cooperation (some competition is accepted in sports)	Competition on individual and group levels
Individual less important than group	Rugged individualism
Nonaggressive	Aggressive
Discipline consists largely of ostracism	Discipline is carried out publicly
Nonmaterialistic	Materialistic
Generosity and sharing are valued	Generosity is institutionalized
Manners (American Indians find it useless to say hello and goodbye)	Small talk is often the measure of friendliness
Child rearing is natural (no coercion)	Physical coercion is common
Religion is a way of life	Religion is one more institution

abilities valued by the individual in both the minority culture and the majority culture. The purpose of a program for the gifted was to provide a bridge between the individual's cultural strengths and the requirements of the majority culture. Such a program would include bilingualism and biculturalism.

I agree with Garrison that the teacher is a key individual in building programs for gifted American Indian students. The teacher needs positive knowledge of both American Indian culture and heritage. Even if the teacher has no minority children in the classroom, this knowledge plays an important role by projecting a positive knowledge of minority people and reduces and circumvents prejudice, stereotyping, and ignorance.

CURRICULUM CONTENT

To meet the socioemotional, academic, and leadership needs of American Indian youths, an emphasis should be placed on learning about American Indian culture, including contemporary American Indian life, federal laws, and programs (Deloria & Lytle, 1984).

Using the conceptual approach as suggested by Garrison is quite appropriate for American Indian youths, as they are more responsive to large ideas than to specific facts.

RECOMMENDATION FOR EARLY EDUCATION

Another important recommendation for education of American Indian children is to implement early education, particularly if the education is carried out in American Indian communities and participation of parents and community leaders is encouraged. In addition, Anglo-American and American Indian teachers need to be selected carefully to espouse the philosophy and to use the strategies that were suggested by Garrison to help build a large cultural range. Young children think and act in their language, and if they are taken from their homes, they may become cultural misfits. As Garrison mentioned, the family environment for American Indian children is very different from the majority culture, especially in its lack of pressure to learn quickly. Consequently, American Indian children often experience difficulty if pressured to learn and perform at a pace more rapid than their own.

ROLE MODELS

A major difference between majority and minority cultures is that no cultural heroes are recognized in the American Indian culture. Sitting Bull and other outstanding American Indian heroes were created by the majority culture (Stedman, 1984). Without models, exemplary individuals do not exist, relationships are diffuse, and strong ties to individuals are lacking.

NEED FOR LEADERSHIP DEVELOPMENT AND DROPOUT PREVENTION

American Indians are among the nation's most depressed minorities, and they have a great need for tribal self-government. Some tribes have been remunerated for use of land and these funds have been invested wisely; but the leadership must be developed more among American Indians. The average educational level of American Indians is eighth grade, 1 month; and the dropout rate is over 50 percent. One very important reason for the high dropout rate is the lack of relevance in education as it is currently provided for American Indian youths. In addition, greater involvement of minority leadership is needed. For example, American Indians need to direct American Indian studies, such as what occurs at the University of Minnesota where an Objibway is Director of the Library Services Institute for Minnesota Indians. This library holds an extensive, nationally acclaimed bibliography of American Indian books, materials, media, speakers, and American Indian organizations in Minnesota.

INVOLVEMENT OF FAMILY

The family is the most important unit in the American Indian culture; therefore family involvement in the school is critical. Educators need to realize, though, that many American Indians prefer to remain American Indian. One American Indian expressed it this way, "It is the question of Indians liking education when it is defined as being Indian, as opposed to education defined as to stop being Indian." Many American Indian parents state that they are not involved in their children's education primarily because in their own education (often boarding school) they experienced academic, spiritual, and economic suffering (Beuf, 1977).

Many times American Indians do not participate in school affairs because of geographic obstacles—the schools are far removed from their homes; anti-American Indian attitudes that exist or are thought to exist; punishment, reprisal, and ridicule that is real or imagined; absence of American Indian culture and history in the school curriculum; and exclusion from decisionmaking. Further, school board members frequently do not understand their American Indian constituents. For example, Acoma Pueblo parents in Grants, New Mexico, reported that one school board member who was completely insensitive to the fact that he was addressing Pueblos, not Navajos, told the parents: "Forget about being Indian, forget your language and outdated customs. You can't order a washing machine in Navajo. You can't earn a living making sand paintings."

In summary, the American Indians who attended the 1979 OGT/OIE conference stated that American Indians are often alienated from schools, and are not involved in schools in meaningful ways because schools are not responsive to them or to their culture. Many described their children as hopelessly confused by the two different societies.

TEACHING/LEARNING MODELS FOR AMERICAN INDIAN STUDENTS

As stated by Garrison (and citing Maker's [1982b] review of teaching models), the Hilda Taba model is particularly appropriate for American Indian children and youths because the concepts in her social studies curriculum are based on examples of different cultures and use a conceptual approach. In addition, the Parnes-Osborne Creative Problem Solving (CPS) model helps students pool or share ideas. The CPS model also can provide opportunities for students to communicate with one another in a nonthreatening and nonevaluative way during brainstorming. I also agree with her suggestion that the Structure of Intellect and Self-Directed Learning models be used.

However, a model not listed by Garrison that provides for a broad spectrum of talent development is that of Calvin Taylor (1986). In the hands of a skillful teacher, the Taylor model provides for multiple modalities, learning from peers, open-ended approaches, and the use of student knowledge as an information base—all methods Garrison notes as assisting American Indian students to learn more effectively.

DIFFERENTIATED CURRICULUM

Garrison's chapter is particularly useful in that she addresses a number of curriculum principles identified by Kaplan (1975): Open-ended, doing-centered, and process-oriented. The curriculum suggested by Garrison should mobilize the American Indian student into satisfying intellectual and personal action.

When planning the curriculum for gifted American Indians, Stedman (1984) suggests that teachers ask themselves some simple questions for selecting content and planning activities: Is American Indian humaneness recognized? Is the tone patronizing? Are the American Indians either noble or savage? Is the wording demeaning? Throughout the past, the problem for most Anglo-Americans has been that the American Indian of imagination and technology has been as real as, and perhaps more real than, the American Indian of actual existence and contact (Hirschfelder, 1982).

IN CONCLUSION

Programs for gifted American Indian students should capitalize on their strengths and use interest areas as motivators. Teachers must understand that being forced to accept values that are antithetical to their culture is dangerous to the mental health of gifted American Indian students. The skillful teacher, however, can encourage and guide American Indian youths to experience the skills of the majority culture to increase their cultural range. This is a real challenge to educators. Teachers also must realize that many of the characteristics of gifted American Indians are similar to those generated by educators of the typical gifted student, but that several characteristics, such as desire to excel, dominating peers or others, being individualistic or competitive (Locke, 1979), have been identified by American Indian leaders as having a negative value. The gifted American Indian has much talent to offer to the American Indian culture as well as the majority culture and identification and development of these gifts and this talent must continue to be an educational priority.

18

Give Me the Bow,
I've Got the Arrow

Charmaine Bradley, M.A.
Texas A&M University

"Give Me the Bow, I've Got the Arrow"; an unusual title, indeed, but a strong one. It came to me as I stood and looked over the city lights of Dallas during an evening get-together at the 1986 National Association for Gifted Children (NAGC) Mid-Winter Conference. Surrounded by experts, well known and even famous, in the education of the gifted and talented, I stood surveying and observing people in the small, exquisitely decorated room of the Fairmont Hotel. I listened and watched in awe and amazement, and . . . in loneliness. I was the only American Indian there. Probably no one else took notice of this, but I did—and that is what matters. And "that is what matters" is what the title of my chapter is about: Listening, watching, awe, amazement, loneliness, and all the other feelings encompassed by being "an Indian in a White man's world."

This chapter is not about me, but about American Indians—gifted and talented American Indian youths who, like myself, live in two worlds (to whatever degree we choose to interact in the two different worlds). This chapter is about being able to mingle, fit in, participate, even contribute to the world of the dominant society and the Indian world in which we live. It is about occasional feelings and thoughts of confusion and conflict that arise from living in two worlds. "Give Me the Bow, I've Got the Arrow" is about the social and emotional needs of gifted and talented American Indian youths.

CONFLICTING CULTURAL VALUES

Gifted and talented American Indian youths from across the United States and Canada, from metropolis to reservation, are individuals who in today's world are in dire need of assistance, guidance and direction from parents, teachers, community

133

leaders, and organizations. This assistance can help youths in their struggle to survive and exist in two worlds—the Anglo-American world and the American Indian world. Full of determination and courage, American Indian youths are trying to save their heritage and remain Indian while learning to take a successful place in the dominant culture. The key word is successful; but successful in whose eyes, and by whose standards?

For gifted and talented American Indian youths the achievement of success can be a double-edged sword. Success can cut deep and do irreversible damage to feelings of self-worth and ethnic identity if success (or to be successful) is not favorably valued or perceived by individuals and/or significant others in their world (e.g., success that is confined to educational or academic achievement).

While success or to be successful is a worthy goal for American Indians, it bears a heavy price. The concern, then, is whether success is worth the price and how success complements or conflicts with American Indian cultural values.

One traditional cultural value of American Indians is an emphasis on group solidarity, cohesiveness, and/or cooperation (Eyster, 1980; Hanson & Eisenbise, 1983; Miller & Garcia, 1974; Skupaka, 1972). Many American Indian families and tribes inadvertently and overtly continue to emphasize this value through social, cultural, and religious activities, and clan and kinship relationships.

An important fact to consider is that individuals who may influence the gifted and talented American Indian youth are not limited exclusively to parents and grandparents. In many, but not all, American Indian households, influence also is exerted by other biologically related people, such as sisters, brothers, aunts, uncles and, unlike the Anglo-American family structure, clan brothers, sisters, aunts, uncles, parents, and grandparents. In many traditional American Indian households, sisters and brothers of grandparents are recognized as grandparents, not great-aunts and great-uncles. Clan brothers, sisters, and others also are recognized as brothers and sisters. Cousins, no matter how distantly related to the American Indian youth, also are recognized as brothers and sisters. This recognizing and referring to relatives and relations as brothers and sisters instead of cousins, and great-aunts, great-uncles, and other elders as grand-parents, reinforces and strengthens the American Indian's cultural value of group cohesiveness and increases social conformity among families.

Group cohesiveness and social conformity are especially evident at cultural, social, and religious activities attended by American Indians. Cultural attitudes, values, and beliefs are strengthened and handed down as the young American Indian children observe the verbal and nonverbal communication that occurs at these functions. Powwows, corn dances, social dances, feasts, tribal fairs, basketball games, and even rodeos all provide the opportunity for grandparents, parents, aunts, and uncles to teach American Indian children their roles in the family and tribe. At these activities children are taught who their relatives are and how to greet them properly. Allowed to run around freely and playfully at most of these activities, the children grow up with a feeling of belonging and of being part of a group. A relative is nearby who protectively watches and cares for the well-being of each child.

Other cultural values, such as the American Indian's concept of time and the value of patience also are taught at tribal and cultural activities. Many of the events begin early in the morning, last for long periods of time, and do not begin at the "scheduled" time. Additionally, talking and questioning are encouraged at certain times and silence is required at other times. This helps to develop an attitude of respect for others and reinforces social conformity of members of the group.

For young children, learning to be silent and patient can be difficult. For gifted and talented American Indian children the task is no less difficult. Filled with mounting curiosity and abounding questions, they quickly learn to resort to their heightened senses to obtain the information they are seeking in the most unobtrusive manner possible. Taught not to interrupt or impose their wills on others, gifted and talented American Indian children watch with discretion and listen with intensity to the behaviors and words of others, thus learning by example or in indirect ways. As a learning method, being unobtrusive is different from what is taught in the classroom.

THE CLASSROOM: CONFLICTS AND CONFUSION

When American Indian children enter the world of academia, they enter a new world, a different world. They are no longer asked to be quiet, but to be assertive, vocally inquisitive, and independent. They are taught to question, to excel individually, and to see the value of books and productivity for the betterment of self, not necessarily others. Gifted and talented American Indian youths may begin to experience frustration, anxiety, confusion, and low self-worth as they recognize a conflict between the two value systems.

Families' level of acculturation and the degree to which they actively practice their traditional tribal ways will determine the degree of conflict and confusion felt by gifted and talented American Indian youths. As youths grow from childhood to adolescence, their participation in tribal activities changes. Youths may choose to become more involved than before in traditional activities, or they may withdraw from participation. They may choose to become involved with their families, or seek independence from family and tribe. The choices are difficult. At this same time, gifted and talented American Indian youths may begin to question their ethnic identity and how they fit, or do not fit.

LIVING IN TWO WORLDS

Counselors, teachers, and parents need to be aware of the personal conflicts and perplexing emotions that gifted and talented American Indian youths may experience. Gifted and talented youths, in general, are said to possess a heightened sensitivity to self and others; and this heightened self-awareness is often accompanied by feelings of being "different" (Clark, 1979). American Indian youths, gifted or not, already possess an awareness of being different; they are not Anglo-American. When American Indian youths are identified as gifted or talented, the feelings of differentness are accentuated, and can become an additional area of personal conflict. These youths need guidance to help them clarify and define their own personal values and determine how they can live effectively and successfully in two worlds.

In the Indian world, quick learning skills; resourcefulness; acute awareness of the sensitivities and the importance of American Indian rituals; readiness; and, possibly, eagerness to learn the songs, dances, traditional tribal arts and crafts, and sacred prayers and rituals, are attributes that can make the gifted and talented American Indian youth valued and sought after. Superior memories, long attention spans, and keen knowledge of how to perform or conduct the various aspects of the cultural, social, or religious activities also are valued and recognized in the Indian world.

How to perform the ceremonies is important; but the person most valued knows why these ceremonies are held, why they are performed the way they are, and why they have been the same for centuries. The all important "whys" behind the ceremonies are the foundation of the culture. Individuals who know the whys may be viewed as the bearers of the culture. These individuals are then viewed as gifted. They are considered gifted, not necessarily for intellectual abilities assessed in the Anglo-American culture, but for their wisdom and love of learning. Heightened curiosity and desire to learn are respected in the American Indian culture.

In the dominant society these same qualities and learning characteristics also can be deemed noteworthy. Gifted and talented American Indian youths also may be sought after for their great skills and keen knowledge, but in the areas of academics rather than cultural practices.

The important difference between cultures is that, although gifted and talented American Indian youths are recognized and valued for their abilities and skills, they are not publicly set apart from the group in the American Indian world. Not separating a person from the group does not mean that acknowledgments of selected, noteworthy individuals are not made. Credits and acknowledgments are given, not only to individuals, but also to their families and other people who have helped them become what they are. An excellent example is observed at powwows in which the Head Boy and Head Girl dancers are honored. The family of the selected individual stands beside the youth while gifts of thanks for being acknowledged and chosen as an exceptional powwow dancer are given away to friends and other family members who have helped the American Indian youth, and the youth's family.

Difficulties, confusion, and conflict arise if individuals place themselves above the group or bring individual acknowledgment to their achievements. Placement in a program for the gifted and talented that stresses individualism and independence can become an impairing, damaging factor instead of a cultivating, enriching one for American Indian youths.

Some gifted and talented American Indian youths may feel caught between maintaining or further developing an ethnic identity with their heritage and participating in a program that emphasizes values in conflict with their own. Other American Indians, possibly the same individuals who made a child feel a part of the group, may shun or make fun of the gifted and talented American Indian because of the separation from the group implied by identification as gifted and talented. The youths may then experience, to different degrees, feelings of anomie, depression, and confusion. Gifted and talented American Indian youths may, at this time, question their ethnic identity and how they view themselves as American Indians, and as persons of American Indian descent.

DEVELOPMENT OF AN ETHNIC IDENTITY

Throughout this chapter gifted and talented American Indian youths have been described as if they all are the same, which is not true. They are individuals who are as varied and different as their tribes and their families. The degree of ethnic identity assumed, and the degree of cultural conflict felt, is different for each of them.

Not all gifted and talented American Indian youths, nor their families or tribes, adhere to traditional American Indian ways. Recognition of this diversity of traditionalism among gifted and talented American Indian youths is necessary and provides important information for those who educate this population.

To function comfortably as a bicultural individual is an ideal state many American Indians strive to attain. Many gifted and talented American Indian youths have difficulty attaining this state if they have questions and concerns about who they are and from where they have come. Educators, parents, and those who develop programs for these youths can help by being aware of the confusion ensuing from living in two worlds.

Counseling that evolves around and addresses the maintenance of cultural values and the part they play in the development of one's social and emotional growth is important. Such help also can serve as a tool to help American Indian youths gain better insight and self-awareness; nullify the cultural conflict and their identity crisis; and help them become successful, productive contributors—to both worlds.

Gifted and talented American Indian youths are children who are descendents of a proud, strong, enduring culture. These youths have the same characteristics as other gifted and talented children; however, they display their giftedness and talent in a way that people unfamiliar with the American Indian world may not understand.

These youths have "the arrow"; that is, the ammunition to go forward; the capability to be productive, noteworthy individuals. Let's give them the bow; that is, the services, curricula, programs, books, music, arts, and listening ear so they can mingle, participate, and even contribute to both worlds. American Indian youths need teachers and mentors who will rejuvenate their spirits and support them as they endeavor to be gifted and talented in two worlds.

19

Implications for Administering Programs for Gifted and Talented American Indian Students

Deena Lyn Brooks, M.A.
Englewood, Colorado

Before administrative implications regarding gifted and talented American Indian students can be discussed, one must examine the numbers of American Indians in the population of students we are addressing. Programming will be very different in a school population where those numbers are minimal as opposed to schools where they constitute a majority.

Initially I will address program purpose, identification, programming, and staffing for areas with large numbers of American Indian students. Then I will discuss identification, programming, and administrative implications in schools in which American Indians do not constitute a majority of the population.

HOMOGENEOUS SETTINGS

Program Purpose

Pfeiffer (see Chapter 13) offers a variety of considerations related to program purpose. Too little attention has been drawn to the problem of bilingualism as an overlying factor. The practicality of providing leadership for an advisory group whose members may vary from similar language background to very little understanding in either their American Indian language or English is no small problem. Before such an advisory group can consider whether a program should lean toward traditional or nontraditional values, be academically oriented, or include a wider range of offerings, that group must develop a common conceptual base tied to language. Administrators may be dealing with groups of parents and community leaders who have very different ideas about what constitutes giftedness at the same time that two or more languages are represented in the group.

Bilingualism relates to program purpose. Is fluency in two languages a necessary skill for future leaders who will help their community to develop financial stability, self-determination, and the ability to deal with world issues?

Identification

As Montgomery suggests (see Chapter 11), the identification process will need to vary depending on whether one identifies all or any combination of the categories of giftedness, including leadership, as "dominant culture" gifted or gifted in the traditional culture. Clearly, the psychometric approach is not sufficient. A pluralistic or culturally neutral test seems to be philosophically sound. Since such tests do not exist in the pure sense, the practical administrative question is, Should a test be developed, or will an existing measure serve as a partial solution? Time and financial considerations surely would limit development of a new instrument even if doing so is viable.

The ethnographic approach also is philosophically appealing, but Montgomery's careful analysis of this approach reveals both strengths and weaknesses. Her final suggestions for screening, referral, naturalistic observation, specific talent recognition, and diagnosis are inclusive and thorough. They also require considerable time and trained personnel for implementation. If little financial support exists for this purpose, such a detailed process may prove impractical, or further searches for funds may be necessary.

Programming

With regard to programming for the gifted American Indian, Garrison (see Chapter 16) has studied thoughtfully the general characteristics of American Indians and in a detailed manner made very specific and important recommendations for teaching strategies and classroom climate. A program for American Indians also would benefit from curriculum based on cognitive education theories. Students who have language deficits should be taught and should practice concept attainment in their use of both languages and vocabulary. An understanding of theorists, such as Gardner (1983), could lead to the identification of students with nontraditional types of giftedness.

Staffing

Staffing a program for gifted American Indian students is the most difficult administrative problem, and this problem has not yet been addressed. Even if the program purpose is clear, identification is in place, and an appropriate curriculum is written, how does an administrator find teachers with the necessary sensitivity and knowledge base to put Garrison's suggestions into practice?

Many of the people trained in the education of gifted and talented students have a traditional academic orientation. Recruiting people who have a more flexible approach is difficult in and of itself. Additionally, teachers in this program should be bilingual. Finding an American Indian with this background would be ideal. If this is not possible, teachers may be working in an environment where they may not be accepted into the culture. Clearly, teacher selection is difficult, but crucial to success.

Staff development is also a necessary part of the implementation of a successful program even though it is a slow process and requires time and financial support. Ideally, teachers should have an extensive repertoire of teaching strategies, but this might not be the case, given other traits needed. If a repertoire of strategies were lacking, a staff development plan with the objective of slowly increasing the knowledge base of the teacher would need to be developed, and could include peer coaching (Showers, in press; Joyce & Showers, 1980, 1981). Ideally, teacher training might take place concurrently with some of the initial stages of defining purpose and identification to allow time to sharpen skills before a full-fledged program is implemented.

HETEROGENEOUS POPULATIONS

Program Purpose

Program purpose should be matched with the population being served. If American Indians constitute a minority of the population, especially careful consideration must be given to identification and programming because a match of needs to the program is not accomplished easily.

Identification

If American Indians constitute a minority of the population, some of the suggestions given by Montgomery probably would not be feasible from a standpoint of staff time. This factor undoubtedly contributes to the lack of identified American Indians in programs for the gifted and talented in heterogeneous populations, but still should not be allowed to exist.

I have several suggestions for the inclusion of American Indians in the identification process. First, the staff needs to be made aware of the special needs and characteristics of this ethnic group. Next, a list of the names of all members of this group needs to be generated. These identified students, then, need to be considered individually, looking carefully at background, academic needs, cultural needs, and general characteristics. The rule of thumb should be inclusion rather than exclusion. Observations should be made as students are performing various tasks in many subject areas, including art and music as well as academic areas.

Programming

Many of the suggestions made by Garrison would meet adequately the needs of a heterogeneous group of gifted students. The key is the teacher, who should have some basic knowledge of the major characteristics of this group of students and consider many of the strategies outlined in providing for them. In systems where bilingual programs exist, using the consultative expertise of that staff, along with the teachers of the gifted, certainly would be an advantage.

IN CONCLUSION

Clearly, the needs of American Indians are not being met in many areas throughout the country. As educators of the gifted, one of our challenges is to consider the specialness of this group of individuals, from cultural aspects to academic ones. We need to encourage our gifted American Indian students to become the next leaders in their communities, to feel positive about themselves within and outside their cultural group, and to help them develop the skills to seek solutions to the many problems that may affect their tribes, localities, and country.

The potential of any individual that goes untapped diminishes each and every one of us. Our responsibility as educators in a democratic society is to work toward solutions that ensure that this does not happen.

20

Summary of American Indian Section

C. June Maker, Ph.D.
Shirley W. Schiever, Ph.D.
University of Arizona

GENERAL STATEMENTS

Certain ideas and philosophies were expressed by all authors in this section. Many used the same words to express a concept; others expressed similar underlying philosophies, but approached them from different perspectives. General statements will be presented, and then examples and perspectives explained.

1. *American Indians have certain similarities; but, because of the many groups and varied levels of acculturation, generalizations about their characteristics must be made with caution.*

Pfeiffer notes that American Indian tribes are different in their economic, linguistic, cultural, social, political, and religious concerns. They believe they are unique, sovereign, and contributors to the nation, state, and world. They are similar in kinship orientation, reservation status, unique trust relationships with state and federal governments, traditions of child-rearing practices, customary law, and tribal government. Both Garrison and Bradley suggest a need to recognize the degree of assimilation of each tribe and each individual in addition to their tribal differences. Garrison discusses the degree of relationship to the "core culture," while Bradley places differences along a continuum from "traditional orientation" to "assimilated," with "acculturated" in the middle of this continuum. Students closer to the traditional end of the continuum will exhibit many characteristics different from those in the mainstream culture, while those closer to the assimilated end of the continuum may exhibit very few or no differences. Montgomery and Kirschenbaum discuss these differences and similarities, and demonstrate how they can affect the identification of gifted American Indian children. George reminds us of the important differences between tribes and families; and Kirschenbaum and Brooks note that whether American Indian students constitute a minority or a majority (e.g., on or off the reservation) is an important factor in definition, identification, program goals, and the curriculum. Pfeiffer's contribution to the introduction to this section provides us with an important historical context in which to view the development of programs both on and off the reservation, demonstrating why American Indians are protective of their recently granted ability to influence and develop policies to govern the education of their children.

2. *Many American Indian tribes and their members place a high value on group membership and cohesiveness, which implies that even though individuals may be recognized and valued for their abilities and skills, they are not publicly set apart or separated from the group.*

All authors in this section recognize this value and the possible implications for special programs. However, as Pfeiffer notes, American Indians are beginning to recognize that their survival as tribes and as a culture depends on developing leadership from within their members, and that this leadership development requires selecting and providing special experiences for some of their members. Montgomery and George both suggest that by focusing on a concept or definition of giftedness, either developed by the tribes or based on abilities valued by (and needed to survive in) the tribes, special programs will more likely be accepted than if their focus is only on a definition of giftedness related to mainstream values. Montgomery and Kirschenbaum both discuss how this cultural value can mitigate against the identification of gifted and talented American Indian students.

Garrison provides many examples of how this cultural characteristic influences students in the classroom, especially when misunderstood by teachers, and provides examples of teacher behavior that can minimize problems. Based on her own experiences, Bradley notes that gifted American Indians may question their ethnic identity when separated from the group by being identified as gifted and talented, but provides a context for solutions. She instructs us that credits and acknowledgments for abilities and skills are given to the family, friends, and others who have helped those persons become who they are.

3. *A definition of giftedness must be developed, and this definition needs to reflect cultural values and needs.*

All authors except Kirschenbaum agree with this principle, but use different words to describe an appropriate definition. Montgomery takes a neutral position, and suggests that the first step educators must take is to develop a definition of giftedness, and suggests a variety of ways to develop it. Her approach would be consistent with the first philosophical approach, described by Garrison, in which students are selected by how they exhibit giftedness as defined within cultural norms. A second philosophical approach has the goal of developing high-ability students' educational and career opportunities to a maximum level and would imply that students who have intellectual and academic skills should be selected. Kirschenbaum advocates this philosophical approach, and provides definitions of giftedness and talent that can be applied to all cultural groups.

Pfeiffer's and George's recommendations are consistent with Garrison's first philosophical approach. Pfeiffer discussed three categories of students who should be provided with a special educational program designed to "strengthen the quality of life of various American Indian tribes." George provides an example of a definition developed by one American Indian community, and discusses its implications.

Bradley's definition demonstrates a philosophical orientation similar to Pfeiffer's and George's, and provides a listing of qualities valued and recognized in American Indian cultures. She goes on to suggest that even though knowing how to perform ceremonies is valued, the individual who understands *why* these ceremonies are important is the gifted one. Certainly, these individuals would be able to work toward the perpetuation of their culture, one of the purposes suggested by Garrison and the philosophy Pfeiffer espouses.

4. *Although standardized tests of intelligence and ability may be appropriate for identification of certain types of ability, other procedures are necessary, both to supplement identification of abilities measured by standardized instruments and to determine other abilities. Regardless of the instruments used, children's performance should be viewed from a cultural and experiential perspective, and must be consistent with the philosophy, purposes, and curriculum of the program.*

All authors provide the reader with information about American Indian cultures that can be useful in interpreting student behavior on standardized instruments and helpful when designing other procedures. Sisk notes that certain characteristics usually included on lists of traits of gifted students are perceived as negative by American Indians and would not be expected in children; and Garrison discusses similar characteristics and their influence on the learning process.

Bradley provides lists of traits valued by American Indians, some of which can be measured in standardized testing situations and some that are specific to the culture and tribe. All remind us that the students' degree of acculturation and the specific characteristics of their families and tribes will determine which of these culture-related traits we can expect to find in any child.

Montgomery and Kirschenbaum present different, but not incompatible, perspectives with regard to identification. Montgomery recommends development of a unique process to fit each situation, in which the first step is development of a definition, and discusses the differences between psychometric and ethnographic approaches. She provides several alternatives for use in an identification process that are developed from both these perspectives, but notes that a choice of one perspective must be made. Kirschenbaum disagrees on this point, and recommends that a "funnel approach" combining ethnographic and psychometric perspectives be used, and makes very specific suggestions for instruments, procedures, and steps to follow.

Kirschenbaum discusses the concepts of flexibility and specificity as aspects of an identification procedure that must be examined, and states that his recommended process has a moderate amount of both. Brooks agrees that comprehensive identification processes are needed, but reminds us of the resources and time necessary for implementation.

5. *A major purpose of programs for gifted American Indian students is to develop abilities necessary for survival of the culture and tribe, including abilities valued by the tribe, necessary for individual success, and required to enable students to be successful in both their own and mainstream cultures.*

All authors allude to these purposes, but recommend varying degrees of emphasis on abilities valued and needed by the culture and those valued and needed by individuals. Pfeiffer states that the primary purpose of a program is to strengthen the quality of life of various American Indian tribes. Montgomery notes that tribes in Oklahoma recognize the need to increase their sovereignty and become less dependent on non-American Indians for leadership. George's recommendations are similar to those of Pfeiffer, Montgomery, and Sisk, but she focuses first on development of individual abilities, then states that purposes must be congruent with the goals and expectations of the individual's cultural community. Much of the focus of Bradley's chapter is on the development of abilities needed to "remain American Indian while learning to take a successful place in the dominant culture." In her view, one important aspect of success for many American Indians is to function comfortably as bicultural individuals.

Garrison outlines two philosophical positions that can be assumed, stating that these are usually distinguishable. However, she may be alerting us to different program foci or emphasis rather than a true dichotomy. One philosophical position, for example, is to ensure the perpetuation of students' native culture, while the other is to "maximize" high-ability students' educational and career opportunities. Certainly, these purposes are not incompatible, since development of certain individual abilities can ensure the perpetuation of students' native culture. Garrison demonstrates the compatibility of these approaches, and shows the similarity of her ideas with those of Bradley, Pfeiffer, and George when she states that the teacher's "job" is to "determine the cultural range within which students can move comfortably and then provide educational programming that will increase that range."

As former director of the federal Office for the Gifted and Talented, Sisk reports that a joint team of individuals from her office and the Office of Indian Education identified the primary purpose of such programs as "to develop the abilities valued by the individual in both the minority culture and the majority culture. . . . to provide a bridge between the individual's cultural strengths and the requirements of the majority culture."

Finally, Kirschenbaum seems to present a different perspective. Although he does not address directly the question of program purpose, based on his statement that definitions of giftedness and talent should not be contingent on the cultural characteristics of any ethnic group and his information-processing definition, Kirschenbaum clearly subscribes to the idea that programs should be designed to enhance the educational and career opportunities of high-ability students. By stating his position related to definitions of giftedness, Kirschenbaum reminds us of the importance of recognizing individual abilities of children regardless of whether or not these abilities are valued by a particular culture.

Although most of the authors in this section do not address in a direct way the differences between programs for American Indian students on reservations and those off reservations, the differences in emphasis regarding program purposes are related to reservation status. Pfeiffer, for example, serves on the board of directors of a school for gifted Navajo students designed and operated by the tribe. Montgomery works extensively with tribes in Oklahoma, assisting them in development of their own educational programs. Bradley is an American Indian in a doctoral program in education of gifted students. George presents examples from experiences in developing public school programs near reservations. Kirschenbaum is a school psychologist who directed a special education program on a reservation in Arizona and now selects students for a special program in a multi-ethnic situation in a public school. Garrison is a teacher of gifted students in Anchorage, Alaska, where no "majority" and many divergent "minorities" exist. Sisk, as director of a federal office, developed a perspective in which the needs of American Indians in both situations needed to be met. Brooks discusses the different program choices that must be made when Indian students constitute a majority or a minority. If the tribe is responsible for a program, it should have the option of selecting students, making its own survival the primary consideration; but if a public school is responsible for a program, it must respond to the needs of a variety of populations. The perspective of enhancement of individual opportunities for students with high ability is a very appropriate focus when students from a variety of cultural backgrounds are being served in a program.

6. *The program should begin with the strengths of the students, and then build on these strengths to develop needed skills.*

Beginning a program with emphasis on development of strengths demonstrates a positive attitude toward American Indian students. Various strengths of American Indian students are listed by Sisk, Kirschenbaum, George, and Garrison, but all recognize biculturalism as a present strength and one that is necessary in the future. It provides an appropriate beginning focus for programs. Garrison's teaching suggestions center on the development of bicultural "comfort," as does much of Bradley's chapter. Pfeiffer provides many suggestions for building on students' knowledge of their own tribes, strengthening this knowledge, and supplementing it with information about other cultures, countries, and nations. Armed with these understandings, the problem solving she believes should be strengthened, and the critical thinking skills she believes need to be developed, gifted American Indian students will possess what is needed to help their tribes survive and to be successful personally. Garrison's ideas for building on the cultural knowledge of students is similar to those recommendations by Pfeiffer, and she provides suggested teaching strategies for accomplishing the agreed-upon goal of biculturalism.

7. *Extensive involvement of families in programs for gifted American Indians is very important to the success of the programs and the students.*

Because extended families play a large part in children's education in American Indian cultures, inclusion of this group of individuals is imperative. Pfeiffer calls attention to the fact that strength and support for a student can be provided by an extended family, and recommends that parents be considered partners with the school. Both Kirschenbaum and Montgomery recommend that parents be consulted during the process of identifying gifted students.

Both George and Bradley provide examples of the differences between the mainstream and American Indian cultures in their family and kinship orientation. In traditional American Indian households, for example, sisters and brothers of grandparents are referred to as grandparents, cousins are recognized as brothers and sisters, and clan brothers and sisters are referred to as brothers and sisters. Finally, Sisk lists obstacles to the involvement of American Indian parents, and recommends that these be eliminated whenever possible. Brooks notes that both language and cultural differences may make the administrator's task of managing a parent advisory committee in a multi-ethnic school district difficult, but seems to value this participation despite its problems.

OTHER IMPORTANT IDEAS

Several other concepts were addressed by only one or two authors, and as such are not areas of general consensus. However, their importance is justified by the authors, and some are similar to suggestions made in other sections.

Role Models

Sisk notes that cultural heroes are not abundant, and Pfeiffer recommends that community resources be tapped to extend students' learning through mentorships, apprenticeships, and work-study programs. Kirschenbaum notes that girls are especially in need of role models. Garrison reminds us that teachers are models for their students. In American Indian cultures, what people do speaks louder than what they say, so teachers' behavior is doubly important.

Cooperative Learning

To capitalize on the American Indian students' desire for group membership and cooperation rather than competition as a learning strategy, use of cooperative learning techniques is important. Garrison suggests that cooperation with a small collection of one's peers be arranged in competitive situations. Peers are then put into a teaching position, a learning method with which American Indian students are comfortable.

Counseling and Affective Development

Even though all authors did not specifically recommend counseling to assist in students' affective development, George and Pfeiffer noted the need to include counseling components, and Garrison focused much of her discussion on ways to meet the affective needs of gifted American Indian students within the classroom setting.

Conceptual Approach

Pfeiffer presents a strong rationale and many excellent suggestions for using a conceptually based approach to the study of cultures, nations, and countries. Garrison recommends a similar strategy and provides specific examples of teaching techniques, models, and materials that can be used.

The Teacher

Garrison, George, Sisk, and Brooks discuss the important role of the teacher. Garrison discusses the teacher's role as a model, and all emphasize the importance of teachers' development of an understanding of American Indians' behavior in classroom situations. Brooks notes the difficulties administrators may encounter in locating such teachers, and recommends staff development to supplement selection.

IN CONCLUSION

Throughout this section, an important theme was "self-determination." All authors recognize this as a historical need, and an important trend in American Indian education. Most suggestions for education of gifted American Indian students are based on the recognition that "[e]ach tribal group, regardless of the cultural changes, wants to maintain its culture, language, and land" (Pfeiffer), and the need for leadership from within the cultural group. To these authors, self-determination is not just a political phrase, as George cautions us: Empowerment of people brings positive attitudes and contributions, and we must serve as *tools, not architects,* of education for gifted American Indian students.

PART III

ASIAN-AMERICANS

THE PROBLEM OF DEFINING ASIAN-AMERICANS

In the census of 1980, 3.47 million Asian-Americans are listed and demographers expect that number to continue to increase. Bouvier, vice-president of the Population Reference Bureau, predicts that the population will consist of almost 10 million Asian-Americans at the turn of the century (Butterfield, 1986). The number of Asian-Americans in schools also is increasing as Asian-Americans tend to continue their formal education past the legal requisite. Asian-Americans have a higher rate of entry into postsecondary education than any other racial or ethnic group (Peng, 1985). An author in *Phi Delta Kappan* notes that Asian-Americans graduate from high school and college more often than their Anglo, Black, or Hispanic counterparts ("Asian-Americans Lead," 1986). Although Asian-Americans make up only 2.1 percent of the population of the United States, undergraduate enrollments of Asian-Americans make up 8 percent of the student body at Harvard; 19 percent at Massachusetts Institute of Technology; 25 percent at University of California, Berkeley; and more than 33 percent at University of California, Irvine (Butterfield, 1986). The evidence that the Asian-American student population is becoming a significant proportion of the American school population is overwhelming; however, few studies concerning these students have been published (Peng, Owings, & Fetters, 1984).

The term Asian-American encompasses a growing number of ethnic groups. The relatively well known Japanese and Chinese immigrants have been joined by Korean,

The editors wish to thank Mary Meeker for her contribution to this introduction; and Chris Hasegawa, Rosina Gallagher, Margie Kitano, and Kazuko Tanaka for permitting us to use information about Asians that was originally included in their chapters.

Vietnamese, Philippine, Laotian, Cambodian, and other, smaller, immigrant groups to constitute the burgeoning classification of Asian-American. In the census of 1980, the term "Asian and Pacific Americans" is used to encompass ten categories including Hawaiian, Guamanian, and Samoan (Chan & Kitano, 1986).

Another aspect of the problem of defining Asian-Americans is the question of citizenship. Defined precisely, the term Asian-American should describe only individuals born in the United States or naturalized citizens. Recent immigrants or visitors to the country should not be included statistically in Asian-American demographics, but little clear differentiation can be found between Asian-Americans and Asians in America in the literature. Statistically, the lack of distinction in the literature is a small problem largely mitigated by the introduction of terms such as immigrants and native-born citizens. However, the lack of distinction among groups is a very important point when considering the formation of self-image for Asian-American youths. During World War II, the difference between being perceived as Japanese rather than Japanese-American was crucial, and continues to be important in view of the economic competition today between Japan and the United States.

The very lack of specificity of the designation has significant consequences for Asian-Americans because most feel more comfortable with specific ethnic identifications. Confusion about the larger group's definition has made people unlikely to identify themselves as Asian-Americans, which makes formation of coalitions difficult. Certainly, circumstances exist in which the concerns of specific ethnic groups must be addressed, but concerns common to all groups are important considerations for an educator interacting with any Asian-American population.

Of the 3.5 million Asian-Americans, more than half immigrated to the United States since the passage of the Immigration Act of 1965, which eliminated restrictive Asian quotas. In 1980, the Chinese population emerged as the largest, the Filipino ranked second, and the Japanese third. Since 1970 the Korean population has increased phenomenally; and Asian-Indians, Vietnamese, and Pacific Islanders have become distinct and identifiable groups.

EXPERIENCE IN THE UNITED STATES

Early immigrants were oppressed, segregated, and feared as "yellow peril." To survive, they adhered to cultural values such as *arugama* or *akirame,* the Japanese mature self-control or resignation to "accept things as they are" (Weisz, Rothbaum, & Blackburn, 1984). These Asians assimilated into the mainstream through the strategy of "accommodation," adapting to social and economic conditions and avoiding direct confrontation with dominant groups (Endo, 1980). After World War II and the humiliating period of incarceration for thousands, Asians took advantage of the limited opportunities for higher education. A tenacious participation in the educational system followed the enactment of the civil rights laws that ensured equality of educational opportunity. Through their accommodation of the existing situation and the public education system Asians achieved meteoric upward mobility.

THE POPULATION

Most Asian immigrants who have entered the United States since the Korean and Vietnam wars wanted to become Americans because they hoped to be free from political or economic tyranny. The sociological aspects of their entrance, however, are quite different from those of the early Irish, Italian, and Jewish immigrants who saw America not only as a haven from religious persecution and poverty, but also as a new country with frontiers to explore. The earlier immigrants saw education not only as a means of achieving relief but also as a way of improving their "class." Education was not mandatory for these first influxes of immigrants. They worked; they sacrificed their cultures, their languages, their ways to make their children Americans. Because of the newness of the cities to which they migrated, much more opportunity existed to mix with the majority, especially when the immigrants or their children became financially successful. Many of these immigrants, dissatisfied with the poverty of the cities, took the opportunity to migrate across the country, which opened other opportunities and eliminated many barriers to success.

The early Asian immigrants came to the United States because of economic necessity. Young men from China and Japan were willing to leave their homeland to labor primarily in railroad and lumber camps. These young men were not educated—some became farmers and merchants—but all had plans to make money and return to the homeland. However, few were able to go back and tended to stay together for economic, housing, and security reasons. Education was not a priority for these immigrants, although many tried to learn English from sympathetic Caucasians. "Baishakunin marriages" (arranged marriages) brought Japanese and Chinese women to America, and the children resulting from these marriages were significant factors in the acculturation process because they attended public school.

The Japanese internment in relocation camps during World War II was the low point of Japanese history in the United States. The internment shattered the lives of people who had been here for 20 to 40 years and who had begun to make some progress in assimilation and economic stability. The term *shigata ganai* ("it can't be helped") helped the Japanese to endure, but may have had a negative influence. Watanabe (1973) sees the *shigata ganai* attitude as a contributing factor to thwarting the development of a strong sense of individuality and of individual control of personal destiny—qualities that underlie forceful self-expression. In an alien culture that encouraged, indeed demanded, aggressive, outspoken individualism and self-expression, the Asian responded only with silence.

The new Asian immigrants come for economic and political reasons and, therefore, possess wide ranges of education and degrees of wealth. The status of Asian countries ranges from the fairly advanced countries such as Taiwan and South Korea, to those impoverished by war, such as Cambodia and Vietnam. The situation now is very different for new immigrants; they are seen as competitors for space and jobs. Sociological factors such as competition contribute to the pocketing and stability of ethnic groups in one part of a city.

Most Asian-American parents who are unable to assimilate into the job market, though qualified, see education as a major key to advancement. When questioned by their children as to why they work long hours under sweatshop conditions, they reply, "This is why you are going to school." These parents know if the work ethic is accompanied by dogged determination, a basis is laid for their children's success. If children work hard enough and long enough at getting educated, and assiduously study to achieve perfection, they can compete successfully. Whether this attitude stems from Confucianism or a need to survive is immaterial. The end result of such determination and valuing of education is a desirable student, many times a student identified as gifted.

UNIQUE BEHAVIORS OF GIFTED ASIAN-AMERICAN STUDENTS

Based on the premise that gifted individuals possess certain absolute aspects of giftedness and these absolute aspects are filtered through a cultural context that produces unique behaviors, the editors of this volume developed Table III-1. In the first column are listed selected characteristics or absolute aspects of giftedness; in the second, Asian

Table III-1 Characteristics of Giftedness and Cultural Values of Asians, and the Behaviors Resulting from Their Interactive Influence

Absolute Aspects of Giftedness	Cultural Values Often Characteristic of Asians	Behavioral Differences
Strong need for consistency between abstract values and personal actions	*Arugama* or *akirame* (mature self-control or resignation)	Passivity, lack of assertiveness
High expectations of self	Confucianist ethic—people can be improved by proper effort and instruction	Academic orientation and achievement
Unusual sensitivity to expectations and feelings of others	Family honor and tradition, personal responsibility	Self-discipline, self-motivation, preference for structure and defined limits
Perfectionism	Conformity, correctness, respect for and obedience to authority	Patience and willingness for drill and rote exercises; decreased risk taking and creative expression
Persistent, goal-directed behavior	Educational achievement, the work ethic	Concentration and persistence on academic tasks

cultural values; and in the third, behavioral differences of gifted Asian-American students.

As with other special populations addressed in this volume, the education of gifted Asian-American students presents a complex challenge. Of course, no simple answers are available; but the following section is offered to provide direction and food for thought.

21

Identification of Gifted Asian-American Students

Jocelyn Chen, Ph.D.
Bethlehem, Connecticut

WHO ARE OUR ASIAN-AMERICAN STUDENTS AND WHY THE NEED FOR SPECIAL CONSIDERATION IN IDENTIFYING THE GIFTED IN THIS POPULATION?

Over the past few years, increased attention has been given in the media to the success of Asian-Americans in the United States, and a *New York Times Special Section* cover story was entitled, "Why Are Asians Going to the Head of the Class?" (Butterfield, 1986). This and other articles collectively report that although Asians make up only 2.1 percent of the U.S. population, their academic performance and entrance into the nation's best colleges surpass that of their fellow minority and Anglo-American counterparts.

This select group of successful Asian-American students consists of essentially first- and second-generation offspring of parents who first came to the United States as students but remained after the Communist takeover of China in 1949. Also, with the Korean War imminent, many physicians, engineers, scientists, and scholars fled Southeast Asia for a better life in America. Thus, with well-educated parents and middle-class backgrounds for at least two generations, these successful Asian-American youths were raised with a strong regard for the Confucianist ethic that people can be improved by proper effort and instruction. When coupled with pride in upholding family honor and tradition, the Confucianist ethic increases the likelihood for achievement and success among Asian-American students in this country.

However, not all Asian-Americans share these advantages, as evidenced by researchers in the early 1970s who describe the reality of social and economic conditions faced by many Asians in this country (Fersch, 1972; Kagiwada & Fugimoto, 1973; Sue & Sue, 1973; Watanabe, 1973). Many Asian-Americans live in the crowded, urban-poor communities of large cities on the East and West coasts. Because they are racially, ethnically, and linguistically different from the dominant American culture, these families are reluctant and fearful to move away from the security and familiarity of their ethnic communities. The high demand for employment by community residents in such areas as Chinatown is often met by nonunion jobs, without the benefits of union wages and employee protection. Job security, then, is for the one who can work the longest for the least wages.

The family's struggle for survival encumbers the children as well, because they are depended upon to care for younger siblings, even when that may require their staying home from school. When extra "piece-work" is brought home from the factory, the children often are required to help when possible.

In spite of the potential barriers to success in school for these disadvantaged Asian-American students of low socioeconomic status, Chen and Goon (1978) found that the incidence of giftedness, even as indicated by the use of traditional achievement measures, is relatively higher than normally would be expected in the general population. Thus, Asian-American students are more likely to achieve academically than are other ethnic minority groups, regardless of social class and family background. However, rather than overgeneralizing Asian-Americans as a successful minority in this country, special consideration should be given to those among them who do not meet traditional criteria for defining giftedness.

DEFINITION AND CHARACTERISTICS OF GIFTED ASIAN-AMERICAN STUDENTS

A general definition of giftedness applicable to individuals from any population describes those who perform above the level expected for their age and background or who have the potential for superior performance if given the encouragement and resources.

This performance may be multidimensional in nature involving an interaction of both cognitive (verbal and nonverbal) and behavioral traits as suggested by Renzulli's (1979) three-ring conception of giftedness. Individuals' performance is compared to specific reference groups so that superior ability is judged relative to what might be expected for an individual of similar age and experience. Thus, criteria for determining giftedness should be based on local norms for the school district and for the specific population in question.

A multidimensional definition of giftedness offers needed flexibility in identifying bilingual and bicultural children, because variables that may be less biased than measures of intelligence (IQ) or achievement are considered. Defining giftedness in a multidimensional manner also allows diverse populations such as gifted Asian-Americans to be measured along a continuum of abilities, which is how human behavior and development occur. Giftedness should be defined by varying patterns of abilities and strengths, rather than discrete scores on tests.

In a survey of teachers and guidance counselors who work in schools in a predominantly Asian-American community, Chen and Goon (1978) found consensus in their observations of intellectual capabilities of the gifted Asian-American students. The characteristics most often cited were (a) excels in work; (b) displays good academic skills; (c) has excellent problem-solving ability; (d) demonstrates creativity in writing, art, or poetry; (e) formulates pertinent questions; (f) interprets information; and (g) has a keen awareness of the environment and of the people around him or her.

With regard to behavioral characteristics, however, variability was evident in the descriptions of the gifted Asian-American student. On the one hand, some students were identified on the basis of individual, introvertive behaviors such as stability, maturity in being able to take responsibility, ability to work independently, high internal motivation to achieve, taking initiative, perseverance at a task until its completion, self-criticism, assertiveness, and acting appropriately. On the other, the gifted student was described in terms of social, extrovertive behaviors such as working well with others, demonstrating leadership qualities, being outgoing, showing enthusiasm in class discussions, and communicating effectively.

On the whole, when compared with gifted non–Asian-American students, these gifted Asian-Americans were described as getting along better with others, particularly adults; working more diligently; demonstrating a good sense of humor; and achieving higher scores in math. Though English is a second language for all of the gifted Asian-American students in this sample, their verbal abilities tended to be equal to or better than those of their gifted non–Asian-American peers in the school district.

SCREENING ASIAN-AMERICAN STUDENTS FOR GIFTEDNESS

Teachers often are asked to recommend students for further assessment of their potential on the basis of a preliminary screening. Familiarity with all the factors in students' lives—including how they relate to their families and, in turn, how the family interacts with the community—is essential to determine what is exceptional behavior.

Daily observations and anecdotal records should be kept for all observable behaviors of students during independent work, when interacting with peers, and when working with adults. Target behaviors to observe include: (a) initiative, organization, self-direction, self-evaluation, perseverance, task commitment, sustained interest, ingenuity, and creativity during independent work; (b) leadership and/or the ability to work cooperatively as part of a team effort toward a common goal when working with peers; and (c) ability to interact appropriately, to follow through on directions when given, and to incorporate new information into an existing schema of ideas when working with adults. Longitudinal comparisons of students' behavior and development also should be made to establish evidence of early onset and stability of those observed behaviors.

The use of sociometric techniques serves as a check on teacher judgment and opens possibilities for further study. Such techniques focus on class preferences by way of peer nomination. Questions regarding who is the most likely to succeed; who is the best in mathematics, reading, and other subjects; who would be the best worker on a committee; who is the most congenial; who is the best leader; and who is the most dependable may tap both leadership/influence and academic qualities of individual students, as perceived by their peers.

In classrooms or schools where Asian-American students constitute a minority, they may appear to be more reticent than when they represent the majority in the school (Chen & Goon, 1978). Behaviors indicative of giftedness may be expressed more during quiet, independent work than in the social interactions likely to capture a teacher's attention. Therefore, a teacher working with Asian-American students may be required to spend time in close observation of the child in independent work and during teacher-pupil interaction to determine giftedness.

The use of structured tasks also may be helpful in eliciting higher level cognitive abilities associated with giftedness. Careful observation and documentation of behaviors, such as creative problem solving, insight, deductive reasoning, transformational thinking, and conceptual organization, are important leads to understanding how a student processes information.

During the screening process, teachers should observe the cognitive and behavioral indicators of giftedness. Some cognitive indicators are rapid learning rate; flexibility in making necessary response shifts to changes in task demands; ability to apply information once learned; and higher order thinking skills, such as making associations, forming abstract concepts, testing hypotheses, thinking critically, analyzing patterns, and solving both verbal and nonverbal problems. Some behavioral indicators include initiative and follow-through; self-discipline; intense, sustained interest in one or more areas; and self-direction toward a goal.

By focusing on the processes used by students, rather than on their attainment of culture-specific factual information, one can better identify students who may be gifted. A focus on processes is particularly relevant to the assessment of bilingual students whose native language ability is limited because of the level spoken in the home or neighborhood. Proficiency in English can be evaluated effectively only when one knows the number of years students have attended school in an English-speaking environment. Children's instruction in English in their native country should not be considered equivalent to instruction in this country. Language proficiency (especially expressive vocabulary), either in the native tongue or in English, should not be the determinant of giftedness in the bilingual child. The learning processes students use and their rate of learning are more important variables to consider than are vocabulary or knowledge of factual information.

EVALUATION OF GIFTED ASIAN-AMERICAN STUDENTS

Using Standardized IQ and Achievement Instruments

The purpose of evaluation is to uncover data that either will verify or discount the observations obtained during the screening phase of the selection process. Evaluation instruments must be both reliable (repeated administrations of the instrument on similar populations will yield similar results) and valid (the instrument measures what it is intended to measure). Also, the standardization group on which norms for performance are established should include the group using the instrument. The number of instruments that meet these qualifications for evaluating Asian-American children is limited.

Most of the standardized IQ and achievement tests commonly used to identify giftedness (both group and individually administered) have very few, if any, Asian-Americans in their normative sample populations. When minority group comparisons of test results are made, attention has been given primarily to Blacks and Hispanics, with Asian-Americans grouped collectively in the category "Other." This category also includes Pacific Islanders, Alaskan Eskimos, and American Indians—groups that are vastly different. Those who develop tests attempt to include Asian-Americans in their standardization groups, but the test items are of questionable validity for the recent Asian immigrant child.

The *Kaufman Assessment Battery for Children (K-ABC)* published by Kaufman and Kaufman (1983) is representative of the trend toward assessing the processes involved in intelligence. As they describe, "mental processing scales measure the child's ability to solve problems sequentially and simultaneously, with emphasis on the process used to produce correct solutions, not on the specific content of the items" (p. 1). The *K-ABC* also includes an achievement scale with subtests that focus on acquired facts and applied skills attained at home and school. Even though the *K-ABC* offers a greater number of culture-fair, nonverbal items than traditional IQ measures, the norming population includes only Blacks and Anglo-Americans from 2.5 to 12.5 years of age.

Another process test is the *Bloomer Learning Test* (Bloomer, 1980). It includes ten verbal subtests that measure the underlying cognitive and emotional factors affecting school learning. However, this test requires basic decoding skills in beginning reading because simple words and letters of the alphabet are used in each subtest. Norms are based predominantly on the performance of Anglo-American and larger (i.e., Black and Hispanic) minority populations.

Use of process-based tests is especially appropriate for the culturally different gifted, because the common denominator for all human learners is a set of cognitive processes enabling them to acquire information from the environment, regardless of the culture-specific content. Instruments to evaluate the process dimension of human ability should be an integral part of assessment to determine giftedness and creativity.

Both the Kaufman and Bloomer tests (which are comprehensive process tests) have shortcomings, however, which pose a dilemma in selecting standardized instruments for evaluating Asian-Americans. If a process test is used and compared with an IQ or achievement test, one can evaluate students' processing potential against their acquired knowledge as measured by the content items of either IQ or achievement tests. This comparison of scores provides a good index of how efficient a learner is relative to innate ability and environmental exposure factors. Measures of learning efficiency, given a child's past experiences in and out of school, lend validity to an evaluation of ability, and are more important for a bicultural child than for one from the majority culture.

Until a greater variety of process-based tests becomes available, standardized IQ and achievement tests can provide useful information for evaluations of Asian-American populations. Administering individual IQ tests enables the examiner to observe directly strategies used by a student to solve a problem, thus providing information about processes. Achievement test data, when used to determine placement, rather than to determine whether or not a student is gifted, can be valuable and should be used.

Achievement tests provide information for establishing a basal point of instruction by which progress during a period of time can be assessed. The progress in achievement made over a period of time should have greater importance than the level of achievement at one point in time. For example, if a child who entered this country two years ago knowing no English has not received any formal instruction, even though the child is nine years old, a grade-equivalent achievement test score of 2.0 in reading should be considered average. For Asian-American children who have recently immigrated to the United States, judgments of superior ability should be based on both academic and social rate of progress.

Analysis of subtest scores on traditional IQ tests also should be considered as a method for determining giftedness, as opposed to reliance on whole test scores. Different patterns or profiles of giftedness can be discovered only if one examines the underlying skills and abilities measured by each subtest and notes similarities or differences across subtests.

A within-group analysis of test scores, with separate norms for various ethnic groups, could be used to identify superior abilities. Patterns of strengths and weaknesses are important indicators of cognitive abilities in disadvantaged children, because less homogeneity of abilities may be found than among children from middle-class backgrounds. Measures of memory, conceptual thinking, and problem solving are more reliable and valid assessments of ability for Asian-American children than are vocabulary and knowledge of factual information.

Using Other Standardized Instruments

Other tests are useful in assessing students from disadvantaged populations to determine giftedness, but they are not employed as often as IQ and achievement tests. These tests, however, may provide more valid information than instruments usually employed, and include *Goodenough-Harris Human Figure Drawing Test, Columbia Mental Maturity Scale, Preschool Talent Checklist, Self-concept and Motivation Inventory,* and *Torrance Tests of Creative Thinking—Verbal and Figural* (Richert, 1985).

These tests are designed to measure a broad range of mental functioning and behavioral traits that should be considered when selecting gifted students for special programming. In the absence of adequate norms for Asian-Americans, any data obtained will have to be compared with knowledge of what other Asian-American students in the class or school can do.

Using Other Than Standardized Instruments

Greater use of multiple criteria and multiple sources of information assures more accuracy in the evaluation process. Techniques such as case studies; interviews; work samples; observational and anecdotal records; criterion-referenced testing (to determine the extent a student has mastered or surpassed the training objective); inventories and checklists; developmental histories obtained from parent interviews (to determine precocity in achieving physical or intellectual developmental milestones); and biographical inventories of the student's present and past activities, preferences, plans, and future goals, enable the evaluator to gain a broad profile of a student's abilities across a wide range of situations.

Recommendations

Until a greater variety of instruments with norms including Asian-American samples becomes available, the use of instruments and procedures similar to those used with mainstream populations will continue. Alternatives include the selection of certain subtests rather than using a whole test, the use of nonverbal cognitive tasks, curriculum/process-based assessment techniques, drawings, evaluation of work produced, observations, and interviews. These alternative procedures provide a more thorough picture of an Asian-American student's abilities than any one type of test or data collection technique.

Test scores should be outweighed by observational data that are collected on a daily basis. Interactive teaching models for teacher and pupil provide more relevant information on how a student learns than the number of correct answers obtained on a group-administered achievement test.

Increased interest in curriculum-based assessment, in which diagnosis of students is based on the materials they use in the classroom, suggests that educators desire hands-on teaching approaches to assessment rather than the kind of data obtained from a test score. That is, instead of relying on test data with questionable norms, a more valid practice may be to see what students can do when given challenging tasks above their expected level. Thus, simulation activities and challenging tasks should be devised to determine giftedness in action rather than continuing to use static scores obtained under testing conditions.

Of utmost importance in establishing a set of criteria for determining giftedness among Asian-American students is weighing the data collected with background information available on the students. How students function outside school in familiar settings, and their "streetwiseness," and responsibility levels in the family are reflective of innate ability and intelligence. The criteria used for determining giftedness in Asian-American populations is not as important a consideration as the weight and interpretation given to the data collected. Greater weight should be given in the selection process to Asian-American children's nonverbal performance, processing skills, and creativity in the performing or fine arts than to the amount of information they have acquired.

ASSUMPTIONS AND FACTORS INVOLVED IN IDENTIFYING GIFTED ASIAN-AMERICAN STUDENTS

Whether school personnel will actually be committed to identifying gifted Asian American students rests on three major factors within the particular school system.

1. *School budget allowances for special education programs for the gifted must be considered.*

In communities with strong public and parental support of programs for the gifted, funding for these programs will stay in the budget.

2. *The number of above-average ability students in the school system often influences decisions about the need for special programs for any group.*

If the student population in a given school district is above average in ability and performance as a whole, then the criteria for inclusion in programs for the gifted may be more stringent than in school systems with a small percentage of above-average ability students, because a limited number of students can be accommodated in most programs.

3. *The number of Asian-American students in the school district has an impact on decisions.*

Whether Asian-Americans are given special consideration for inclusion in programs for the gifted often depends on the number of Asian-American students enrolled in the school district; their performance or class standing relative to other students; the ethnic composition of the student population as a whole; and the extent of active participation in and support from the local community.

Teacher familiarity with the variations among Asian-American students is greater in densely populated Asian-American communities than in communities with few Asian-American people. In school districts with a high percentage of Asian-Americans, teachers are able to make fine discriminations among students and are in a position to give special consideration to the Asian-American student.

In school districts where the Asian-American student is a rare individual, teachers often are not familiar with Asian-Americans and are likely to make erroneous generalizations on the basis of the one or two students with whom they have had contact. When Asian-American students are few in number, teachers may see no need for special consideration, as they may feel these students just should fit in with everyone else.

IN CONCLUSION

In this chapter, I seek to dispel the belief that Asian-Americans always do well in school and, therefore, do not need special consideration in assessment and educational programming. The fact is, not all Asian-Americans are alike. They have many intergroup differences, as well as intragroup racial, ethnic, and linguistic differences. As a group, Asian-Americans share many sociocultural problems with other ethnic minorities in their attempt to assimilate into the mainstream of American life.

Ongoing attention in the media highlighting the success of many Asian-Americans in this country serves only to perpetuate the myth of the successful Asian-American. Successful Asian-Americans often come from educated, middle-class backgrounds in Asia or the United States, as exemplified by the continuing success of many first- and second-generation Asians. However, the fact that a large proportion of Asian-Americans come from low socioeconomic, disadvantaged communities within the large urban cities of the country makes necessary the use of alternative methods of identifying the gifted.

A multidimensional approach to identification emphasizing the analysis of cognitive processes, curriculum-based assessment, and data obtained through observation and interviews should be used with consideration of sociocultural factors for a more valid evaluation of Asian-American children.

Future researchers should focus on determining what factors enable some Asian-Americans to overcome barriers to success that other minorities face, so as to develop preventive or remedial strategies for those who are not yet successful. Further, a closer look at the abilities and talents of the bilingual and bicultural gifted Asian-American child may offer insight and direction in constructing programs to enhance capabilities that contribute to success in adulthood. Such programs would benefit not only the gifted, but also all children.

22

Critique of "Identification of Gifted Asian-American Students"

Margie K. Kitano, Ph.D.
San Diego State University

In her chapter on identifying gifted Asian-American students, Chen challenges educators, administrators, and communities to "become knowledgeable of the socioeducational issues facing Asian-American youths in the country and use this knowledge to develop a commitment toward more flexible educational programming that meets the needs of ethnic minorities." Toward this end, she argues a need for special considerations in identifying the gifted of this population and recommends several alternatives to traditional assessment procedures, including analysis of subtest patterns, use of nonverbal tasks, assessment of processes, and use of observational data, all interpreted within the context of the student's background.

I generally agree with Chen's conclusions regarding the need for a multidimensional approach to identification. However, the major assumptions underlying Chen's suggestions and conclusions are open to question, based on extant literature and her inherent logic. I have evaluated Chen's definition of gifted Asian-American students and her rationale for special consideration, and as a result, provide additional recommendations for identifying such students.

DEFINING GIFTED ASIAN-AMERICAN STUDENTS

Understanding the term gifted Asian-American students requires defining the terms Asian and gifted. Chen has adopted Renzulli's (1979) three-ring conception of giftedness, which permits flexibility in identifying bilingual and bicultural children, as indicated by Chen. However, the parameters of "Asian" remain unclear.

To help educators and the community become knowledgeable about Asians in America, no concept is more critical than an understanding of the rich variety and heterogeneity of languages, cultures, and people encompassed in the category. Chen understates the diversity among Asian-Americans. Information is included in the introduction to Section III demonstrating the wide variety of ethnicities included in the category Asian-American, but needs to be supplemented by additional data.

In addition to the diversity of ethnic groups considered Asian, the members differ within and across groups in culture, language, place of birth, age, level of acculturation, social class, immigration experience (voluntary or refugee), and educational background. For example, individuals within one ethnic group may speak different languages or dialects. Moreover, some Asian-American groups in the United States speak mostly English (e.g., Japanese, 86 percent) while others (e.g., Vietnamese, 60 percent) are largely Asian language speakers. Southeast Asians, who comprise the largest influx of immigrants over the last decade, include Cambodians, Laotians, and Vietnamese. Each of these groups includes a variety of ethnic and linguistic subgroups. For example, the Montagnards, a minority group in Vietnam, speak 20 languages (Chinn & Plata, 1986).

While the majority of Asian-Americans are foreign born (e.g., Koreans, 82 percent; Vietnamese, 90 percent), each group contains members whose families have been in this country for as many as three or four generations. The point is clear: The title Asian-American represents a variety of ethnic and cultural groups whose members differ widely in language, social, and educational background.

RATIONALE FOR SPECIAL CONSIDERATION IN IDENTIFYING GIFTED ASIAN-AMERICAN STUDENTS

A number of Asian-American writers (including this author) seem to harbor a need to acknowledge the academic achievements of Asian-Americans as a group while simultaneously identifying with the sociocultural problems of other ethnic minorities in their attempt to assimilate into the mainstream American life. Academic success and sociocultural problems (e.g., racism) can and do coexist for individuals and for groups. However, the existence of sociocultural problems does not necessarily justify special educational consideration, especially when the individuals or groups in question demonstrate success in educational achievement. Yet because of vast within-group differences for any cultural group, some children in every group need and deserve special consideration to accomplish appropriate identification. Thus, arguing against special consideration for the cultural group he or she represents would be untenable for any educator.

Chen's arguments in support of special consideration for identifying gifted Asian-American children reflect this dilemma, and are summarized below.

1. Asian-Americans who project the media's successful Asian-American stereotype are from well-educated, middle-class backgrounds.
2. Not all Asians in America are socioeconomically advantaged. Many live in crowded, urban, poor communities.
3. The incidence of giftedness among disadvantaged Asians is high relative to that expected in the general population, even when traditional achievement measures are used as indicators of giftedness.

4. A large proportion of Asian-Americans come from low socioeconomic, disadvantaged communities; thus, educators need to use alternative methods for identifying the gifted.

Chen seems to be arguing for special consideration in the assessment of socioeconomically disadvantaged Asian-Americans even while this group contains a relatively high proportion of gifted students identified using traditional measures. I propose the following, alternative rationale.

1. While Asian-American children from all economic strata are being identified as gifted in relatively high proportions and using traditional measures, alternative approaches are needed to identify those gifted children in this group who do not meet traditional criteria for determining giftedness.
2. Given the great variety of people labeled Asian-Americans, traditional measures are unlikely to be appropriate for all.

The above points appear more logical than those presented by Chen, and they can be applied to every cultural group, including the majority.

A more fruitful and objective approach than that offered for answering the question about the need for special consideration would be to examine empirical data concerning relative proportions of groups identified as gifted, taking into account socioeconomic status, English language proficiency, and other relevant variables. The only data I have been able to find are those provided by a 1980 Civil Rights survey, which indicated that while the broad category of Asian-American children comprised only 2.2 percent of the total school enrollment, these children constituted 4.4 percent of the identified gifted (Chan & Kitano, 1986). Asian-American children as a group are overrepresented among the identified gifted relative to their proportions in the school population. However, these data cannot be generalized across subgroups. Hawaiian native children, for example, tend to be underrepresented among the identified gifted in Hawaii.

RECOMMENDATIONS FOR ASSESSMENT

Kitano (1986) observed that although Asian-American cultures differ in many ways from the majority culture, the value placed on educational attainment and obedience to authority by some of these cultures clearly supports achievement in American schools (e.g., the Filipino culture, Santos [1983]; the Japanese, Yamamoto & Iga [1983]; the Chinese, Sue, Sue, & Sue [1983]; the Korean, Yu & Kim [1983]; and the Vietnamese, Chinn & Plata [1986]). Assessment procedures designed to identify high achievers are consistent with these values and, in fact, may be biased in favor of Asian-American students. Yet, given the heterogeneity of background and experience presented by Asian-American children, Chen's recommendations for a multidimensional approach and curriculum-based assessment procedures are appropriate. I offer additional recommendations.

Identification Criteria

Chen's recommendation that criteria for determining giftedness be guided by local norms for the school district and for the specific populations should be considered in areas where Asian-Americans are underrepresented in programs for the gifted relative to their incidence in the school population. Use of multiple norms in areas where Asian-Americans are overidentified can lead to establishment of quotas that limit the numbers of Asian-American students who can be served by programs for the gifted. The rationale for use of multiple norms and for limited quotas is the same: All cultures have the same underlying cognitive abilities but manifest these abilities in different ways. Thus, a single identification procedure will not be equally effective for all.

However, use of limited quotas assumes that for groups whose proportion of identified gifted exceeds their expected proportion, some nongifted children are being identified as gifted. While this assumption may be true, at this time distinguishing the truly gifted from those who are not gifted is not possible when all have met established criteria. In short, overidentifying is better than underidentifying. Performance in programs for gifted students (e.g., Renzulli's Revolving Door model) can be used to evaluate identification procedures.

Assessment Methods

Chen's recommendations favoring process- and curriculum-based assessment generally are well suited to identification of culturally different gifted children. The test-teach-test or pretest-coaching-posttest method has been recommended by a number of authors to achieve a more accurate assessment of minority children's abilities (e.g., Leung [1986]; Padilla & Wyatt [1983]). One cautionary note is important: Children whose culturally determined learning styles conflict with the school's instructional methods may require adaptations in the test-teach-test approach. Specifically, the teaching method must accommodate children's learning styles. For example, among some Pacific American cultures, values are oriented toward cooperation rather than competition and toward support of family needs, which sometimes take precedence over children's education (Munoz, 1983). The successful experiences of the Kamehameha Early Education Project with Hawaiian children indicate that instructional strategies compatible with cultural values of cooperation and sharing are more effective than traditional teaching methods in fostering academic achievement (Jordan, 1981).

Chen's emphasis on nonverbal measures for children who have limited English proficiency is appropriate and also requires qualification. Again, given the diverse characteristics of Asian-American children, some of these children's strengths or areas of giftedness may be verbal rather than nonverbal. Verbally gifted children would be penalized by use of mainly nonverbal measures, unless they also possess strengths in nonverbal areas of functioning. Asian-American children whose major strengths lie in the verbal domain and who have limited proficiency in English may be identified using standardized instruments administered in their first language.

As Chen suggests, measures of creativity (informal observations and Torrance Tests) provide additional data for identification of gifted children, especially when Renzulli's three-ring definition of giftedness has been adopted. However, creativity data must be evaluated in the context of the individual child's background and experience. The child-rearing practices of some Asian-American families, which emphasize conformity, correctness, and obedience (Chan, 1986), tend to reinforce convergent rather than divergent thinking. The memorization/recitation style used in some Asian-American school systems (Dinh, 1976) also fails to encourage risk-taking attitudes needed to score at a high level on tests of creative thinking.

Test Administration

A final recommendation regarding the assessment of giftedness in Asian-American children concerns the tester's sensitivity to the child's linguistic and affective characteristics and needs during test administration. (Readers interested in interviews of parents should consult Chan [1986].) Given the variety of first languages spoken by limited English proficient Asian-American children, use of an interpreter/translator (I/T) can be an option during assessment. According to Leung (1986), the *Wechsler Intelligence Scale for Children–Revised (WISC-R)* has been translated and normed in both Hong Kong and Taiwan. He cautions that the utility of these translations is limited to recent immigrants from these areas and to testers with high levels of Chinese proficiency. Leung suggests that administration of standardized assessment devices through an I/T can yield useful information, provided that I/Ts are credentialed and experienced bilingual professionals or, at minimum, carefully selected and trained paraprofessionals. Leung offers guidelines for use of I/Ts.

Asian-American children who have been raised in families emphasizing obedience to authority and placing a high value on educational achievement may bring to the testing situation an affective set that influences their performance. The sometimes excessively high achievement motivation may create anxiety and internal pressure. Such children also may be reluctant to guess on tests (Leung, 1986). Examiners must make clear to students how they are expected to respond in the test situation.

IN CONCLUSION

Chen's chapter on identifying gifted Asian-American students provides useful and appropriate suggestions regarding a multidimensional approach, including process- and curriculum-based assessment. The rationale given for special consideration in identifying gifted Asian-American children is that even though high numbers of disadvantaged Asian-Americans are identified using traditional measures, some remain unidentified. Perhaps a more cogent argument may be based on the recognition that Asian-Americans constitute a conglomeration of widely heterogeneous groups for which no single identification approach would be effective. Multidimensional assessment is appropriate for identifying gifted Asian-American children because it is appropriate for gifted children of any ethnicity who would not be identified accurately using traditional assessment methods.

Additional considerations for identifying gifted Asian-American children include cautions in employing multiple norms and exclusively nonverbal measures. Appropriate use of interpreter/translators provides another option for administration of standardized assessment devices.

Perhaps the most important concept in helping educators and administrators become knowledgeable about Asian-American children is that a wide variety of cultures and experiences of individuals is subsumed under the term Asian-American. Until data become available regarding the effectiveness of traditional identification methods for the various cultural and economic subgroups, the heterogeneity of Asian-Americans requires that identification and programming approaches be designed to consider the background of each child, a recommendation applicable to gifted children from all cultural groups.

23

Are We Meeting the Needs of Gifted Asian-Americans?

Rosina M. Gallagher, Ph.D.
St. Augustine College

The term Asian-American has been used generically since the late 1960s to classify not only the early immigrants from China (1850s) and Japan (1890s) but also the recent waves from the Philippines and Korea (1970s) as well as refugees from Vietnam, Laos, and Cambodia (1975 to present). On one hand, the term is useful, as it unifies areas of concern common to all Asian-American groups. On the other, the composite is unfortunate, as it undermines the rich, distinct culture and historical experience that each group represents. The reader is referred to the introduction to Section III for a description of the problems in defining this diverse population, as well as its experience, historically, of becoming part of the American culture and the role of education in this immersion.

Judging from the popular press, Asian-Americans are the "model minority." Feature articles extol salient qualities of hard work, frugality, self-discipline, determination, and academic achievement. These qualities are inherent in Asian family life and culture. The popular success image, however, has been criticized by Asian-American psychologists, social scientists, and researchers on several counts (Hsia, 1985; Sue & Morishima, 1982; Suzuki, 1977).

First, the oppression and suffering early Asian-American groups have endured, and the precarious existence of the poor, elderly, and new immigrants is ignored. Second, the fact that Asian-American communities are atrophying due to the erosion of languages and subsequent abandonment of traditions is disregarded. Third, the utopian image oversimplifies the issue of academic success. While results of research show that mathematical skills par excellence occur among Asians, they also confirm deficiencies in oral language and writing abilities even among second, third, and fourth generations (Hsia, 1985; Peng, Owings, & Fetters, 1984; Tsang & Wing, 1985; Watanabe, 1973; Wong, 1985).

Based on a review of summary data from the College Board *Scholastic Aptitude Test (SAT)* administered to college candidates, Hsia (1983) concluded that mathematics and verbal skills are more differentiated within Asian-American groups than among all other populations. A case in point is the student from Australia, Terence Tao. According to Stanley (Gross, 1986), at the age of eight years, ten months, Terry achieved one of the highest *SAT*-Math scores (760 out of 800 possible) ever recorded for a child his age, but a much lower score (290 out of 800, a chance score being about 230) on the *SAT*-Verbal.

Data from the *SAT* generally show that a greater proportion of Asian-American students falls into the highest *SAT-M* range, while a greater proportion of Anglo-American students falls into the highest *SAT-V* range. Hsia (1983) also reports that in studies of young children from five ethnic groups (Lesser, 1964; Stodolsky & Lesser, 1967), Chinese children excelled in reasoning and spatial conceptualization, but ranked next to the lowest in verbal performance.

The reality that predominant specialization in quantitative and technical fields is limiting the career and vocational opportunities for Asian-Americans is related to the educational success myth (Cesa, 1982). As cited by Hsia (1983), Weyl found Asian-Americans to be vastly overrepresented among accountants, engineers, architects, physicians, natural scientists, university professors, school teachers and technicians, but underrepresented among social scientists, lawyers, judges, and clergy.

Fourth, the "model minority" stereotype also implies Asian-Americans experience few adjustment problems in society. This is not the case. The mental health literature reports common sources of severe depression, alienation and somatic involvement for Asian-Americans, including parental and community pressures to excel, confusion over cultural identity, conflict between individual and group values, and difficulty in establishing close, interpersonal relationships.

A final objection is that "model" suggests Asian-Americans must continue to be silent in the political, social, and economic arenas. That is, Asian-Americans should raise no voice in government to lobby for educational or affirmative action programs. Further, this group should acquiesce to underemployment, lower salaries than those received by professional counterparts, and less than equal opportunities for top level management promotions (Urban Associates, 1974; Young, 1977).

PROGRAMS FOR THE GIFTED AND THE ASIAN-AMERICAN CHILD

Given the previous considerations, how can educators meet the needs of gifted Asian-Americans? Before dealing directly with this question, a review of the primary goals of special programs for gifted students is helpful.

Gowan (1975) believed that these programs should incorporate an environment wherein gifted children could develop their potential to become creative adults. Ward (1980) emphasizes the development of original thinkers who will be directed by "enduring methods and sources of learning" (p. 156). Clark (1983) adds the requirement of active and cooperative interaction with peers and adults to promote self-discovery, definition of abilities, and unique contributions to an interdependent world society.

Baldwin (1985) cites respect for cultural differences, awareness of ethnic histories and traditions, knowledge of resources available to minorities, and flexible organization as essential considerations for those who plan programs for gifted minority students. Particular to Asian-Americans and in light of the issues previously outlined, three areas warrant attention: identification, curriculum design, and counseling.

Identification of Gifted Students

Persons who develop identification procedures need to take into account an ever increasing number of limited English proficient (LEP) students who exhibit high ability in specific areas.

A case comes to mind of a bright Korean six-year-old girl who scored within the 99th percentile on the *Otis Lennon School Abilities Test* administered in English. When the administrator of the program for gifted students was informed that this child spoke little English and had no reading readiness skills, the immediate consensus was that she enroll in a bilingual program until she gained proficiency in English. The girl was born and raised in the Midwest (United States) but had spent her kindergarten year in Seoul. While she obviously understood English, her expressive language was in limbo at the time her parents apologetically referred her for screening. She was not given the opportunity to demonstrate her potential in a challenging program.

In a second case, a bright young man, who had lived in the United States for only one year, was referred by his sixth-grade teacher to a comprehensive center for gifted students. He completed his elementary school program with honors and successfully competed for a scholarship to attend a private boarding high school. Despite a pronounced Tagalog accent, which may perdure throughout his life, the boy met the expectations for a gifted student.

These anecdotes illustrate the need for flexible programming to enable the inclusion of precocious LEP students. Special English language instruction for the first year might have brought the young girl's performance to an acceptable level. Within a multifaceted identification and selection model, such as that described by Gallagher (1983), minority youngsters are not penalized for not knowing content they may not have mastered for reasons intrinsic or extrinsic to their individual educational experience.

Curriculum Designed To Develop Functional Bilingualism

If a long-term goal of education for gifted students is to develop world citizens, the curriculum should be designed to nurture verbal competency in English, and in a second or third language. This nurturance requires a revamping of motivational techniques to improve verbal reasoning and expressive abilities to develop, ideally, functional bilingualism. (Note: The term ''functional bilingualism'' refers to individuals who are bilingual/biliterate and who have an appreciation of their two cultures. Also, the term "bilingualism" may be used interchangeably with "multilingualism.")

We need to become advocates of bilingualism not only for language minorities but for *all* students. However, the tendency toward monolingualism in the United States is alarming, as the President's Commission on Foreign and International Studies reports. Psycholinguist Hakuta (1986) has compared the rate of loss of language diversity in the United States with that of other nations and concludes that "it would take 350 years for the average nation to experience the loss witnessed in just one generation in the United States" (p. 167).

In summer programs for gifted junior high school students offered by a prominent university in the Midwest, usually 20 percent of the participants are Asian. However, one summer a course in Chinese had to be dropped for lack of enrollment. Another summer, in a Japanese class, not one of the 20 students enrolled was Asian.

Second and third generations of Asian-Americans are not only losing the home language but also are failing to become truly proficient in English. Although Asian-American students at all levels are generally aware of weak oral and written communication skills in English, they seem to do little if anything about it. Investigators (Hsia, 1985; Peng, Owings, & Fetters, 1984) report that, on the average, elementary and high school students spend less time studying English and social studies than mathematics or science. This focus helps them to develop high achievement scores that will get them into college and graduate or technical schools. For the same reasons college students avoid courses that emphasize student-centered discussion, concentrating instead on mathematics and the sciences.

While avoiding courses that develop language may be manifestation of *arugama* or *akirame,* Asian-Americans must be made aware that they are limiting not only future educational and career options, but also full participation in an ever changing competitive society. Verbal competency in oral and written communication is a requirement for top administrative positions in business, government, or academic settings.

One way language diversity and proficiency can be encouraged is through the Counseling-Learning® Approach to Community Language Learning (C-L/CLL). In this approach (Curran 1972, 1977), principles from counseling and psychotherapy are integrated into a philosophy of education that engages both learners and teacher in creative affiliation. Six key principles are embraced in the approach: (a) Individuals learn as whole persons; (b) Human learning is investment in values; (c) Learning is persons; that is, ideas are learned not as abstractions but as they are embodied in the person of the teacher; (d) Counseling, whether about self or about ideas enables learning; (e) Education is the process whereby teacher and learners, through mature self-discipline, acquire the art and skill of understanding; and (f) Personal learning leads to community, the environment wherein each person has a proper and vital responsibility to integrate concepts and bring forth new ideas (Rardin, Tirone, & Tranel, 1987).

In practice, in the Community Language Learning (CLL) model, a client-learner/counselor-teacher relationship guides language learners sensitively through five developmental stages, from total dependence on the language counselor-teacher to independent and free communication in the target language. A multilingual program developed around C-L/CLL would be a challenging model to offer gifted students.

Counseling for Cultural Identity and Career Choice

A need for counseling techniques and strategies exists to (a) resolve confusions about cultural identity or individual versus group values; (b) cultivate the robust self-concept that the term Asian-American connotes; and (c) expand career choices. These needs are not unique to the gifted or to Asian-Americans. However, by understanding the needs of a particular ethnic group, insight into subtle aspects of human behavior may be gained.

Objections to educational programs providing for the affective needs of participants are voiced; this is understandable if one accepts a dichotomized view of the person—that is, intellect and psyche operate independently of one another. While this seventeenth century philosophical perspective remains palpable in our educational system, more holistic and humanistic theories of education are being defined. Counseling-Learning (described earlier) enables counseling issues to become an integral part of the educative process. To illustrate, using CLL in a foreign language class, discussions in the target language (e.g., Japanese) could center around issues such as family customs and traditions, or what students admire and find difficult to accept in role models of that culture. Other topics might include occupations that various ethnic groups tend to select, career alternatives to which students aspire, interpretation of literature selections or magazine articles and popular aphorisms such as *Makeru ga kachi*, which in Japanese means "To lose is to win."

CONCLUSIONS AND FUTURE DIRECTIONS

The historical experiences of Asian-Americans are complex and change too rapidly to be documented readily or understood fully. Nevertheless, a sensitive awareness of the past will help educators to evaluate and shape the present, and will offer guidelines for the future. Specific provisions need to be established to accommodate the gifted limited English proficient student. Rather than channel Asian-American students into mathematical and technical fields, as well-meaning educators tend to do, ample opportunity should be provided to develop communication skills.

Gifted students from minority populations have the potential to become world ambassadors in whatever field of endeavor they choose, and becoming functionally bilingual would be a step in that direction. When acknowledging the significant progress Asian-Americans have made, care should be exercised to avoid alienating this group from other minorities, and excluding those in need from participating in affirmative action. Finally, those who develop programs for the gifted should evaluate current holistic and humanistic philosophies of education to guide their efforts in continuing to meet the needs of the gifted and talented.

24

A Response to "Are We Meeting the Needs of Gifted Asian-Americans?"

Kazuko Tanaka, M.A.
Montebello Unified School District,
California

Gallagher recognizes the distinct cultural and historical experiences and diversity of Asian-Americans; yet, we are still confronted with generalizations being applied to whole groups of people. These generalizations ignore the balance of talents within each culture. (For example, Japanese are not all scientists and mathematicians; language, art, music, history, and religion are integral parts of their culture as well.)

The myth of the "model minority" or popular image of success of Asian-Americans was well addressed and countered with five significant contradictions to the stereotype. My response consists of discussion of identification procedures and suggestions for educational strategies for gifted Asian-Americans.

IDENTIFICATION OF GIFTED AND TALENTED ASIAN-AMERICAN STUDENTS

Every culture has natural leaders, creative individuals, artists, and performers who should be identified as having special gifts, in addition to the academically gifted who are most commonly identified for special programs. The Asian-American culture is no exception; but for many school districts, serving students other than the academically gifted is not economically feasible. Therefore, Asian-American students are not fully served in all of their areas of giftedness. I am not confident we even serve the academic needs of Asian-American students due to our stereotypic expectations and the differences between new immigrants and third- or fourth-generation, assimilated students.

In Montebello Unified School District, the total population is 8 percent Asian-American, and current participation in the program for gifted students is 40 percent Asian-American. The majority has been identified in the high achievement category, using standardized tests and teacher judgment with intellectual (as determined by tests such as the *WISC-R, Stanford-Binet,* or *Leiter International Performance Scale*) being the next most frequent area of giftedness identified. The intelligence quotients (IQs) range from 123, for those students in the high achievement category, to 172, which is in the highly gifted range (above 140). In other words, large numbers of Asian-American students are being identified as gifted, and these students are primarily high achievers.

In the Montebello Unified School District, we are piloting a Bilingual Identification Project (BIP) that focuses on identification of gifted students without an individual test. We look at characteristics of giftedness as indicated by a variety of data. School data, which include information such as teacher comments and test scores from cumulative records; teacher, aide, and peer nominations; as well as parent interviews; are evaluated and brought to the Placement Committee, which is composed of the BIP project facilitator, teacher, administrator, district consultant, and psychologist. This process was developed primarily to identify underrepresented minority populations, in this case Hispanic, for the program for gifted and talented students, but is open to all. The consultants for programs for the bilingual/bicultural and for the gifted and talented worked together, and shared costs, resources, and expertise to develop this project of mutual concern and interest.

STRATEGIES TO MEET THE EDUCATIONAL NEEDS OF ASIAN-AMERICAN STUDENTS

The following are limiting, culturally supported attitudes and experiences that children may bring to the learning situation. These attitudes are mentioned here to develop a heightened awareness and provide direction for program planning.

- Attitudes unfavorable to participation in discussion groups
- Little experience with independent thinking
- Strong valuing of conformity, which inhibits creative activity or divergent thinking
- Quiet manner, which may foster unrealistic expectations and inappropriate assessments
- Attitude of perfectionism, which makes using mistakes as learning experiences quite difficult
- Sex role differentiation—male more desirable and dominant sex
- Critical self-concept (Clark, 1979).

To do well in school is commendable, but unfortunately many immigrant Asian-American students become like robots. The teachers assign and the students complete—they do not question, they merely memorize without always understanding. These students delve no farther than necessary for the assignment, because they must go on to the next subject. The highly gifted Asian-American student or the assimilated Asian who does not conform to this achiever mold is criticized and not served appropriately.

Third- and fourth-generation Asian-American students are changing. One such student, currently a senior in college, made the following comments when asked to reflect on an appropriate education for gifted students.

> I would remove them completely from the unmotivating brain, [and] soul crushing environment public education in suburbia fosters so well. Send them abroad to study Western civilization at its roots. Some students at the far end (gifted) are not able to develop to where they could and should be. A contextual environment for them to have community with others of like ability and interests must be provided. I would have liked a mentor . . . there were not attractive role models and [there was] no introduction to see my potential in a meaningful way. The social atmosphere inhibits one from learning. The pressure a group can bring to bear on an individual's values and goals is great. Even if that is not what an individual wants, the social side of them ends up wanting that, especially in the intensive social age of high school.
>
> The thing to do is to align the gifted child's abilities and interest with a social group whose interest and abilities will encourage them. It would have been helpful to have known the ability level I had. It would have been a self-fulfilling prophecy. The most important point is to have the social group to reinforce [each other].
>
> None of my friends in this Asian subculture are majoring in humanities. They are in business, science, and engineering. Asians have respect for education, but not for learning. There is no integration of their learning nor a curiosity. (1987)

This young man is third-generation Japanese, feels integrated into the mainstream, and is glad to be Asian-American. He feels that being distinctive in his background and self is more interesting than being like everyone else. He feels at home with Asian-Americans and would not have been adverse to an all-Asian-American school; but he also feels that values and beliefs, more than nationality or background, unify people. This young man ventured out of his community while his friends chose to remain in the secure neighborhood environment; and his experiences and comments uncover concerns worthy of comment and consideration.

Students from a subculture must learn about the mainstream culture—Western civilization. Music and art appreciation are not automatically provided; yet, if we propose to develop total persons these are necessary elements of a curriculum. Music and art can be added to a curriculum, for example, by a high school teacher sponsorship of an "Unclub," so named because it has no name and is not a service organization. ("Culture vultures" is another name used at a neighboring high school.) The purpose of the clubs is to allow students to attend plays, musicals, and orchestral performances in Los Angeles throughout the school year. The students pay for their own tickets, bring enough money for dinner at a restaurant of their choice near the theater, and become culturally enriched as a group. The teacher provides background for understanding the performance and guides subsequent discussion.

Asian-American children need to be taught to express their feelings, verbally and in writing. This means writing, writing, and more writing; verbal practice, practice, and more practice. The word processor is a wonderful tool for writing, and a strong vocabulary program is a necessity. The Montebello Unified School District provides such an extensive vocabulary program, and College Board *PSAT* and *SAT* scores have risen a mean of 100 points on the verbal section of the tests since the program was developed. With skills and confidence, third- and fourth-generation Asian-Americans will be able to express feelings, as well as depth, in their writing. Writing also is an essential skill for scientists and mathematicians, who must communicate findings and concepts for presentation. A case in point is a young Asian-American at the managerial level in a science-oriented field who agonizes over writing reports. The lack of writing skills could prohibit his advancement in his field; others with the same level of scientific expertise also may possess effective writing skills.

Torrance (1977) has made reference to nurturing giftedness in Black children, but his guidelines for nurturing culturally different gifted students are apropos for Asian-American students: "A special characteristic of programs for culturally different gifted students should make heavy reliance on learning and working in teams or small groups. These should include both teacher initiated and pupil initiated activities, planned as well as impromptu experiences" (p. 72).

Torrance (1977) continues that culturally different gifted children, especially disadvantaged ones, need sponsors or mentors who encourage and protect their rights when they are frustrated, discouraged, or abused. These students need someone special who can see that the students get a chance. The role of the Asian-American parent, who characteristically has been very supportive, is not minimized by this recommendation; mentors fulfill different needs from parents.

The different learning styles of Asian-American students must be given consideration. Torrance (cited in Gallagher, 1985), after visiting Japan, noticed sharp contrasts between students in Japan and the United States. When compared with students in the United States (a) more than twice as many Japanese students preferred to solve problems intuitively rather than logically; (b) twice as many preferred synthesizing to analyzing; (c) more than twice as many enjoyed drawing and manipulating objects; and (d) less than half considered themselves more intellectual than creative.

Asian-Americans are becoming as prone to social and emotional problems as mainstream gifted students, and require the support system available to mainstream students without criticism, loss of face, or feelings of failure. Stereotypes must be broken down and reality accepted. Understanding of cultural factors is crucial (Kaneshige, 1973). Such a stereotypical view of social and emotional support is particularly Asian; this cultural barrier must be overcome.

IN CONCLUSION

We recognize and acknowledge the diversity of the Asian-American population and also the differences between newly arrived immigrants and third- and fourth-generation Asian-Americans who have assimilated into the mainstream. We need to know from where these students come and the circumstances of their immigration. The number and, therefore, the visibility of Asian-Americans is increasing on the streets and in schools.

When designing identification procedures and programs, educators must consider the learning styles of each student and the wide range of giftedness in the population. Thus, many ways must be available to place a student in a special program.

Awareness of specific characteristics of the Asian-American population that may limit success will help in designing appropriate programs. Talking to students who have graduated from programs for gifted students also is helpful. Such conversations reveal specific student needs, such as mentors for role models.

The purpose of programs for gifted Asian-American students should include broadening their knowledge of the mainstream culture and nurturing appreciation of their own culture. Students must be helped to build bridges from one culture to another. Activities such as vocabulary building and an emphasis on oral and written verbal tasks should be included in programs for gifted Asian-American students.

Gallagher has clearly expressed, and I agree, that, along with gifted students from all cultures, Asian-American students have the potential to make vital and positive contributions in the future. These students deserve the most appropriate education we can provide.

25

Personal Reflections on the Purpose of Special Education for Gifted Asian-Americans

Elaine Woo, B.A.
Los Angeles Times

At age 33, I am a successful staff writer for one of the country's top metropolitan daily newspapers. In my more reflective moments, I sometimes wonder how I made it this far because, when I look back on my public education, I see weaknesses in the system that should have resulted in my pursuing a more conventional, less risky career path.

Born in Los Angeles, I attended public schools during the 1960s and 1970s in a suburban school district that was predominantly Anglo-American, although both Latinos and Asian-Americans were increasing in numbers. In most ways, I fit my (Asian) cultural stereotype: I was a quiet, shy, obedient, and very studious pupil. Not surprisingly, teachers liked me. I personified the "model minority" years before the term became commonplace.

I was raised in a traditional Chinese household, headed by my loving, though stern, grandparents who laid down the law with unwavering authority. My grandparents impressed upon my siblings and me the importance of earning the best grades, for to achieve anything less would bring shame on the family. Shame was and is a guiding influence in most Asian cultures.

My grandparents also taught us that rewards only follow hard work, a basically Confucianist philosophy. We children spent, I'm sure, significantly more time doing homework and extra credit assignments than the average student. I earned mostly As and Bs throughout my school career. While the children in my family certainly worked hard, we took few risks.

Did I receive a good education? If one believes in a holistic purpose for education, then I think the system failed me in important ways. I agree with Gallagher that strong communication skills are not taught in schools, and this is an area of weakness among many Asian-Americans.

Unlike many Asian-Americans, I had little problem with writing; for me, writing became a safe way to express private thoughts. Where my education was lacking was in oral development. Speaking in class was a traumatic experience for me because it raised the possibility of conflict with another person's opinion, or the chance that I might say "the wrong thing." Culturally, I was not prepared to deal with such possibilities. I was raised to obey, not question, authority figures, and to yield to the majority view. My grade school and high school teachers allowed me to hide behind my writing skills; but in college—a small liberal arts school where participation in classroom discussion was rated highly—my silence became a terrible burden. As a reporter, I have struggled hard to overcome this reticence and succeeded, though with no help from my school teachers or counselors.

How could I have been helped? Gallagher may be right in suggesting a need for counseling "to resolve confusions about cultural identity or individual versus group values." Many minority children suffer from a strong sense of being different, and not in the mainstream; and I believe this sense of differentness contributes to public reticence and the image of Asian-Americans as passive. This sense of being set apart also encourages a kind of deceit; I spent many years pretending that I was not different.

Remember studying about the four basic food groups in elementary school? I do, because I lied when my teacher asked the class to identify which items from the four groups we ate for dinner the previous night. Instead of listing what I really ate— fermented eggs, tofu and fish with black bean sauce—I made up a menu that seemed more American—hamburgers and french fries and pork chops. Now, of course, I can see how much energy I wasted in denying my cultural identity.

Wouldn't it be wonderful if schools truly offered multicultural education so that children could grow up learning that people come in all different shapes and colors and have varied but equally valid customs and cultures? Simply holding a Chinese New Year festival would not be enough. True multicultural education would mean a literature class including a play by Frank Chin or David Huang, or an art class that mentions the architecture of I.M. Pei as well as Frank Lloyd Wright. When primary school children learn about the family unit, their lessons should include a discussion of Asian extended families or a comparison of family customs and traditions in several cultures.

Finally, I can't emphasize enough the importance of role models. I previously mentioned my amazement at my success in a nontraditional field; I am amazed because I received little direct support from my family for my goals. In high school, however, I was fortunate to take journalism classes from a gifted teacher who happened to be Japanese-American. He was articulate, outspoken, and he encouraged me to hone my budding talent as a writer.

Many Asian-Americans have been stereotyped as having little creative ability, and thus have been channeled into careers in science and mathematics that emphasize technical expertise. Asian-American parents, who tend to err on the side of conservatism and practicality, can be blamed as much as the schools for restricting the goals and dreams of their children. I have known many Asian-American physicians and engineers who are frustrated actors, writers, and inventors because, as Gallagher so ably states, they were never afforded the opportunity to develop strong communication skills—the kind of skills that might have made them feel more comfortable about exploring themselves and the world of choices that are open to people with the self-assuredness to seek such opportunities.

At a time when the school population is changing so rapidly—soon approaching, at least in California, a majority of ethnic "minority" students—the development of strong communication skills seems to me a mission that ought to receive top priority in our schools.

26

Teaching Strategies and Practices for the Education of Gifted Cantonese Students

Sally Young Wong, B.A.
Pauline Renee Wong, M.A.
Los Angeles Unified School District

CULTURE-SPECIFIC FACTORS AFFECTING GIFTEDNESS IN CANTONESE STUDENTS

Culture-specific factors affecting Cantonese-speaking students in general are applicable to gifted Cantonese speakers as well. Examining these factors not only provides insight into the characteristics of Cantonese-speaking gifted students, but also determines the strategies to be used with these students. The influence of Confucianism is seen in the interdependence of the child with parents and teachers. Characteristics may be viewed as strengths or weaknesses; the effective teacher expands on strengths and shores up weaknesses using culture-specific factors to determine eclectic teaching strategies. A variety of challenging experiences to foster social skills, problem solving, critical thinking, values awareness, and self-esteem may be developed based on culture-specific factors.

When identifying culture-specific factors commonly found among Cantonese-speaking gifted students, no discussion would be complete without first acknowledging the influence of the family and its espousal of traditional values for the students. Many traditional family values have been cited before in various studies, and, in the opinion of the authors, have a danger of appearing almost stereotypically rigid with regard to Chinese families and students. However, to avoid digression into sociological or psychological explanations of traditional values, we will recognize and comment on these values as they are evidenced in conferences with parents and by student behaviors

---

This chapter on teaching strategies for gifted Asian-American children is limited to practices and techniques found successful for Cantonese-speaking children of Chinese descent. The student population to whom this discussion refers does not represent all Asian-American school children, nor are our students' characteristics deemed typical of Asian-American populations in general. Cultural characteristics and applicable teaching strategies are considered broadly valid to the highlighted student population, that is, first-generation American Cantonese-speaking school children of Chinese descent.

within the classroom. Certain culture-specific characteristics related to these values are deemed influential to the students' academic performance.

As first-generation Chinese-Americans, many of whom belong to immigrant families, children of the highlighted student population respect the authority of the parent. Parents set the tone and the rule for acceptable behaviors, and children learn to abide by those prescriptions at a young age. Standards, roles, and personal responsibility are established at an early age, and children enter school with a predisposition for structure and self-management. Traditional Confucianist ethics are encouraged strongly, and among those most emphasized are (a) the value of an education, (b) the work ethic, (c) personal responsibility, and (d) a respect for authority and order.

The Value of an Education

Based on numerous discussions with both parents and students, the authors know that a high premium is placed by the family on student academic performance and school success. Beyond Confucianist traditions of valuing an education, most parents view education more practically as a means of self-advancement in American society. Menial jobs are common employment for these parents, but they desire better career opportunities for their children. Thus, at an early age students view school as a stepping stone to the betterment of both their own personal positions and the position of their entire family. Emphasis is placed on the future welfare of the family, and what each member can do to contribute to its promotion. Long-term goals are delineated by parents, and high scholastic expectations are shouldered by students. From the parents' point of view, being "good in school" is defined as scholarship, with emphasis being placed on traditional measurements of academic achievement. This attitude is reflected during parent conferences, when parents exhibit a pronounced interest in their children's grades rather than in their social development.

As a result of this mind-set, and in conjunction with economic pressures, parents instill in their children a respect for learning as a means of achieving material gains rather than as an end in itself. The future is discussed between parents and children, and a sense of the future is evident in the thinking of students. A common expression among Chinese parents is "saving for the future," and this applies not only to monetary savings, but also to education. The expression is a reminder that an investment in the rigors of an education is a maturing process that will pay long-term rewards, if not immediate dividends. The thrift children witness daily in their parents' lives is applied to their own school experiences, and learning time is not squandered. Parents educate their children to value each day in school, and avoid wasting educational opportunities. Each day with the teacher, therefore, must be used to its fullest extent.

The Work Ethic

As strict proponents of the work ethic, Chinese parents believe that individual effort is a greater factor in success than innate intelligence or talent. Many times during parent conferences, parents will indicate that their child's progress in school is due more to concentration and persistence than to ability. Where improvement is necessary, parents often cite "laziness" as the cause and "hard work" as the remedy. Students are saturated with this philosophy of effort righting all things, and are reminded by their parents that their intellectual accomplishments are merely a reflection of that effort. Esteeming one's intelligence over one's hard work is considered foolish and proud.

A seeming inconsistency exists in this work ethic: Parents have a strong preference for professional rather than vocational education. Due to economic hardships and a great desire for upward mobility, parents exert a strong influence on their children's choice of profession, and usually opt for the most financially lucrative careers. Trade professions are regarded in an unfavorable light, and students are dissuaded from pursuing such options. The inconsistency in this line of reasoning lies in the fact that the intellectual abilities that parents have not acknowledged previously throughout their child's school career are the very same traits that are vital to success in preferred professions. Parents have failed to realize that both hard work and innate intelligence are necessary for the type of self-advancement they have prescribed for their children.

Personal Responsibility

Following traditional Confucianist values of group interdependence, Chinese children of immigrant parents are reared with a deep sense of personal responsibility to their families. Unlike American children from Western backgrounds, Chinese children are taught that the family group's well-being is more important than personal liberty, and that a hierarchy of authority exists within relationships and has predominance over personal voice. As a survival response to economic hardship, each member within the family is expected to contribute toward its maintenance and well-being; and this standard of responsibility also is extended to the children. Thus, seeing children rearing younger siblings, caring for the household, and even helping their parents to earn menial wages is not uncommon.

What this home training does academically for the student is to preset a noticeable disposition toward structure and defined limits, self-discipline and self-motivation. Students bring to the classroom the same high level of personal responsibility they practice at home. Responsibility is manifested in such attributes as perfect attendance, consistently completed assignments, and concentrated time on task with minimal teacher direction. In contrast with Western children who tend to question the purpose of an assignment before starting, Chinese children will begin assignments without questioning the intent and accept them as responsibilities for which they are personally liable. The children take pride in taking care of themselves.

A Respect for Authority and Order

Much has been said about the respect accorded to teachers by Chinese children. This respect results not from a stereotyped view of the adult as an authority figure, but rather from the view of a teacher as a "master" of knowledge. Teachers are revered for their vast body of knowledge, which the children hope to acquire. Within this frame of mind, teachers become analogous to piano virtuosos the students hope to emulate. Imitation of the "master" is considered an important first step toward developing one's own personal style. What the "master" has to offer serves only as the foundation on which student creativity is developed in a precise and organized progression. Given their preference for structure and order, then, Chinese students regard their teacher's knowledge as a valuable resource to be mined and modeled for their own ultimate individual purposes.

Not surprising, therefore, is the fact that drill and rote exercises are not considered monotonous or as worthless busy work. Just as a serious piano student does not regard playing piano scales as boring and useless practice, Chinese students have a readiness and patience for drill and rote exercises as skill repetitions in mastering a concept. Drill in itself is not considered productive, but is a means to form a base for more advanced and sophisticated activities.

Imitation of the "master" teacher and conscientious adherence to drill and rote exercises finally merge in the pursuit of a structured, traditional, and rigorous academic curriculum that emphasizes innovations based on these principles. With mastery of basic skills firmly established within their repertoire of academic competencies, students are confident in their undertaking of problem-solving and situational learning exercises that require higher levels of critical and creative thinking. This self-assurance would not be possible if students were not open to an acceptance of the teacher as a "master" and willing to follow through on drill and rote exercises.

SUCCESSFUL TEACHING STRATEGIES

Through our experiences as educators of the gifted, we have come to recognize two recurrent traits found in gifted students: Low self-esteem and academic underachievement. Based on professional literature concerning these problems, we have provided suggestions for forming a teaching style and classroom environment that may be appropriate for Asian-American students.

Cooperative Learning

In the cooperative learning model, with three to five students grouped heterogeneously by gender, ethnicity, and ability, gifted students may improve their social skills, use the higher levels of thinking in explanations to students of lesser abilities, and interact positively with students of different cultures and sex.

In cooperative learning, teachers place as much emphasis on the social skills to be used as on the task to be accomplished. Oral expressive skills and social amenities can be improved through this strategy. The cooperative learning environment allows teachers to foster the formation of trusting relationships, create situations in which gifted students may resolve conflicts, and allow students to share their knowledge. Cross-cultural and gender relationships are improved through cooperative learning.

Cooperative learning within heterogeneous groups is invaluable in promoting students' self-esteem, and in exposing them to the abilities of pupils who are not gifted. It relieves those students not wishing to be in the spotlight and/or not ready to be leaders to share the responsibility for group and individual success. Because of the standards imposed by cooperative learning tenets, gifted students in this learning situation are given opportunities to lead with their strong points. It allows gifted students, in a nonthreatening, less burdensome atmosphere, to shine in their areas of special interest and expertise while providing opportunities for invaluable peer interaction with students not identified as gifted who may have superior abilities in different areas.

Self-paced Instruction

Self-paced instruction seemingly is contradictory to the cooperative learning concept. Use of cooperative learning exclusively would not develop all the tools gifted students need to be well rounded. To extend themselves students also need to develop self-motivation and work independently and creatively through using self-checking kits, completing independent projects, or designing original research.

Limited use of self-paced instruction is especially helpful in remediation of basic skills. Many gifted students do not exhibit the standard achievement skills of their prescribed grade level. However, they do not work well in a group of students not identified as gifted who also are not performing at grade level. This arrangement seems to be injurious to self-esteem. Limited and strictly monitored self-paced instruction is a better strategy for remediating basic skills, as students seem more favorably motivated to improve their basic skills at their own pace, although in compliance with the general time frame outlined by the teacher. Drill and rote exercises, when used minimally, help to promote a structured foundation, which gifted students find necessary as a base for advancement.

Clustering of Gifted Students

To structure an environment of challenge, teachers also need to cluster gifted students according to ability, talents, or interests. This strategy may seem contradictory to the self-paced instruction and cooperative learning group strategies, but serves the purpose of challenging students.

Clustering of gifted students provides opportunities for peer interaction, which also sparks their creativity and intellectual curiosity. Clustering of gifted students is an effective follow-up to a whole-class discussion. In this grouping, students elaborate on the preceding discussion and refine their perceptions by using a more sophisticated vocabulary and higher critical and creative thinking skills. This verbalization is then extended to problem-solving situational learning that will draw on students' entire body of knowledge, skills, and abilities. Many projects and in-depth reports can be conceived and developed through clustering gifted students; this is especially effective in the teaching of social studies and science.

Student Coaching

Student coaching encourages students to be autonomous. Components of student coaching include having one student read another's work and discuss other options, checking the work for possible errors, and developing trust to the point of being able to accept constructive criticism from peers. The teacher acts as a facilitator, and structures the situations for the students to give constructive suggestions to one another for improvement.

A variation of peer tutoring uses gifted students as student coaches; gifted students must draw on deeper levels of understanding to instruct or make explanations to those who are not gifted. Many times gifted students are able to complete their assignments without realizing the mental process they used to arrive at their solutions. Gifted students in a student-coaching role must articulate and rationalize consciously their own mental procedures in the explanation process. They must convey their own understanding so that other students with varying ability can comprehend. In this manner, they reinforce their own deeper levels of understanding and perception.

Values Awareness

Values awareness strategies help students to understand they have values that may be different from those of others. Students also come to understand that those values, although different, may be no better or worse than the values of others. Through interaction with peers and greater experience, students may add, alter, or delete aspects of their values; develop a code of ethics; and appreciate the value differences of others.

Gifted students are sensitive to ethical questions and global issues. Values awareness discussions are successful in developing and broadening a sense of moral values, and fostering questioning about ethical issues. Discussions should be supplemented by essays on ethical issues that focus on universal questions and emphasize the refinement of the students' own set of values as these values relate to the society at large. Values awareness discussions combined with essays on ethics have proved to be very successful, not only in developing intellectual maturity, but also in improving self-esteem.

PARENT-TEACHER DIALOGUE

Cantonese parents have revealed in conferences with the authors that they do not view themselves as primary and valuable role models in their child's education, nor as priceless resources from which their children can derive vital knowledge. The education of parents about the necessity of assuming the role of the primary teacher in their child's life education will be enhanced by the following suggestions.

1. Parents should be alerted to upcoming units of study and input on how they can help facilitate and supplement the lesson objectives should be sought. In particular, homework assignments should be geared to mining the knowledge that parents can bring to a specific lesson objective.
2. Parents should be encouraged to tutor their children in their primary home language, and promote bilingualism in their children. Many parents feel scholastically incompetent because of their English deficiencies. This misconception of their abilities should be discussed, and parents should be helped to realize the importance of maintaining bilingualism in their children. Bilingualism is not only a cultural birthright, but also is a vital and necessary skill in an increasingly polyglot world.
3. Parents need to be encouraged to be the primary role models for their child's education. For those who may lack formal education, their management and survival skills should be highlighted in teacher-parent dialogue. Parents should share their capabilities with their children in a variety of situational learning activities.
4. Parents should be advised to realize the potential of their children and the variety of possibilities open to their children. Parents need to be encouraged to consider and discuss the future with their children, and to set realistic life goals. Humanities education and social science careers should be discussed as viable alternatives to the more traditional science and technology options.
5. Parents possess a desire for their children to recognize them as vital sources of knowledge. Parent-student-teacher dialogue can be discussed as a means of communicating to the student the necessity of forming an educational partnership that includes the parent as an integral element in the learning process.

IN CONCLUSION

Cantonese-speaking gifted students have the value of education instilled in them at home. These students are expected to work diligently, expending time and energy to the fullest; they have a responsibility not only to themselves, but also to their family. Great respect for the teacher leads these students to emulate the teacher without question.

Attendance and motivation for completion of assignments are strengths of gifted Cantonese students. The tendency of these students to emulate their teacher and their preference for rote and drill exercises suggest the need for strategies that will provide opportunities for creativity, critical thinking, and other higher levels of thinking. Motivation for academic success is evident; however, less emphasis is placed on social development than on academic success in the home, so curriculum should be structured to provide for social interaction. Due to the influence of parents and the valuable resources they have to offer, a dialogue and interaction among parents, teacher, and student is critical to the success of a program for gifted Cantonese students.

27

The Gifted Asian-American Child: A General Response to a Specific Issue

Sandra N. Kaplan, Ed.D.
National/State Leadership Training
Institute on the Gifted and Talented

A specific critique of the chapter addressing the gifted Asian-American child could have been submitted, but the separate treatment of cultural groups negates the meaning of cultural pluralism and a belief in a global perspective. Both cultural pluralism and a global perspective dominate my approach to students who represent the cultural diversity of our schools and society. Therefore in this chapter a philosophical orientation to educating gifted students from any cultural group is presented; concentration on educating students from any one cultural group is not its purpose.

The factors included within this orientation follow. These factors center on a question that has plagued those who are charged with the responsibility of educating children from diverse backgrounds: How can we educate gifted children from varying cultural groups, without sacrificing the uniqueness of their differences or depreciating either their giftedness or cultural ties? The answer to this question may lie in the following principles.

1. *Knowledge about the nature of giftedness should be related to an understanding of cultural diversity to enable acceptance and understanding of such differences.*

The recognition and support of individual and group differences constitute the philosophical foundation for education of the gifted. Literature in the field is replete with statements that advocate the existence and maintenance of differences between individuals. Issues of equity and democracy underlie the rationale for allocating resources to provide for gifted students. Because the acceptance of individual and group differences parallels an understanding of giftedness, a reasonable assumption is that those who are cognizant of the value of individual and group differences as they pertain to gifted students also would be sympathetic to the value of differences as they apply to cultural groups. Thus, acceptance of the differences that govern education of the gifted should be applied to accepting and educating children whose uniqueness stems from their cultural background.

2. *Commonalities that exist between and among students should be defined.*

An acknowledged set of general, universal, or commonly held characteristics defines gifted individuals, regardless of culture. Such a characteristic is curiosity. Cultural background might mediate or influence how traits are manifested, but such traits of giftedness are universal and enable culturally different students to be identified as gifted.

Underscoring the commonalities of traits that exist within the gifted population increases the danger of evoking stereotypical thinking and endangers individuality. Effective education of students who are gifted and culturally different demands that educators understand both universal and commonly held traits of the groups to which these students belong. Educators must observe these groups collectively and individually, and see universal as well as unique traits of the individuals who comprise the groups.

3. *Differences should be regarded as positive, rather than negative, attributes.*

Perceptions of and appreciations for differences often are shaped by the kind and amount of learning experiences individuals have had. Some attempts to teach about differences between cultures are solicitous, rather than respectful. In these instances, educators define differences as disadvantages or handicaps. Such definitions of differences designate the different individual as deviant, rather than as an individual who differs from others, and obliterate the fact that such differences can be assets, not liabilities. Indeed, evidence exists that the differences noted between gifted Asian-American and gifted Anglo-American students have served as assets to the Asian-American child in schools.

4. *Fixed ends or outcomes, and multiple means or activities to attain these ends, should be established.*

One of the controversial issues regarding culturally different gifted students is whether adjustments in ends (objectives of learning) or means (activities) are more effective and appropriate. Many people believe that any change or adjustment in the ends outlined for gifted students within the majority population is tantamount to changing (or demeaning) the concept of giftedness for those who also are members of minority groups. Other people subscribe to the idea that unless ends and means are changed for gifted students of different cultural backgrounds, these students will be treated unfairly, and such treatment is equated with prejudice or bias.

Adjustments in the ends generally held for all gifted students do not seem necessary. For example, an anticipated end or outcome of an educational program for gifted students is an understanding of self. Such an understanding will enable students to respond positively to their potential and, subsequently, to translate that potential into performance. Productive performance is equally important for a gifted Asian-American, Anglo-American, or Hispanic student. Respect and concern for individual differences implies that altering the means or activities by which gifted students attain fixed ends is more valid than altering ends for some students because they are culturally different. Provision for a variety of means to accommodate the varied needs, interests, and abilities of the gifted population represents a commitment to individual differences, regardless of the origin of those differences.

IN CONCLUSION

In the complex society of school, students have multiple group memberships, and each of these groups in some way attests to the individual differences that distinguish human beings. A culturally pluralistic and global perspective enables the educator to view differences as assets. This perspective allows educators to recognize that times exist when an understanding of commonly held traits takes precedence over the recognition of individual differences, and times exist when this situation is reversed. Most important, educators of the gifted must perceive culturally different gifted students as simultaneously similar to and different from all other gifted students.

28

The Unmentioned Minority

Chris Hasegawa, M.A.
University of Oregon

> Everywhere I grew up I was always a minority. I was always the only Japanese-American, practically, in the whole group. And I never mentioned it too much. And that bothered me for a long time, and was one of the things I had to get over. (Kometani, 1986, p. 10)

In American educational circles, Asian-Americans often are not mentioned. Kometani (1986) was bothered by the fact that he never mentioned being Japanese-American and that even after World War II ended, he still felt "like a guest in my own country" (p. 10).

In many ways, Asian-Americans have been treated like temporary visitors in the United States with little provision made for their permanent residence. Whereas civil rights for Blacks and bilingual education for Hispanics have made headlines, very little national attention has been paid to Asian-Americans in schools. However, all educators need to be conscious of this minority group if they are to serve these students effectively.

DISCRIMINATION

In an address to the U.S. Commission on Civil Rights, Dr. K. Patrick Okura stated,

> There's a widespread belief that Asian and Pacific Americans do not suffer the discrimination and disadvantages associated with other minority groups. The stereotyping of Asian-Pacific Americans among minority groups by virtue of hard work, education, thrift, and initiatives, has lulled the general public into an attitude of what we call benign neglect to the extent that Asian-

American concerns are secondary to the problems of other minority groups. (U.S. Commission on Civil Rights, 1979, p. 669)

Teachers must be aware of the distinctive problems and conditions faced by Asian-American students. The black hair, dark eyes, tawny tan (some anthropologists call it yellow) skin, and distinctive facial characteristics make Asian-Americans as easy to identify as any of the racial groups in America.

Instructors need to understand the subtle, yet consistent, traces of prejudice faced by Asian-American students. Native-born Asian-Americans report being complimented on their use of English, even though many of these students know no other language. Many Asian-American students report they feel pressure to behave in class because they are so easily identified. But while Asian-Americans are quite easy to identify and classify on an individual basis, scant attention has been paid to these students as a group in educational literature.

FIRST-GENERATION IMMIGRANT STUDENTS

Being a first-generation immigrant in an isolated setting is clearly the most difficult situation for a new student. According to the census of 1980, about 59 percent of Asian-Americans are foreign born (Chan & Kitano, 1986). Often, students must learn the language on their own while attending to the subject matter of the class. Although students from many other countries study English as a regular part of their education, most foreign-born Asian students have not spoken English and are not able to use the language effectively.

A gifted student, who was learning English as he went through my junior high science class, suggested that I provide as much reading material as possible because most Japanese-Americans have studied English in school and are more comfortable with the written form of the language.

Immigrant parents have the often well-earned reputation of being individuals with whom it is difficult to communicate. This situation provides the potential for problems on either end of the special education continuum—gifted or remedial. Many of these parents also are so eager for their children to succeed that no extra program will be refused whether or not the student is ready for the work. On the other hand, parents from households where little or no English is spoken often misinterpret the purposes of testing and refuse to give permission, believing that special programming of any sort represents a weakness in the student and reflects badly on the family.

NATIVE-BORN ASIAN-AMERICANS

While facility with English varies substantially among ethnic groups included in the general category of native-born Asian-Americans, these students generally are more fluent in spoken, than in written, English because they learned the language in conversation as they played with other children. In fact, the student may be the primary communication conduit for the parents who speak little or no English.

Native-born Asian-American students often are extremely academically oriented. Some educators, parents, and students credit "Oriental discipline" or "family pride" as motivating factors. Whatever the reason, Asian-American students seem to work harder at school than their classmates.

SPECIAL EDUCATION STUDENTS

Language difficulties make identification of any special education student, gifted or remedial, difficult at best. Standardized testing, though sometimes controversial (even in cases of native-born minority students), provides results that are even more questionable when used with students from different cultures.

On the other hand, Asian-American students who are handicapped may not be identified as learning disabled or educable mentally retarded because their difficulties are mistakenly attributed to language problems.

Because testing is often inadequate, misplacement in special education programs can occur at both ends (gifted and remedial) of the range of exceptional students. Teachers may incorrectly identify immigrant students as gifted because of their superior work habits and attitudes. The statistical overrepresentation of Asian-Americans in programs for the gifted and talented (Chan & Kitano, 1986) may be due to inaccurate assessment, and many students who are not gifted are experiencing frustration from being in programs for the gifted.

CULTURAL CONSIDERATIONS

Some sociologists suggest that people who emigrate to the United States will lose their cultural identities and adopt that of the most dominant existing culture. Japanese-Americans who grew up in the era of World War II are particularly careful to "fully Americanize" their children in the hope that these children will be able to avoid the racial problems faced by their parents.

Because Asian cultures are often non-Christian, students may have to make significant adjustments to accommodate both ethnic heritage and social acceptance. Gifted students may feel this conflict more acutely than other students of a similar cultural background because of their enhanced understanding and reflection.

Accommodation of cultural differences also has important implications in teaching exceptional Asian-American students. For example, Asian-American students might not look directly at the teacher in a culturally learned show of respect. The teacher might perceive this as a lack of confidence in abilities or an uncooperative attitude.

As role models for Asian immigrants, teachers must take special care, because insular family structures may allow for little or no adult contact outside the family. Many Asian-American students, both first-generation immigrants and native-born Asian-Americans, point to favorite teachers as the most significant role models in their lives.

ASIAN-AMERICANS AND THE FIELDS OF MATHEMATICS AND SCIENCE

Asian-American students report that they are expected to perform well in science and mathematics because of their ethnic appearance. This situation is similar to having an outstanding older sibling precede you through school, except in this case the big brother or big sister is the generic reputation of Asian students. At American universities and colleges, non-Asian-American students have been known to transfer out of those mathematics or technical course sections with high numbers of Asian-American students enrolled because of a fear that the grading "curve" will be higher in that section than in others. First-generation immigrants may be most comfortable in the mathematics, science, and technical fields, but gifted Asian-Americans report frustration at being channeled automatically in those directions.

While their highly regarded work ethic makes Asian-Americans models of successful students, undue concentration on this aspect of education may serve to hinder the development of a truly gifted student. Educators need to be aware that traditional enrichment activities for the gifted student, particularly those centered on mathematics or science, may not be the most beneficial to gifted Asian-American students and should not be the sole focus of such programs. Kitano (1986) suggests that while gifted Asian-American students would benefit from the same teaching strategies used with any other gifted students, "an environment conducive to creative or divergent thinking and selected techniques for developing creative potential" (p. 56) should be used to counterbalance cultural influences.

RECOMMENDATIONS FOR EDUCATORS

Asian-American students require careful and sensitive handling on an individual basis. In addition to being aware of and avoiding the persistent, albeit often unintentional, discriminatory gestures faced by Asian-American students in their classrooms, teachers need to attend carefully to several points when dealing with these students: (a) whether or not the student has been raised primarily in America, (b) consideration of the student's English language background, (c) examination of the Asian-American student's reputation for exemplary work and any attendant pressures and possible misinterpretations, (d) the bias of the mathematics and science prowess, and (e) cultural and social role modeling.

As Asian-American students continue to be successful and gain greater recognition, more academic attention will come their way. Today, awareness that Asian-Americans are significant contributors to the success story of American education is increasing. Funding must be found for preparation of intercultural programs designed to increase the classroom teacher's awareness of this growing population. To serve Asian-American students most effectively, teachers must have a level of consciousness that matches their awareness of the concerns of Blacks and Hispanics. Solomon (1985) suggests that teachers analyze their classrooms for nonpluralistic attitudes and select goals and strategies that will "promote intercultural standards, understanding, and cooperation that grow out of a general appreciation and respect for human differences." Institutions that provide for training of teachers would seem to be the most appropriate agencies to provide instruction in the area of human differences for both prospective and active educators. The benefits of such instruction would accrue not just to Asian-Americans or other minority groups but to our entire society.

29

Administrative Implications in Developing Programs for Gifted Asian-American Students

Paul D. Larson, Ph.D.
Steamboat Springs Public Schools,
Colorado

What administrative implications are suggested in the chapters on gifted Asian-American students? As pointed out, gifted Asian-American students constitute a variety of individuals and specific groups from diverse backgrounds. Probably as many intra-group differences exist among these students as intergroup differences. The combination of such distinct cultural and ethnic groups appears to be artificial. Asian-American heterogeneity is particularly important in administrative planning. Combining Asian-Americans into one composite group has the potential to cover up individual groups, thus making the estimation of educational progress of Asian-Americans generally a rather inaccurate activity. Therefore, one administrative implication follows: Educational planning should be conducted individually for each Asian-American group and/or specific student.

A general theme or trend throughout the chapters is a lack of consensus as to what provisions should be made for the education of gifted Asian-American children. I believe that programming should not be ''categorical''; that is, we need to look at the unique needs of all gifted Asian-American children. At times, a general reluctance to support special provisions for the education of gifted students exists due to categorization and definitions of what constitutes giftedness in children. Thus, a second administrative implication follows: Strong management practices are needed and should include the following.

- Review of existing practices, with an assessment of immediate and long-range goals
- Planned procedure for screening and identification using multiple data

- Tailored program (kindergarten through grade 12) with appropriate curricular accommodations
- Designated program staff
- Planned district-wide staff development program
- Communication procedure for disseminating information
- Planned procedure for program evaluation

Wong and Wong identify two traits common to gifted Asian-American children—academic underachievement and low self-esteem. The inclusion of these traits is questionable and suggests that administrators should review the parameters of inclusion in their programs. The appropriate focus for self-esteem issues is the counseling component within the program. Further, I question whether these traits are characteristic of this gifted population.

Several special administrative considerations should be mentioned. Providing for basic skills improvement for gifted Asian-American pupils who may be underachieving or lacking certain basic skills is essential. After reviewing and analyzing the chapters in this section, I have concluded that a strong counseling program for Asian-American students with specific social and/or emotional needs is a critical program component.

I find a dichotomy of thought between Wong and Wong's major introductory premises and their statement, ''Parents do not view themselves as primary and valuable role models in their child's education.'' The other contributing authors tend to stress parental involvement as being extremely positive. I make the following administrative recommendation: Differentiate between parent role at school and parent role at home. Family values concerning home and school need to be known by educators.

I found Gallagher's first consideration falling short procedurally when she suggested that awareness of the history of oppression would help educators develop guidelines for the future. Awareness is too nebulous to give direction or structure to the planning phase. The related administrative implication follows: Actions need to go beyond the awareness level. A synthesis and evaluation of issues is needed to offer guidelines for the future.

The question of whether studying bilingual and bicultural gifted Asian-American children will offer insight and benefits for all children as stated by Chen is at best a weak programming rationale. Such research rarely produces definitive findings or results that change existing practices. The administrative implication for bilingual populations is: Review all children on an individual language and cultural basis.

A review of the recommendations contained in the book, *Educating Able Learners* (Cox, Daniel, & Boston, 1985), is most appropriate. As stated therein, many recommendations have implications for all learners; ''Insofar as these practices allow for more individualization, they will enable us to do a better job with all students'' (p. 152).

Administrative implications also include providing a program for gifted Asian-American students that includes an awareness of and commitment to changing current practices to make accommodations for the individual learner. That is, how is the issue of acceleration versus enrichment addressed? Does a balance between academic emphasis and affective education exist?

Regular classroom teachers need to have specific training and inservice regarding the unique characteristics and qualities of gifted Asian-American students. This inservice can provide support to the regular classroom teacher who is providing individual programming. Teachers also need to understand and make adaptations within the classroom for individual learning styles and to use a variety of teaching/learning models. Understanding how children learn is important in planning educational methodology and choosing materials, because children's learning styles will dictate how they approach tasks. All children come to school with preferred learning styles and those styles may be culturally related. Identification of culture-related learning styles provides a basis for developing curriculum materials that meet the needs of gifted Asian-American children.

Certainly the issue of creativity and its relationship to other factors for the identification of students for programs for the gifted and talented should be addressed. Renzulli's (1977) model indicates gifted individuals possess high task commitment, creativity, and above-average intelligence. If this is the case, one administrative implication follows: Education of gifted individuals should include development of all three characteristics in each individual. However, investigations of creativity lead to conflicting predictions about the creative abilities of Asian-American students. Based on my experience and reading, I believe that creative children come from less inhibited, less dependable, and less structured family environments that encourage diversity and risk taking. Achieving children, in contrast, have more authoritarian families that encourage conformity and minimize risk taking. When these findings are compared to Asian-American child-rearing practices, one can conclude that Asian-American families may be more likely to foster academic achievement than creativity. This has major administrative implications for providing programs that foster creativity and affective development of gifted Asian-American students.

Teaching strategies generally recommended for gifted students can be used appropriately with gifted Asian-American students. These students usually are taught the values of correctness and conformity within the family structure. Asian-American pupils may be most comfortable performing tasks that require convergent thinking; that is, solving problems with a single correct answer. Gifted Asian-American students may experience difficulty when performing tasks that require divergent thinking or solving problems that have a wide variety of acceptable responses. Consequently, teachers need to provide an atmosphere for Asian-American students that supports and encourages divergent thinking while also providing for emotional needs relating to risk taking and creativity. Gifted Asian-American children may demonstrate high ability in task commitment but need support for development of creativity.

Budgetary issues dictate a further administrative implication. The development of an interest, identified need, and commitment by those with decision-making authority is of utmost necessity. This commitment, in turn, can result in monetary support for program development. The administrative implication: A balance should be struck between funding programs for gifted and talented students and the support for other programs within school districts.

Identifying special considerations for any specific group and stating subsequent administrative implications can result in undesirable singling out of, in this case, gifted Asian-American students. The authors in this section refer indirectly to what possibly may be the major administrative implication in providing appropriate programs for the gifted. Thomas Jefferson once stated that nothing is so unequal as the equal treatment of unequals. Individualized student programming, whatever the population, is the true goal of, and direction for, education of gifted students.

30

Summary of Asian-American Section

C. June Maker, Ph.D.
Shirley W. Schiever, Ph.D.
University of Arizona

GENERAL STATEMENTS

Underlying themes and principles in the writing of authors in this section are identified and discussed. The major focus of this section is on analysis of similarities and differences among the concepts presented.

1. *The category of people labeled Asian or Asian-American varies widely in culture, language, place of birth, age, level of acculturation, social class, immigration experience, and educational background.*

Many of these differences were introduced at the beginning of the section, and they will not be repeated here. Five factors are viewed as important by the authors because of their direct and strong influence in the educational process. Both Chen and Kitano discuss how these factors can influence the process of identification. For example, if students learned English in another country, they cannot be expected to have the same level of proficiency as those who have studied English in this country for the same length of time. Gallagher and Tanaka review the historical context of Asians in this country, and discuss how educators should conceptualize the goals for programs for the gifted based on the differences in the Asian population. Because of the noted differences in Asians, Wong and Wong state that their comments can be generalized only to the population of first-generation Cantonese-speaking school children of Chinese descent. However, the editors note that the four values they discuss as being common to their specific populations also are values noted by Hasegawa, Woo, Chen, Gallagher, and Tanaka. Based on these similarities, we would suggest that Wong and Wong's recommendations have wide applicability to Asian-American children. Certainly teachers must determine whether these common values apply to individual students, rather than assume automatically that they do. At the administrative level, Larson recommends planning for Asian-Americans (and all students) on an individual rather than group basis.

In her chapter, Woo focuses on her personal traits and how they interacted with her educational experience and influenced her career development. Hasegawa provides an excellent review of the general influences such traits can have on the educational process—including classroom instruction, program focus, counseling needs, and identification.

2. *Asians have become stereotyped as the "model minority" because they have achieved high levels of success in the American educational system. This perception has both positive and negative implications.*

Several authors call attention to articles in popular journals and newspapers in which the success of Asians in school is recognized. They report (a) overrepresentation of Asians in programs for gifted students; (b) underrepresentation of students in special education programs; and (c) overrepresentation in higher education programs, especially those in some of the most prestigious academic institutions in this country. Gallagher demonstrates how this "stereotype" perception of Asians as the model minority has serious implications for the education of gifted Asian-American students in her listing of five results.

First, like Kitano and Hasegawa, Gallagher states that this stereotype leads to an ignoring of the many differences among Asian populations (Kitano and Chen); and some subgroups of Asians are seriously underrepresented in programs for the gifted and institutions of higher learning (Kitano).

A second result of the stereotype discussed by Gallagher, Wong and Wong, and Tanaka is that it ignores the fact that many Asian communities are losing their language and their distinctiveness as a cultural group.

Third, as Gallagher states, this image "oversimplifies the issue of academic success." Hasegawa, Woo, Chen, and Kitano acknowledge the strengths and interests of many Asians in mathematics, science, and other technical areas, but point to the fact that many Asian-American students have weaknesses in areas such as the humanities and others in which verbal communication abilities are necessary. Because of the child-rearing practices of some Asian families, the recitation/memorization style of some Asian school systems, and the values placed on authority and order, many Asian students also lack creativity and innovativeness. Woo notes that she personified the model minority years before the term became commonplace; that she worked hard and "took few risks;" and that she has known "many Asian-American physicians and engineers who are frustrated actors, writers, and inventors"—all examples of the stereotype in action. Hasegawa also suggests that the statistical overrepresentation of Asian-Americans in programs for the gifted may be due to teachers equating hard work and respect for the teacher's authority with giftedness, and may result in many nongifted students becoming frustrated with the academic pressure of "keeping up" in classes for which they are not qualified. In Tanaka's chapter, an Asian youth notes that many "Asian-American students become like robots. . . . students delve no farther than necessary for the assignment because they must go on to the next subject."

Fourth, Gallagher states that the model minority stereotype implies that Asian-Americans experience few adjustment problems in society, and lists many problems of Asians as do Hasegawa, Chen, Wong and Wong, Tanaka, and Kitano. Woo expresses regret for the amount of energy she "wasted" in denying her cultural identity, a problem also noted by others. Hasegawa provides many examples of discrimination experienced by Asian-American students and notes that the sensitivity of gifted students would cause them to notice this discrimination and need counseling or at least special assistance from teachers to deal with their feelings.

Finally, a result of the stereotype is to suggest that Asian-Americans should continue to be silent in political arenas. Indeed, many of the authors in this section, themselves Asian, have made special attempts to justify their concern about this population. Every Asian author in this section has in some way addressed the negative implications of the model minority stereotype.

3. *Overreliance on standardized tests in identification of gifted Asian-Americans may result in overlooking children who need and can benefit from special programs, especially those from low socioeconomic status families and recent immigrants.*

Chen recognizes that the incidence of giftedness, when using traditional achievement tests, is higher in the Asian population than normally would be expected, even in disadvantaged populations. She continues to advocate the use of nontraditional and nontest measures to supplement the use of tests. Kitano notes that the rationale for use of alternative measures includes the fact that traditional measures are unlikely to be appropriate for all individuals labeled Asian-Americans, and calls attention to the fact that many subgroups of Asians are underrepresented in programs for gifted students. Tanaka states that the majority of Asian students in her school district have been identified in the "high achievement" category. Kitano provides corroboration for this statement by noting that assessment procedures designed to identify high achievers are consistent with Asians' emphasis on educational attainment and obedience to authority and, in fact, may be biased in favor of Asians. She also notes that overidentification is better than underidentification, but Hasegawa's caution that some students may be experiencing undue pressure because of their inappropriate placement is important to note. Woo's observation that her parents impressed on her the importance of earning the best grades because achieving less would bring shame on the family, and her further observation that "shame was and is a guiding influence in most Asian cultures," provide support for Hasegawa's caution.

Because many people have contact with Asians who have been in this country for many years, and many of these individuals have never spoken a language other than English, the fact that certain subgroups of Asians speak little or no English is a surprise to many educators (Hasegawa). Because of the influence of English proficiency on test results, and because of the various languages spoken by Asians, limited English proficient (LEP) students present a special problem. To solve the problem of identifying LEP students, Chen proposes (a) a focus on processes and learning rate rather than the attainment of culture-specific factual information; (b) use of language proficiency, either in a child's native tongue or English, not as a determinant of giftedness but as a factor to consider; and (c) more weight given to nonverbal abilities than verbal abilities. Kitano agrees that assessment of processes and rate of progress are important means for identifying LEP Asian-American students who are gifted, but cautions that the use of nonverbal measures and criteria would be ineffective in identifying verbally gifted students. She recommends administration of a verbal test in the child's first language, and using interpreter/translators. Larson stresses the need to review all students on an individual language and cultural basis.

All authors who discuss identification recommend that standardized tests be included in the process, but suggest that the results of these tests be supplemented with other data. Chen provides excellent recommendations for teachers to use when observing students to determine their abilities. Kitano agrees with the use of process- and curriculum-based assessment, but cautions that we must be aware of the learning styles and culture—specific traits of students in this context as well—and make certain that observations are made in appropriate learning situations.

In this section, the issue seems not to be whether to use standardized tests, but how to use them and which ones are more appropriate. Chen recommends, and Kitano agrees, that tests used with this population be chosen carefully. Chen also provides excellent recommendations for analyzing subtest patterns, comparing performance on different types of tests (such as learning potential and achievement), and interpreting test results in the context of cultural traits of Asians.

Finally, Chen, Kitano, Tanaka, and Hasegawa recommend strongly that the results of tests and assessments be "weighed in the context of the whole picture of the student" (Chen). Kitano reminds us that high achievement motivation and desire to perform well to meet parental expectations may create anxiety and internal pressure in the testing situation. All four authors discuss the cultural influences on Asian-American children's performance on tests of creativity. Chen provides an extensive discussion and excellent guidelines for interpreting scores based on her assumption that "test scores should be outweighed by observational data that are collected on a daily basis."

4. *An important goal of a program for gifted Asian-American students is development of biculturalism, especially "comfort" with being different.*

Several authors emphasized the fact that Asian-American students often are not comfortable with the fact that they are different from mainstream culture students, and gave examples of students denying their cultural heritage to appear like others (Woo, Hasegawa, Tanaka). To help combat this problem, a recommendation made by Kaplan, Woo, Tanaka, Wong and Wong, and Hasegawa is that students study the similarities and differences among a variety of cultures.

Hasegawa and Kaplan both recommend the development of a multicultural classroom. Hasegawa presents words of caution about "tread[ing] carefully the line between education and indoctrination," and suggests that teachers select goals that promote intercultural standards and evolve from a general respect for human differences. Kaplan notes the importance of education with a multicultural focus, but takes a different perspective. She advocates that educators relate knowledge about the nature of giftedness to an understanding of cultural diversity as a way to help students understand differences. Emphasizing that students have similarities because of their giftedness, but differences because of their cultural backgrounds, helps students to be more comfortable with their differences.

Tanaka, and Wong and Wong, emphasize the importance of acceptance of themselves and development of individuality as elements necessary for the success of Asian-American students. Differences, Tanaka notes, can be sources of personal and intellectual strength. Wong and Wong note that parents of Chinese children (and many other Asian children) view schooling as a means for self-advancement in American society. If it is a means for advancement, and advancement is important, Asian-American students will value each day in school and not waste any opportunities to learn skills that will be useful to them. To accomplish goals so important in the education of gifted Asian-Americans, Larson states that teachers in regular classrooms need extensive inservice training to help them go beyond an awareness level and develop strategies for accommodating cultural differences in learning styles and other traits.

Gallagher, Tanaka, and Wong and Wong focus on the need to develop not only biculturalism but also bilingualism. These authors recommend a parent involvement program in which parents of Asian-American students are reminded of the values of bilingualism and encouraged to use their strengths in becoming educational role models for their children. Gallagher and Tanaka agree that bilingualism (and, by implication, biculturalism) is important for all people because multilingualism is important in developing a more harmonious global society.

5. *Even though Asian-American students have many strengths and have been successful in school, they also have weaknesses that must be developed so they can realize their potential in future careers.*

Unlike the authors in other sections, most writers in this section focused on the development of what are perceived as weaknesses, rather than strengths, of gifted Asian-American students. Exceptions to that statement are Wong and Wong, who state that the characteristics they list could be perceived as either strengths or weaknesses, and that the effective teacher "expands on strengths and shores up weaknesses using culture-specific factors to determine eclectic teaching strategies." Kaplan recommends that differences be regarded as positive rather than negative attributes; Chen closes her chapter by suggesting that future research should focus on determining what factors enable some Asians to overcome barriers to success that other minorities face, so that preventive or remedial strategies can be developed for those not yet successful. Her recommendation is similar in philosophy to Larson's suggestion that educators use Renzulli's definition of giftedness as a guide, and that three clusters of behavior described as components (e.g., ability, creativity, task commitment) be developed in all gifted students to enable them to be successful.

Wong and Wong emphasize Asian students' disposition toward structure and defined limits, self-discipline, and self-motivation, traits that can be very important in a program for gifted students. Tanaka begins her discussion of strategies to meet the educational needs of Asian-American students with a list of limiting culturally supported attitudes Asian children may bring to the learning situation. Following this scenario are many excellent suggestions for developing the missing dimensions. Gallagher takes a similar approach and recommends that verbal competency in both English and another language be included in the curriculum because second and third generations of Asian-Americans are not only losing the home language, but also failing to become truly proficient in English. Woo agrees with Gallagher's analysis and discusses it from her own perspective as one who, unlike many Asians, possesses strong writing skills (developed because writing became a safe way to express private thoughts). However, her oral communication skills were lacking. She notes that her elementary and high school teachers allowed her to "hide behind" her writing skills, but in college classes where participation in class discussions was necessary, she faced many problems. Gallagher supports the fact that many Asians have the same difficulties by citing statistics about the avoidance of classes where discussions are held.

Hasegawa, like Kaplan, states that Asians' highly regarded work ethic makes them models of successful students; but undue emphasis on this aspect of education may hinder the development of a truly gifted student. He, like Woo, notes educators are so focused on the successful traits of Asian-American students that they "lose track" of the "insufficiencies" in other areas of life. He recommends "relaxation from academic pressures" to allow creative talents to develop, a suggestion similar to that of Woo, when she notes that Asians work hard, but fail to take risks.

The authors in this section seem to be reacting again to the negative effects of the "model minority" stereotype, and focusing on the weaknesses of Asian-American students because much attention has been paid to their strengths in the popular literature. They are attempting to counterbalance this image rather than suggesting a total focus on student weaknesses. They seem to believe that educators are already doing a good job of developing the strengths of most Asian-American students.

6. *Counseling and affective development are essential aspects of an effective program for gifted Asian-American students.*

All authors who address programming emphasize the need for affective components, either counseling outside the classroom or directing attention to affective needs within the classroom. All authors list affective needs that must be addressed. Techniques explained and advocated for addressing these affective needs range from a focus on multicultural awareness through the actual content of instruction (Kaplan, Woo, Hasegawa), to specific teaching strategies that recognize and build on the different learning styles of Asian-American students (Kitano, Hasegawa, Kaplan, Tanaka, Wong and Wong), to teaching and counseling techniques designed to address specific needs (Gallagher, Wong and Wong).

OTHER IMPORTANT IDEAS

Although no consensus was present regarding certain other ideas, several points were made that deserve mention as well as analysis. These ideas are presented briefly below.

Family Involvement

Not as much emphasis was placed in this section as in others on the need to involve families in the educational process for gifted Asian-American students, although Chen and Kitano note that parents should be asked to supply information about their children's abilities. Only Wong and Wong provide guidelines for parent involvement. Based on their discussion, Larson recommends that educators differentiate between parent role at home and parent role at school. A program such as the one described by Wong and Wong would have been of great benefit to Woo, who notes that she had no support from her family in her choice of a career as a writer.

Role Models, Mentors, and Sponsors

In three of the chapters, authors note the need for role models, mentors, or sponsors. Wong and Wong emphasize the need for parents to be role models for their children, while others focus more on the teacher as a role model and sponsor. Woo states that she was fortunate to have a gifted journalism teacher (who was Japanese), who encouraged her to develop her writing talent. Tanaka notes the need for mentors or sponsors who "encourage and protect their rights when they are frustrated, discouraged, or abused," and notes that mentors fulfill needs different from those met by parents. Finally, Hasegawa notes that teachers must exercise care in their roles as models because teachers often are the only adult contacts Asian-American children have outside the family structure.

Cooperative Learning

Three authors discussed the use of cooperative learning techniques. Kitano recognized the cooperative learning styles of some Pacific Islanders as important to accommodate when using a curriculum-based approach to identification of giftedness. Tanaka recommends using teams or small groups as advocated by Torrance, and Wong and Wong described cooperative learning with three to five students in a heterogeneous group as an important learning strategy for gifted Asian-American students.

Gifted Girls

Interestingly enough, only one author discussed gifted girls. Tanaka mentions briefly that one of the "limiting, culturally supported attitudes" Asian-American students may bring to the learning situation is that the male is the "more desirable and dominant sex."

IN CONCLUSION

In this section, authors relate a common concern that the popular image of Asians as the "model minority" and successful in school has negative implications for the education of gifted Asian-American students. Because they are overrepresented in programs for gifted students as a group, educators often fail to recognize that many Asians who may be gifted are not being identified—particularly those from low socioeconomic status communities, those from certain subgroups, and those with abilities in other areas besides science and mathematics. Even though the cultural and family values of Asians contribute to their achievement in academic areas, these same attitudes may interfere with development in some other, very important areas. To be effective in providing programs to meet the needs of this minority, we must develop an awareness of the limiting attitudes of educators, families, and students, and give students the tools necessary to overcome these limits so they can become successful, contributing members of society. All authors recognize that most, if not all, of these strategies would be beneficial to all children, regardless of giftedness, talent, or cultural background.

Part IV

BLACKS

BLACK-AMERICANS

The Black population can be defined as a group only by two common elements: (a) physical features (skin color and hair texture); and (b) a common heritage of denied opportunities. Beyond these commonalities, however, environmental factors have resulted in subgroups of the Black population that show as great a variance among groups as between Blacks and other groups.

The cultural legacy of Blacks is unique; the circumstances of their arrival in this country wrenched from them their connection to known origins and specific ancestors in other lands. Other immigrants voluntarily have sacrificed established roots and traditions for a perceived value to be gained; the Black slaves were sacrificed involuntarily for the perceived good of the dominant class of American society. Since the end of slavery, Blacks have strived to belong and to establish cultural rootedness; however, the fragile connections this ethnic group has established are endangered by the effects of 300 years of racism.

Perhaps nowhere are the results of the above factors more apparent than in programs for gifted students. A survey conducted by the Office of Civil Rights (DBS Corporation, 1982) revealed that while Blacks accounted for 20.1 percent of total school enrollment, they only accounted for 11.1 percent of enrollment in programs for the gifted and talented.

Blacks are one of the few minority populations in the United States whose percentage in the population is not dramatically increasing. After declining from 1790 to 1950, the percentage of Blacks in this country is slowly increasing with a projected net increase of 1.5 percent by 1990. Blacks are young, with a median age of 26.3, compared to 32.2 for Anglo-Americans and 31.3 for the total U.S. population. This young population also is a poor one, with 35.7 percent of Black families below the poverty level, compared with 15.2 percent of all families in the United States (U.S. Department of Commerce, 1986).

DISTINCTIVENESS OF THE BLACK SITUATION

The uniqueness of the Black population in this country was demonstrated forcefully to the editors of this volume as they wrote this introductory section. Examination of the chapters on gifted Black students revealed a distinct difference when compared to other sections; none of the chapters allude to cultural values specific to and typical of Blacks. After some reflection and discussion, the decision was made to explore (briefly) the phenomenon of the missing cultural values. Reexamining the chapters with a different focus provided a possible explanation that may help the reader to make implications and to do some insightful thinking.

The original Black people in the United States were brought here against their will. Family and community units were destroyed, and people from different tribes and regions were distributed almost randomly throughout the slave states. Once situated, the Blacks were locked into a brutal system that did not allow for any lingering cultural values or customs to be remembered or observed, much less developed or enhanced. Further, slavery, as practiced in Africa and the New World, prohibited the emergence of a newly developing cultural identity. The essential difference between New World slavery and that of ancient Greece and Rome was the dehumanization of the laborer to a commodity (Low & Clift, 1981). This dehumanization also allowed and/or encouraged only those ethnic strengths and practices found to be entertaining, such as Black music and folklore. Minority populations in the United States have experienced discrimination and subjugation throughout our history, but certainly no group other than Blacks has been subjected to events and situations that, in effect, destroy *immediately* its entire cultural heritage. The internment of the Japanese in this country during World War II was traumatic and shattering, but did not destroy cultural identity. American Indians have been uprooted and moved, and their children taken from them to be educated in alien ways, but even this uprooting did not destroy immediately their cultural heritage, as did the kidnapping, enslavement, and dehumanization of Black Africans in the United States.

Baldwin (Chapter 33) alludes to the fragile Black "cultural rootedness" and the never-ending pursuit to belong. The implication may be that having had their original cultural value system annihilated, Blacks reach out to the values of the dominant society as they struggle to develop their own unique cultural identity. The Catch-22 is that the dominant class is still for the most part reluctant to allow Blacks to enter the mainstream and thus fully participate in mainstream life and values.

Cohen's (Chapter 34) premise is that the basic issue is not racial (Black), but socioeconomic (poverty). Frasier's (Chapter 31) classification of Black family types contains socioeconomic status as a primary factor, and Baldwin (Chapter 33) includes socioeconomic status as one of the three causal and interacting variables that affect students. Cronbach (1977) believes that with many variables, social class (socioeconomic status) makes a far greater difference than ethnicity; and Rokeach (1973) found that when social class is equated, Black-White differences in values disappear. While socioeconomic factors are recognized widely as contributing to school achievement and societal power, the Black population may be the only group struggling to attain upward mobility without the unifying and empowering stability offered by an established cultural identity.

Because the culture of poverty is such a pervasive influence on the development and school behavior of a child, the editors developed Table IV-1 in an attempt to show how the absolute aspects of giftedness, when filtered through the cultural values typical of low socioeconomic status homes, may result in behaviors different from the mainstream norm. This is not an attempt to lump all Black families in one (low socioeconomic status) group, but merely to recognize the influence of this factor on the behavior of *many* children. (See Table IV-1.) In fact, this table can be useful as a supplement to those offered in other introductory sections because it shows differences among students within a particular cultural group.

IN CONCLUSION

Authors of the chapters in the section on Blacks do not indicate the presence of unique cultural influences on the gifted Black child. Rather, evidence indicates that poverty and discrimination continue to hinder the development of a strong cultural

Table IV-1 Characteristics of Giftedness and Cultural Values of Low Socioeconomic Status Groups, and the Behaviors Resulting from Their Interactive Influence

Absolute Aspects of Giftedness	Cultural Values Generally Characteristic of Low Socioeconomic Status Groups (Cronbach, 1977)	Behavioral Differences
Flexible thought processes	Conformity, mastery of minimum academic essentials	Acting out
Accelerated pace of thought processes	Physical punishment, blunt orders rather than discussion	Manipulative behavior, scapegoating
Unusual sensitivity to the expectations and feelings of others	Parental pressure conduct oriented, rather than task oriented	Compliant behavior, lack of academic achievement
Leadership	Immediate or short-term gratification	Leadership in street gangs, delinquency
Persistent, goal-directed behavior	Survival in circumstances	"Streetwiseness," community-based entrepreneurship

identity. Poverty has its own insidious effects on children's behavior, and its influence on Black and other students must be remembered. As concerned educators, our task is (a) to conceptualize the differentness of Black people when compared to other minority groups; (b) to become aware of the effects of poverty and discrimination; and (c) to act on the suggestions of the authors in this section so that Black people may take their rightful place in society. Personal, professional, and societal ethics and justice require no less.

31

Identification of Gifted Black Students: Developing New Perspectives

Mary M. Frasier, Ph.D.
University of Georgia

"Nature never rhymes her children, nor makes two men alike."
—Ralph Waldo Emerson

Any answer to the question, "Who are gifted Black students and how are they identified?" must be presented against a background of deliberations on definitions of giftedness. Definitions of the gifted and giftedness abound. For example, gifted (and/or giftedness) has been defined as indicated below:

- Performance in the upper 1 percent on a test of intelligence (Terman, 1925);
- Demonstrated achievement or the potential ability to perform at a superior level as determined by professionally qualified persons (Marland, 1972);
- Exceptional level of performance based on a combination of above-average ability, task commitment, and creativity (Renzulli, 1978);
- Potential for critically acclaimed performance or exemplary production of ideas in a variety of spheres that enhance the life of humanity (Tannenbaum, 1983);
- Exceptional competence in one or more domains of ability with interests, personality traits, and environment fixing the orientation of the individual toward a particular field of talent, and motivation fixing the intensity of the talent (Gagne, 1985); and
- Superior general abilities, special focused talents, and a special view of self that includes high-level creative achievement or production as attainable (Feldhusen & Hoover, 1986).

Many professionals have stated repeatedly that all the abilities listed above can be found in every ethnic and racial group and at all socioeconomic levels (Clark, 1983; Davis & Rimm, 1985; Gallagher, 1985; Kitano & Kirby, 1986; Marland, 1972). One must, therefore, conclude that definitions of the gifted and giftedness refer to Black students as well as students from other cultural groups.

The number of Black students identified as gifted, however, remains small. Adler (1967) observed that the lowest proportion of children being identified as gifted come from Black, Italian, Mexican-American, and American Indian populations.

What are the factors that account for this underrepresentation of gifted Black students? What have been the results of using procedures and instruments developed to overcome the inhibiting effects of these factors? Do new approaches to identifying the gifted Black student exist that we should consider?

The purposes of this chapter follow: (a) Identify factors that have inhibited our identification of gifted Black students; (b) review research findings and other reports on instruments and procedures designed to increase our ability to identify these students; and (c) provide new perspectives on the problems associated with this identification. The chapter has two parts. In part one, current recommendations for using certain procedures, standardized instruments, and rating scales are reviewed and evaluated according to "best practices" in the identification of gifted students. In part two, components of the Creative Problem Solving (CPS) model are used to generate new perspectives on the identification of gifted Black students.

Best practices are defined as commonly agreed upon principles of identification derived from research and practice. To determine what constituted a best practice I conducted an extensive review of the literature on identification procedures and found the following consistencies.

1. The focus should be on the diversity within gifted populations.
2. The goal should be inclusion, rather than exclusion, of students.
3. Data should be gathered from multiple sources; a single criterion of giftedness should be avoided.
4. Both objective and subjective data should be collected.
5. Professionals and nonprofessionals who represent various areas of expertise and who are knowledgeable about behavioral indicators of giftedness should be involved.
6. Identification of giftedness should occur as early as possible, should consist of a series of steps, and should be continuous.
7. Special attention should be given to the different ways in which children from different cultures manifest behavioral indicators of giftedness.
8. Decisionmaking should be delayed until all pertinent data on a student have been reviewed.
9. Data collected during the identification process should be used in determining curriculum.

The topics around which discussions are arranged in this chapter include: (a) a working definition of gifted Black students; (b) screening procedures and use of standardized instruments and test scores; (c) similarities and/or differences in criteria for determining giftedness and instruments and procedures used with Black students and students from mainstream populations; and (d) guidelines for developing new perspectives for identification. The focus is on intellectually gifted Black students.

PART I: THE CURRENT STATE OF AFFAIRS

Working Definition

Gifted people are present in all racial, ethnic, and socioeconomic groups. Therefore, a logical conclusion is that the definition of gifted (and giftedness) refers to all students. Several factors hinder the identification of Black students.

- Definitions of giftedness that reflect middle-class, majority-culture values and perceptions (Maker, 1983);
- Standardized tests that do not reflect the exceptional abilities of minority students (Davis & Rimm, 1985; Kitano & Kirby, 1986; MacMillan, 1982; Richert, Alvino, & McDonnel, 1982);
- Low referral rates for assessment of giftedness from parents and teachers (Clark, 1983; Davis & Rimm, 1985; Kitano & Kirby, 1986);
- Low socioeconomic status causing differences in environmental opportunities that enhance intellectual achievement (Clark, 1983; Gallagher, 1985; Kitano & Kirby, 1986; Maker, 1983); and
- Cultural and class differences in the manifestation of behaviors indicative of giftedness (Baldwin, 1985a; Clark, 1983; Davis & Rimm, 1985; Frierson, 1965; Gay, 1978; Kitano & Kirby, 1986; Torrance, 1977).

Screening Procedures

Nominations

Entrance into programs for the gifted traditionally begins with some method for screening a target population. Nominations by teachers continue to be the first step in identifying students to participate in programs for the gifted, even though reliance on teacher nominations may severely penalize minority children. Nominations should be sought from multiple sources within and outside the school (Clark, 1983; Davis & Rimm, 1985; Kitano & Kirby, 1986).

Nominations from community leaders (Davis, 1978), peers (Blackshear, 1979), and self, especially through the use of biographical inventories (Taylor & Ellison, 1983), exemplify best practices because they represent a way to collect data from multiple sources.

Checklists and Rating Scales

Culturally different children may not always demonstrate their high abilities in ways that are typical for children from majority cultures (Baldwin, 1985a; Gay, 1978; Kitano & Kirby, 1986; Passow, 1981). Thus, the use of checklists and rating scales designed to assess potential based on culture-specific behavioral indicators is recommended.

Gay (1978) devised a checklist to evaluate different manifestations of giftedness in Black children. For example, a typical descriptor of gifted children, "interest and ability in perceiving relationships" was modified: "seeks structure and organization in required tasks; may be slow to motivate in abstract thinking" (Gay, 1978, p. 354).

Descriptors of exceptional mental ability in children who were experiencing the effects of cultural diversity, socioeconomic deprivation, and geographic isolation compiled by Baldwin (1985) included "physical resiliency to environmental hardships, language rich in imagery and symbolism, logical reasoning skills, creative ability and social intelligence" (p. 47). The authors suggested that to observe these abilities in potentially gifted minority students, we might look for behavioral indicators, such as a good memory, high tolerance for ambiguity, inventiveness, and revolutionary ideas. These recommendations by Baldwin, Gear, and Lucito, (1978) and Gay (1978) reflect the best practices of being sensitive to the diversity within gifted populations and the difference in manifesting behavioral indicators of giftedness in different cultural groups.

The "Who" and "O" checklists were developed by Hilliard (1976) to screen for giftedness in Black populations. These checklists reflect his view of the synthetic-personal or relational style exhibited by Afro-Americans. This style was represented in his conclusion that Afro-American people

1. tend to view things in their entirety and not in isolated parts,
2. seem to prefer inferential reasoning to deductive or inductive reasoning,
3. appear to focus on people and their activities rather than objects,
4. tend to prefer novelty, personal freedom and distinctiveness,
5. tend to approximate space, number, and time instead of aiming for complete accuracy,
6. have a keen sense of justice and quickly perceive injustice, and
7. in general tend not to be "word" dependent, but are proficient in non-verbal as well as verbal communication. (Hilliard, 1976, p. 36)

The "Who" and "O" checklists are recommended as supplements to traditional assessment procedures.

The Checklist of Creative Positives (CCP) (Torrance, 1977) was developed from Torrance's experiences as an instructor and observer of low-income, primarily Black, children engaging in problem-solving tasks. The 18 areas of the checklist included traits such as ability to improvise with commonplace materials, expression of feelings and emotions, use of expressive speech, humor, and originality of ideas in problem solving.

The checklists by Hilliard (1976) and Torrance (1977) exemplify best practices because they are culture-specific examples of relevant subjective data to be considered in the identification process.

Adaptations of Conventional Models

Fitz-Gibbon (1975) developed a procedure to identify inner-city eighth graders in the top 2 percent in ability on the *Wechsler Intelligence Scale for Children (WISC)*. Several conventional methods and measures were used to screen students to take the *WISC:* (a) Teacher nominations; (b) a conventional group intelligence (IQ) test—the

California Test of Mental Maturity (CTMM), 1963 edition, short form, level 3; (c) a "culture-fair" intelligence test, the *Raven Standard Progressive Matrices (SPM);* and (d) the *California Achievement Tests (CAT),* 1970 edition, level 4, form A, in mathematics and reading. The *Advanced Progressive Matrices (AdvPM,* 1962 edition) measure was added to differentiate more clearly among students who scored in the upper ability range.

Though the method used by Fitz-Gibbon (1975) proved to be both effective (100 percent) and efficient (90 percent), she concluded that an even simpler method could have been used:

1. Screening: Administer the *SPM* to all students as a 30-minute classroom test.
2. Selection: Administer the *AdvPM* to the top 6 percent on the *SPM* and to any student strongly recommended by parents or teachers.
3. Identification: Administer the *WISC* to students whose *AdvPM* scores were in the top half of the sample and to students who were in the top 2 percent on the *SPM.*

The identification procedure developed by Fitz-Gibbon exemplifies best practices, for it illustrates collecting data from multiple sources and emphasizes inclusion and delayed identification until all pertinent data have been gathered and reviewed.

Witty and Jenkins (1934) also demonstrated that some gifted Black students could be located using conventional methods. Using selection methods similar to those used by Terman (1925), they identified 26 superior Negro students in grades 3 to 8. While Witty and Jenkins' study did not particularly support current best practices, it did demonstrate that some gifted Black students can be found even when traditional procedures are used.

Standardized Instruments

Van Tassel-Baska (1986) argued emphatically for the use of standardized tests and against their alleged bias. She noted that the use of the College Board *Scholastic Aptitude Test (SAT)* not only aided in the identification of academically able disadvantaged gifted students, but also created an important talent pool of individuals in need of scholarship assistance to gain educational advantages.

Considerable documentation, however, still exists regarding the inappropriateness of traditional intelligence tests with Blacks (Black, 1963; Bruch, 1975; Davis, Gardner, & Gardner, 1941; Hoffman, 1962; Torrance, 1971; Williams, 1974). Nonetheless, some standardized tests are believed to be appropriate. Each of the instruments described below allows for culturally different manifestations and interpretations of intellectual ability through its design.

Torrance Tests of Creative Thinking (TTCT)

Extensive empirical research on the *TTCT* has revealed little or no difference in performance between Black and Anglo-American students. Though the validity of the

TTCT and other measures of creativity has been questioned (Tannenbaum, 1983), the tests remain widely accepted measures for inclusion in identification procedures to locate gifted Black children.

Kaufman Assessment Battery for Children (K-ABC)

Considerable evidence is accumulating that the *K-ABC,* developed by Kaufman and Kaufman (1983), is fair to minorities. Kaufman (1984) reported that the higher scores achieved by Blacks and other minority groups on the *K-ABC* may be due to the "deemphasis on acquired facts, applied skills, and verbal expression . . . and the inclusion of tasks that tap a broader range of mental functions . . . than is usually associated with IQ tests" (p. 86).

Raven Standard (and Advanced) Progressive Matrices

In school systems where special efforts have been made to locate gifted minority students the *Raven Standard Progressive Matrices* (Raven, 1956) is included frequently as one of the selection devices. Baska (1986a,b) especially has endorsed the *Advanced Progressive Matrices* (Raven, 1962) because of its high correlation with formal IQ measures and because minimum verbal content is needed to understand instructions.

Abbreviated Binet for Disadvantaged Children (ABDA)

Bruch (1971) devised a differentiated scoring plan for the *Stanford-Binet* as a way to identify giftedness among Blacks. Called *ABDA,* it was intended to assess only those abilities of Blacks that coincided with identified strengths on the *Stanford-Binet.*

Stallings' Environmentally Based Screen (SEBS)

This test, developed by Stallings (1972; revised 1975), was designed as a supplementary procedure to identify gifted minority children. The intent of the author was to test children on information from their environment, with which they were familiar. His thesis was that minority children often missed test items because the material was unfamiliar. By allowing the content of a test instrument to be words and concepts that the child had experienced, children would miss an item for the right reason. When a child missed an item with familiar information, one could conclude that the child could not handle the level of reasoning or abstraction necessary to complete the task.

Models as Adjuncts to Identification

A Matrix Model

Matrices have been used as effective models to gather and interpret information from multiple sources. The *Baldwin Identification Matrix (BIM)* (Baldwin, 1984; Baldwin & Wooster, 1977) is recommended frequently as a way to plot results from a variety of objective and subjective identification measures. Though the *BIM* has been criticized for giving equal weight to data from dissimilar sources (Feldhusen, Baska, & Womble, 1981), its effectiveness as a tool for increasing the number of Black students identified for programs for the gifted has been reported in several school districts (Dabney, 1983; Long, 1981; McBeath, Blackshear, & Smart, 1981).

The *BIM* exemplifies a best practice because it allows both objective and subjective data to be collected and used and provides a method for delaying decisionmaking until all pertinent data can be reviewed at one time.

A Culture-specific Model

The *System of Multicultural Pluralistic Assessment (SOMPA)* (Mercer, 1981; Mercer & Lewis, 1978) was designed to be culture specific; that is, the intelligence of each person was evaluated "only in relation to others who come from similar socio-cultural backgrounds and who have had approximately the same opportunity to acquire the knowledge and skills needed to answer questions on an intelligence test designed for an Anglo-American society" (Mercer, 1971, p. 335).

The use of *SOMPA* illustrates best practices by (a) focusing on inclusion regardless of socioeconomic status; (b) following a series of steps that results in a comprehensive assessment of a child; and (c) being sensitive to achievement differences within a population as well as in comparison with others.

A Quota System Model

Kitano and Kirby (1986) suggested that when all students have been screened or identified through an effective referral system, the quota approach helps ensure delivery of special services to talented students from each cultural group. The major problem with the quota system, in their opinion, is that some low-scoring students from one cultural group may eliminate high scorers in another. Further, they noted that children who rank at the top in their group at one school might not be in the top group at another school.

An identification procedure developed by Mitchell (1982) illustrated the use of a modified quota system to increase the number of low-income and culturally different children identified for programs for the gifted. In the model, a series of steps began with nominations solicited from parents, students, teachers, principals, and peers. Then, students were screened through the use of an intelligence test with a recommended cutoff of 110, or an achievement test with a recommended cutoff at the 75th percentile. Finally, teachers rated students on a behavioral checklist developed by Mitchell, who recommended that approximately 10 to 15 percent of the slots available for gifted students be reserved for "low income/culturally different students who survive the 'first cut'" (p. 110). He also recommended that the 10 to 15 percent figure be "raised when school districts had unusually large percentages of low income and/or culturally different children" (p. 116). Mitchell stated that use of this procedure allowed program decisionmakers to be sensitive to racial representations without relying on a pure quota system.

While a quota system does seem to be sensitive to the best practice of inclusion rather than exclusion, some important considerations are not addressed in this system. Identifying children through the use of appropriate procedures does not mean artificially forcing them into a program. The use of a quota system supports the concept that *one* correct standard exists by which *all* children capable of performance at a gifted level should be measured. Finally, by implication, use of a quota system suggests that certain gifted children may be "second-class gifted."

An Identification and Instructional Model

Davis and Rimm (1985) noted that "reducing basic skills deficits of gifted disadvantaged youngsters is indeed an important step, but one that is preliminary to identifying these children and providing programs for them" (p. 258). Exemplary of such an approach is the Program of Assessment, Diagnosis and Instruction (PADI), developed to identify and nurture Black and Hispanic students with potential who were being overlooked (Johnson, Starnes, Gregory, & Blaylock, 1985). The barriers children not being identified were facing were those of poverty, lack of early enrichment experiences, developmental delays, or differences in language and/or culture. The instructional component was designed to increase academic skills and to refine thinking skills needed to be successful in a program for gifted students.

Several aspects of the PADI program reflect best practices in identification of gifted students. The diagnostic battery was developed deliberately to focus on the diversity within a group of students with previously unrecognized abilities. The emphasis was on early identification and supported the concept of inclusion, for each child in grades two and three who had not been identified as gifted was administered all measures in the diagnostic battery. The diagnostic battery included data collection measures from objective and subjective sources. An "identification through teaching" process was used wherein project staff refined "their judgments about individual students based on observation of their ability to meet the cognitive demands of the program over time" (Johnson, Starnes, Gregory, & Blaylock, 1985, p. 418).

Issues Regarding Different Standards and Procedures

Other issues center around some basic concerns related to the application of standards and procedures: (a) Should the instruments or procedures used with Black students be the same as those used with students from the mainstream culture?; and (b) Should the criteria used to identify gifted Black students be the same as those used to identify mainstream populations?

My review of current practices has indicated a general consensus that instruments, procedures, and criteria used to identify gifted Black students should be either different from those used with mainstream populations or, if not different, modified. The principle underlying this belief is that some adjustment must be made to account for deficits caused by low SES or cultural differences in ability to achieve.

PART II: COMMENTS ON A FUTURE STATE OF AFFAIRS

Probably with no other subpopulation have the definition and identification of giftedness been more complex and seemingly inextricably interwoven with environmental factors, performance on standardized tests, deviation from mainstream cultures, and ambiguous attitudes regarding the degree of academic acuity possessed by Black students. In the vernacular of the Creative Problem Solving (CPS) process (Isaksen & Treffinger, 1985), the situation is a "mess."

A new perspective must be taken. Approaches thus far have tended to revisit traditional causes and/or refurbish traditional solutions to address the cause of difficulties in identifying gifted Black students.

Using Creative Problem Solving (CPS) To Develop a New Perspective

Use of the CPS structure may be an effective way to extricate the real problem from the fuzziness created by inappropriately intermingling the definition and identification of gifted Black students with the obstacles of cultural differences and economic disadvantage. Certainly some new perspective must be taken or some new conceptual and operational model must be developed, because, despite efforts that have been made, Blacks continue to be one of the populations largely underrepresented in programs for the gifted. What approach might be used to develop new perspectives? What type of information should be considered in developing new perspectives? In what ways might old information be used differently?

Isaksen & Treffinger (1985) have listed several blocks that inhibit creative thinking. Germane to this discussion is that "scientific reasoning provides a panacea—this attitude promotes the view that reason, logic, numbers utility, practicality and tradition are good; feeling, intuition, qualitative judgments, pleasure, and change are bad" (p. Three-6). When scientific reasoning is allowed to block creative thinking, faulty syllogisms may occur. For example, *if* test scores and other traditional measures of achievement are viewed as the only credible evidence of a person's ability to achieve, *then* one could conclude that few Blacks are gifted because they tend to score, on the average, 15 points lower on IQ tests than do majority-culture groups.

This faulty syllogism may be a result of what Isaksen and Treffinger (1985) described as "the natural tendency to 'leap to solution'" (p. Three-1). *If* we consider that new approaches might be developed by avoiding blocks to creative thinking; and *if* we apply the principles of deferred judgment, we might, then, be in a better position to develop new perspectives.

Deferring Judgment

By deferring judgments about the totality of the effects of low SES on achievement, our thinking could proceed in another manner. As a result of deferring judgment, we would acknowledge that "there are many well-adjusted, well-cared for children even in inner city environments who are reinforced in their intellectual pursuits" (Frasier, 1980, p. 58). We would acknowledge the heterogeneity in the Black population by recognizing the existence of at least four socioeconomic levels (Frasier, 1980; see Figure 31-1).

Students most often overlooked, even though they may have the potential to succeed in a program for the gifted, are usually in levels B and C. Overwhelming attention in research literature, and in practice, however, is given to the achievement barriers described in level D. Children at this level have appeared to be the prototype for recommended adjustments or modifications in identification procedures to locate gifted Black children. By acknowledging heterogeneity within the Black population we would begin to see that "a major problem to avoid is the indiscriminate application of stereotypical descriptors to each minority or low-income individual encountered" (Kitano & Kirby, 1986, p. 294).

Making a Complex Problem Manageable

Does the identification of children from level D of Figure 31-1 suggest that we give limited or no attention to the debilitating effects a limited environment can have? No,

Source: Copyright © Mary M. Frasier, University of Georgia, 1980.

Figure 31-1 Black Family Types. *Source*: Copyright © Mary M. Frasier, University of Georgia, 1980.

it does not. It does, however, suggest that if we follow the CPS process a little further, ways of making what has been a complex problem more manageable may emerge.

In line with the suggestion of Isaksen and Treffinger (1985), I propose that new perspectives on the identification of gifted Black students be developed by asking, *I wonder what would happen if . . . ?* (IWWWHI)?

Recognizing Traits of Gifted Black Students

IWWWHI we considered that gifted students from all cultures held the following mental talents in common:

1. The ability to meaningfully manipulate some symbol system held valuable in the subculture.
2. The ability to think logically, given appropriate information.
3. The ability to use stored knowledge to solve problems.
4. The ability to reason by analogy; and
5. The ability to extend or extrapolate knowledge to new situations or unique applications. (Gallagher & Kinney, 1974, p. 16)

IWWWHI we considered data by Shade (1978) on Black high achievers when defining appropriate indicators of giftedness among Black students? Shade's (1978) summary of studies on Black achievers revealed that they were goal oriented, possessed great self-confidence, felt positive about themselves, felt in control of their destiny, had high levels of aspirations, and possessed confidence in their ability to accomplish their goals. While they were portrayed as demonstrating a need to be cautious, controlled, less trusting, and constricting in their approach to their environment, they also were highly original and creative in their ideas and tended to be shrewd in the manipulation of situations in which they found themselves.

IWWWHI we observed for gifted behaviors among Black children by reflecting on the 14 traits identified by Glaser and Ross (1970) that characterize successful students from seriously disadvantaged backgrounds?

IWWWHI we compared those traits typically attributed to gifted children with traits attributed to gifted disadvantaged students (Frasier, 1983). (See Table 31-1.)

Data Finding

Once we have defined indicators of potential giftedness, Hagen (1980) suggested that sources of information for each indicator be identified. A review of typical characteristics of giftedness immediately confirms the need to use a variety of sources to evaluate adequately these behaviors. When the principles of data finding (the second step in the CPS process) are applied, a greater variety of approaches may become apparent.

Current research supporting the multifaceted concept of intelligence (Gardner, 1983; Sternberg, 1982a, 1982b, 1986) compels us to apply data-finding techniques to the

Table 31-1 Comparison of Traits Attributed to Gifted, versus Gifted Disadvantaged, Children

Gifted Children (Clark, 1983)	Gifted Disadvantaged Children (Baldwin, Gear, & Lucito, 1978; Gay, 1978; Torrance, 1977)
Extraordinary quantity of information; unusual retentiveness	Alertness, curiosity
	Learning quickly through experience
Unusually varied interest and curiosity	Retaining and using ideas and information well
Accelerated pace of thought processes	
Early ability to delay closure	Originality and creativity in thinking
Ability to generate original ideas and solutions	Ability to generalize learning to other areas and to show relationships among apparently unrelated ideas
Early differential patterns for thought processing	
Early ability to use and form conceptual frameworks	Resourcefulness, ability to solve problems by ingenious methods

Source: From "A Comparison of General Traits and Behaviors Attributed to the Gifted with Traits and Behaviors Attributed to the Gifted Disadvantaged" by M.M. Frasier, unpublished manuscript, University of Georgia, Athens, Georgia.

identification of gifted students. This becomes especially important for Blacks and other subpopulations who may be overlooked when traditional procedures are used.

IWWWHI we allowed ourselves to use "different tests to identify children from different groups . . . [when they] have been shown to be more appropriate" (Maker, 1983, p. 137)? IWWWHI we evaluated a "student's use of language" (Hagen, 1980, p. 23) as well as the extent of his or her vocabulary? IWWWHI we asked nominators of students for special programs to recommend students on the basis of the "quality of questions" (Hagen, 1980, p. 23) they ask, as well as the quantity of questions? IWWWHI we evaluated a "student's ability to devise or adopt a systematic strategy for solving problems and to change that strategy if it is not working" (Hagen, 1980, p. 24)? IWWWHI we solicited nominations by using "descriptive vignettes or problem situations . . . rather than trait names or psychological constructs" (Hagen, 1980, p. 27)?

The evaluation of characteristics of potential giftedness suggested by Hagen (1980) represents an action-oriented, "nonentrenched" (Sternberg, 1982a) approach. Observing for characteristics of giftedness in this manner might help teachers look beyond their perceptions of giftedness and possibly their preconceived notions of who is and who is not gifted. By applying as many data-finding techniques as possible, we can make better decisions than before about who the gifted are and what kinds of programs they need.

SUMMARY AND RECOMMENDATIONS

If we now look at the critical issues raised regarding the identification of gifted Black students, we can respond to these issues from a different perspective. The following three principles are offered as a guide to developing this new perspective. These principles are based on conclusions drawn from the review of current procedures and their compatibility with best practices (offered in part one).

Principle 1. The gifted are diverse individuals capable of diverse expression of their talents at the upper end of a variety of talent continua; therefore, we must use diverse procedures to identify and educate them. Adherence to principle one is consistent with best practices in which the recommendation is that we (a) focus on diversity within gifted populations; (b) emphasize inclusion rather than exclusion; and (c) recognize that behavioral indicators of giftedness may be expressed differently in different cultural groups.

Principle 2. Methods of locating children and youths capable of performance at a high level can be varied without eroding quality and without requiring excessive data collection or expenditure of time. Soliciting information from a variety of sources does not compromise a decision; it enriches the decision. Adherence to principle two is consistent with best practices that advise us (a) to gather data from multiple sources, (b) to gather data that are both subjective and objective, (c) to use knowledgeable professionals and nonprofessionals within and without the school setting, and (d) to delay decisionmaking until all data on a student have been reviewed and evaluated.

Principle 3. Data on certain personality traits, socioeconomic factors, and physical traits should be considered only as they affect performance when determining curriculum, not to determine giftedness. Adherence to principle three means that we will not let a priori beliefs about racial or ethnic background and socioeconomic status stand in the way of determining giftedness. Factors related to environment, language development, and levels of skill development in areas other than language should be used to provide clues for planning curriculum to nurture potential.

The three principles for developing a new perspective are compatible with recommendations by Renzulli (1984)—that identification requires use of a variety of techniques applied over a period of time. Renzulli further recommended that "identification of gifted and talented individuals should be based on knowledge of the individual, the cultural-experiential context in which the individual has developed, and the fields of activity in which he or she performs" (p. 164). Adopting these three principles would represent the spirit of Treffinger's (1984) admonition that we take an affirmative approach to problems associated with identifying giftedness if we are to develop new perspectives and resolve the critical issues we face.

Only when we adhere to the principles and recommendations outlined above can we proceed to identify all gifted children. At that time we can begin to acknowledge the validity of Emerson's statement: "Nature never rhymes her children, nor makes two men alike."

32

Standardized Testing for Minority Students: Is It Fair?

Leland Baska, M.M.Ed.
Williamsburg Public Schools,
Virginia

The underlying assumption in Frasier's chapter is quite valid; that is, the crux of the problem regarding gifted Black children in our schools is that they are not being identified in representative numbers that match their overall representation in a given contextual population. Her belief about the cause of the problem, however, may be debatable.

Frasier believes that the root of the problem is an inappropriate identification system. I view the problem in a broader context. If we are to examine seriously what is responsible for the underrepresentation of Blacks in programs for the gifted, then we must be concerned about several issues.

First, because sufficient evidence is available to suggest that low socioeconomic status (SES) plays an important role in how even highly able students may score on tests (Van Tassel-Baska, in press), we must view the home environment as a critical factor in understanding and interpreting the phenomenon.

Second, lowering entrance scores, even in a well-defined program for gifted students, may not prevent those scoring at lower levels from succeeding in the class (Olszewski, in preparation). We need to consider carefully the "match" between identification and program so that we are not excluding peremptorily students who can succeed by establishing higher cutoff scores than necessary.

Third, we are forced also to examine the purposes of existing special programs and inferences that can be made about levels or types of intellectual functioning required for participation. For example, if a given program requires students to engage in original production requiring rigorous high-level analytic and interpretive skills, then only students with these readiness skills should be exposed to such a challenging intervention. If, however, the program only provides mild enrichment through, for example, a special unit on archaeology where the expectations are open ended, then insisting on high threshhold scores for entry is inappropriate.

Finally, we also must maintain logical consistency in procedures for identifying Black students. If we are willing to entertain not only a multiple criteria model of identification, but also a quota system, are we equally willing to entertain the idea of multiple program options based on aptitude and interest? If we accept Frasier's premise that gifted Black students (or at least those from lower SES levels) have characteristics and needs different from those of gifted Anglo-American students, then we also must accept the premise that differential programming for these students will be required to meet differential needs. A question then becomes important: What program interventions are most needed by Black students and what are the implications of providing for Black students differentially? Should the focus of programs for gifted Black students be less academic and more creative and open ended than for Anglo-American students? Or should all gifted students be immersed in a multifaceted set of program opportunities that allow for wide deviations among individual profiles? This central program concern is much larger than identification and becomes a critical area worth close scrutiny. To broaden identification criteria to include more able Blacks, only to funnel them into a narrowly conceptualized program, is to do the ultimate disservice—attach a label conveying the opposite impression from the reality of the program experience.

These programming issues are central to gaining an appropriate perspective on representational numbers of Blacks and other minority children in special programs. We need to examine our fundamental purposes for special programs, our capacities to manage individual differences and needs within them, and our willingness to operate multiple program options and to define student outcomes before we look at adjusting the inequities of identification protocols. For in reality, effective identification procedures must interact in significant ways with program expectations. Thus, the fundamental premise in this chapter, unlike Frasier's, is that the problem of underrepresentation of Black students in programs for the gifted is due to several factors more comprehensive than identification alone, and that faulty visions of programming can seriously impede reasonable progress in solving the problem.

If, however, we view the solution-finding model within the purview of identification systems, Frasier's ideas about approaching identification have merit in several areas:

- Using multiple criteria that include inventories and checklists corresponding to traits characteristic of gifted Black students;
- Using the diagnostic-prescriptive teaching approach to improving test performance popularized by Feuerstein's (1979) notion of test-teach-test;
- Broadening the data-finding procedures for students, including peer nomination, self-nomination, and recommendations of personnel other than teachers;
- Considering broad ranges of scores for entrance into programs; and
- Using standardized tests shown historically to be effective in identifying Black students.

Thus, my overall response to Frasier's chapter is positive toward those areas she believes need to be changed. What is less comforting is her focus on the process of identification as the heart of the problem without considering antecedents and consequences of altering such procedures.

THE LARGER VIEW

Casting a different light on the issues may be helpful before returning to the identification issue per se. In Figure 32-1 are represented the issues discussed earlier in a broader context of individual lives beyond the kindergarten through grade twelve schooling years. Because much attention has been focused on the identification process, educators may have lost sight of related fundamental issues, and the purpose behind ensuring that Black students have access to educational advantages.

Level I—Family. The family and home environment are very important in providing the foundation to traverse the levels of society in adulthood on the positive side of the continuum. Parents' educational and occupational levels are predictive of positive mobility (Jencks, 1972), but the value they perceive for education also becomes critical.

Level II—Schooling. The kindergarten through grade twelve public school training that students receive in American society is crucial. The important issue in this context for many students is achievement. High achievement guarantees a place at the next level, while low achievement presages limited access to advanced training.

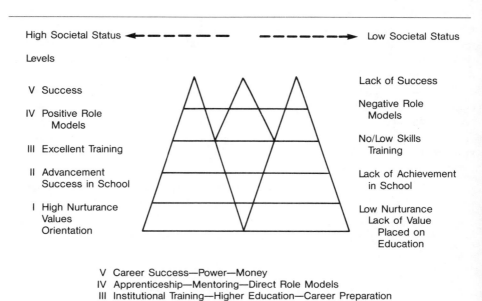

Figure 32-1 models the following:

High Societal Status ◄ — — — — — — — — — — — ► Low Societal Status

Levels

Positive (left)	Negative (right)
V Success	Lack of Success
IV Positive Role Models	Negative Role Models
III Excellent Training	No/Low Skills Training
II Advancement Success in School	Lack of Achievement in School
I High Nurturance Values Orientation	Low Nurturance Lack of Value Placed on Education

V Career Success—Power—Money
IV Apprenticeship—Mentoring—Direct Role Models
III Institutional Training—Higher Education—Career Preparation
II Schooling—Access to Institutional Training
I Family—Nurturance—Value Orientation

Figure 32-1 A Model of Level of and Continua of Influence on Perceived Upward Mobility in Society.

Level III—Institutional Training. The nature of occupational training and the linkage to university or college work vary widely with modern occupations; yet, the key is skills training—Can students leave this level with the requisite skills to succeed in the workplace?

Level IV—Role Models. The role modeling and mentor training at this level again are linked closely to value orientation and the hero-myth structure within the individual. The adult models chosen at this level of societal mobility, or emulated based on earlier choices, will determine ultimately the individual's perception of mainstream society in adulthood career paths. The key to this level is the power or influence of those role models.

Level V—Success. The adult model for success in our society becomes a potent motivator for shaping behavior. The key is in viewing power, money, and prestige as important attainments within the mainstream culture as opposed to seeking success outside the system. The paths to preparation for divergence at this level have been set at prior stages in the individual's life. For any subgroup operating in American society, including Blacks, the lure of quick rewards for illegal activities, albeit accompanied with high risks, is strong. Thus, a need exists to focus at earlier stages of development on turnkey areas that can possibly influence a Black student toward attaining high levels of career success within the sanction of the mainstream societal structure. Our need to see more Black students in programs for the gifted is one small manifestation of the larger phenomenon. As educators, our tools may be limited; but we do have them. They are the tools of achievement and success in schooling—experiences fostered, direct and indirect influence and role models provided, and linkages to the family advocated—that encourage continued educational growth and positive performance.

BACK TO TESTING

The nationwide influx of minority students into large city school systems has raised several issues regarding appropriate testing and program intervention, especially for students of high or low ability from these cultures. Are minority students in urban centers receiving a free and appropriate education based on measures adequate to assess their ability? I have examined the demography of one urban center to assist in understanding the extent of the problem.

In the October 31, 1986, racial/ethnic survey of the Chicago public schools, the school population is divided into five ethnic groups for identification purposes: (a) White, Non-Hispanic; (b) Black, Non-Hispanic; (c) American Indian/Alaskan Native; (d) Asian or Pacific Islander; and (e) Hispanic (subdivided into Mexican, Puerto Rican, Cuban, and other Hispanic origins). A survey has been published yearly to describe the demographic composition of the public schools. The 1986 school population of 431,298 students is slightly larger than 1985's, but considerably lower than the 1980 population. In Table 32-1 the numbers and percentages of racial/ethnic groups are listed and contrasted with the 1986 survey results.

Based on these figures, the White Non-Hispanic category, which was almost equal to the Hispanic group in 1980, clearly is now the third largest group, losing 5 percentage

Table 32-1 Comparison of Numbers (1986) and Percentages (1980 and 1986)
of Racial/Ethnic Groups

| | | Percentage | |
Category	Number 1986	1986	1980
White, Non-Hispanic	58,313	13.5	18.6
Black, Non-Hispanic	259,555	60.1	60.8
American Indian/Alaskan Native	706	0.2	0.1
Asian or Pacific Islander	12,088	2.8	2.1
Hispanic	100,636	23.4	18.4
Total	431,298		

points between 1980 and 1986. The Hispanic category has gained 5 percentage points. Blacks as a group remained stable in this period at about 60 percent of the total.

The ethnic balance of programs for gifted students follows these percentages, which means that ethnic percentage limits have been set for programs with open admission to ensure compliance with desegregation guidelines in schools. Generally a 65% minority and 35% majority guideline has been used in comprehensive programs for the gifted in the City of Chicago.

The commentary in *Education Week* (Riles et al., 1987) from participants in litigation related to using intelligence tests to determine special education placement gives some insight into issues surrounding use of intelligence (IQ) tests for minority gifted students as well. California School Superintendent Riles chose to become a defendant in the case of *Larry P. v. Riles* because he viewed the banning of tests as a simplistic solution to a complex problem. In his opinion, due to the lack of objective data, teacher judgment had the danger of being even more biased or prejudicial for minority students. For gifted minority students who are reluctant to demonstrate publicly their true ability as a means of avoiding ostracism of the peer group, this kind of objective measure may be the truest indication of the child's disguised ability. Superintendent Riles states that without objective data the result would be "more special education misplacement or no placement at all for needy students" (Riles et al., 1987, p. 28).

The judge in the case of *Larry P. v. Riles* was concerned with the lack of validity data (from special education classes) to demonstrate a clear link to the testing process. Thus, claims of educational remediation made for special education were not resulting in benefits for the children placed. However, a program for gifted students offers concerned parents a perceived hope for change.

Another view of the case of *Larry P. v. Riles* came from a California school psychologist who pointed to the need for reliable instruments with a known research base to help make informed decisions that will meet the needs of children. The logical extension of banning IQ tests is to ban all standardized tests. This would be problematic for schools, because IQ tests have been used over the years to link testing to predicted achievement in the mainstream school curriculum, and other standardized achievement measures have been used as a way to validate achievement predictions.

Benefits of Testing for Black Students

The benefits of testing for many Black students have been obscured in attacks on intelligence tests in particular and standardized tests in general. The large number of Outstanding Negro Achievement awardees from the Chicago public schools every year attests to their high performance on a nationally standardized examination. The lists of semifinalists on the *PSAT-NMSQT* published each fall include 1,500 high school seniors nationwide from 995 schools across 46 states. Furthermore, substantial numbers of Black students are identified in Chicago each year through the talent search testing using the *Scholastic Aptitude Test*. These data from standardized tests then provide the basis for a series of programs, including museology options and university course-work on eight campuses.

The Astor Program in New York City (Ehrlich, 1978) demonstrated the power of using an intelligence scale as an admission criterion for programs for preschool gifted students. One troubling aspect of psychometric information over the years, however, has been its relationship to the essential knowledge base associated with schooling. To develop intelligence tests without obvious achievement items that measure the same fundamental ability is the goal of testmakers. Testing the validity of that prediction of academic success leading to the long-term goal of professional competency is crucial, and often is not considered in validity studies. A second troubling aspect of the psychometric information is the mean score differences that appear between subgroups of students if we look at racial data.

The Issue of Differences between Groups on Standardized Tests

The score discrepancy between ethnic groups on tests (see, e.g., Jensen, 1969) has led to (a) general criticisms of intelligence tests; (b) a search for other instruments that might, by eliminating the discrepancy, be "truer" measures of the intelligence construct; and (c) claims of reduced bias by developers of tests such as the *Kaufman Assessment Battery for Children* (*K-ABC*) (Kaufman & Kaufman, 1983). The reduced differential between groups reported in the norms has been the basis of claims of reduced bias. One of the criticisms of the *K-ABC* (Bracken, 1985), however, is based on the underrepresentation of low SES Blacks and Hispanics in the norm sample and the overrepresentation of students whose parents have high educational attainment levels. Socioeconomic status differences, cultural patterns, family expectations, family interactions, and the early learning environment of the child are complex factors that may be perceived as ethnic group differences.

THE ROLE OF THE FAMILY

Clark (1983) cited a number of home and family patterns that contribute to Black students' success in schools: high involvement of parents in the child's schooling pattern; fundamentally positive parent-child relationship; and clear parental expectations for behaviors and performance in all areas of the child's life. Clark's full comparison between Black high and low achievers is found in Table 32-2. The similarity between Clark's findings and those of researchers who have studied the background of talented individuals from the mainstream culture (Bloom, 1985) is interesting to note: Parents play a dominant nurturing role in the school achievement of their children. These variables critical to high achievement are less related to being Black than to the positive psychological, emotional, and expectational environment of the family. Therefore, working with Black parents to establish facilitative learning environments in the home may be a better long-term strategy for educators than looking for the "best" test, because the most important factors in determining the child's success in school may be concentrated within the family structure.

In this chapter a critique of Frasier's commentary has been presented, a generic model for viewing access to societal mobility has been provided, and the issue of testing minority Black children in the context of urban settings has been presented. Now, I will recommend some specific procedures for identification of minority children.

DEFINITIONAL FRAMEWORK

Defining giftedness as "the demonstrated need for educational treatment beyond that provided the average student in school so that potential may be realized in adult performance," is the heart of credible programs for gifted students. Creating a special category of giftedness for each subgroup or subpopulation is inappropriate as long as success in the mainstream culture is measured by professional competency or eminence in a given line of work. The long-term view of giftedness realistically must consider developing the child's ability to compete effectively in the established culture rather than redefining giftedness to realign group differences and allow students to pursue programs that do not prepare them for the transition to the next level of education.

SCREENING PROCEDURES

Screening of available records is a first step in implementing appropriate identification procedures. Standardized test scores in addition to reports of significant observers in the child's environment need to be examined. Reports from observers could include anecdotal data from medical or school personnel and parents.

Traditional approaches in which only yearly standardized achievement test scores are used have sometimes been criticized because they "screen out" students who avoid making themselves targets for peer disapproval by demonstrating their abilities in ways acceptable to their peers. In an environment that fosters "It's not cool to be smart,"

Table 32-2 A Comparison of the Quality of Success-Producing Patterns in Homes of High Achievers and Low Achievers

High Achievers	Low Achievers
1. Frequent school contact initiated by parent	Infrequent school contact initiated by parent
2. Child has had some stimulating, supportive school teachers	Child has had no stimulating, supportive school teachers
3. Parents psychologically and emotionally calm with child	Parents in psychological and emotional upheaval with child
4. Students psychologically and emotionally calm with parents	Students less psychologically and emotionally calm with parents
5. Parents expect to play major role in child's schooling	Parents have lower expectation of playing role in child's schooling
6. Parents expect child to play major role in child's schooling	Parents have lower expectation of child's role in child's schooling
7. Parents expect child to get postsecondary training	Parents have lower expectation that child will get postsecondary training
8. Parents have explicit achievement-centered rules and norms	Parents have less explicit achievement-centered rules and norms
9. Students show long-term acceptance of norms as legitimate	Students have less long-term acceptance of norms
10. Parents establish clear, specific role boundaries and status structures with parents as dominant authority	Parents establish more blurred role boundaries and status structures
11. Siblings interact as organized subgroup	Siblings are a less structured, interactive subgroup
12. Conflict between family members is infrequent	Conflict between some family members is frequent
13. Parents frequently engage in deliberate achievement-training activities	Parents seldom engage in deliberate achievement-training activities
14. Parents frequently engage in implicit achievement-training activities	Parents engage less frequently in implicit achievement-training activities
15. Parents exercise firm, consistent monitoring and rules enforcement	Parents have inconsistent standards and exercise less monitoring of child's time and space
16. Parents provide liberal nurturance and support	Parents are less liberal with nurturance and support
17. Parents defer to child's knowledge in intellectual matters	Parents do not defer to child in intellectual matters

Source: From *Family Life and School Achievement: Why Poor Black Children Succeed or Fail* (p. 200) by R. Clark, 1983, Chicago, Ill.: University of Chicago Press. Copyright 1983 by University of Chicago Press. Reprinted by permission.

the gifted minority child possibly finds going along with the dominant group easier than standing out from the crowd.

One important contribution that can be made through programs for gifted students is to legitimize the slogan, "It's cool to be smart." By starting a program we are not guaranteeing admission to major university or college programs but introducing the notion that academic challenge is possible and success probable for the children chosen. Special programs that prepare and entitle students to participate fully in educational advantages may be viewed as essential aspects of upward educational mobility for minority students. As more programs come into being, self-nomination by students also may become part of a screening process that allows for trial placement. Before admission, conditions for continued placement and length of the trial period need to be specified through some form of contract that involves the child, parent, and possibly guidance personnel of the school.

APPROPRIATE STANDARDIZED INSTRUMENTS

The most reliable, well written test items available, which have documentation to support their use in the general population, need to be used with all subpopulations. Knowing the psychometric properties of the examination gives us a way of tracking the other variables associated with differences in group performance. The major IQ tests used for predicting school success, such as the *Stanford-Binet* and the *Wechsler Intelligence Scale for Children–Revised (WISC-R)*, are individually administered measures that meet this criterion and have a research base supporting their use. The *Cognitive Abilities Test* and *Otis-Lennon School Ability Index* are similar examples of group administered paper-and-pencil tests that have earned the respect of the testing community and have been used successfully in school-based settings to help identify gifted minority children. The series of *Raven Matrices* cover a wide spectrum of age and ability levels with a measure that minimizes language demands. A frequent criticism of this instrument has been the lack of American norms; however, these have been developed for the *Coloured and Standard Matrices* through a network of cooperating psychologists (Raven, 1986).

OTHER TYPES OF DATA

For very young children the use of singing games and educational toys yields information about differences within groups or classes of kindergarten children. Games, such as Simon, that require the child to repeat a gradually lengthening pattern of electronic beeps associated with color are good informal measures that can be introduced as play activities and will help with ranking children on performance of memory tasks. Singing games and the lengthy rhymes associated with jump rope activities also can be used to find children with particular ability.

For older children word games, such as Scrabble, help develop an interest in words and vocabulary in all students while helping to pinpoint children of high ability. Board games, such as chess, can be introduced to groups of students as leisure activities and can help to find those students who excel consistently at developing complex strategies for winning.

The increased use of microcomputers in schools has helped identify children who have the logic skills necessary for programming. The new proliferation of educational software for microcomputers has high potential for use with groups of children as a standard presentation format demonstrating or comparing how much and how quickly children learn. Art and music activities may reveal which children have a special talent or good perceptual skills.

Sociograms—the students' perception of who is the smartest, or best in various areas of endeavor—are other informal measures that need to be part of an identification package. Teacher nomination is probably the most common type of informal identification used for programs for gifted students, but it needs to be broadened to include other personnel who have the opportunity to observe groups of children during the school day.

THE ISSUE OF DIFFERENTIAL TREATMENT

Not using the same instruments to identify gifted Black students as those to identify other gifted students will have the potential effect of reducing them to second-class status. Evidence exists that these students can compete with "advantaged" students in programs for gifted students and magnet high school programs in large metropolitan areas, and even in suburban areas where the percentage of Black students is smaller. Not to be tested for or included in traditional programs for the gifted is a detriment to Black students. The lower percentage of Black students in programs for the gifted compared to their percentage in a given population is troubling, but only exacerbated by changing the structure of testing or programming.

Lowering thresholds for minorities to enter programs, rather than changing the structure of testing or programming, seems a better strategy for gaining full representation. The ranking of each defined subgroup of students on mainstream tests is a more reasonable way to begin programs leading to the ultimate goal of accessing the institutions associated with adult success.

Achievement test scores for minority children need to be separated by subtests so that ranks can be assigned for verbal, quantitative, nonverbal, and other ability dimensions. Through development of a learning profile, particular strengths and/or weaknesses can be identified and accommodated in programming.

If the mainstream standards of professional excellence are accepted as long-term goals, the parallel process for selection for special programs needs to be considered. Using ethnic quotas for the numbers of program seats available is one strategy to ensure representation of all groups, and is being used as part of desegregation policy in large cities. A quota system requires a delineation of groups on ethnic guidelines whose boundaries are becoming increasingly blurred and that may be less defensible than grouping on variables related to SES, cultural differences, or the amount of parental involvement in the child's education.

One unresolved issue for the Chicago magnet high school program is how to eliminate the frequent, initial adjustment problems of the high-scoring child who has not developed study skills or good work habits because of a lack of challenge in the first six grades. In contrast, another child may be scoring at lower levels but has developed in those same six years the skills to keep up with brighter children. How lengthy a period is reasonable for the child to develop study skills and work habits? What is a reasonable standard for the teacher to set as an absolute goal for the lowest score a child can have in a class? These decisions often need to be supported by a case study by skilled observers connected with the program for gifted students rather than the ancillary staff for special education programs.

USING TEST INFORMATION APPROPRIATELY

Historically tests have been useful as a way to measure a child's knowledge acquisition and to identify particular teaching/instructional needs. The use of tests by school personnel for public relations, political purposes, and teacher accountability also has led to abuse. Placing children who are marginally below average in special education classes is a misuse of test data that has met with nationwide criticism and litigation. The difficulty for Blacks in accessing employment positions in numbers that reflect their percentages in the general population has resulted in numerous civil rights tests of fairness in employment practices and a close examination of the numbers of Black students in business and professional schools. An extension of this reasoning to the domain of the public school introduces the spectrum of litigation that may discourage the creation of special programs for gifted students for fear of not meeting the courts' interpretations of equity.

IN CONCLUSION

As we move into the next century, the information revolution, and a future that will place ever greater demands on students to achieve academic success, we need to look closely at issues related to equal opportunity for educational advantage. Programs for gifted students and good schools are only a small part of a process that prepares children for mainstream, societal success. Creating school environments that increase the child's chances for success in the mainstream may be our best route to reducing the societal inequities that have been the rule in the history of our country. The extent of our ability to provide a free and appropriate education for all our citizens will determine the direction of our society's commitment to education and the future of our democracy.

33

The Purpose of Education for Gifted Black Students

Alexinia Y. Baldwin, Ph.D.
State University of New York
at Albany

The purposes, or ultimate goals, of programs for gifted Black-American students should be the same as those proposed for all gifted students. However, the process for meeting these goals might be different. An explication of this point of view will help clarify the issues involved in providing appropriate programs for gifted black students.

When educators discuss the purpose of education, they are usually considering those end objectives deemed appropriate for this society and the good life of the individual. Concomitantly, an analysis of the values and historical artifacts considered to be important by the population being served is necessary. This analysis must be followed by an adjustment of the curricula and instructional plans to the purposes being established and values considered important by the group being served.

Writers (Lyon, 1979; Start, 1985) have characterized gifted students as an overlooked minority. Extended, this premise can characterize the gifted Black student as an overlooked minority within this minority; not simply because of skin color or race, but because of the variances and inadequacies in defining and identifying giftedness. The cultural legacy of this gifted minority within a minority—gifted Black child—is unique. Since the end of slavery, the never-ending pursuit to belong and to span the years of neglect have been sources of determination and frustration. Consequently, the cushion of support and pride inherent in cultural rootedness remains fragile, contributing generally to lowered self-esteem. In large measure the lack of cultural rootedness creates a uniqueness among Black-Americans not experienced by other minorities, even those Blacks from Jamaica or other West Indian countries.

The purpose of educational planning for gifted Black children cannot be unidimensional. The culture does not produce certain prototypical children; instead, children actively select from the environment the features that help them to adapt. The adaptive behavior exhibited by some Black children is related not necessarily to Black culture, but rather to the circumstances of the environment. A swaggering "hip" walk, for instance, can be used to assert the person's uniqueness in an environment where little attention is being paid to the individual. The intellectual skills used by gifted Black students in adjusting to the environment are the cognitive processing skills used by gifted students of any racial or ethnic group. Those who are gifted within the Black population use these cognitive processing skills more effectively and efficiently than average individuals within the same environment.

A lack of consensus exists about appropriate programs for gifted Black students. Some program designers have argued that programs for gifted Black students should emphasize leadership skills because the basic problems of the Black population could be addressed more readily under the guidance of great gifted leaders. I do not agree that leadership should be the basis of a program for gifted Blacks.

Some argue that programs for gifted Black students produce an elitist mentality that seriously inhibits the effective understanding of, and ability to deal with, the realities of life among those who are average or below average in their school achievement. Some also fear that attention to the groups of gifted Blacks would diminish the attention given to those Blacks who are dropping out of school or receiving failing grades.

I would respond to these arguments by stating that the mental energy generated in a fertile mind will be used constructively or destructively. Thus, we must nurture this ability and provide gifted students options to use their abilities constructively. Programs for gifted Black students should include exposure to as many knowledge trajectories as possible. Many of these students need a new awareness of what growth possibilities exist in the world today.

PROGRAM DESIGN

Program Planning Concepts

Although the needs of gifted Black students vary greatly, a primary need is the development of a positive self-concept. One pertinent objective is to develop a feeling of pride and self-worth through study of the courage and ingenuity of Blacks' forefathers during their enslavement. This bravery and ingenuity should be a part of the curriculum for children of all ethnic groups, because self-respect of an ethnic group is enhanced when others recognize the important legacies left for subsequent generations.

Many questions exist regarding the focus of a program specifically designed for gifted Black students. Should the program's focus be on individual strengths; the basic culture of the child; or, the skills necessary for success in the majority culture? All three are important areas with which planners should be concerned, and none should be the main focus. In fact, a program in which all these factors are not incorporated is ineffective.

In published guidelines for the development of programs for the gifted, an emphasis is placed on providing programs that are qualitatively different, or differentiated in content taught (Baldwin, 1978; Kaplan, 1974; Maker, 1982a; Renzulli, 1977; Ward, 1980). According to these guidelines, the purpose of such programs is threefold: (a) to extend the capabilities of gifted students; (b) to eliminate the boredom of lock-step vertical progression; and (c) to develop special abilities for individuals' personal development and their possible contributions to society. If these statements of purpose constitute a general intent of programs for the gifted child and a philosophically sound rationale for the stated purpose can be identified, then these same statements of purpose should guide a program designed for gifted Black students.

Concept I

To design programs that will help students who are gifted or show great potential for giftedness attain goals set for all gifted students, attention must be given to adaptive behaviors, which can serve as a vehicle to attain the larger goals. Table 33-1 (Baldwin, 1985b) is a summary of some of the adaptive behaviors exhibited by Blacks, the possible causes, the intellectual processing abilities manifested, and some possible strategies for achieving the larger goals in programs for the gifted. For example, students who exhibit logical reasoning ability and pragmatic problem-solving ability (number five of Table 33-1) think in logical systems. They have had to survive and to live by "wit and grit." These students should be able to grow and to develop through an introduction to logic and problem solving. These two abilities are important in many subject areas and a first step in developing skills for future careers.

The process of identification becomes a crucial aspect of program design if one considers the permutations of giftedness suggested by the information in Table 33-1. Regardless of whether the identification of exceptional ability is accomplished using qualitative or quantitative measures, a complete analysis of students' abilities must be made. From this information, a profile of strengths and weaknesses can be drawn. This profile gives the planner decision-making data for program emphases (Baldwin, 1984). In Figure 33-1, a profile of a Black student is presented. From this matrix profile and the narrative data received from parents and teachers, diagnosticians determined that the strengths of this student were in the creative problem-solving and psychosocial areas. His weaknesses were in the cognitive area, particularly mathematics and science. For this student great emphasis should be placed on developing further his creative problem-solving skills and introducing him to the processes of scientific analysis and logic using practical problems of science with which the student might be familiar in his own environment.

Concept II

An important note is that a cross section of profiles of Black students from across this nation will show a variance in common strengths. In Figure 33-2, a possible grouping of gifted or potentially gifted students is shown with the interaction of three causal variables along a continuum from least desirable to most desirable. The strengths that might appear common among students from rural southern towns might be quite different from those common among students from midwestern cities. However, when we look at the profiles of students that fall at a certain level on the continuum within a particular causal category, we will find common trends. One could, for instance, find a trend toward higher levels of creativity in the figural area among students of

Table 33-1 The Most Common Descriptors for Children Affected by Cultural Diversity, Socioeconomic Deprivation, and Geographic Isolation

Descriptors	External and Internal Deficit	Possible Environmental Causality
1. Outer locus of control rather than inner locus of control	1. Inability to attend to task without supervision	1. Discipline does not encourage inner locus of control. Child is given directions. Tradition dictates strict adherence to directions
2. Loyalty to peer group	2. Inability to externalize behavioral cues	2. A need to belong: empathy for those in similar situation
3. Physical resiliency to hardships encountered in the environment	3. Inability to trust or consider beauty in life	3. Environment dictates need to survive. Anger and frustration increase animalistic desire to survive. Alternatives, solutions are forced
4. Language rich in imagery and humor rich with symbolism; persuasive language	4. Perhaps only avenue of communication; standard language skills not used	4. A need to use subterfuge in environment to get message across; a lack of dominant language skills; a need to fantasize through language; acute awareness of environment due to its effect on individual
5. Logical reasoning; planning ability and pragmatic problem-solving ability	5. Opinions disallowed in school situation	5. Early responsibility related to survival
6. Creative ability	6. Lack of directed development of ability	6. Need to use items of environment as substitute, e.g., dolls, balls out of tin cans; wagons, sleds out of packing boxes; dolls out of corn husks

Table 33-1 continued

Descriptors	External and Internal Deficit	Possible Environmental Causality
7. Social intelligence and feeling of responsibility for the community: rebellious regarding inequities	7. No opportunity to exercise behavior in community without censorship	7. Social reforms needed to help community; high regard for moral obligation to fellow human; religious influence, tradition, survival dictate awareness of social elements related to survival
8. Sensitivity and alertness to movement	8. Lack of training and development	8. Need to excel, toughness of environment, family emphasis on physical prowess to substitute for lack of educational input

Exceptional Characteristics to Look for	Intellectual Processing Ability Indicators	Horizontal/Vertical Program Adaptation
1. Academic: good memory	1. Convergent production of semantic units	1. Contract activities; directed level development; counseling for trust–skill development
2. Psychosocial: sense of humor; intuitive grasp of situations; understanding of compromise	2. Affective behavior: possible indication of convergent production of behavioral units or classification	2. Group activity, debating, counseling seminars, philosophy, logic, process and skill development
3. Creative: tolerance for ambiguities, insight, inventiveness, revolutionary ideas	3. Divergent production	3. Creative activities, counseling, mentor relationship; process/skill development
4. Creative: fluency, flexibility, ability to elaborate, originality Academic: good memory, ability to think systematically	4. Divergent production of semantic classifications, systems, relations, and transformations; fluency of thought; evaluation of behavioral implications	4. Writing and speaking emphases. Debating, rhetoric analysis, contemporary and historical literary comparisons, literary product development

continues

Table 33-1 continued

Exceptional Characteristics to Look for	Intellectual Processing Ability Indicators	Horizontal/Vertical Program Adaptation
5. Thinks in logical systems, uncluttered thinking, insightfulness, understanding cause and effect	5. Systems analysis, decision-making skills	5. Exposure to systematically developed strategies for solving problems, logic
6. Flexibility of thinking, fluency, special aptitudes in music, drama, creative writing	6. Divergent production of symbolic transformation, flexibility of thought	6. Special classes in creative aptitudes, independent study, mentor, process and content skills development
7. Intuitive grasp of situations, sensitiveness to right and wrong	7. Affective domain: Kohlberg's upper levels of moral development	7. Leadership seminars, community service participation, counseling, historical antecedents, process and content skills
8. Hand-eye coordination, physical stamina, skilled body movements	8. Divergent production, convergent production of behavioral implications	8. Special developmental classes, Olympic participation, physical culture classes

Source: From *The Gifted and Talented Developmental Perspectives* (pp. 232–233) by F. Horowitz and M. O'Brien (Eds.), 1985, Washington, D.C.: American Psychological Association. Copyright 1985 by American Psychological Association. Reprinted by permission.

low socioeconomic status. Generalizations that apply across the board are difficult to make, however, because many exceptions exist.

Considering Figure 33-2 further, students in group one will be gifted in ways not readily evidenced on the usual intelligence (IQ) and achievement tests. For instance, while using nonstandard English, students in group one exhibit extremely meaningful figurative language. Specific skills in mathematics might be below grade level, but general problem-solving and problem-finding abilities are far above average. Forecasting and planning abilities are extremely high, although these skills might be used in situations other than classrooms. Academic scores might not be high, but evidence from subjective or qualitative measures—such as observations, performance scales (Baldwin, 1984), and/or peer and parental rating scales—documents the fact that students in group one have the potential for success in academic areas. Inclusion of students from group one in programs for the gifted requires support from teachers and administrators with well-thought-out program designs.

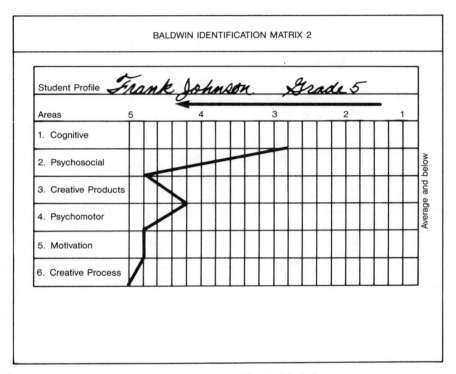

Figure 33-1 Student's Profile Form from Baldwin Identification Matrix 2.

Students in group two of Figure 33-2 are those who might be gifted in creative (graphic or performing) arts, leadership, or psychomotor areas. Students in group two might not be succeeding in regular classwork but are highly task committed and capable in their interest areas. The difficulty for those who have the responsibility of identifying the gifted Black child is in the lack of insight into the mental processes used in the high-level abilities exhibited in these nonacademic areas.

In an attempt to identify the relationship of certain creative activities to cognitive and affective areas, Lang and Ryba (1976) tried to identify parameters of creative thinking common to the artistic and musical personality. Their research conclusions did "lend credence to the notion that creative individuals regardless of their avocation, share a heightened perceptual discrimination across sensory modalities that is not masked by superior acuity in their preferred modality" (p. 277).

This finding can be interpreted to mean that the perceptual discrimination abilities found in persons with creative abilities can be applied to the everyday school room tasks expected of students who are gifted. In other words, Black students who show abilities in areas of the creative arts can be guided to express their giftedness in other areas as well. An ability to discriminate perceptually could be used to develop skills in several subject areas. As an example, a study of jazz could involve history, politics, and mathematical activities. Students can be motivated to explore the parallels between

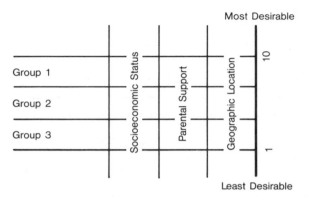

Figure 33-2 Groupings of Gifted Black Students and Possible Interacting Variables of Socioeconomic Status, Parental Support, and Geographic Location.

the socioeconomic conditions of a particular era in history and the type of jazz popular at that time. Their ability to discriminate perceptually will aid their analysis of musical trends and historical or economic conditions of various periods in the history of jazz. The uniqueness of the jazz scale and the rhythmic structure of jazz lend themselves to an analysis of the unusual mathematical arrangement of notes in a measure.

Students who fit into group three in Figure 33-2 have strong parental support, and/or socioeconomic strength in the home and community environment. This support has afforded them experiences and the positive self-concept needed for maximum development of abilities. Parental support is a significant variable in group three and should not be equated with money or environment. Many Black students who grow up in the least desirable circumstances have parental or other mentor support and encouragement. Many of these students will be selected by the usual criteria for determining giftedness and will be successful in school work. In spite of their resulting ego strength, however, the students in group three need to learn the rich history of the courage, strength, ingenuity, and contributions of their forefathers during the early decades of this country's development. This history should be an integral part of the history being taught to all children in classes for the gifted.

Meeting the needs of students in all three groups depends on the development of high-interest programs starting with the strengths discovered during identification. However, the carry-over of these strengths will take more time and stimulation in group one and, in some cases, in group two. Two case studies (Baldwin, 1977; Dabney, 1980) that included Black students of all three groups attest to the importance of focusing on the strengths or positives in identification and program development for gifted students.

In the Baldwin (1977) case study, over 80 percent of the children selected for the program (organized as a self-contained class) were scoring below the usual IQ required for admittance to the program, and approximately 20 percent were achieving at or below grade level. Immediate high-level changes were seen within six months of the program's inception. In two years, the students were operating at two to six years above grade level in many subject areas. Based on observations of parents, supervisors, and students, the flexibility of the classroom situation, the enriched environment, and the development of independence in the students were seen as contributing in large measure to their success. After two years, standardized achievement tests and measures of creativity (student products in class projects and science and mathematics fairs) indicated 90 percent of the group could be classified as gifted (supporting the planners' assessment of giftedness). The other 10 percent of the group, while good performers, could not be classified as gifted.

In the Baldwin (1977) case study, the primary objective was to unlock the creative potential of these students. The secondary and tertiary objectives, respectively, were (a) to develop self-confidence through sharpened skills necessary for making the greatest use of potential (i.e., students were given a "key" to unlock the door of accomplishment); and (b) to translate their honed skills into creative, intellectual pursuits above and beyond the classroom fare.

The Dabney (1980) case study involved gifted Black adolescents. For this group, great emphasis was placed on the positives each student brought to the high school program. Extensive use of mentors, or role models, along with a flexible program helped to accomplish the purpose and objectives of this program.

Two variables were common in these case studies: (a) total programming was evident; and (b) flexibility was allowed. These two case studies document the subsequent successes of students enrolled in the program and suggest that Black students who can be categorized in groups one and two of Figure 33-2 would be accommodated appropriately in self-contained programs with great flexibility.

IN CONCLUSION

This discussion of the purpose of programs for gifted Black students began with the premise that the purposes or ultimate goals of programs designed for gifted Black-American students should be the same as those proposed for all gifted students. The argument that the processes used in programming for gifted Blacks might not be the same as for all gifted and talented children, but that the expected results should be the same, centered around the fact that Black-Americans cannot be placed in a particular category generalizable to the entire Black population.

The historical artifacts showing the strength, pride, and exceptional abilities of Blacks are inspiring and should be a part of the program for all gifted students. Two concepts are proposed for planning such programs: (a) an awareness of the causal factors of low achievement and the adaptive or behavioral characteristics that indicate high levels of intellectual processing ability; and (b) a recognition of the variability within the Black population that draws attention to the need for alternative programming ideas, yet does not suggest the same program for all Black children.

Vestiges of past barriers and inequities, in many instances, have limited access to the many trajectories that enlightened knowledge can provide. These trajectories must be provided for young gifted Black students, because as a part of the growing minority population in this country, much of the decision-making responsibility for the future will rest in their hands.

34

What the Children Taught Me: Comments on "The Purpose of Education for Gifted Black Students"

Leonora M. Cohen, Ed.D.
University of Oregon

I will never forget when Frankie W.'s mother came to our seventh-grade class one day. Frankie created problems; he cheated, put his feet on other kids' desks, sassed the teachers, threatened to beat up classmates, and was a general nuisance. I guess his mother had been called into school once too often. She marched into the room, ordered him to take off his belt, and beat him in front of the class. Then they both ran from the room crying. Several of us put our heads on our desks and wept also.

Whether Frankie was Black, Anglo-American, Hispanic, or Asian-American does not matter; he was poor, as were most of us. Kids in this class for the most part were children of recent immigrants, ashamed of their heritage, and trying to belong by emulating jitterbuggers on "American Bandstand." These kids understood Frankie's stories about beatings his mother and siblings received from his drunken father and had their own stories to tell. Poverty, drunkenness, stressed families, and overcrowded living conditions were characteristic, as was yearning to belong to the mainstream culture.

How does this incident tie in to the purpose of programs for gifted Black children? The basic issue is not Black, but poor. I submit that middle-class Black children are more similar to middle-class children of any ethnic or racial group than to poor Black children. I hypothesize that Baldwin's group one gifted Black children share a culture of poverty with and are similar to others whose common bond is low socioeconomic status (SES), lack of parental support, and limited environment. My argument thus focuses on poverty and giftedness related to the Black population.

AGREEMENTS WITH BALDWIN

I agree with Baldwin's primary premises: (a) The ultimate purposes of special programs for gifted Black children should be the same as those for all gifted children;

however, the process for attaining these goals may be different. (b) The focus of programs for gifted Black children must encompass three areas—individual strengths and interests, skills needed in the mainstream culture, *and* specific culture of the child. (c) Educational planning for gifted Black children cannot be unidimensional, because variances within the Black population are as great as those between Blacks and other groups.

Baldwin makes strong points about the uniqueness of the Black-American child's cultural legacy, rootlessness, and concomitant lowered self-esteem; their minority as Blacks among the minority of gifted; and the enormous variance within the Black population. She is on target in calling for programs that build a positive self-concept. She suggests that all children study the courage and ingenuity of the slaves to foster respect for the Black experience. I agree that programs for these children must be total and flexible, that extensive use of mentors and role models is valuable, and that the focus should be on the positives in each child. I agree with Baldwin's use of high-interest programs that focus on a child's strengths, as abilities in one area suggest possible transfer to other areas. I am intrigued with her idea of looking at how Black children adapt successfully to their environment, particularly when identifying group one students who may be gifted.

Baldwin presents the notion that variance in the strength of gifted Black children depends on geographical location, SES, and parental support. She suggests three levels of groups, from undesirable (group one) to desirable (group three). Group one students are lowest on the three variables and must be identified through subjective tests and observations. Group two students fall somewhere between groups one and three, and may exhibit strengths in psychomotor skills, visual and performing arts, leadership, or task commitment. I have difficulty with this level, as the way the variables affect strengths of gifted Black children is not clear. Group three students appear to have more desirable backgrounds with parental support, higher SES, and/or better geographical location. Baldwin points out that a child can be poor and still have much family support, therefore qualifying for group three categorization. I believe that these same variables—poverty, lack of parental support, limited environment, and poor geographical location—apply to strengths of all children, Black or other.

DISAGREEMENTS WITH BALDWIN

I disagree with Baldwin on three points.[1]

Point 1: Self-Contained Classrooms for Groups One and Two—Gifted Black Children. Although Baldwin suggests these children might be better served in self-contained

---

[1] In response to Cohen's points 1 and 2, Baldwin has clarified her intended meaning.

(1) Self-contained classes represent one type of organizational pattern for programs that serve gifted students. The recommendation of self-contained classes for groups one and two does not imply nor assume segregation by ethnic or racial group.

(2) The self-concept of Black students is enhanced when all students are knowledgeable about and accepting of the value of the Black heritage. Therefore, the curriculum for all students should include the study of Black heritage.

programs that give greater flexibility than other programs, I do not believe gifted children should be separated by race or ethnicity. A mix of children leads to appreciation of diversity, exposure to other values and interests, and interactions.

While coordinating Philadelphia's Mentally Gifted Program, I received two grants from the U.S. Office of Education to identify and serve Hispanic and Title I (now Chapter I) children (Cohen, Revol, & McGreevey, 1981; Cohen & Shorter, 1981). We decided not to separate Spanish-dominant children from others in a predominantly Puerto Rican community. The subdivision, where the great bulk of mostly low SES Hispanic pupils lived, was sandwiched between separate sections of poor Blacks and poor Anglo-Americans. Usually children from each zone did not cross each others' turf. A very creative teacher brought them together to build a Japanese teahouse in the corner of her classroom. Each morning Black, Anglo-American, and Hispanic children took off their shoes, bowed to each other, and entered the teahouse to enjoy a ceremony while discussing events of their lives, planning their day, and learning more about Japanese culture. The study of this fourth culture served to focus on awareness and appreciation of culture, and was a neutral bridge to studying each of their own cultures. The children made great strides in their thinking and creative abilities and improved in regular class work.

Group one children of diverse backgounds, however, might be served better in full-time programs. These children probably differ more from children of poverty who are not gifted than middle-class gifted children differ from their low SES peers. A very bright child in an impoverished community may have to conform to peer pressure by appearing not to be overly intelligent. Examples are the capable child who distracts himself on a test to avoid a perfect paper and the gifted girl who tells her classmates that she cheated when she received an "A."

I advocate full-time programs that provide flexibility, total program planning possibilities, and mutual support of bright peers for what Baldwin calls groups one and two children of diverse backgrounds. These children should be in mixed groups, not separated by skin color or ethnic background.

Point 2: Development of Positive Self-concept through the Study of Courage and Ingenuity of the Slaves. I do not believe cultural heritage affects self-concept as much as daily interactions with parents and peers and success in one's own endeavors. A child of any background of poverty, with poor parental support and an unstimulating or dangerous environment, is more likely to suffer low self-esteem from these factors than from lack of cultural identification. Studying Black history is important in developing pride in one's heritage, but it is too removed from the immediate "me-ness" to develop self-esteem.

Point 3: Emphasis on Creative Development. This major purpose of programs for gifted Black children will be discussed in greater depth later. It was discussed only tangentially by Baldwin.

OTHER PURPOSES OF PROGRAMS FOR GIFTED STUDENTS

Baldwin advocates that educational programs for gifted Black children be individualized because of variations among Blacks, particularly considering economic factors, and that these programs should stress the building of self-esteem through appreciation of strengths of Black slave ancestors. To these I would add (a) identifying Black students who may be gifted; (b) developing a vision of possibilities; (c) dealing with being Black and gifted; (d) providing role models; and (e) developing creative potential.

Identification

Because many children in the lowest SES group who may be gifted are not identified (Maker, 1983), the issue of identification is crucial. The first purpose of programs for gifted Black children must be to look diligently for children whose abilities could be developed with appropriate support.

First, we should look for children when they are very young. Although Philadelphia's public school population is 63.6 percent Black and 57.3 percent of the schools are eligible for Chapter I funds, the first-grade standardized test scores have a higher percentile (60 reading, 50 mathematics) than the national averages. By the third grade, these scores drop considerably (33 reading, 40 mathematics). In my research on identification of both Hispanics and Chapter I children, intelligence (IQ) was negatively correlated with age on the *WISC-R* and on the *DeAvila Cartoon Conservation Scales* (a NeoPiagetian test).

Second, Horowitz and O'Brien's (1985) notion of vulnerability in development of giftedness contains a postulate that strengths arise through an interaction of organism (heredity) and environment, but that a third variable is one of vulnerability. Children of parents of relatively low intelligence and very impoverished environment possibly could be gifted. Horowitz and O'Brien consider these children to be less vulnerable to circumstances in their background. We must look for both those who are sensitive and vulnerable to the hardships of environment, and those who exhibit extraordinary strengths in spite of these hardships. Perhaps the notion of vulnerability may clarify Baldwin's strength development, group one being more vulnerable and group two being less vulnerable.

Third, developmental tests such as the *DeAvila Cartoon Conservation Scale* should be used to identify gifted children in the Black population at the kindergarten level or immediately following developmental transition points. These transition points mask the movement between Piagetian stages (e.g., between the ages of five and seven, when children are developing the ability to conserve). DeAvila notes (1976) that what is seen in testing children with developmental instruments is the false negatives—those youngsters who do not score high on IQ tests due to environmental or language handicaps.

Fourth, programs for gifted Black students should reflect the population of any given area. A concerted effort must be made to find children in nonmainstream populations. Baldwin's suggestions for looking at adaptiveness and building extensive profiles are excellent.

Finally, working intensively in a school is advantageous because teachers become aware of the identification process and begin to search actively for additional children. "If you think Jemal is gifted, you have to test Latonya!" When children of a particular racial or ethnic group are sought, they are found.

Vision of Possibilities

The second major purpose of programs for gifted Black children is to increase the vision of possibilities for these children. One purpose could be to secure sponsorship for groups of poor bright children. Other resources to help a child of an impoverished background, such as scholarships for shoes, books, and transportation, should be sought from local Rotary Clubs, Black business persons, or Parent-Teacher Associations. A school/business consortium might be a most useful avenue to explore.

We must find the strengths—the sparks of confidence in each child—and then allow the child to pursue these interests like craftsmen honing their trades. After determining directions for students by developing extensive profiles (as Baldwin suggests) and carefully ascertaining interests (Cohen, 1987a, 1987b), we can support interest development in three ways.

1. *Exposing children to all the possibilities of interest—people, places, ideas, things, events—open to them*. Charlie, a sixth-grade pupil, became engrossed in a study of Latin American history after we began to prepare our class for a trip to Mexico. He read all the textbooks and school library materials available and came to me with further questions. I brought my college texts and shared these with him. I was amazed at his ability to plow through such difficult works. Although he had not been an exceptional student prior to this experience, the engagement in this area was complete.

2. *Facilitating direct requests for help or offering help to children hesitant in asking, and encouraging use of journals* (Farley & Farley, 1987) *in which children can ask for help and materials*. Kim asks, "How can I say this in a more interesting way?" The teacher might brainstorm possibilities with her.

3. *Thinking about questions children are trying to answer (through their interests), and facilitating development*. When children consistently write about being heroes and having super friends, their fantasies tell us they are trying to deal with their own feelings of powerlessness and to answer the question of how they can become more powerful. We might find ways to help students feel a sense of power, for example, by giving them a leadership role in a class project.

We should explore career choices, especially with groups one and two gifted Black children, to help them develop an awareness of the many different career possibilities and to envision themselves in those careers. Career explorations to awaken possibilities and the raising of aspirations should be a major goal of programs for gifted Black students.

Along with opening visions of possibilities in the world come visions of possibilities within the self: awareness of one's strengths and values, overcoming fears and anxieties, developing self-trust and self-esteem, and establishing one's place in the world and in one's own culture. Counseling, good role models and mentors, and teachers who love children in a growth-supporting way, as well as success in class projects and activities, facilitate this development.

Being Black and Gifted

The third major purpose of programs for gifted Black children is to help those students deal with what Baldwin describes as the minority within the minority—being a Black minority within a gifted minority. As Baldwin notes, one way is to help Black children become aware of the strengths of their ancestors. They also should become aware of the strengths of Blacks in present society; that is, strong religious faith, importance of family ties (including those of the extended family), and zeal for freedom and for self-realization. Gifted Black students also should deal honestly and openly with problems facing Blacks today, as they will likely be the ones to solve them.

Gifted Black children, especially groups one and two, need to be aware that standard English is a necessary skill for functioning successfully in the mainstream culture. According to DeHaven (1983), standard English should be considered a second language to children who speak Black English. They should be taught English like children of Hispanic or other linguistically different groups.

Also important to stress is values development. Breaking away from middle-class materialistic values and outward trappings is essential. Values can be discussed through moral dilemmas, such as those offered through Stanford and Stanford's (1969) classic, "Lost on the Moon"; other simulations (Horn & Cleaves, 1980; Sisk, 1987); or Lipman, Sharp, and Oscanyan's (1980) "Philosophy for Children." Stressing the positive values that Blacks share and introducing Black children to famous Black people whose values and contributions have been outstanding are important.

Role Models

The fourth purpose of programs for gifted Black students, offering role models, requires a word of caution. Positive aspects include exposing Black students to outstanding Black teachers. Mentors, famous Black people, older Black students, counselors, and caring individuals of whatever background also can be role models.

The remarkable portrait of a young Black boxer (Foster & Seltzer, 1986) showed that the coach (his mentor) served as the central figure in the young man's success. For children in groups one and two, where parental support often is lacking, finding adults who can serve as role models that offer support and encouragement over extensive time periods becomes increasingly important for realization of abilities in Black students.

Using gifted Black students in special programs as role models for peers who are not gifted must be approached with caution. Too often, as Colangelo and Zaffron (1979) noted, students of racial minority groups underachieve academically to stay in the group. Gifted children may be "put down" by their peers if they try to achieve. Rowan (1987) describes this as a particularly destructive form of peer pressure in which Black youngsters who strive to get good grades or excel in speaking or writing are accused of "acting White." He notes that such peer ostracism may prevent Black intellectual achievement. Kenya, a gifted and very sensitive fifth grader at a school for academically talented, decided to return to her local school because she could not bear being called "stuck up" by neighborhood children.

In contrast, the young boxer (described by Foster & Seltzer, 1986) was determined to be a role model like his coach was for him, a symbol of success for others in his ghetto community. Unfortunately, academic and intellectual abilities often are not valued by those whose experiences in academics are negative. Important purposes of

Table 34-1 Continuum of Adaptive Creative Behaviors

	Infants and All New Learners; Individual Benefit	Degree of Novelty and Value to the World			Extraordinary Adults, Mature Creativity; Group Benefit
	Universal Novelty	*Problem Solving*	*Demonstration of Talents*	*Creativity— by Extending a Field*	*Creativity—by Revolutionizing a Field*
Definition of constructions or products	Individuals construct relationships new to them but not to the world. Everyone who learns a field must make the same constructions, which remain in the realm of thought. The construction is of personal value.	Individuals develop alternatives; think flexibly, fluently, originally, and elaboratively; make transformations; use critical thinking; systematically use problem-solving processes, including relaxation in a variety of subject areas. The product is of limited value to others.	Individuals develop products or ideas that are rare compared to peers, but not new to the world, in a field of endeavor that is being mastered. The product may be of high value, perhaps as an anomaly (as seen in prodigies), or of some value to others.	Individuals add something new to a field of endeavor that they have mastered, thereby extending it.* The product is of value, especially to those in the field.	Individuals reconceptualize and revolutionize the field in which they function so that it is passed to new learners in its revised state.* The product is of value to those in and outside the field.
Examples	A tot constructs the idea of number . . . that four objects means 1, 1, 1, 1 always; an adult discovers the rule for a perfect soufflé.	A group of middle-school students designs a landscape for a small school courtyard; or businessmen decide on a way to make toothpaste more appealing to children.	A four-year-old invents the idea of a stencil from cutting folded paper; or, a 10-year-old produces an exquisite poem or story.	An individual designs a massive sculpture for the foyer of a public building; or, a physician invents a new procedure for an operation.	Piaget's theory about how children think; or Darwin's theory of evolution.

Characteristic of the creator	Curiosity and pleasure in novelties. Play is important.	Solving problems, usually suggested by others. Can move toward self-set investigations of problems real to the individual. Becomes producer rather than consumer.**	Inventiveness and originality. Compulsion to work in area of interest. Internally motivated.	Problem finding. An awareness of a gap or need in the field and a need to work on it. Internally motivated.	Vision of the possible—an awareness of what could be done and total commitment to create. A Renaissance person who constructs relationships between fields.
Structural aspects	Modify the internal structure to adjust to contradictions in the environment through simple assimilation and accommodation.	Put things into relationships, using reflective abstractions. Coordinate schemes and subsystems (reciprocal equilibrations).	Coordinate schemes and subsystems to see new uses in their combinations (reciprocal equilibrations). Systems of affect and purpose involved.	Develop a frame of reference. Results in a partial Type 3 hierarchical equilibration of totalities. Systems of affect and purpose involved.	Frame of reference completed with unique point of view.** Type 3 hierarchical equilibration of totalities completed. See relationships among disciplines—universal becomes universality. Use networks of enterprises.
Speed	Rapid—seconds to hours, although preparation for insights may take time.	Hours, days, or, at most, a few months.	Ongoing and developing. Seen repeatedly.	Usually takes long periods of time.	Takes many years.***
Result	"Aha!"—the insight experienced in constructing relationships between objects or ideas.	Solution to problems, usually of short duration.	Products or acts are rare compared to peers, but not new to the world.	Intraparadigm creativity.	Inter- or extraparadigm creativity resulting in a paradigm shift.
	Level I	Level II	Level III	Level IV	Level V

Mature Creativity (Level IV and Level V)

*Feldman, 1982.
**Renzulli, 1977.
***Gruber, 1981.

253

programs for gifted Black children are to provide role models that can support full development and to help children deal with feelings of isolation when their gifts (academic or intellectual) are not valued by their own community.

Creative Potential

The final purpose of programs for gifted Black students is to help them realize their creative potential. Baldwin considers this the major goal for the self-contained class she described in her case study. I believe she also would consider it a major program purpose.

I suggest a continuum of creative behaviors that can be both a purpose for education of gifted students and a description of the movement from the universal creativity of the infant to the revolutionizing creativity of the genius. (See Table 34-1.) This continuum can be viewed as an adaptation—the farther along one moves on the continuum, the more one is in control of the environment.

An essential focus of educational provisions for gifted Black students is on critical and creative thinking strategies, problem-solving tools, and research and communication skills that allow for optimum development, provide skills needed to function in the society at large, and help in coping with the strengths and weaknesses of the students' own cultural group.

Gifted Black students must be taught how to find alternative ways to succeed when the going is rough. They need to learn to solve problems, and even more important, to pose them by asking the right questions. Lindstrom and Van Sant (1986) point out that for children from an impoverished background, planning and thinking about the future often is eclipsed by experiences of daily living. Thinking creatively is difficult when one is hungry. Attitudes about long-range planning and purposes may be affected by poverty. Support from teachers and mentors is needed to help students carry out their creative ideas.

In conclusion, I would like to include a letter written to me the last day of school by Tamika, a beautiful fifth grader of group one background. She wrote:

> Dear Dr. Cohen,
>   I have learned a lot about solving problems in this class, so if you have any problem please call me. My telephone number is. . . .

My best teachers of the purposes of education for the gifted have been my remarkable gifted Black students.

35

Successful Adult Response to "The Purpose of Education for Gifted Black Students"

Doris Jefferies Ford, Ph.D.
University of Arizona

Baldwin has framed intellectually the soul-stirring lyrics of the song made popular by Aretha Franklin, "To Be Young, Gifted, and Black." This was one of the songs that came to symbolize the Black Pride Reawakening of the 1960s. For me, the song set forth in a public arena feelings and thoughts that I had already felt as a member of my family unit. The recognition that many more people outside my small circle also were gifted and Black was exciting. This refreshing new beginning enabled me to gain a perception of myself within a Black nationalistic context. Gifted Black people were being heard from in large numbers. Acknowledgments of Black cultural contributions to the larger social structure were being made. The act of inclusion of the strengths of Blacks enhanced our group self-esteem.

In my early public school education in Detroit the contributions of my people were excluded from all subject matter. The only story the teacher read where the character shared my African heritage was "Little Black Sambo." At that time, during the forties and fifties, the neighborhood was in transition with the exit of Jewish people and the entry of Black people. Access to better housing and schools was the focus of social change for Blacks, rather than curriculum issues. My parents reminded us more than once that we went to school to learn and that we would be loved at home. Undoubtedly, learning from a curriculum in which everyone was respected would have been not only to my psychological advantage but also to my classmates' political-social advantage. At a young age, embarrassed by the stupidity of Little Black Sambo and the cannibalistic natives whom Tarzan conquered in the Saturday matinee movies, I tried to distance myself from my African heritage. Without a doubt, the gifted Black student, like all other students, can benefit from the program design presented by Baldwin where "pride and self-worth through study of the courage and ingenuity of Blacks' forefathers" is integrated into the curriculum.

Giftedness, however, cannot be limited to a discussion within the school context. For the Black child, a somewhat dangerous assumption is that only the school can enhance intellectual achievement. Such an assumption will continue to contribute to the dropout rate of gifted Black students. In a study by Ford (1976) on the family characteristics of high-achieving Black children, among his conclusions were the following:

1. The home atmosphere is neat and orderly with a variety of educational material and recreational equipment.
2. The parents are achievement-oriented, as evidenced by their school-related experiences; they place a high value on education.
3. The parents not only read to their children but also read extensively themselves.
4. The parents are knowledgeable about what efforts they should put forth in assisting their children to do well in school.
5. While few Black awareness materials are in the home, evidence indicated that the families prefer and listen to Black music.

My own experiences show the need for cooperative linkages among the family, school, and community, with all serving crucial educational enhancement roles. I consider myself not as a gifted person but rather as one who had the ability, socialization, and motivation to achieve extremely well in the formal school setting. Factors contributing to my academic success included being from a family in which education was valued highly and in which the home life was structured to be supportive of the efforts of my teachers. I also entered kindergarten with the advantage of being the fifth of six children. For many, many evenings of those preschool years, I sat at the kitchen table while my parents supervised the completion of homework assignments by my older siblings. I listened and was encouraged to participate. The expectation for my achievement was set within my blue collar, lower socioeconomic family group and not in the classroom where I was only one of two Black students. Thus, the importance of the family support system, whether traditional or nontraditional, cannot be recognized only cursorily. That sense of family in most, but certainly not in all, cases increases the educational success of gifted students who otherwise might become lost while trying to find their way in the mainstream.

Because I lived up to my family's expectations and had some teachers who reinforced my ability to achieve, I was accelerated from the second half of the third grade to the second half of the fourth grade. After that, I was placed in split sections with students who were a grade higher. While most of my academic needs were being met, my social security and physical development lagged behind that of my classmates. The problems created from the acceleration haunted me for many years. I was painfully shy and ashamed of my little-girl physical appearance. Not until the eleventh grade did I begin to catch up with the others both physically and socially, but the die had been cast for my social label. Through it all, the joy of learning and the reward of kisses and hugs from my father and mother made me stronger.

Could I have benefited from the program for gifted students outlined by Baldwin? Probably. The program she proposes would have added to my self-esteem within the school environment where I could have been treated as a whole person, rather than as a too shy bright child. My heritage, like that of my classmates, would have been accepted, thus increasing my self-acceptance. Baldwin also implies that the gifted student participates in a homogeneous group rather than with other gifted students, which would reduce the social maturation and physical development problems I encountered from the old model of grade acceleration. However, programs that totally separate the gifted group from other students also have a social cost important to young people. Perhaps the best method is to have a few special classes or tutoring during the day for the gifted child, just as the child needing remedial work has special time. My high school had a system that I reflect upon quite favorably. It had "x" sections for classes in English and mathematics, which were available for the accelerated students. The students could have their academic challenges met in the essential subject areas while intermingling with the mainstream of students in their other classes. The potential for elitism is greatly reduced. All students learn that some people have gifts and talents in certain areas, but certainly not in all areas.

Individualized assessment to determine the strengths and weaknesses of the student is an acceptable approach. However, the practice of individualization appears difficult to implement in public schools. The example given of introducing a student with strengths in creative problem solving to processes that would increase analytic skills in the areas of science and logic is laudatory. For the self-starter and independent student, the teacher could spend a brief time providing direction, and then the student could become nearly self-taught in learning the process. However, if the gifted Black student is not a self-starter in school work, the individualized approach requires much more time than most teachers humanly can give. Also, the highly assertive gifted Black student often will engage the teacher in time-consuming, mentally challenging confrontations until the teacher becomes exhausted and labels the student "a behavior problem." The student, needing the highly interactive individualized approach, typically will lose the designation "gifted" and get placed in less challenging academic tracks. I was "lucky." I was an obedient, shy, and passive learner thanks to my kindergarten teacher. She had made me sit under her desk for squealing too loudly while building a structure out of large wooden blocks. I remember the traumatic experience vividly. During those preschool years at the kitchen table, my family forgot to tell me that school was a place where you spoke when you were spoken to. I learned my lesson well. My elementary school, junior high, and high school autograph books signed by my classmates attest to what a nice, shy, and smart girl I was. An individualized approach for me would have helped me learn to be more courageous in expressing creative thought within the school environment, rather than sharing such thoughts only at home.

I cannot even begin to imagine what my school experience would have been like if I had the opportunity, as Baldwin suggests, to integrate my love for Black blues (which my father sang and played on the guitar) with history, politics, and mathematics. The curriculum of yesterday and today cannot tolerate that which is Black and "lower-class" as an acceptable area of study. I wish my love for the unwritten blues my father and his friends played had not been a family secret because it was not socially accepted. I wish I had been encouraged to research the meanings of the phraseology, its geometric forms, and the psychological history so that I could have memorialized my father for the gifts he and my mother passed on to me.

The discussion of gifted Black students does not extend far enough to include the gift of talent. Many Black students have talents that go unrecognized and unrewarded in the school environment. Just as care is taken through testing and other assessments to identify and nurture intellectual development, that same care should be taken to heighten the talents of Black students. Historically, the talents of Black students are designated for street expression only; and, many of these students display the talent in the street rather than in the school. Society continues to be willing to pay the cost for Black dropouts, while seizing their cultural contributions without just compensation.

My husband was able to use his talent as an athlete to secure his education. As a young boy growing up in a small Black township in Louisiana, he had limited educational resources. His advantage was that his Black teachers continually encouraged him and made the school environment more interesting than the call to the fishing or swimming hole. The contributions of Blacks to society were a part of his curriculum, which did not place his self-concept into a compromising position. The broad range of educational resources was not available to him as it was for me, but he was not fearful of asserting himself. As an adult he became an elected official, in a city where Blacks are approximately 3 percent of the population. His achievement is attributable to a self-concept that was never forced into compromise in order to succeed. Our relationship of mutual respect takes the best of both our experiences.

Would I have a more productive life had I had the advantage of the model for gifted Black students as presented by Baldwin? I don't know. My life is highly productive, but I always feel that I could be doing more. I have not written a great book, nor have I been able to eradicate singlehandedly racism and sexism. However, I remain committed to helping make the world a better place than I found it by using whatever gifts and talents I have.

36

Gifted Black Students: Curriculum and Teaching Strategies

Saundra Scott Sparling, Ph.D.
California State University,
Bakersfield

A question arises about specific curriculum and teaching strategies for gifted Black students: Are they necessary, and why? The answer is both yes and no. Yes, because the school motivation and performance patterns of Black students are lower than those of Anglo-American students (Cooper & Tom, 1984; Hare, 1985), indicating a need for curriculum and teaching strategies that better meet the needs of Black students. No, because too many troubling patterns of difference exist both within and between Anglo-American and a number of stigmatized minority groups.[1] Such patterns of difference are related to language, socioeconomic status (SES), gender, and criteria for identifying giftedness (Clark, 1979, 1981; Cooper & Tom, 1984; Hare, 1985; Torrance, 1970b; Wood, 1983). Providing curriculum and teaching strategies to meet each different need would place an incredible burden on the capabilities of curriculum developers; on teachers, to learn and to apply differentially so many instructional approaches; and, more important, on stigmatized minority and poor students, by placing them in the role of eternally hopeless victims needing to be provided for and removing from them an essential element in their educational growth—their right to share responsibility for meeting their own needs.

Curriculum and teaching strategies are needed, then, that meet, but are not limited to, the differing needs of gifted Black students. These curricula and teaching strategies must be difference-sensitive and (a) address a range of learning needs across racial, gender, and socioeconomic group lines; (b) allow students to share responsibility for meeting their own learning needs; and (c) simplify the task of curriculum developers

---

[1]The term stigmatized minority is a designation used for Black, Hispanic, and other racial groups to whom a stigma has been attached by systematic discrimination and bigotry in this country. It is so designated in Word, C.O., Zanna, M.P., & Cooper, J. (1984). Non-verbal mediation of self-fullfilling prophecies in interaction. *Journal of Experimental Social Psychology, 10,* 109–120.

and teachers. Though the concept may seem idealistic, a project underway in the Los Angeles area involves testing difference-sensitive curriculum and teaching strategies with culturally and socioeconomically different gifted and nongifted students in both integrated and isolated programs. In the project, Clark's (1981, 1986) Integrative Education Model of brain-compatible instruction is combined with Sparling's (1985, 1986) Shared Responsibility Model approach to classroom and behavior management. A major goal of the project is to ensure that student and teacher participants are more sensitive to cultural differences but, at the same time, understand and address differences in learning needs based on principles of human function rather than on characteristics of culture, gender, and SES. The objective of this chapter is to present the curriculum and teaching strategies forthcoming from Clark's and Sparling's work. Though final results from this research are not yet available, theoretical backgrounds of both models, descriptions and guidelines for their implementation, and some preliminary results of the project are discussed.

THEORETICAL BACKGROUND

Integrative Education Model (IEM)

The Integrative Education Model (Clark, 1981, 1985, 1986) is described as a model of "learning and teaching that is highly structured, complex, decentralized, and individualized, allowing for variations in pace, level and grouping" (Clark, 1985, p. 2). The model works well in mainstream programs, where it allows for the range of intellectual abilities, and in programs for the gifted, where it allows for the learning characteristics of culturally different students who may have been identified by non-academic (e.g., creativity, leadership) as well academic (e.g., school achievement, mathematics aptitude) criteria (Baldwin, 1973; Benson, 1978; Sparling, 1984; Torrance, 1970b, 1977; Wood, 1983). Based on a Jungian model (positing four areas of human function) and on brain research, the goal of the IEM is to combine four functions—thinking, feeling, physical sensing, and intuition—in the teaching of each subject area and to allow each function of the brain to support the others.

The thinking function (cognitive) involves the left brain specializations of analyzing, problem solving, sequencing, and evaluating and the spatial/gestalt orientations of the right brain. Clark suggests that two factors in the brain—higher synaptic activity and increased density of the dendrites—are the basis for complex thought and that these and their related advanced capacity to generalize, conceptualize, and reason abstractly are promoted by stimulating environments.

The feeling function (affective) affects every part of the brain/mind system. Feelings are regulated primarily by the limbic area of the brain, and their influence can enhance or limit higher cognitive functions. Clark posits that "worthwhile academic programs integrate emotional growth" (1985, p. 1).

The physical function (senses) involves movement, physical encoding, sight, hearing, smell, taste, and touch. Clark states, "We know our world through our senses, so how our bodies integrate sensory cues determines how we perceive" (1985, p. 1).

Finally, *the intuitive function (insightful, creative)* is centered in the prefrontal cortex of the brain and is described as "a sense of total understanding, of directly and immediately gaining a concept in its whole, living existence" (1985, p. 1). This function is in part the result of a high-level synthesis of all brain functions. In educational settings, concentration and unusual clarity during complex tasks are two activities believed to be related to intuition. Clark suggests that intuition is operant in the planning, future thinking, and insight necessary to intelligence.

In summarizing the elements necessary for a brain-compatible curriculum and teaching strategies, Clark (1985) states, "Learning is optimal when thinking—both linear and spatial—feeling, physical/sensing, and intuition are all part of the learning experience. Such experiences must be novel, complex, pleasurable, relatively free of tension, and challenging if they are to be brain compatible" (p. 2).

Shared Responsibility Model (SRM)

The Shared Responsibility Model (Sparling, 1985, 1986) was originally developed (Benson, 1979) (a) to build school-related self-esteem, (b) to foster increased responsible behavior, (c) to increase a sense of personal causation and control, and (d) to build self-management skills among low SES gifted Black students. Though Benson (1979) found these to be areas of need for Black students, the model appears to be effective with students differing in motivational, academic, cultural, and economic backgrounds. As a model of student/teacher interaction and classroom management, its purpose is to help teachers increase student self-direction. The model allows gradual replacement of total teacher control with a balance of teacher and student responsibility. The SRM is posited to have an impact in three areas: Students' relationships with each other and their own learning; the teachers' relationships with students; and parents' relationships with the school.

For students, personal valuing of learning activities and choice and decisionmaking are promoted through use of the model. Personal valuing, or that experience when students feel that what they are doing has meaning, is related directly to their willingness to accomplish (Maehr, 1984). Choice and decisionmaking involve students in selecting from among meaningful alternatives and judging for themselves what is the best alternative. By making choices and decisions, students gain a perception of control over their learning outcomes (deCharms, 1984). Perceived control influences three major aspects of responsible behavior: motivation to initiate, continue, and follow through with learning tasks (Sparling, 1985).

For teachers, the model helps provide relief from a primary source of frustration and burnout; that is, the conflicting sense of needing to control what goes on in the classroom versus the goal of having students be more responsible for that activity. In the SRM model, responsible behavior is conceptualized as falling on a continuum between the two extreme ends of total teacher control and total student control. A sharing of responsibility with optimum freedom and structure for both works best. Seven elements of the learning environment inhibit the sharing of responsibility for learning:

1. Low beliefs and limited expectations about the feasibility of sharing responsibility
2. Negative feelings and attitudes
3. Lack of dreams and goals for learning and achieving
4. Limited willingness and commitment to do what works and to follow through on tasks and commitments
5. Lack of perceived control over results
6. Poor skills and strategies for producing results
7. Inability to monitor one's progress (Sparling, 1985)

In the classroom, three factors contribute to these inhibiting elements: teachers' and students' negative past experiences (Weiner, 1984); nonsupportive classroom relationships (Ginott, 1972); and the design and organization of learning activities (e.g., competitive activities, grading on a curve) (Maehr, 1984). The SRM model is designed to help teachers supplant these factors with those that enhance beliefs and expectations, generate positive feelings and attitudes, elicit dreams for future achievement, promote willingness and commitment, expand skills and strategies, provide for self-monitoring, and foster mastery-enhancing goals (described by Maehr [1984] as resulting from task involvement, in which students' attention is focused on developing skills, rather than from ego involvement, in which attention is focused on protecting self-esteem).

For parents, potentially significant changes in the way some children conduct themselves can operate in concert, or in conflict, with at-home expectations of children. Parents, therefore, have been involved in SRM implementation. When parents are involved in or at least informed of what is happening with their children at school, the resulting growth process more often is seen by them as beneficial, is given more at-home support, and happens much more rapidly than when parents are not involved. Parents can be involved and informed in many ways:

- several hours of group training before the beginning of school, featuring ways to support and to follow through with shared responsibility at home; followed by signing of contracts of agreement
- short parent meeting prior to, or at the beginning of, school explaining the program and indicating specific areas of needed at-home support; followed by signing of contracts of agreement
- letter-contracts sent home; followed by individual telephone conferences in which teachers and parents review the nature of the child's participation and agree on the form of at-home support
- letter-contracts without telephone conferences, which are simply read by parents, signed, and returned to school

Several types of at-home support are desirable: (a) Providing accessory tools that enhance academic progress (e.g., consistent time and quiet place to study, dictionary and access to reference materials—at home or the library, library card and library accessibility); (b) focusing on the positives in the parent-child relationship and the uniqueness of children and what they do (e.g., acknowledging what is done right rather than admonishing what is done wrong, reading the child's stories for enjoyment rather than for correction, providing outside information on subjects of interest to the child, one-to-one time for activities other than discipline such as reading, playing games, talking over problems); and (c) using empowering language and behavior (defined as any verbal, nonverbal, and/or overt physical response that results in the experience of positive challenge, competence, support, closeness, appreciation, and/or the receiving of helpful feedback). "I-centered" messages, affirmations, and humor are examples of empowering language and behavior.

MODEL DESCRIPTIONS AND IMPLEMENTATION GUIDELINES

Integrative Education Model

Seven components have been proposed to meet the objectives of the IEM, and each is discussed below.

Responsive learning environment involves establishing the context for learning, emphasizing the creation of a supportive socioemotional and physical home/school environment and engaging teachers, parents, and students in working together as a team. The following are some guidelines teachers have found effective in establishing responsive learning environments (Clark, 1985):

- display an abundance of student activities, products, and ideas around the classroom
- conduct cooperative planning sessions with teachers, students, and parents
- keep notes and histories on each student's intellectual, emotional, and physical development
- use evaluation as feedback for the student and as a way to guide the student's instruction
- arrange a variety of simultaneous individual and small-group activities for the student's participation
- group students for lessons directed at specific needs
- have students voluntarily group and regroup themselves
- provide a diversity of materials readily accessible to the students, including many levels and manipulatives
- include in the environment materials developed by the students and teachers
- supply many different books
- encourage students to write and to use "books" written by their classmates
- provide all students with a personal storage space (not necessarily their own desks)
- encourage parents to carry over into the home environment activities and outcomes, such as cooperative parent/child planning and diverse and numerous books

Relaxation and tension reduction has as its focus increasing relaxation and reducing tension to levels optimal for processing and retaining information. To achieve optimal levels, use relaxation techniques—such as cleansing breaths, stretching exercises, and visualization. Model for students a relaxed, calm manner. As much as possible, eliminate interruptions and maintain low and purposeful noise levels. Relaxation and tension reduction procedures help to develop coherence, to prepare students for tests, and to facilitate calm during periods of transition.

Movement and physical encoding, which relate to the physical function, involve body action in the understanding and retention of abstract concepts. For example, if one has driven a route, physically made the turns, and seen the landmarks, one remembers the route much longer than if one has simply heard the route described. To implement this component, teachers can (a) limit movement in the room to that which is purposeful, (b) use physical sensing (e.g., touch, smell) in learning activities, and (c) incorporate body movement in the development of concepts (e.g., choreographing a representation of cell division in which students play the role of different structures in the cell).

The purpose of the fourth (*empowering language and behavior*) and fifth (*choice and perceived control*) components is to influence responsible behavior. They are related to the feeling function. According to Clark (1985) "emotions trigger the brain's production of biochemistry, which enhances or inhibits the thinking function" (p. 2). Language and behavioral interchanges between teachers and students and among students facilitate empowering or debilitating emotional responses. The use of empowering language and behavior builds a sense of community and "helps develop positive interpersonal and intrapersonal communication" (Clark, 1985, p. 2). Choice and perceived control motivate achievement striving and persistence (deCharms, 1984; Deiner & Dweck, 1978). Without striving and persistence, children do not initiate or follow through with learning activities. Positive interpersonal and intrapersonal communication, initiative, and follow-through are the focus of these two components. (Because many aspects of both components were developed by Sparling [1985, 1986] as a part of the SRM, they also will be presented with that model.)

Complex and challenging activities relate to the thinking (cognitive) function. The focus of this component is on the two ways to process thinking—linear/rational and spatial/gestalt—facilitating the integration of the functions of the left and right hemispheres of the brain. "By allowing the linear/rational and spatial/gestalt specializations to support each other, teachers take advantage of the brain's associative nature. Providing novelty, complexity, variety, and challenge as the standard for each lesson makes the educational process more brain compatible" (Clark, 1985, p. 4). Sufficient complexity and challenge can be established through certain activities:

a. Use pre- and post-testing and continuous assessment.
b. Develop lessons at the learner's level paced to meet each individual's need.
c. Use interesting and experiental tasks.
d. Use both the rational/linear and the spatial/gestalt processes.
e. Give students choice and allow them to share responsibility for planning learning experiences. (Clark, 1985, p. 5)

Intuition and integration relate to the intuitive function. Clark (1985) states, "Intuition, future planning, and creativity are brain processes considered unique to human beings. They may be the most powerful of the brain functions. Many educational researchers believe that activities which allow their use are essential for optimizing learning. Because they are highly synthetic functions, however, they require teaching opportunities that are multi-sensory" (p. 6).

Conditions believed to foster intuition are relaxed states, silence, focused attention, and receptive and nonjudgmental attitudes. Especially important are teachers who (a) value and encourage intuitive processes, and hypothesis and probability testing; (b) are comfortable with both the students' and their own mistakes; and (c) emphasize personal discovery over memorization of facts. To develop or capitalize on intuitive processing, the following strategies can be used:

- provide students with a minimum amount of known information and encourage them to reorganize, hypothesize, and suggest solutions
- help students use known information plus hunches to establish probabilities
- give students opportunities to synthesize many known and unknown sources in creating new information and artistic products
- use imagery, fantasy, and visualization
- use "what if" and open-ended future-thinking strategies
- encourage creativity
- emphasize real-world problems and their solutions

Shared Responsibility Model

Like the IEM, the SRM has seven components, and a discussion of each follows. *Task-involving context* fosters belief in and expectations of success by focusing teachers' and students' attention on what can be done. Teachers who believe that children can behave responsibly will set goals to enable them to do so. Students who believe they can control themselves will elicit support from those in authority around them. To motivate their own beliefs and expectations, teachers can provide themselves with opportunities to observe their own responses in different learning contexts. In this way, teachers can note (a) how their own responsible behavior occurs naturally when they are task involved; (b) how differently they think, feel, and act when task involved as opposed to ego involved; and (c) how these two types of involvement (task and ego) affect both their expectations for, and actual, personal success or failure. To provide a task-involving context for students, teachers can

- model how personal limitations and failures can be turned into learning opportunities, and support students in doing the same
- practice behavior in which blaming themselves and students for limitations and failures is seldom an influence
- provide students with fewer competitive and more cooperative-learning activities

- use grading and evaluation systems that do not compare one student to another
- give students negative evaluations in a private setting
- provide student learning activities frequently that foster competition with (challenge of) self, rather than competition with others
- provide few external rewards (e.g., tokens, candies, money) and more feedback on skills
- provide enough rewards (when offered) for everyone to earn
- involve students in problem-solving strategies, such as brainstorming or the Five Question Method—that is, What is the problem? What do you want (or is wanted)? What are you doing (or is being done) about it? Is it working? What will you do now (or can be done) that might work? (Sparling, 1986).

Empowering language and behavior are used to create a classroom atmosphere of mutual trust and respect where mistakes that are a natural part of learning can be seen as valuable learning tools, rather than as failures. To ensure that empowering language and behavior are operating, teachers can use questions to foster personal valuing, to aid in choice and decisionmaking, and to encourage the sharing of ideas. They also can avoid cross-messages, in which body language and verbal communication give conflicting information, and can avoid giving excessive help, praise, or sympathy for easy work that is poorly done. Both teachers and students can use the following strategies:

- communicate appreciation and empathy for positive *and* negative thoughts and feelings
- use "I-centered" messages, affirmations, humor, and constructive feedback
- minimize use of terms such as should, shouldn't, must, mustn't, always, and never
- increase use of percentage words, such as often, seldom, and frequently
- acknowledge successes and contributions

Dreaming and goal setting activities such as those below give students direction.

- share dreams and goals for the future
- identify and share what can be done today and tomorrow (short-range goals) that might lead to the realization of life dreams and goals
- make the objective of every classroom activity clear
- set time aside (as often as possible) for students to create and to link personal goals to lesson goals (e.g., brainstorm and share personal goals that can be achieved through a learning activity)
- help students understand that every goal has ground rules (i.e., steps necessary and sufficient to achieve the goal)
- practice identifying the ground rules inherent in goals
- apply classroom learning to real-life nonacademic problems

Valuing and renewal experiences are focused on overcoming loss of interest and enthusiasm. After the novelty of new insights and skills wanes, motivation to apply skills often decreases. Use of strategies from this component helps maintain and rekindle students' and teachers' willingness and commitment to do whatever works to achieve goals and realize dreams. To create the experience of valuing and renewal, the following strategies are effective:

- help students identify what actions work (and do not work) in achieving goals
- share the feelings associated with effective and ineffective actions
- acknowledge the similarities and differences between what works (and does not work) for teachers, and for students
- discuss frequently results that feel good
- encourage the sharing of ways in which students and teachers sabotage their motivation, willingness, and commitment
- use the classroom as a laboratory for experimenting with ways to overcome motivation, behavior, and learning problems
- use verbal or written affirmation to renew motivation, commitment, and willingness to follow through on tasks

Choice and decisionmaking help establish and maintain perceived control. Perceived control is sensing that one already possesses, or can attain, the skills necessary to achieve one's goals. The extent to which teachers help students maintain this sense of control partly determines how much responsibility students will take. Making choices and making decisions are powerful contributors to the perception of control. To make choice and decisionmaking a part of classroom activities, teachers should work with students to establish agreements for appropriate behavior rather than imposing rules of behavior. Following are examples of effective strategies to accomplish this goal:

- model alternative thinking
- help students to see that they have choices about how to respond to any situation
- train students to make choices and decisions
- give students parameters of requisite knowledge, and allow them to choose how they will demonstrate mastery of that knowledge
- offer only choices that are acceptable
- encourage learning in small steps

Skills and strategy development is focused on increasing the means that teachers and students have available for sharing responsibility. The procedures help teachers organize lessons so that students learn to do as much as possible for themselves. Because many instructional strategies are designed to foster compliant (i.e., instruction-following) student behavior, students often are poorly equipped to behave responsibly. To develop skills and strategies for responsible behavior, the following strategies are recommended:

- help students brainstorm and keep track of ways that work to accomplish their learning goals
- have students create attractive, simple, and efficient systems to organize, store, and/or display the materials and information for which they are responsible
- use simple instructions and agendas
- have students help create instructions and agendas
- encourage planning ahead to identify possible barriers to achieving goals, and to assess potential consequences of action
- allow students to experience the consequences of their own actions
- use brainstorming and other nonjudgmental methods to help students generate strategies
- have students share their coping and problem-solving strategies
- help students evaluate the effectiveness of the skills and strategies they use
- model all of these strategies

Finally, in the *self-monitoring and acknowledgment* component, students' independence and self-direction are supported. Controlling one's own behavior requires knowing when that behavior meets (or does not meet) standards of appropriateness. Students' rates of responsible behavior increase in relation to their opportunities to monitor and acknowledge their own progress and to evaluate their own results. To implement this component, the following strategies are effective:

- make expectations clear, consistent, and based on goals and ground rules
- provide clear evaluation criteria
- involve students in determining evaluation criteria
- give students immediate feedback whenever possible
- share with students the scope and sequence of content and skills, and discuss with them (individually) their growth
- give, or have students design, checklists for monitoring their progress and evaluating their products
- analyze differences between teacher and student evaluation outcomes
- give students opportunities to improve assignments, tests, and projects before final evaluation
- encourage students to evaluate classroom activities and suggest changes
- encourage students to acknowledge regularly their own and others' progress

PRELIMINARY PROJECT RESULTS

Although preliminary data on the IEM are not yet available, student observations from pilot testing of the SRM indicate increases in (a) attendance; (b) number of required and extra-credit assignments completed; (c) quality of assignments (as indicated by letter grades); (d) receptivity to constructive criticism; (d) degree of initiation, self-direction, and follow-through on learning activities; and (e) feelings and sense of enjoyment and satisfaction with classroom activities. Gradual decreases also are apparent in interpersonal relationship problems, need for authoritarian teacher control, and teachers' experience of frustration and stress. The changes seem to be significant and consistent across cultural and socioeconomic groups. The significance of changes seems to bear an inverse relationship to each student's past achievement patterns, with greater increases or decreases for students with the greatest past performance-potential discrepancies.

IN CONCLUSION

Because gifted Black students seem to have special learning needs and because too many groups with special needs exist to provide curriculum and teaching strategies for each one, difference-sensitive curriculum and teaching strategies are recommended as viable alternatives. They are being developed out of the combined instructional and management models of Clark (1981, 1986) and Sparling (1985, 1986), and are posited to offer teachers the advantage of a single instructional approach to address the individual needs of gifted students across a range of motivational, cultural, academic, and socioeconomic backgrounds.

In comparing self-reports from students who are, and who are not, being instructed through use of the combined Integrative Education and Shared Responsibility Models, students who are being instructed with these models (in contrast to their counterparts) report feeling *more*

- relaxed;
- at ease with themselves and others;
- positive, caring, and respectful of each other and their teachers;
- creative;
- positive and enthusiastic about their learning;
- independent;
- apt to try unusual solutions; and
- likely to engage in alternative and higher level cognitive activities (Clark, 1985).

Though self-report data alone are insufficient to give strong evidence of the effectiveness of these models, results are still encouraging and affirm that difference-sensitive curriculum and teaching strategies are fruitful avenues for future research and development.

37

A Reaction to "Gifted Black Students: Curriculum and Teaching Strategies"

E. Paul Torrance, Ph.D.
Distinguished Professor Emeritus
University of Georgia

Sparling offers two exciting models for educating gifted Black children: the Integrative Education Model (IEM) and the Shared Responsibility Model (SRM). Both models are challenging, and both contain ingredients I have pioneered and advocated over the last 30 years (Torrance, 1958, 1962, 1965a, 1965c, 1970a, 1977, 1979a; Torrance & Myers, 1970). These models include practices such as developing a responsive environment; teaching and learning that is integrative (or whole-brain); integrating intuition, future planning, and creativity; sharing responsibility (creative student/teacher relationship); decisionmaking; giving feedback; emphasizing cooperative learning; grouping and regrouping; using relaxation and tension reduction exercises; motivating achievement striving and persistence; incorporating challenging activities; guiding imagery, fantasy, and visualization; brainstorming (Creative Problem Solving); and dreaming and setting goals. Sparling has added empowering language and behavior, and physical encoding.

Some rightfully might complain that these models and their ingredients are appropriate for all children, not just gifted Black children. While this contention is true, I believe that the elements in these models are especially appropriate for the gifted and, furthermore, for gifted Black students. To make the models more specifically appropriate, we have to consider specific characteristics (abilities, skills, and motivations) of gifted Black students. I wish Sparling had addressed more of these specifics, though I realize this would be difficult to do in a short chapter.

SPECIAL STRENGTHS OF BLACKS

I have referred to the abilities, skills, and motivations Blacks demonstrate at levels as high or higher than others, as their "creative positives" (Torrance, 1972, 1974a, 1977). My research (Torrance, 1977) indicated that Blacks possess these characteristics to a high degree and frequently attain fame for outstanding achievement in related areas. I contend that successful educational programs for Blacks must be based on their strengths, rather than their deficits. Characteristics or positives identified include the following (Torrance, 1970b, 1977):

- ability to express feelings and emotions
- ability to improvise with common materials
- articulateness in role playing and storytelling
- enjoyment of and ability in visual art
- enjoyment of and ability in creative movement, dance, and dramatics
- enjoyment of and ability in music and rhythm
- expressive and colorful speech
- fluency and flexibility in nonverbal media
- enjoyment of and skill in small-group (cooperative) learning and problem solving
- responsiveness to the concrete
- responsiveness to the kinesthetic (movement)
- expressiveness of gestures and body language
- humor
- richness of imagery in informal language
- orginality of ideas in problem solving, invention
- problem centeredness
- quickness of "warm-up"

Along with these characteristics, I have maintained steadfastly that creativeness always should be one of the criteria considered in searching for giftedness among Blacks, though not the sole criterion. Two major reasons can be cited for my belief: (a) Creativity is a key characteristic of almost every person who has made outstanding social contributions, and (b) creativity is one of the greatest and most common strengths of Blacks. Because people generally are motivated most to do the things that they do best, Blacks are most motivated to achieve in the areas that emphasize these strengths.

The admonitions of my "manifesto" emphasize developing strengths, and are especially appropriate for gifted Black children. (See Figure 37-1.)

The need for mentors for gifted Black students cannot be emphasized too strongly. Disadvantaged (poor) Black students especially need mentors who can encourage them during times of frustration, discouragement, or abuse, and protect their rights if necessary. Poor Black students need someone who is special to them who can see that they get a chance. The purpose of this chance is not to give Black students "something for nothing," but rather to see that they have opportunities "to work for it."

TEACHING STRATEGY

As Glasser (in Gough, 1987, p. 660) says, "Teachers can't make students learn, but they can certainly set things up so that students want to learn." I contend that creative learning is self-motivating and that this kind of motivation will persevere

Figure 37-1 Manifesto for Children. *Source*: Designed by Morgan Henderson & Jack Presbury for Georgia Studies of Creative Behavior + Full Circle Counseling, Inc. © Copyright 1983. All Rights Reserved by Henderson, Presbury, Torrance.

(Torrance, 1965c, 1970a, 1979b; Torrance & Myers, 1970). My instructional model contains elements to arouse and to sustain motivation and offers a strategy that is especially suitable for gifted Black children because it makes use of their special strengths and learning styles. This instructional model is represented in Figure 37-2.

The model is a strategy for teaching lessons but also may be used in organizing a course, module, or other unit of instruction. As a strategy for teaching a lesson, it offers guidance for creating or selecting learning activities to be used before, during, and after (or at the end of) a lesson. The model has been described in some detail elsewhere (Torrance, 1969a, 1969c, 1970a, 1979a, 1979b, 1987a, 1987b) and is amply illustrated in the *Reading 360* and *Reading 720 Programs* (Clymer, 1969, 1976) and other sources (Torrance, 1969a, 1969c). Only the highlights are presented here.

The purpose of the activities before (or at the beginning of) a lesson (stage one) is to heighten anticipation and expectations, to create a desire to know, to find out, to understand. The emphasis is on anticipatory learning (Botkin, Elmandjra, & Malitza, 1979).

The purpose of the activities during a lesson (stage two) is to sustain motivation and deepen expectations. This involves alternating between anticipatory and participatory learning.

After a lesson (or at the end; stage three) keeping the processes going and promoting continued learning and thinking are important. The emphasis is on participatory learning. Intuitive, creative thinking is involved at every stage, but is given full rein here.

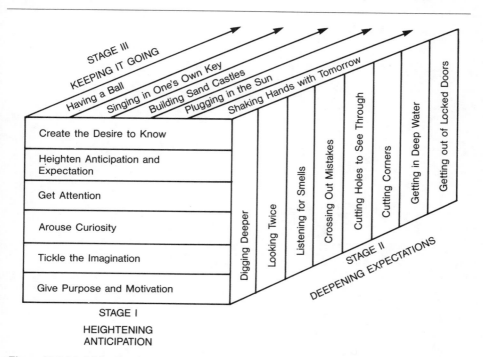

Figure 37-2 Model for Creative Learning and Teaching. *Source*: Copyright © E. Paul Torrance, 1987.

I have designed a simple lesson planning form that many of my students (and their students as well) have found useful and simple, though powerful. It may be used in designing instruction in any subject matter area at any educational level. The planner first states a dominant subject matter objective and a dominant creative skill objective, and then lists learning and thinking activities hypothesized to accomplish those objectives. Much serendipitous learning usually accompanies the use of this design.

Individual feedback is an important element of instruction. My students and I have found the model sketched by de Bono (1974) in his *Thinking Course for Juniors* very useful and exciting. This model involves sequential talk or writing in four areas: (a) praise, (b) clarification, (c) criticism, and (d) amplification. As in the instructional model, use of this feedback plan arouses and sustains motivation, and it seems to be easy to learn and execute.

IN CONCLUSION

Gifted Black students possess abilities, skills, and motivations that I have called Creative Positives. These Creative Positives not only are useful in identifying gifted students from ethnic minorities, but also serve as guides to curriculum development. Using the Creative Positives in these ways offers the promise of moving away from deficit-based procedures to those based on (student) strengths.

38

Black Students and Education: Points for Consideration

Carl A. Grant, Ph.D.
University of Wisconsin at Madison

Initially, I wish to point out that Black students (and I would argue students of other groups of color) are not in need of *special* considerations nor do they see themselves as a special population. Rather, Black students are in need of understanding and *equal* considerations. This point is important because educational literature is replete with ethnocentric phrases or terms that make Blacks (and other students of color) seem inferior to Anglo-American students, and make Anglo-American students the normative group in schools. If Blacks were given equal consideration, then the question of special considerations might become moot.

With this important observation stated, I now will turn to the charge at hand. I have defined the task in this chapter as discussing educational programs and practices that may be particularly relevant to gifted Black students. To perform my task, I decided not to rely solely on my own thinking. I conducted an informal interview survey with sixteen individuals. Fourteen are Blacks, four of whom are professional educators; and ten are college seniors. Eight of the ten seniors were in programs for gifted students sometime during their kindergarten through grade 12 educational experience. The other two people interviewed are Anglo-Americans. One is a tutor for athletes at a large Big Ten university; many of her students are gifted Black athletes trying to be successful, both academically and athletically. The other is an educator who works with Black students at the secondary and college level. I asked these individuals, "If you had to address Black students and their teachers about the education of gifted Blacks, what would you say to them?" Their suggestions can be grouped under three major ideas: (a) the need to develop in students the skills and attitudes needed for them to take charge of their own destiny; (b) the need to work actively to assure that students are a part of the mainstream of school and society; and (c) the need to *really* know your students well.

TAKING CHARGE OF DESTINY

The majority of those interviewed stated that gifted Black students need to be taught to take charge of their destiny to enable them to change life circumstances for themselves and the many Blacks who are poor and powerless. This means that learning the three Rs is not enough. For example, too often reading, writing, arithmetic, and other subjects are taught in a classroom context that is irrelevant to the needs and interests of Black students. Teachers or textbook authors (residing in some distant university) determine what issues Black students will address, the nature of the problems they will solve, what analytic and conceptual frameworks will be used, and the subjects of their reading and writing.

Teaching Black students to take charge of their destiny also means that Black students, especially those in predominantly Anglo-American environments, need to learn to deal with authority, which is often Anglo-American. One of the college students, who also works with Black youths, noted that many Black children have not learned how to ask for help when it is important and can make a difference. Anglo-American authority figures feel threatened when Black children do not respond to them. They think the child is rebellious, or that the lack of response is associated with guilt or ignorance. Many Anglo-Americans, the college student stated, are not aware that many Black children have been raised not to challenge authority.

Those I interviewed observed that Black students need to learn to use the basic skills to help them understand and change the cycle of poverty and powerlessness in which they often are trapped. For example, in a language arts class, Black female students should help decide what literature is worth studying, especially because so much of what is considered "good" literature is still the literature about Anglo-Americans, written by Anglo-American males. The Black female in particular often is treated as if she does not exist or is invisible. She may wish to read about "her" story, "how society sees her," how other Black women have lived, suffered, and/or enjoyed life. As topics and issues to be studied are identified, Black students should help formulate ways to study them and to evaluate the worthiness and appropriateness of their learning and problem solving. Involving students in decisionmaking about their own learning would help Black students to acquire the three Rs, and also teach them how to use these skills to understand better and to change their own life circumstances.

A number of those interviewed discussed the importance of Black students knowing their own culture and history. Interviewees noted that a good knowledge of the facts of Black history, in relationship to those of Anglo-American history, is important to a Black person's self-esteem and their ability to argue in this racist, classist, and sexist society that Blacks are neither superior nor inferior to any other racial group that makes up the U.S. society. Those interviewed also said that obtaining a knowledge of Black history is difficult, because a racist, classist, and sexist curriculum is still provided in schools (see, e.g., Butterfield, Demos, Grant, Moy, & Perez, 1979; Grant & Grant, 1981; Scott, 1981). If Black students are going to learn about their history and contributions to the United States society, they may have to do so on their own. Most of the college seniors stated that their own knowledge about Black history was extremely poor, not formal or sophisticated, and that only when they were able to choose electives at the university were they able to take courses informing them about their history.

Two of the educators stated that Black students should start to consider a career as early as the seventh grade. Discovering early what they need to become, for example, an engineer, lawyer, or educator, will provide direction in helping Black students to work hard and choose the courses they need to achieve their ambition. Often Black students are not given the counseling and guidance needed to achieve career goals. Grant and Sleeter (1986) found that many parents of color send their children to school with the belief that students will be provided automatically with necessary information and encouragement to achieve career dreams. This is a flawed belief. Often, after students have completed state requirements for graduation, their course selection and its relationship to career goals is not monitored in schools. The sooner Black students are informed about the hard work and course requirements needed for certain careers, the sooner they can participate more actively in decisions that will affect their futures.

One educator who has worked with numerous gifted students pointed to the importance of actively encouraging gifted Black students to stay in school. He observed that just because students are gifted does not mean that we should relax our encouragement of their staying in school. Quite the contrary; too many gifted Black students become fed up with boredom and the uninteresting school curriculum and drop out or are pushed out of school. This educator observed that gifted Black students (along with all others) should be challenged academically and shown how education can help them to achieve a more fulfilling life.

The same person also indicated that educators need personally to encourage the gifted Black student to stay away from drugs. He noted that students who are especially gifted in athletics or academics also want to be accepted by their peers. The self-confidence they display on the sports field or in the classroom may not carry over to other areas of life, and therefore these students are vulnerable and will often accede to group pressure to conform. He also noted that gifted individuals may think they are special and can therefore handle drugs. Informing gifted Black students that all people are mere mortals when it comes to drugs that can kill is important.

Several of the college students discussed the importance of encouraging gifted Black students to choose their friends wisely. Although teachers or other educators cannot tell students whom to select as friends, these students advised that teachers should not hesitate to speak with a student (at any grade level) if that student begins to associate with individuals who are not taking school seriously. Teachers should make certain that the student who seems to be "sliding" has the opportunity to work on group projects with other students who are serious about their studies.

Concerning friendships, one of the college students said that, when she was in high school, she felt very much alone because she was the only Black female in the honor class. Other Black students did not think she was regular, and the Anglo-American students in her honor class did not view her as one of them. She said she would have been helped if someone had explained student culture and had talked with her about what she was experiencing. She said, "I knew what was going on, and about the cliques—jocks, nerds, and others—but it would have been helpful if someone in the school would have let me know they understood what I was going through."

BECOMING A PART OF THE MAINSTREAM

Educators responsible for programs that include Black students, especially where Black student enrollment is low, must work actively to assure that Blacks are a part of the mainstream. This does not mean getting Black students to adopt the Anglo-American way, but making certain that the mainstream school programs and practices are multicultural. A recent study (Grant & Sleeter, 1986) of a desegregated upper-middle-class high school revealed that Black students bussed to this school from the inner-city area were not accepted into the mainstream of the school; and that no serious effort was being made to help the Black students become a part of the mainstream of the school. Several Anglo-American students told us that they were pleased to see the Black students in the school, but time and a rigorous academic program did not allow them an opportunity to get to know the Black students. Many of the Black students believed it was the Anglo-American students' school, and therefore they should form their own cliques and stay to themselves.

All of those interviewed discussed the importance of Blacks having role models in school, not only to have someone with whom students can identify, but also to have teachers with whom they can talk and who understand what it means to be Black, especially when only a few other Black students are in attendance in a school or class. One of the students said that often "White teachers are so busy trying to be fair and to treat Blacks like the other White students that they ignore your ethnic background." Another student described being the only Black student in the "smart" class when she was in the fourth grade. She reports that she was treated very fairly in school by the teacher and her classmates, but when the students went to recess they played a game called "boys chase the girls." She said none of the Anglo-American boys ever chased her and she did not understand why. She really wished she had a Black female teacher with whom to talk about the situation. She said she thought something was wrong with her. A related concern is to make certain that Black females are not made second class citizens to Anglo-American females. In spite of the feminist movement, female beauty is still esteemed. This beauty is standardized on the Anglo-American female almost entirely. The curriculum, selection of cheerleaders, queen of the school, and pictures on the wall need to give equal complimentary treatment to Black females (and other female students of color).

Hard work and perseverance are supposed to be the watchwords of success in school and in careers. To work hard and to persevere are two abilities that those interviewed often mentioned Black students need to develop. However, university students said that Black students also need mentors who are straightforward with them, know the system, and have contacts to help when information is needed or problems arise. I recently was told the story of a Black female student who had been trying to complete a graduate degree in the psychology department of a large West Coast university. The student was not interested in doing the typical empirical behavioral research that was standard practice in the department. She was interested in conducting research on the attitudes of teachers working with students of color in an urban area. The student was made to feel that her ideas were not worthy; she was given very little assistance by her major professor in getting her proposed study accepted by the school. Just when she decided to give up on her idea and "play ball" with her advisor, she met a new faculty member in the department who was very interested in her research topic. The student is now completing her study, and a good possibility exists that the study will be published as a book. Mentorship (and some degree of sponsorship) and development of the ability to work hard often are important in helping Black students move from the periphery of involvement and activity into the mainstream.

University students also emphasized the importance of Black students being able to participate in organizations and activities that will allow them to gain knowledge about how groups work and how to use parliamentary procedure, which will help them to develop their leadership potential. In desegregated schools in which Anglo-Americans are in the majority, Black students often believe that they stand little chance of being elected student body president or school king or queen. Nevertheless, providing students other leadership opportunities is good preparation for career development. Joining school clubs will provide Black students some opportunities for learning about parliamentary procedure and for developing leadership skills. Similarly, many of the college students also stated that Black students should be encouraged to join discussion groups, such as the Great Books or the debate team, or take courses in speech or theater, which would help them gain confidence and skills in oral communication. Black college students said that for a Black student to be the only person of color in a class or on a committee is not unusual. Therefore, to handle better the pressure this aloneness often brings, they should be very confident in their oral communication ability and skill. Similarly these college students noted that because Blacks often are in the minority, if they do not develop good, effective communication, Anglo-Americans will be more readily able to convince others to listen to them and accept their ideas.

GETTING TO KNOW THE STUDENTS

Educators interviewed indicated that teachers should get to know the students' parents. Parents should not be mere spectators who attend school events, such as open house, sports events, or Parent-Teacher Association (PTA) meetings, but should be active partners in their child's education. This partnership, educators of Black students believe, is a key factor in getting to know the students well, establishing two-way communication between the home and school, and making certain that the teacher's expectations of the student are consistent with the parents' expectations and the student's ability. One educator stated that the teacher is often in the best position to alert parents to the range of possibilities open to their son or daughter. Information about career opportunities is important in helping the parents to plan for their children's futures.

The majority of those interviewed emphasized the importance of a teacher getting to know students as individuals and their interests, dislikes, and home background. They discussed the importance of the teacher knowing what students do at home. For example, do students have the major responsibility for caring for a younger sibling or an elderly grandparent? Do they have the opportunity to study when they wish, or do living conditions make studying extremely difficult? The teacher should know if students have had travel experiences, where they have been or where they would like to go. How do the students spend their weekends? Do they take advantage of attending a free concert, or going to the museum or art gallery? Have they ever been to a "proper" restaurant? What are the career goals of their older sisters or brothers? The reason for collecting these data is not to be nosey, but to be informed so one can help the students.

The fact that all Blacks do not look alike and are not the same finally has been accepted by most people. However, the educators and students I interviewed believed that another stereotype about Blacks is being perpetuated: That all Blacks (except celebrities, sports figures, and a few others) are poor and grew up in a ghetto. Although only a small Black middle class exists, a teacher would be wrong to assume that just because people are Black, they have grown up in poverty and have lived in the ghetto.

IN CONCLUSION

As I listened to the statements made during the interviews, I increasingly became aware that the interviewees were not offering specific or innovative teaching strategies or techniques for working with gifted Black students. They were discussing common-sense ideas that would promote a positive, challenging, and understanding learning environment for Black students. When I pressed them on this point, especially the educators, asking them if they did not have some special teaching tips or ideas for working with gifted Black students, one said, "Nothing special is really needed. Like most students, they need to know you care, understand, are fair, and will give them the chance to make it." That statement captured the beliefs of the others interviewed.

39

Administrative Reactions to Chapters About Programs for Gifted Black Students

Richard W. Ronvik, M.A.
Chicago Public Schools

Many practitioners in the field of education for gifted students have long been concerned with the particular problems related to gifted minority students. Unfortunately, much of the literature on the subject has not been particularly helpful in solving these problems, and often is general rather than specific, political rather than educational, and applicable to all students rather than to gifted students.

While the four areas addressed in this section, dealing with identification, purpose, curriculum, and special considerations for gifted Black students, suffer from some of these same flaws, they do offer some possibilities for improving the design of programs and services for gifted minority students.

IDENTIFICATION

In Frasier's chapter on identification (Chapter 31), what should be avoided—traditional testing—is clear, but what should be embraced—"I wonder what would happen if. . . ? (IWWWHI)"—is not clear. Certainly the criticism of defining giftedness solely as a score on an intelligence test is well taken, but the aversion shown by Frasier to reliance on any testing procedure for identifying Black children for programs for gifted students would, in my opinion, lead to more confusion than clarity on the issue of properly identifying and serving any underserved group.

Children need to be included in a program for gifted students when the regular program fails to serve their needs, and the alternate intervention (special program) requires differentiation to meet these needs. Therefore, a test that proves, verifies, or substantiates ability level is a reasonable part of the identification process. If such tests continue to show depressed scores by minority children, this information should be considered of consequence to educators and to society. The elimination of tests as a solution to the problem is akin to beheading the bearer of bad tidings.

Reasonable educators agree that no reason exists for the belief that intelligence is not evenly distributed throughout all races and ethnic groups. Yet, standardized tests show a score depression for many minority students, especially those falling into the low socioeconomic status group rooted in large urban areas. Therefore, a case surely could be made that testing is not the problem so much as the fact that 300 years of racism has exacted an unfair toll on our minority children.

The identification procedures described by Frasier, while rich in ideas for supplementary criteria, have their own inadequacies, and tend to draw the identification process down unacceptable paths. Alternate strategies that involve testing minorities in different domains are setting up students for failure if the program activities that follow are not related to the areas screened (e.g., screening minority children on an alternate basis in areas of leadership or creativity and then scheduling them into accelerated programs in traditional content areas).

If we avoid this error by designing program activities for minority students that are directly related to the alternative area screened, we are setting up separate curricula for minority and nonminority gifted students. This would seem to be an unacceptably racist path. I concur with Baldwin when she states, "I do not agree that leadership should be the basis of a program for gifted Blacks."

Two procedures mentioned by Frasier, lacking subtlety and elegance, but dealing directly with the problem, are those advocated by Mitchell (1982), and Kitano and Kirby (1986). These procedures resemble quota systems, and, as such, have their own limitations. Students with scores lower than the scores of some who are placed are excluded from the program because of their ethnic background (nonminority).

CURRICULUM

Most of the authors in this section refer to the imposition of Anglo-American or middle-class values on Black children. Frasier (Chapter 31) refers to definitions of giftedness that reflect middle-class, majority-culture values and perceptions; Baldwin (Chapter 33) refers to an adjustment of curricula to the values considered important by the group being served; Sparling (Chapter 36) touches lightly on the need for curricula that better meet the needs of Black students; and Grant (Chapter 38) mentions the need for educators to assure that Blacks are a part of the mainstream, but "not [by] getting Black students to adopt the Anglo-American way."

When these authors imply that work must be done to include in the curriculum that which has been systematically left out since the beginning of public education in this country, the point is well taken. However, when authors imply that identification procedures, curriculum, or teaching strategies developed around Anglo-American, middle-class values have been, and should not be, imposed on Black students, the specific offensive values should be delineated. This demand for specificity whenever the issue of Anglo-American, middle-class values is raised would yield either some practical corrective steps for practitioners or end an overused educational cliché.

Some of the writers in this section suggest that identification procedures or curriculum focus should reflect the culturally accepted values of the community being served; this is a popular view in the literature and is in some degree defensible and desirable. When culturally accepted values, however, interfere with a student's social, emotional, or educational development, those values not only should not be woven into the educational fabric, but also should be discouraged by the school system. Educators need not tolerate, much less cater to, (a) the philosophy of "machismo," the concept of male superiority; (b) the idea that higher education is unnecessary for girls; (c) the practice of discouraging young girls to consider professional careers on the grounds that a young woman's role is to stay near home to assume the care of aging parents; (d) the overprotection of females from optional programs that require new settings; (e) the notion that scholarliness is "square"; (f) the working class ethic that discourages advanced education; (g) the practice of seeking out athletes rather than scholars as role models; or (h) the habit of Anglo-America to espouse justice for all, while systematically denying it to all minorities. An illustration of student-accepted values that should not be incorporated into the curriculum is Grant's example of the girl who felt alone because she was the only Black female in her honor class. "Other Black students did not think she was regular, and the Anglo-American students in her honor class did not view her as one of them."

Baldwin and Grant (Chapters 33 and 38) point out the importance of developing in Black students an understanding of Black history and culture. Baldwin's comments on cultural rootedness underscore the significance of adding neglected material to the curriculum. Though this addition would be important for all students, it presumably would have particular implications for gifted Black students.

TEACHING STRATEGIES

In the chapter on curriculum (Chapter 36), rather than a focus specifically on content and teaching strategies for gifted Black students, a combination of two models is presented for consideration and, because results from the research are not yet available, perhaps it is presented prematurely. The Integrative Education Model, somewhat esoteric because of its author's fascination with higher synaptic activity, increased density of the dendrites, limbic and prefrontal cortex areas of the brain (see Chapter 36), results from a "brain-compatible" curriculum. The most charitable view that could be offered is that to the general program practitioner, a curriculum that is brain compatible certainly would seem to be in order.

The Shared Responsibility Model offers excellent guidance to teachers in the areas of student relationships, teacher's relationships with students, and parents' relationships with school. The inclusion of the model in the context of issues related to gifted Black students is somewhat questionable, because a program practitioner would not see either half of the combined model as related particularly to gifted students, let alone gifted Black students.

IN CONCLUSION

Whether all commentary on identification, purpose, and curriculum, and special considerations for gifted Black students possibly could relate exclusively to that one group or not, the material presented in this section offers some positive ideas for program planners. In addition to using the ideas presented here, educators must have a commitment to providing appropriate education for gifted Black students. Commitment is the most important ingredient in success.

40

Summary of Black Section

C. June Maker, Ph.D.
Shirley W. Schiever, Ph.D.
University of Arizona

GENERAL STATEMENTS

Many concepts underlying ideas presented by authors in this section are the same even though authors' perspectives, examples, and words used to explain the concepts often are different. Generalizations expressing the ideas are presented, then followed by examples and explanations of the various perspectives.

1. *The population labeled Black is not a homogeneous one. Major differences exist in socioeconomic status (SES); commonalities consist of physical features and a common heritage of being denied certain opportunities.*

Both Baldwin and Frasier present descriptions of different groups within the Black population. Baldwin distinguishes three groups ranging from least to most desirable, and notes that differences exist among these groups based on three interacting factors. Baldwin discusses the strengths of students in each group, and demonstrates how educators can capitalize on and develop these abilities. Frasier's four groups roughly correspond to Baldwin's, but she acknowledges the existence of a subgroup of low SES families with positive family organization and parental support (even though parents may have limited educational opportunities).

When commenting on Baldwin's groupings, Cohen states her belief: "I submit that middle-class Black children are more similar to middle-class children of any ethnic or racial group than to poor Black children." The editors cannot resist making an editorial comment, however, supported by many of Grant's examples and those from our own experience. Although we agree that the Black children themselves may be quite similar to other children, the fact is that many of the people they encounter during their education and careers do not perceive them as being the same or even of equal value. Thus, these students will be treated differently, and must be prepared to cope successfully with this different treatment. Like Cohen, Baska believes that basic differences between populations are due to differences in the presence or absence of family support, schooling, institutional training, apprenticeships, and modeling. Finally, Grant urges teachers to get to know their students to discover what characteristics they possess, and not to assume just because a person is Black, that he or she has grown up in poverty and lived in the ghetto.

    2. *Black students often are viewed as being in need of remedial education, rather than as candidates for programs for gifted students.*

Not all authors discussed this issue as a major obstacle in the development of programs. However, the editors chose to address it in this context because all authors provided evidence that either they or others perceive Black students as being more in need of remedial programs than special programs. Baska, for example, alludes to the fact that Black students, as a group, score lower than Anglo-American students on most standardized tests of achievement and ability, and suggests the lowering of criteria for admission into programs for the gifted as a possible solution to the problem of underrepresentation. Ronvik notes also that a quota system or a modified one would be an acceptable solution, but lists as a disadvantage the fact that minority students would be allowed to enter the program with lower scores than majority students.

Grant points out that educational literature contains many ethnocentric phrases or terms that make Black students seem inferior to Anglo-American students, and make Anglo-American students the normative group in the schools. He suggests *equal* rather than *special* treatment. Baldwin cautions against having low expectations for students, and Torrance suggests focusing on creative positives, rather than on weaknesses. Both Baska and Ronvik include as one reason for retaining tests for identification purposes the fact that teachers may not recommend Black children; thus, other means for finding children, such as teacher nomination, may be more biased than standardized tests.

Frasier presents perhaps the strongest case for a need to change perceptions of Black students' abilities. Even though many students from low SES families were selected for a program she describes, and many were in the top group on standardized instruments, only one low SES student was included in the top group based on teacher nominations. This result and others support the statements made by Baska and Ronvik and suggest a definite need to change perceptions of Black students' potential for success in a program for the gifted.

    3. *The use of only standardized tests and the use of only one score on a test as a criterion for determining giftedness are unacceptable practices, and are not appropriate ways to identify gifted Black students.*

Although all authors seem to agree with this statement, the degree of emphasis recommended for standardized tests in the identification process is different. In the lead chapter, Frasier reviews the "best practices" recommended by experts in identification of gifted students. Included in her discussion is the recommendation that certain tests be used because they have a history of success as identifiers of giftedness in Black and low SES children. An underlying premise of her discussion is that giftedness may be expressed differently in different populations. To Frasier, the combination of identifiers, all appropriately selected, seemingly should provide the proof, verification, or substantiation of ability level that Ronvik would like to have from tests.

Perhaps because of their disagreement with these underlying premises of Frasier's, Ronvik and Baska discuss at great length the values of standardized testing and remind educators that eliminating standardized testing from the identification process will have many negative consequences. In the opinion of the editors, Frasier is not advocating an elimination of tests, but instead (a) different emphasis on their results as determiners of placement in a program, and (b) use of different tests, checklists, or procedures because of demonstrated success in revealing the strengths of Black students. Baska also presents a list of alternative strategies for identifying Black students with superior ability.

Baska, Ronvik, Baldwin, and Torrance remind us that the curriculum and teaching strategies must be consistent with the criteria for identifying giftedness, and Ronvik uses this need for consistency as an argument for not following identification processes advocated by Frasier. He states that when the program activities are related directly to the alternative area screened, we are setting up a separate curriculum for minority students and students from the majority culture. If Ronvik is correct in making this prediction, then Baska, Cohen, Baldwin, Frasier, Torrance, and a whole host of other writers and researchers are wrong about the similarities between poor people (i.e., students of low SES families) of *all* racial and ethnic groups. The editors suspect that the assessment of certain "alternative areas" of giftedness would result in finding Black, Anglo-American, Asian-American, Hispanic, and many other groups whose major commonality is being poor, rather than being from a particular minority group. In many other instances, such as in the assessment of creativity (a recommendation made by Frasier because tests of creativity tend to identify strengths of Black children), the most salient commonality will be the abilities measured by the test—not socio-economic, racial, or ethnic traits!

Finally, the issue of predictive ability of tests and procedures must be addressed. Only one author discussed this issue. In his discussion of the benefits of standardized testing for Black students, Baska notes the ability of such tests to predict success *in school,* but fails to review the well-known data regarding the failure of such tests to predict success in careers. He then defines giftedness as a need for special educational programming because of the potential to excel as an *adult.* The editors wonder, what would happen if the alternative procedures and tests recommended by Frasier were found to be more predictive of adult excellence than traditional standardized tests?

4. *The purpose of programs for gifted Black students must be to develop individual strengths, the basic culture of the child, and abilities needed for success in the mainstream culture.*

Although all authors seem to agree with the underlying philosophy of this statement, differing degrees of emphasis and different perspectives of its meaning are evident. Baldwin states, and Cohen agrees, educators of gifted students should focus equally on individual strengths, the culture of the child, and the skills needed for success in the majority culture. Baldwin recommends, and Cohen and Ford concur, that major emphasis should be placed on helping gifted students deal with being gifted and Black. Although Cohen's ideas go beyond the others in this section on this point, her suggestions are similar to those of Grant, Baldwin, and Ronvik, who all recommend the inclusion of studies of Black history and Black culture as ways to help students develop a positive view of themselves, an understanding of present problems, and the ability to deal with future issues. Ford addresses the need to identify and nurture talents of Black students, which are often expressed outside the context of school.

Related to the development of skills necessary for success in the mainstream culture, Cohen also recommends a focus on "increas[ing] the vision of possibilities" for gifted Black children. Cohen recognizes, as Grant also tells us, that many Black children and their families do not know their career possibilities and do not know how to prepare adequately for the careers of interest to them. Torrance recommends that creativity development be a focus for identification of gifted Black students, and that creativity development be a focus for programs. His suggestions follow a line of reasoning similar to the other authors in this approach.

Both Grant and Sparling address another area related to the concept of a triple focus for programs: developing in Black students the ability to "take charge of their own destiny." Grant notes that many Black students perceive themselves as poor and powerless, and that many of their educational experiences perpetuate and enhance this perception.

Ronvik provides an important perspective as well. He notes that a popular view in the literature in general, and in the writing of authors in this section, is that curriculum (and identification procedures) should reflect the culturally accepted values of the community being served. His perspective is that in public schools, values (even when culturally accepted) that interfere with a student's social, emotional, or educational development should not be tolerated nor indulged. Examples of these potentially harmful values include the concept of male superiority, the idea that higher education is not necessary for girls, the notion that scholarliness is "square," or a "working-class" ethic that discourages advanced education.

Finally, Baska addresses the need for a program focus like that discussed by presenting an alternative to Frasier's view of the causes for underrepresentation of minorities in programs for the gifted. Rather than being the result of inappropriate and/or inadequate identification procedures, Baska believes that underrepresentation is part of a larger societal problem.

5. *Families and parents should be partners with the school in the educational process.*

Using Baska's model of factors necessary for upward mobility, family/parent involvement becomes an essential component in any program designed for gifted Black students. In addition to the model, Baska lists factors present in homes of high- and low-achieving students that are similar to those identified by Ford. She attributes much of her academic success to the high value her family placed on education and their support for the teachers' efforts. In the groupings of Black populations by both Frasier and Baldwin, family patterns are important distinguishing factors between desirable and undesirable groups.

Finally, Grant recommends that teachers get to know their students' parents, and that parents should be perceived as partners, rather than spectators, in their child's education. When forming a partnership between schools and parents to benefit gifted Black students, educators can begin with the suggestions of Sparling in her description of the Shared Responsibility Model.

6. *The starting point for program development should be each student's strengths.*
Frasier, Baldwin, Cohen, Torrance, and Sparling addressed this issue directly. Torrance focused on the identification and development of creative strengths, and cites his research demonstrating that Black children score as high or higher than Anglo-American children on these characteristics, and frequently attain fame for outstanding achievements in these areas. Frasier lists these same strengths as characteristics to note during the identification process. Sparling emphasizes student-generated goals and development of creativity and intuition. If Torrance is accurate in both his belief that Black students have creative strengths, and that they will be motivated to develop what they do well, the students will most likely develop goals in these areas. Baldwin presents a different view of the strengths of gifted Black students, suggesting that their strengths may differ depending on factors that identify them as members of the most or least desirable group. Children from the "least desirable" group, for example, who lack parental support, have low SES, and live in impoverished areas have developed many adaptive behaviors necessary for survival, such as logical thinking and analysis.

7. *Although the focal point of a program should be the development of student strengths, their weaknesses should not be ignored.*
This principle is very much related to the earlier statement that programs should be focused on individual strengths, development of the student's culture, and acquisition of the skills necessary for success in the mainstream culture. Like Baldwin and Torrance, Cohen emphasizes the importance of creativity development. She recommends it as a program focus; but, unlike Torrance, Frasier, and Baldwin, she notes that Black children from impoverished backgrounds may have difficulty in long-term creative productivity because planning and thinking about the future are difficult due to the demands of daily living.

Grant's recommendation that educators assist gifted Black students in development of the ability to work hard and persevere provides support for Cohen's belief that Black children will need assistance in developing the skills necessary for applying their creative strengths. He also recommends that educators assist Black students in participating in organizations and activities that allow them to learn parliamentary procedures and to develop discussion skills.

8. *Role models and mentors need to be incorporated into the curriculum.*
All authors discuss or recognize the importance of role models or mentors in the education of gifted Black students. Sparling focuses on the teacher as a model for students in each of the components of her teaching approach, and Ronvik agrees that the Shared Responsibility Model offers excellent guidance for teachers. Baldwin includes role models and mentoring in her case studies of successful programs; positive benefits of role models for gifted Black students are listed by Cohen, Baska, and Torrance. Grant discusses the importance of role models in school—especially those who "know the system" and can help students move successfully through it. Mentors also can be instrumental in helping Black students become and remain a part of the mainstream. Cohen elevates the use of role models and mentors to the level of program purpose because of the many positive benefits for children, and advocates contact for children with a wide range of possible mentors from the community in which they live.

9. *Counseling and affective development are important components of programs for gifted Black students.*

Baldwin introduces the primary goal of a program as development of student self-concept—an affective goal. Many of Grant's suggestions pertain to affective areas, and he calls attention to the importance of teachers and their encouragement. Sparling discusses development and integration of the feeling function with thinking (cognitive), physical, and intuitive functions as a major purpose of the recommended Integrative Education Model. The second model, Shared Responsibility, is designed primarily to achieve affective goals. Many of Cohen's and Torrance's recommendations related to development of creative strengths are in affective areas. Torrance's "Manifesto for Children" (Figure 37-1) and Cohen's section on the topic of "increas[ing] the vision of possibilities for [gifted Black] children" include many excellent suggestions for affective development. Finally, Ford's discussion of her problems resulting from acceleration and her need to develop self-esteem demonstrates that attention to affective development is essential.

10. *The techniques advocated for gifted Black students would be good for all gifted students, and possibly for all students, whether or not they are gifted.*

Torrance addresses this issue directly, and probably expresses a sentiment shared by all, when he states that the models proposed by Sparling would be good for all children, but they are "especially appropriate for the gifted and, furthermore, for gifted Black students." Sparling also addresses the question directly, and states that although a *different* curriculum or program is not needed, *difference-sensitive* curricula and programs are. Ronvik agrees with Torrance that the models proposed by Sparling would be good for all children, but wonders if educators would not want to know why these models are included in a chapter on teaching gifted Black students without documentation of the fact that they are useful for this population.

Both Baldwin and Cohen note that although the purposes for special education of gifted Black children are the same as the purposes for education of all gifted students, the means for achieving these goals may be different. Grant summed up the sentiments of most of us when he quoted one individual he interviewed: "Nothing special is really needed. Like most students, they need to know you care, understand, are fair, and will give them the chance to make it." At the beginning of his chapter, however, Grant reminds us that although Black students are not in need of *special* considerations, they do need *equal* considerations. Ronvik reminds us that our past failure to provide equal treatment may be the cause for our inability to identify many gifted Black children.

OTHER IMPORTANT IDEAS

The authors in this section also introduced other ideas important in the education of gifted Black students. Although not addressed, or perhaps agreed upon, by all, they are important to list.

Consistency of Program Elements

Ronvik, Baska, and Baldwin emphasize the importance of achieving consistency between definitions of giftedness, procedures for identifying giftedness, and the curriculum designed to develop giftedness. Concerns of both Ronvik and Baska center around the inappropriateness of identifying Black children based on "alternative criteria" and then providing the same program and curriculum as we provide for those selected based on "regular" criteria.

Biculturalism

Although most authors noted the importance of studying Black history and Black culture, they did not emphasize the development of biculturalism in the same way as did authors in other sections of this book. Baldwin suggests that a study of Black history and culture can be important in the development of positive self-images of Black students, and Ford provides support for this point of view by describing her embarrassment and need to "distance herself" from her African heritage because of the stupidity of Little Black Sambo and the cannibalistic natives in Tarzan movies, the only Blacks included in literature or the popular media. Cohen agrees that gifted Black students need to study their heritage, but suggests other methods for helping students deal with being Black and gifted.

Gifted Girls—A Special Problem

Grant presents examples of ways gifted Black girls need encouragement, reminds us that female beauty is still important, and notes that because Anglo-American female beauty is often the standard, we need to make certain that the beauty of Black females is recognized. Ronvik emphasizes that educators should discourage values interfering with a student's social, emotional, or educational development, and lists as offending values several that relate to females.

Cooperative Learning

The need for more cooperation and less competition in learning situations is noted by Sparling, Torrance, and Baldwin. Grant also notes the positive effects of having Black students who may be showing signs of low motivation to work on projects with Black students and other students who are "serious about learning."

Channeling of Abilities

Two authors, Baldwin and Baska, recognize the tendency of bright Black students to use their creative energies and strengths in socially unacceptable ways. When discussing dropouts, Baldwin notes that the mental energy generated in a fertile mind will be used constructively or destructively, and recommends that we help students use their creative abilities constructively.

IN CONCLUSION

A consistent theme throughout this section is that the problems facing educators of gifted Black children are multifaceted and complex, and that these problems are part of a larger societal issue in which racial prejudice and economic problems play important roles. Although these problems cannot be corrected in schools, certain tools in the school environment can be used successfully. Of all the tools we have, perhaps the most significant is the second underlying theme of the chapters in this section, that is, development of gifted Black students' belief that they can "control their own destiny." Because of continual discrimination and prejudice, and lack of financial resources, many Blacks (and other minorities) develop a sense of powerlessness—a belief that they are destined to continue in the cycle of poverty in which they are trapped. Helping gifted Black students see that they have capabilities, and that these capabilities are recognized by the mainstream culture, is imperative. They must learn the possibilities of being gifted, Black, and successful.

Part V

VOLUME CONCLUSION

Programs for Gifted Minority Students: A Synthesis of Perspectives

C. June Maker, Ph.D.
University of Arizona

The purpose of this final section is to present an analytic synthesis and a summary of the perspectives of various authors in this volume. In each section, authors writing about similar topics were asked to address the same key questions. These key questions will be used to organize the series editor's synthesis. As readers will note, at the end of the sections addressing each minority group, a summary/synthesis also is presented. In these conclusions, the editors have focused on certain principles common in the writing of all authors in the section. To avoid repetition of comments in section conclusions, my focus in this chapter will be on a comparison of the answers of authors to the key questions for their chapters. For example, the first question addressed in this section is the key question for authors of lead and critique chapters on identification of students from a particular minority group. Although other authors in the section may have addressed the issue of identification, their comments will not be the focus of discussion unless unique perspectives not already included are presented by these authors.

The final synthesizing question was not included in the list of key questions in this volume. It has been added, however, because it provides a mechanism to relate the perspectives of authors in the present volume to the perspectives of authors in volume one of this series, *Defensible Programs for the Gifted*. In the final chapter of the first volume, the editor developed a set of elements necessary to make a program for gifted students defensible. These same elements need to be present in programs for gifted students from the minority groups discussed in this volume, as the perspectives of a wide variety of authors demonstrate. Following each key element is the definition presented in volume one. After this general definition, specific aspects of these elements that relate to minorities will be discussed.

How can students from special populations be identified?

Common principles were discussed by authors who answered this question. First, these authors emphasized that although each group has certain similar traits, many differences are found between subgroups. These differences will influence the characteristics of gifted students and, in turn, must be understood and used to design identification procedures that will be appropriate. Factors distinguishing between subgroups include socioeconomic level (all authors); the degree of assimilation or acculturation of the family or ethnic group as a whole (Montgomery, Kirschenbaum); geographic location, including current residence and country of origin (Zappia, Montgomery, Kirschenbaum, Chen, Kitano); primary language, degree of bilingualism, and level of proficiency in English (Zappia, Chen, Kitano, Perrine); value placed on education (Perrine, Chen, Kitano, Montgomery, Kirschenbaum); and the length of time a family has been in this country (Chen, Kitano).

Each child must be viewed as an individual, with knowledge of inter- and intragroup differences in values and other cultural characteristics used as the means to *interpret the behaviors observed* in students, rather than to predict what behaviors will be exhibited. The important point made by these authors is that individual factors (influencing similarities and differences between cultures and among members of a particular culture) must provide the basis for comparison of people and interpretation of test scores and behaviors, rather than membership in a particular cultural group. Indeed, the observation has been made frequently that economic factors may be more important than cultural ones in producing similarities and differences between individuals.

Before gifted students from minority groups can be identified, stereotypes and narrow (both positive and negative) attitudes must be overcome. Due to a history of underrepresentation in programs for gifted students and lower academic achievement than nonminority peers, minority students often are perceived as having lower intellectual and academic abilities than their Anglo-American peers. This stereotype is perpetuated and even strengthened by some of the traditional identification practices used in programs for gifted students. A common practice, for example, is to lower the achievement criteria required for admission of students from minority populations to a special program to increase the percentages of such students in the program. If programs designed to raise achievement levels are provided for these children, or if high-academic skill achievement levels are not needed for success in the program, and if instructional techniques are compatible with the learning styles of the minority students, these minority students can experience the same levels of success as their peers who began with higher academic achievement. However, the usual case is that accelerated basic skill acquisition is not a part of the program and instruction does not match learning styles. Thus, minority students often drop out of programs for the gifted, are counseled out because of low performance, or continue to achieve at a lower level than their nonminority peers. These facts contribute to the perpetuation of negative stereotypes of minority students' abilities and mitigate against their identification for special services.

Asian-American students also suffer from stereotyping. Because Asian-Americans have been characterized as the "model minority," due to their high academic achievement, Asian-American students all are expected to be high achievers and to be interested in mathematics and science, rather than in humanities. The authors caution us about such stereotypes because we may overlook Asian-American students from under-represented groups and those who have abilities in the verbal and social areas, rather than those abilities generally attributed to Asians. Additionally, we may fail to develop necessary verbal abilities in these students.

To accommodate known differences in individuals and groups, and to avoid harmful stereotyping, several recommendations are common in the writing of authors in all of the sections. Even though recommendations for specific behaviors to observe or tests to employ may vary, the principles are the same.

1. *Use multiple assessment procedures, including objective and subjective data from a variety of sources.*

Application of this principle requires that comprehensive procedures be designed and implemented. A variety of standardized tests must be available to enable the testing of a variety of intellectual abilities. Consistency in identification must not be carried to its extreme through attempts to identify, for example, *one* intelligence test equally appropriate for all individuals or groups being tested. The most common error made in the name of consistency in identification is to choose nonverbal tests of intelligence. However, the major ingredient in many individuals' concept of giftedness is verbal ability, and verbal skills are emphasized in many programs. Thus, the identification procedure is inconsistent with both the definition of giftedness and the curriculum provided for the students. In addition, reliance on only nonverbal measures will penalize students who are verbally gifted.

To avoid some of the problems occurring as a result of biases of individuals against those from certain minority groups, multiple referral sources are recommended by all authors. These sources can include parents, teachers (both past and present), peers, special teachers, individuals from the community, and the students themselves.

As a part of this comprehensive assessment process, authors recommend other procedures, such as interviews with students, presentation of problems to solve in a structured or unstructured situation, and evaluation of student products. Parent interviews, developmental data, educational histories, and other data regarding the student are helpful in providing a context in which to interpret test scores and observational data.

Even though all authors agree on the need to include both objective and subjective data in making decisions about giftedness, they disagree on the importance of these two types of data. Some view observational data collected over a period of time as *more* important than test data while others recommend caution in its use because of the biases of teachers and others making the observations. They suggest that people with negative attitudes or stereotypes may be more biased than standardized tests. Others remind educators that observations need to be made in contexts in which differences in cognitive and learning styles are accommodated.

My conclusion is that we must listen to each of the authors. The fact that their opinions differ regarding the weight of subjective and objective data lends further support to recommendation three, use of a case study approach. Each child and each educational situation is different. Therefore, we must interpret a variety of data in the context of the educational situation and involve several qualified individuals in decisions about which data are most significant.

2. *Include culturally and linguistically appropriate instruments in the referral and testing process.*

To improve the ability of teachers and other observers to identify giftedness in all cultural groups, specific behavioral indicators of giftedness should be provided on checklists or nomination forms. As several authors have noted, even though the "absolute" or underlying traits indicative of giftedness may be the same in all cultures and across all linguistic, geographic, or economic groups, the specific manifestations of giftedness are not always the same.

Instruments must be chosen carefully, and selected because of their appropriateness for both cultural and linguistic characteristics of the children being tested. Because different tests are designed to assess diverse abilities or to emphasize different patterns of abilities, certain instruments may tap the strengths of particular groups better than other instruments. In addition, tests of learning rate may be more appropriate than tests of level of learning because they reduce the impact of differing experiences or lack of exposure to material being tested.

Often, the need for selection of linguistically appropriate tests results in choosing either nonverbal tests or verbal tests translated or developed in the student's primary language. Verbal tests developed and standardized on individuals with characteristics similar to those of the individual being tested are the most appropriate.

The problem of continued development of a child's first language, a primary reason for difficulties in assessing verbal ability, usually is not solved. In this country, our educational systems often fail to provide truly bilingual programs, in which students continue to receive instruction in, and to develop, their primary language while learning a second language. For this reason, many students who enter school speaking a language other than English cannot be assessed appropriately in either their first *or* second language. Since their first language has not continued to develop, these students lack words to express sophisticated concepts in that language. Because language skills at the level necessary to perform well on an intelligence test require five to seven years to develop, children's abilities cannot be assessed adequately in the second language for several years. In such cases, nonverbal assessment must supplement assessment in either or both languages—preferably in both.

3. *Use a case study approach, in which a variety of assessment data is interpreted in the context of a student's individual characteristics, and decisions are made by a team of qualified individuals.*

All authors emphasized the importance of making decisions about admission to programs for gifted students based on all data available for each student, and using information from tests in an appropriate manner. In addition to considering a child's unique traits and experiences, one must consider the historical context of the child's family and ethnic group.

Rather than recommending the lowering of admission requirements (or thresholds for entry) to special programs, some authors advocate (a) searching for the most appropriate tests and procedures for all students, (b) using the most appropriate even though they may be different, and (c) interpreting all information in the context of a student's individual traits. Final decisions about program placement should be based on the match between the student's characteristics and what the program can provide.

To achieve racial and ethnic balance, Baska advocates the use of a quota system. Frasier presents a completely different view of a quota system, noting that some students are denied access to the program because balance is the goal, and that identification procedures should be developed that are consistent with the belief that diversity exists within the gifted population. Most important, she states that a quota system supports the concept that one standard exists by which all children capable of performance at a high level should be measured, and that a quota system suggests that certain children may be "second-class" gifted.

In this volume, the debate still continues: Should we use different measures and different criteria, different measures and the same criteria, the same measures and different criteria, or the same measures and the same criteria for determining giftedness in all populations? Many answers have been given by authors, but the majority seems to favor different measures and different criteria because of the diversity of the populations and subpopulations being evaluated. Thus, a case study approach in which individual, rather than group, decisions are made, is important.

What is the purpose of a special program for gifted students from minority groups?

Among the authors who addressed this question, general agreement exists that the purposes of special programs for gifted students are the same regardless of the populations being considered. The primary purpose advocated is to enable individuals to achieve in ways and at levels they are capable of achieving. An exception to this consensus is the clear statement by Pfeiffer that the purpose of programs for gifted American Indians is to strengthen the quality of life of the tribe. George generally agrees with Pfeiffer, and discusses self-understanding as the important goal to be achieved in such programs.

Often, in programs for gifted students, two interacting philosophies exist. From one perspective, the purpose of a special program is to enable gifted individuals to become "self-actualized," to become what they wish to be and are capable of becoming. From another perspective, because the contributions of gifted people enable our survival as a nation, culture, and world, the purpose of a special program is to develop the talents and abilities of our gifted individuals that will benefit society. Although these perspectives demonstrate a different emphasis, they can interact so that they are not incompatible. Abilities valued by individuals also can be of benefit to society, and a society made up of self-actualized gifted individuals certainly would be a desirable one. The two philosophies result in different emphases when some special programs are designed only for those who are high achievers in areas perceived as critical to our survival as a nation (e.g., the mathematics and science programs that proliferated after the launching of Sputnik) and other programs are designed to develop high-level abilities in the arts, leadership, humanities, and other areas of human competence.

When different cultural or ethnic groups are discussed, two other considerations are evident—benefits to the minority as well as the majority culture, and abilities valued by the minority as well as the majority culture. Although the authors addressing the question of program purpose agree on general issues related to development of individual potential, they disagree on the amount of emphasis or the priority that should be given to development of abilities valued by various groups or by the individual.

A point made by authors addressing other questions (Montgomery, Kirschenbaum, Brooks) is important as a possible reason for the differences in perspectives. The educational context of a special program for gifted students in a school for Navajo Indian students operated by the Navajo nation is different from a public school program in an urban area serving many ethnic and cultural groups. Thus, the purposes of these programs can and should be different. Examination of the experiences of the authors who addressed purposes of programs for the four groups provides support for this explanation of their different perspectives. Pfeiffer, for example, has been deeply involved in the creation of a special school for gifted Navajo students that is completely under the control of the elected officials of the tribe. Banda, on the other hand, comes from a public school perspective in a large urban area.

Related to the purposes outlined by Pfeiffer is a goal articulated by Cohen for programs for Black children, and addressed by many other authors: By developing programs for gifted students from minority groups, and by "searching diligently" for them, we will accomplish important goals for our multicultural society. When gifted students of all ethnic backgrounds participate together in programs in which a diversity of values and abilities is recognized and supported, they will grow up with a positive view of these differences, and eventually contribute to the elimination (or at least reduction) of ethnic and racial stereotypes. The view of differences as positive, or at least neutral, is far more productive for our society than the view of differences as deficits. Successful adults asked to respond to the program purposes outlined by lead authors provided support for such goals by reviewing personal experiences in which they and others would have received many benefits from participation in programs in which differences were respected and valued, rather than viewed as weaknesses to be remediated.

Even though writers addressing the question of program purpose advocate in certain instances different emphases, some goals are common, in addition to the general focus on individually valued, culturally valued, and mainstream society-valued abilities.

First, all authors address in some way the need to develop a sense of self-esteem or self-worth as a goal for programs for gifted minority students. Often, feelings of self-esteem are tied to cultural context because people from minority groups have experienced discrimination and have attempted to "cover" or deny their cultural identities. Woo, Rodriguez, Ford, and Throssell, the successful adults, provide examples of such denial by themselves and/or their families. Other authors in this volume, particularly educators from the target minority groups (Grant, Bradley, Hasegawa, Ruiz), also express a need for cultural heritage to be valued by self and society. They also tell us, loudly and clearly, that individual abilities and talents must be allowed to develop, and indeed be encouraged, even if those abilities are not valued by a particular cultural group or by the individual's family.

A second common goal is the development of functional bilingualism and biculturalism. A part of this goal, or associated with it, is development of appreciation for the contributions of members of one's cultural group and recognition that differences are positive rather than negative. Authors express alarm (especially Rodriguez) at the current movements to make English the official language of this country while many other countries in the world are emphasizing the need for multilingualism (Bernal).

Biculturalism is associated with, but goes beyond, bilingualism. A truly bicultural individual is able to function successfully and comfortably in two cultures. Bicultural individuals must (a) have information about the values and contributions of individuals from their own cultural background, (b) appreciate and value the contributions and beliefs of those from similar cultural backgrounds, (c) have information about the values and contributions of individuals from other cultures, (d) appreciate and value the contributions and beliefs of those from other cultures, and, finally, (e) modify their behavior in ways that are compatible with either or both cultures when such behavior is necessary. While knowledge and understanding of two cultures may be easy to develop (notwithstanding the fact that schools traditionally have been unsuccessful in developing knowledge and understanding of minority cultures), and appreciation or value may accompany knowledge and understanding; developing the ability to modify one's behavior comfortably and successfully is another matter entirely.

Throughout many of the discussions the series editor has held with educators and members of various minority groups, a pervasive belief seems to be that if individuals develop an understanding and appreciation of two cultures, and develop skills enabling them to be successful in the majority culture and comfortable with their cultural or ethnic background, they will be comfortable, fully functioning individuals who "fit" into both cultures equally well. The reality, however, is that "comfort" and "fit" are difficult to achieve. In the words of one individual (not a writer in this volume) who considers himself bicultural, "I am not *both,* I am *neither!*" His statement brings to our attention clearly the fact that cultural values often conflict. Biculturalism is simplified if one believes that the values of two cultures can be accepted equally by a given individual. Certainly, these often disparate values can receive equal respect and understanding, but individuals must make decisions for themselves about which values are the most important guiding principles. Individual decisions may result (and usually do) in definite differences between individuals and their cultural or ethnic group as well as clear differences between individuals and the majority culture. Thus, the result is feeling that one belongs not to both cultures, but to neither.

Throssell's statement that one's feelings of self-worth must be derived from within the self is important. Gifted students, particularly those from minority groups, must be assisted in development of the *courage* to be who they are and who they want to be, regardless of their cultural and ethnic heritage, and without compromising either that heritage or their own personal abilities. Perhaps the key for any individual from a minority group is to develop a *unique* combination of individual, cultural, and societal abilities necessary to succeed in areas of his or her choice. With a sense of self-worth, one will not, as Throssell cautions, "sit and wait for failure to catch up to you."

Discussions of the purposes of education for individuals from cultural and ethnic minorities often begin with the premise that the values developed in school should not conflict with the values of a culture, and that traits valued by a particular culture should be emphasized and developed in its young people. Pfeiffer's and Ronvik's discussions bring out interpretations of the values issue that are somewhat different from those usually heard. Pfeiffer is influenced greatly by the current need of her people to control their own destiny and to assure the survival of their culture. Thus, she places the tribe's needs above those of the individual, and recommends tribal well-being as the primary goal. An important distinction to make, however, is that she is not focusing on abilities *valued* by the tribe, but on abilities *necessary* for its survival and well-being. Ronvik's focus, although similar, is on the survival and well-being of the individual. He expresses general agreement with the idea that programs should be compatible with culturally accepted values of a community. However, he also reminds us that some culturally accepted values actually *interfere* with a student's social, emotional, or educational development, and recommends that such values be discouraged, and certainly not included as a part of the program. He cites as examples the concept of male superiority, the idea that higher education is unnecessary for girls, the notion that advanced education is unnecessary, and "[the ability] of Anglo-America to espouse justice for all, while systematically denying it to all minorities."

In conclusion, the authors in this volume have shown that the goals of programs for gifted minority students are compatible with the goals for all gifted students, and indeed similar to educational goals for all students. Additional purposes are evident as well, such as the development of abilities valued by more than one culture, acquisition of skills in moving between and within at least two cultures, and development of a self-identity. Development of self-identity requires making choices between values of various groups, courage to follow those choices even when one's ethnic group or the majority culture does not agree, and confidence in one's abilities that enable success in the area one has chosen.

Should we provide the same kind of educational program for students from special populations that we provide for mainstream gifted students, or should the program be differentiated?

Answers to this question in the current volume can be arranged on a continuum from "the same" to "different," but cluster around "similar" or "the same." The two extremes are found in the writing of two authors who address the development of curricula for gifted Asian-Americans. Wong and Wong, for example, discuss certain teaching strategies and practices advocated for "first-generation American Cantonese-speaking school children of Chinese descent." They are unwilling to generalize their discussion to other students of Chinese descent and certainly not to others of Asian descent. At the other extreme, Kaplan responds to their chapter by outlining four principles that should guide the development of programs for all gifted students. Sparling's response to the question of differentiation of programs is "yes" and "no." Yes, because learning needs are different, and no, because different strategies specifically for each group would perpetuate cultural stereotypes.

Torrance's perspective provides a way to relate all these points of view. He states that while the models proposed in Sparling's chapter may benefit all children, they are particularly important for gifted children, and especially good for gifted Black children. According to the editors, a similar statement can be made about curricula and teaching strategies advocated in this volume: They may benefit all children, they are important for gifted students, and they are essential for gifted minority students.

Many commonalities exist in the curricula and teaching strategies described for the four minority groups included in this volume. Although the examples and specifics of implementation may be different, the principles are the same. Many of these principles are included in the section summaries, along with summaries of the various authors' recommendations.

1. *Identify students' strengths and plan a curriculum to develop these abilities.*
2. *Provide for development of basic skills and other abilities students lack.*
3. *Regard differences as positive, rather than negative, attributes.*
4. *Provide for involvement of parents, the community, and mentors or role models.*
5. *Create and maintain classrooms with a multicultural emphasis.*

Many of the recommendations in this section can be applied to education for all students, and for all gifted students. Thus, these recommendations constitute part of the answer to the question of whether or not programs should be differentiated for gifted students from ethnic and cultural minorities. Elements common to programs for gifted students are outlined and explanations are given for retaining or strengthening these elements when children from minority groups are included.

If the program should be differentiated, how should it be modified?

The teachers who were asked to contribute to this volume have described many specific strategies designed to respond to the characteristics and learning needs they have observed in their students from particular minority backgrounds. Even though the strategies described can benefit students from backgrounds other than those addressed by the author, the strategies usually are not included as components of programs for gifted students.

Teachers of Hispanic, Asian-American, and American Indian students who are gifted recommend the use of cooperative learning strategies, although their reasons for advocating cooperative learning vary. The common theme is that based on the characteristics of the learners, cooperative learning meets the needs of gifted minority students.

Another instructional strategy usually not included in programs for gifted students is recommended by Garrison as a way to accommodate cultural differences in American Indian students. Teaching students through demonstration and modeling, with no verbal interaction—no instruction, no questions, no answers—is a way to allow the cultural strengths of American Indian students to be demonstrated, and it increases the ability of other students to learn through observation and concentration rather than being able to relax their concentration because they know that later the teacher will provide an explanation of what was missed.

Udall advocates the use of nonverbal tasks and activities because some students may be learning English as a second language and lack verbal skills equal to those of their classmates. Nonverbal activities can give these students a chance to excel, and to develop reasoning abilities not dependent on their language.

Udall also emphasizes the importance of physical warmth and caring in a classroom with Hispanic students. Physical warmth, including touching, probably would not be comfortable for many Asian-American and American Indian students except on special occasions. However, physical closeness, warmth, and contact provide evidence to Hispanic students that the teacher really cares about them as people—not for what they can do, but for who they are. Perrine discusses *abrazo,* the Spanish word for "embrace," as an important concept in teaching Hispanic students, and describes spiritual closeness (sometimes resulting in physical closeness) as an essential quality in teachers who can develop in their Hispanic students the will to achieve.

In this country, as Bernal notes, development of bilingualism usually is not included as a program emphasis for gifted students. However, the learning of English as a second language must be included in programs for gifted minority students when needed, and those who plan programs for gifted students should not repeat the errors of their counterparts in regular education by equating the teaching of English as a second language with the development of bilingualism. The cognitive advantages of bilingualism will not accrue to those who have low levels of proficiency in their native language, because these students have not continued to develop academic skills in that language.

Authors addressing another question have made a recommendation appropriate here. Both Bradley and George recommend involvement of American Indian students' extended families—not just their immediate families—in the educational process. Aunts, uncles, cousins, and grandparents are considered a part of the immediate family. When recognition is given for accomplishments, or when important decisions are being made, educators must remember the close ties among all these significant family members and the gifted student.

Finally, the issue of teacher expectations must be addressed. Usually, this issue does not cause a great deal of concern in a program for gifted students because the effects are positive. The identification of students as gifted usually causes their teachers to have high expectations for performances and achievement. Students often live up to those expectations, so the positive expectations continue to exist. However, if teachers have lowered expectations for student performance based on cultural and ethnic stereotypes, these expectations may prevail even though students have been identified as gifted. In addition, as was discussed previously, students from minority groups often are placed in programs inappropriate to their cultural traits and learning styles and based on "alternative criteria," or standards different from the criteria used for other students. They also are placed in programs based on *lower* achievement criteria. In these cases, when children drop out, achieve at lower levels than others, or fail to succeed in the program, teachers either develop or continue the expectation that minority students will not be as successful as those from the majority culture. These practices may perpetuate lowered teacher expectations that are communicated to students and may become self-fulfilling prophecies. On the other hand, the overly positive expectations teachers may have for Asian-American students based on their levels of achievement and the stereotype of Asians as the "model minority" may result in unreasonably high expectations.

In the answer to the question of how programs for gifted students from minority groups should be different from programs for gifted students from the majority culture, I have attempted to outline instructional strategies advocated by various authors that are *not usually included* as components of programs for gifted students, and are not recommended frequently for such programs. Since the section in which differences are explained is shorter than others, one can infer that very few strategies are unique to each cultural group. Even though some may view this lack of uniqueness as a weakness of theory in the field of education for gifted students, the series editor views it as a strength, both from a practical and a theoretical standpoint. From the practitioner's viewpoint, the fact that certain general principles can be used to guide the development of curricula and teaching strategies that will accommodate cultural differences effectively in the classroom makes the appropriate teaching of multi-ethnic groups (advocated by the experts) possible! If instructional strategies were not useful with groups of students, teachers would be faced with the formidable task of designing a completely different method with every child in the classroom. From a theoretical standpoint, the fact that few exceptions to general practices exist demonstrates the comprehensiveness and validity of models already developed to accommodate the diversity of gifted learners.

Authors in this volume again have emphasized what writers and researchers alike have known for some time: The *teacher* is the most important element in the instructional process. The quality of the teacher's preparation, his or her cultural sensitivity, the ability to understand and respect a variety of cultures, and the willingness and skill needed to translate these understandings into instructional practices all are crucial variables in the success of programs for gifted students from minority cultures.

What special considerations should be addressed, and what are their administrative implications?

Authors from two different perspectives were asked to address this question. The first group, educators and members of the target group, were asked to write from their own experience. They were requested to suggest what educators should consider in the development of provisions for gifted students from this group, other than identification, curriculum development, and curriculum implementation. The second group, administrators with experience working with gifted students in a multicultural setting, were asked to react to all the lead chapters in a given section (e.g., Hispanic, American Indian, Asian-American, Black), and to comment on the administrative implications of the recommendations made for identification procedures, program purposes, curriculum and teaching strategies, and special considerations for a particular ethnic and cultural group.

Because many of the special considerations recommended by the authors of these chapters already have been addressed by others writing about program purposes, identification, and curriculum and teaching strategies, these concepts will not be explained again. The agreement of these authors simply is noted.

When other emphases are suggested, or different perspectives are offered, differences are explained.

Certain elements of programs are perceived to be important and already have been explained:

1. The diversity within each cultural group as well as the differences between cultural groups must be recognized when designing identification procedures as well as the curriculum and instruction (Ruiz, Bradley, Grant, Hasegawa).
2. Stereotypes resulting from attending to the negative or positive traits usually attributed to minorities must be avoided, and each student must be viewed as an individual. Knowledge of group traits must be used for interpreting rather than predicting behavior of individuals (Ruiz, Grant, Hasegawa).
3. The influence of language must not be ignored in the assessment of giftedness (Ruiz, Hasegawa).
4. The primary purpose of educational programs for gifted students from minority cultures should be to enable them to develop abilities valued by them, valued by their culture, and necessary for success in the mainstream culture (Ruiz, Hasegawa, Bradley, Grant).
5. The development of self-esteem and a sense of self-worth is a necessary component of a program for gifted students, and is related to (or perhaps determines) the students' ability to function comfortably and successfully in more than one culture (Ruiz, Bradley, Hasegawa, Grant).
6. Enhancement of bilingual abilities is important (Ruiz, Hasegawa).
7. Increasing the range of career possibilities perceived by gifted minority students should be a program component (Hasegawa, Grant, Ruiz).

Unique emphases and perspectives of the authors asked to address special considerations also need to be noted. Even though the following ideas may be related to those already discussed, each is unique in its expression or its emphasis and needs attention from readers.

Grant expresses a philosophy that easily could be attributed to other authors if one considers underlying principles rather than exact words. He emphasizes that Black students are not in need of *special* considerations, but rather, in need of consideration and understanding *equal* to that of students from other groups. Grant's philosophy relates to the suggestion of other authors that we view differences as positive, or at least neutral, but not as deficits, and that we eliminate racial and ethnic stereotypes in favor of the perception of individuals first and group membership later.

Ruiz presents a unique perspective on the issue of family involvement in programs, and suggests that we view the parents and guardians of Hispanic students as the "clients" for our educational programs rather than viewing the students as the clients.

Both Ruiz and Bradley note the importance of involving the family in any recognition given to gifted students. Families of American Indians are recognized because they have helped the child being recognized to become what he or she is. The child *gives* gifts to those who have helped him or her, rather than *receiving* gifts. An obvious implication is that family recognition is important in this context, and that individual achievements are seen as resulting from the support given by others rather than from the superior abilities of the achiever.

Hasegawa recommends that educators avoid stereotyping Asian-American students as high achievers in math and science. Because of their internal pressures to achieve, Asian-American students also may need relaxation of academic expectations to enable them to develop creative talents necessary for success in a changing world.

Recommendations made by authors in this section support the conclusions of others, and provide additional examples of ways general principles can be applied or implemented. Personal experiences are cited by individuals who were students in the system and have become students *of* the system.

Administrators asked to respond to lead articles have provided their perspectives on the necessary elements of programs for gifted students from various minority groups.

The purpose of a special program for gifted students was the first question posed to authors in the four sections. In response to their answers, the administrators offered quite different perspectives. Ronvik, for example, focused on the suggestion that Anglo-American, middle-class values not be imposed upon minority students. His recommendation is that educators not even tolerate, and indeed even discourage, values that interfere with the emotional, social, or educational development. Larson recommends that educators plan for the development of each student individually rather than for groups based on their ethnicity, and emphasizes that strong management practices include long-range planning, communication, special staff, district-wide staff development, and systematic evaluation. In his response, strong action rather than "awareness" is emphasized as a need if program purposes such as those outlined by the experts are to be achieved. Weiss emphasizes the need to educate parents and other members of minority communities regarding the purpose and importance of special programs for gifted students.

Brooks demonstrates a different perspective by emphasizing that programs may have different purposes depending on the settings in which they exist: homogeneous (e.g., those with a majority of American Indians) and heterogeneous (e.g., those with only a small percentage of American Indians). She recommends the creation of an advisory group in homogeneous settings even though consensus about program purpose may be difficult to reach. In heterogeneous populations, she recommends that emphasis be placed on identification and programming because program purposes may not easily match the needs of a specific group of minority students. The first consideration in programming is how to identify students. To increase the possibility that gifted students from minority cultures will be identified, administrators have several options: (a) establish programs designed to increase the ability of students to achieve at high levels on instruments used for selection; (b) employ a variety of tests and other instruments selected because of their potential to highlight the abilities of particular populations; (c) develop local norms for tests being used, and employ these in the selection process; (d) establish quota systems; and (e) employ the same tests for all students, but lower criteria for entrance into the program for some groups.

Weiss and Ronvik respond to issues regarding identification by describing the approaches taken by their respective school districts. Weiss emphasizes the success of programs in which critical thinking skills are developed in enrichment programs for students not yet identified as gifted, but demonstrating high intellectual or academic abilities. Students are tested for possible placement in programs for the gifted *after* enrichment experiences are provided. The philosophy underlying this approach is similar to that of other experts and practitioners: Students from minority groups may need to develop certain skills prior to assessment if the results of tests are to be considered valid. Language proficiency certainly is one of these skills, and others are important as well.

In Ronvik's response, he emphasizes the success of a quota system in which the same measures are used to assess all populations. In this system, different (e.g., lower) criteria for admission may be employed to assure that all groups have access to special programs in percentages equal to those of the school population.

Brooks and Larson do not describe their own programs, but instead, address the issues regarding identification from a more general administration perspective. Both emphasize that the processes advocated by authors addressing identification will require sound management practices, adequate financial resources, and specially trained personnel. Time is also an important consideration, and some recommendations (e.g., development of ``culturally pluralistic'' measures) may not be possible to implement for several years.

Responses to issues related to curriculum and teaching strategies also were varied. However, three authors did emphasize the importance of a staff development plan for those involved in providing instruction (Larson, Brooks, Weiss). All authors alluded to the fact that the teaching strategies advocated for various minority populations would be good for students from any ethnic or cultural group, but emphasized different aspects of this assumption.

In conclusion, the administrators' responses to the lead articles in each section reflected different emphases and some similar recommendations. Weiss focused on service delivery, Ronvik discussed values and the importance of identification of traits similar across cultural groups, and Brooks emphasized differences in administrative implications depending on whether a particular cultural or ethnic group constituted a minority or majority of the school population. Both Brooks and Larson addressed management concerns and the importance of planning and service delivery on an individual basis.

What are the elements of a defensible program
for gifted students from cultural and ethnic minority groups?

In volume one of this series, *Defensible Programs for the Gifted,* I described eight criteria for development of a defensible program for gifted students. These principles or criteria were derived from the writing of authors in that volume, and resulted from a synthesis of their perspectives. Based on my review of the chapters of this volume, I have concluded that these same principles apply to programs for gifted students from cultural and ethnic minority groups. Each principle is explained in the first volume as it relates to gifted students in general. In this volume, the specific application of each principle to the development of programs for gifted minority students is explained.

Appropriate

Definitions of giftedness must be appropriate for the students to be served. If only one ethnic or cultural group is included, the values and traits of this group can form the basis of a definition, but if several groups must be served, a multidimensional definition should include components appropriate for each group. Identification procedures must be appropriate to the cultural, linguistic, and economic backgrounds and current traits of minority students. Appropriate instructional strategies are those in which the abilities, values, learning styles, and culturally related expressions of giftedness are respected and accommodated. Service delivery and supplementary programs must be viewed as appropriate by families as well as students, and must take into account cultural, linguistic, and economic characteristics of the individuals served. Finally, appropriateness of programs and services must be judged on an individual rather than a group basis.

Articulated

Internal articulation of a program for gifted minority students includes the assurance that both strengths and weaknesses of students are addressed, and that interruptions of services do not occur because criteria for placement of students fluctuate from year to year and school to school. In addition, since services not usually included may be needed by a student, such as instruction in English as a Second Language and an enrichment program in thinking skills, articulation needs special attention. External articulation is necessary, and must include involvement of extended families and minority cultural/ethnic communities and agencies as well as those of the majority culture.

Clear

Clarity of definitions, program purpose, and identification procedures is essential, and most difficult to achieve when values of educators and minority group members differ, or when values of minority group members themselves differ. Purposes and goals of special programs for gifted students must be communicated clearly to families of minority students so informed decisions about involvement can be made. Clarity of communication may necessitate use of the family's primary language.

Consistent

All aspects of a program must be consistent with each other, and with an underlying philosophy regarding the purpose of a special program for gifted individuals in a multicultural society. Consistency between procedures for identification of minority students who are gifted and the curriculum provided for those identified is perhaps the most problematic area. Students who are identified based on alternative criteria or who are admitted to a program with lower achievement or IQ scores than the majority of students in the program (because of the use of a quota system) are ''set up to fail'' if they are not provided a curriculum consistent with their strengths, weaknesses, and/or types of giftedness.

Comprehensive

Comprehensiveness implies that definitions of giftedness include a variety of abilities necessary for success in minority as well as the majority culture, and that identification procedures include a variety of types of data—both objective and subjective—so that biases in instruments and observers do not influence greatly the determination of giftedness. Services need to be comprehensive in their attention to social and emotional needs of students who need to develop self-identity in a world in which minority cultures are often subsumed by the majority, and values often conflict. Comprehensive programs also include curricula in which the contributions of individuals of many cultural groups are studied and services in which mentors and role models from various cultural and ethnic groups are included. A range of types of programs, including services in home schools, magnet programs in centers, special bilingual programs, and programs in regular classrooms, will be necessary to accommodate the variety of cultural values, learning styles, and abilities of a multiethnic population.

Responsive

Educators must be responsive to the differing values, concerns, and behavioral manifestations of giftedness in students from different ethnic and cultural groups. Responsiveness requires first a knowledge that differences exist between various groups, and that individuals within these groups share similar traits but are also different from one another. Next, this knowledge must be translated into skills in providing for the specific differences that exist in a community, a school, or a classroom. Finally, and most important, educators must encourage the expression of these differences, regard them as positive rather than negative, and respond to learning needs in ways that demonstrate genuine respect for cultural and ethnic values different from their own.

Unique

The principle of uniqueness does *not* suggest that programs and services for each ethnic and cultural group be unique. However, it does imply that giftedness be described in a way that gifted students can be viewed as having needs different from those of their peers, including those from their own ethnic or cultural group. For some minority groups, this uniqueness of an individual's potential contribution to the preservation of his or her culture may need to be emphasized as a justification for the provision of special services.

Valid

Validity of instruments and procedures is of primary concern in the assessment of giftedness in students from minority groups. Frequently, the methods used to develop standardized instruments do not account for variations due to cultural, linguistic, or economic differences. Teaching methods and curricula also must be validated for use with a variety of linguistic, cultural, and ethnic groups, but very little information is currently available on this subject. We must demonstrate to some educators as well as many members of the community, that special programs for students from cultural and ethnic minority groups are necessary and valid.

BIBLIOGRAPHY

Abbott, J.A. (undated). An anthropological approach to the identification of Navajo gifted children. Unpublished manuscript. (Available from Unpublished Manuscripts, The Dine Bi'olta Research Institute, Farmington, NM.)

Abbott, J.A. (1983). The Gifted Attitudes Inventory for Navajos: Directions for administering and scoring the GAIN and technical supplement. Unpublished manuscript. (Available from Unpublished Manuscripts, The Dine Bi'olta Research Institute, Farmington, NM.)

Addison, L. (1982). Strengthening the minority and disadvantaged gifted student: Curricula to develop locus of control. In *Identifying and educating the disadvantaged gifted/talented.* Ventura, CA: Office of Superintendent of Schools, Ventura County.

Adler, M. (1967). Reported incidence of giftedness among ethnic groups. *Exceptional Children, 34,* 101–105.

Allen, J. (1977). *The other side of the elephant.* Buffalo, NY: DOK.

Allison, L., & Katz, D. (1983). *Gee whiz: How to mix art and science or the art of thinking scientifically.* New York: Little, Brown.

Aoki, E. (1986). Which party will harvest the new Asian votes? *California Journal,* 545–546.

Argulewicz, E.N., & Kush, J.C. (1984). Concurrent validity of the SRBCSS Creativity Scale for Anglo-American and Mexican-American gifted students. *Educational and Psychological Research, 4,* 81–89.

Asian-Americans lead the way in educational attainment. (1986, March). *Phi Delta Kappan,* p. 546.

Baldwin, A. (1973, March). *Identifying the disadvantaged.* Paper presented at the First National Conference on the Disadvantaged Gifted, Ventura, CA.

Baldwin, A.Y. (1977). Tests can underpredict: A case study. *Phi Delta Kappan, 58*(8), 620–621.

Baldwin, A.Y. (1978). Curriculum and methods—What is the difference? In A.Y. Baldwin, G.H. Gear, & L.J. Lucito (Eds.), *Educational planning for the gifted: Overcoming cultural, geographic, and socioeconomic barriers.* Reston, VA: The Council for Exceptional Children.

Baldwin, A.Y. (1984). *The Baldwin identification matrix 2 for the identification of the gifted and talented: A handbook for its use.* New York: Trillium Press.

Baldwin, A.Y. (1985a). Issues concerning minorities. In F.D. Horowitz & M. O'Brien (Eds.), *The gifted and talented: Developmental perspectives.* Washington, DC: American Psychological Association.

Baldwin, A.Y. (1985b). Programs for the gifted and talented: Issues concerning minority populations. In F.D. Horowitz & M. O'Brien (Eds.), *The gifted and talented: Developmental perspectives* (pp. 223–249). Washington, DC: American Psychological Association.

Baldwin, A.Y., Gear, G.H., & Lucito, L.J. (Eds.). (1978). *Educational planning for the gifted: Overcoming cultural, geographic, and socioeconomic barriers.* Reston, VA: The Council for Exceptional Children.

Baldwin, A., & Wooster, J. (1977). *Baldwin identification matrix inservice kit for the identification of gifted and talented students.* Buffalo, NY: DOK.

Banks, J.A. (1975). *Teaching strategies for ethnic studies.* Boston: Allyn & Bacon.

Banks, J.A. (1979). *Teaching strategies for ethnic studies* (2nd ed.). Boston: Allyn & Bacon.

Barik, H., & Swain, M. (1974). English-French bilingual education in the early grades: The Elgin Study. *Modern Language Journal, 54,* 392.

Barnhardt, C. (1982). Tuning-in: Athabaskan teachers and Athabaskan students. In R. Barnhardt (Ed.), *Cross-cultural issues in Alaskan education: Vol. II*. Fairbanks: University of Alaska, Center for Cross-Cultural Studies.

Barrio, R. (1969). *The plum plum pickers*. Guerneville, CA: Ventura Press.

Baska, L. (in preparation). The use of the Stanford-Binet to validate selection in gifted programs.

Baska, L. (1986a). Alternatives to traditional testing. *Roeper Review, 8*(3), 181–184.

Baska, L. (1986b). The use of Raven Advanced Progressive Matrices for the selection of magnet junior high school students. *Roeper Review, 8*(3), 181–184.

Bauer, M.P., Bock, S., Kennedy, K., Lowe, O., Machotka, M., Moore, E., Scott, R., & Cummings, M.A. (1975). *A supplement to individual differences: An experience in human relations for children*. Madison, WI: Madison Public Schools.

Benson, S.S. (1978). *School-enrichment-parent education program*. Unpublished master's thesis, California State University at Los Angeles.

Benson, S.S. (1979). School enrichment-parent education program. In B. Clark, *Growing up gifted* (pp. 291–303). Columbus, OH: Charles E. Merrill.

Berlak, H. (1985). Testing in a democracy. *Educational Leadership, 43*(2), 16–17.

Bernal, E.M. (1974a). *Analysis of giftedness in Mexican-American children and design of a prototype identification instrument*. Austin, TX: Southwest Education Development Laboratory.

Bernal, E.M. (1974b). Gifted Mexican-American children: An ethno-scientific perspective. *California Journal of Educational Research, 25*, 261–273.

Bernal, E.M. (1976). Gifted programs for the culturally different. *National Association of Secondary School Principals Bulletin, 60*, 67–76.

Bernal, E.M. (1977). Assessment procedures for Chicano children: The sad state of the art. *Aztlan, 8*, 59–81.

Bernal, E.M. (1978). The identification of gifted Chicano children. In A.Y. Baldwin, G.H. Gear, & L.J. Lucito (Eds.), *Educational planning for the gifted: Overcoming cultural, geographic, and socioeconomic barriers*. Reston, VA: The Council for Exceptional Children.

Bernal, E.M. (1981). *Identifying minority gifted students: Special problems and procedures*. Paper presented for The Council for Exceptional Children's Conference on the Exceptional Bilingual Child, New Orleans, LA. (ERIC Document Reproduction Service No. ED 208 785)

Bernal, E.M. (1984a). Bias in mental testing: Evidence for an alternative to the heredity-environment controversy. In C.R. Reynolds & R.T. Brown (Eds.), *Perspectives on bias in mental testing*. New York: Plenum Press.

Bernal, E.M. (1984b). The implications of academic excellence for the culturally different gifted. In L. Kanevsky (Ed.), *Academic excellence: Its role in gifted education* (pp. 65–83). San Diego, CA: San Diego City Schools.

Bernal, E.M., & Reyna, J. (1974). *Analysis of giftedness in Mexican-American children and design of a prototype identification instrument*. Austin, TX: Southwest Education Development Laboratory. (ERIC Document Reproduction Service No. ED 090 743)

Beuf, A. (1977). *Red children in White America*. Philadelphia: University of Pennsylvania Press.

Birch, J.W. (1984). Is any identification procedure necessary? *Gifted Child Quarterly, 28*(4), 157–161.

Black, H. (1963). *They shall not pass*. New York: W.W. Morrow.

Blackshear, P. (1979). *A comparison of peer nomination and teacher nomination in the identification of the academically gifted, Black, primary level student*. Unpublished doctoral dissertation, University of Maryland, College Park.

Block, A.G. (1986). March Fong Eu, a political career stalled near the top? *California Journal*, 547–550.

Bloom, B.S. (Ed.). (1985). *Developing talent in young people*. New York: Ballantine.

Bloom, B.S., & Krathwohl, D.R. (1977). *Taxonomy of educational objectives: Handbook I: Cognitive domain*. New York: Longman.

Bloomer, R.H. (1980). *Bloomer Learning Test*. Livonia, NY: Brador.

Booth, L. (1980). An apprentice-mentor program for gifted students. *Roeper Review, 3*, 11–13.

Borland, J.H. (1986). IQ tests: Throwing out the bathwater, saving the baby. *Roeper Review, 8*(3), 163–167.

Botkin, J.W., Elmandjra, M., & Malitza, M. (1979). *No limits to learning*. New York: Pergamon.

Boyer, E. (1987). Early schooling and the nation's future. *Educational Leadership, 44*(6), 4–6.

Bracken, B. (1985). A critical review of the Kaufman Assessment Battery for Children (K-ABC). *School Psychology Review, 14*(1).

Briggs, J. (1984). The genius mind. *Science Digest, 92*(12), 75–103.

Bronfenbrenner, U. (1976). The experimental ecology of education. *Educational Researcher, 5*, 5–15.

Brooks, P.R. (1984). *A teacher's guide for Project Step: Strategies for targeting early potential*. (ERIC Document Reproduction Service No. ED 254 015)

Brown, A.D. (1980). Cherokee culture and school achievement. *American Indian Culture and Research Journal, 4,* 55–74.

Brown, S.R. (1980). *Political subjectivity: Applications of Q methodology in political science.* New Haven: Yale University.

Bruch, C.B. (1971). Modification of procedures for identification of the disadvantaged gifted. *Gifted Child Quarterly, 15,* 267–272.

Bruch, C.B. (1975). Assessment of creativity in culturally different children. *Gifted Child Quarterly, 19,* 164–174.

Bruch, C.B. (1978). Recent insights on the culturally different gifted. *Gifted Child Quarterly, 22,* 374–385.

Bureau of the Census. (1980). *Race of the population by states: 1980* (Supplementary Reports, PC80-S1-3, 1981). Washington, DC: Author.

Bureau of Indian Affairs. (1974). *The American Indians* (Stock No. 2402-000-40). Washington, DC: U.S. Government Printing Office.

Bureau of Indian Affairs. (1984). *American Indians: U.S. Indian policy, tribes and reservations, BIA past and present, economic development.* Washington, DC: Department of the Interior.

Bureau of Indian Affairs. (1985). *Indian service population and labor force estimates.* Washington, DC: Department of the Interior.

Bureau of Indian Affairs. (1986). *American Indians today.* Washington, DC: Department of the Interior.

Butterfield, F. (1986, August 3). Why are Asians going to the head of the class? *New York Times Special Section,* pp. 18–23.

Butterfield, R.A., Demos, E.S., Grant, G.W., Moy, P.S., & Perez, A.L. (1979). A multicultural analysis of a popular basal reading series in the International Year of the Child. *Journal of Negro Education, 48,* 382–389.

Calfee, R.C., Cazden, C.B., Duran, R.P., Griffin, M.P., Martus, M., & Willis, H.D. (1981). *Designing reading instruction for cultural minorities: The case of the Kamehameha early education program* (Unpublished report). (Available from Dr. C.B. Cazden, Harvard Graduate School of Education, Cambridge, MA)

Campos, & Keating, B. (1984). *The Carpenteria preschool program: Title VII second year evaluation report.* Washington, DC: Department of Education.

Cantu, R., Trevino, D., & Walther, K.P. (1982). Meeting the needs of the Hispanic gifted. In *Identifying and educating the disadvantaged gifted/talented: Selected proceedings from the Fifth National Conference on Disadvantaged Gifted/Talented.* Ventura, CA: Office of Ventura County Superintendent of Schools.

Castaneda, A. (1976). Cultural democracy and the educational needs of Mexican American children. In R.L. Jones (Ed.), *Mainstreaming and the minority child.* Reston, VA: The Council for Exceptional Children.

Cattell, R.B. (1963). Theory of fluid and crystallized intelligence: A critical experiment. *Journal of Educational Psychology, 54,* 1–22.

Cesa, T.A. (1982). *Language background survey of foreign born Asian undergraduates at the University of California, Berkeley.* Berkeley, CA: University of California Press. (ERIC Document Reproduction Service No. ED 223 152).

Chambers, J., Barron, F., & Spencer, J. (1986). Identifying gifted Mexican-American students. *Gifted Child Quarterly, 24,* 123–128.

Chamot, A.U. (1981). Applications of second language acquisition research to the bilingual classroom. *Focus,* No. 8.

Chan, S. (1986). Parents of exceptional Asian children. In M.K. Kitano & P.C. Chinn (Eds.), *Exceptional Asian children and youth* (pp. 36–53). Reston, VA: The Council for Exceptional Children.

Chan, K.S., & Kitano, M.K. (1986). Demographic characteristics of exceptional Asian students. In M.K. Kitano & P.C. Chinn (Eds.), *Exceptional Asian children and youth* (pp. 1–11). Reston, VA: The Council for Exceptional Children.

Charlesworth, W.R. (1976). An ethology of intelligence. In L.B. Resnick (Ed.), *The nature of intelligence.* Hillsdale, NJ: Lawrence Erlbaum Associates.

Charlesworth, W.R. (1979). An ethological approach to studying intelligence. *Human Development, 22,* 212–216.

Chavers, D. (1982–83). False promises, in American Indian education, *Integrateducation, 19–20,* 13.

Chen, J., & Goon, S. (1978). Recognition of the gifted from among disadvantaged Asian children. *Gifted Child Quarterly, 20,* 157–164.

Chinn, P.C., & Plata, M. (1986). Perspectives and educational implications of Southeast Asian students. In M.K. Kitano & P.C. Chinn (Eds.), *Exceptional Asian children and youth* (pp. 12–28). Reston, VA: The Council for Exceptional Children.

Chomsky, N. (1968). *Language and mind.* New York: Hartcourt, Brace & World.

Clarizo, H.F. (1982). Intellectual assessment of Hispanic children. *Psychology in the Schools, 19,* 61–71.

Clark, B. (1979). *Growing up gifted.* Columbus, OH: Charles E. Merrill.
Clark, B. (1983). *Growing up gifted: Developing the potential of children at home and at school* (2nd ed.). Columbus, OH: Charles E. Merrill.
Clark, B. (1985). *The integrative education model (IEM).* Unpublished manuscript, California State University, Los Angeles, CA.
Clark, B. (1986). *Optimizing learning: The integrative education model in the classroom.* Columbus, OH: Charles E. Merrill.
Clark, B., & Kaplan, S. (1981). *Improving differentiated curricula for the gifted/talented.* Los Angeles: California Association for the Gifted.
Clark, E.R. (1981). A double minority: The gifted Mexican-American child. In T. Escobedo (Ed.), *Education and Research Monograph 8.* Los Angeles, CA: University of California, Spanish Speaking Mental Health Research Center.
Clark, R. (1983). *Family life and school achievement: Why poor black children succeed or fail.* Chicago, IL: University of Chicago Press.
Clymer, T. (Ed.). (1969). *Reading 360 program.* Boston: Ginn.
Clymer, T. (Ed.). (1976). *Reading 720 program.* Lexington, MA: Ginn.
Coburn, J. (Ed.). (1981). *Native American education: Topic summary report* (p. 8). Portland, OR: Northwest Regional Educational Laboratory.
Cohen, L.M. (1987a). Infant interests: Seeds of creative development. Unpublished manuscript. Available from author, University of Oregon, Eugene, Oregon 97403.
Cohen, L.M. (1987b). Techniques for studying the interests of infants and young children. *Gifted International, 4*(2), 15–32.
Cohen, L.M., Revo, S.K., & McGreevey, P. (1981). *Identification of elementary Spanish-speaking (Puerto Rican) gifted: Final performance report* (Report submitted to U.S. Office of Education for Grant No. G00-770-1838). School District of Philadelphia. (Available from Cohen, University of Oregon, Eugene, Oregon, 97403.)
Cohen, L.M., & Shorter, E. (1981). *The use of Piagetian based tests for the identification of disadvantaged gifted* (Report submitted to the U.S. Office of Education for Grant No. 1236004102A1). School District of Philadelphia. (Available from Cohen, University of Oregon, Eugene, Oregon 97403.)
Colangelo, N., & Brower, P. (1986, November). *Long-term impact of labeling on gifted youngsters and their families.* Paper presented at the Thirty-third Annual Convention of the National Association for the Gifted and Talented, Las Vegas, NV.
Colangelo, N., & Zaffron, R. (1979). Special issues in counseling the gifted. *Counseling and Human Development, 2*(5), 1–12.
Coleman, L.J. (1985). *Schooling the gifted.* Reading, MA: Addison-Wesley.
Collins, N. (1983). *Professional women and their mentors.* Englewood Cliffs, NJ: Prentice-Hall.
Committee on Policy for Racial Justice (1987). *Black initiative and governmental responsibility: A policy framework for racial justice.* Washington, DC: Joint Center for Political Studies.
Cooper, H., & Tom, Y.H. (1984). Socio-economic status and ethnic group differences in achievement motivation. In R.E. Ames & C. Ames (Eds.), *Research on motivation in education: Vol. 1. Student motivation* (pp. 209–244). New York: Academic Press.
Cordova, R.H. (1985, February). U.S. schools mired in monocultural past. *Rocky Mountain News,* p. 91.
Cox, J., Daniel, N., & Boston, B.O. (1985). *Educating able learners: Programs & promising practices.* Austin, TX: University of Texas Press.
Crawford, T., & George, K. (1980, December). *Identifying and serving Native American gifted students: A position paper.* Paper presented to United Indians of All Tribes Foundation, Seattle, WA.
Cronbach, L.J., (1977). *Educational psychology* (3rd ed.). New York: Harcourt, Brace & Jovanovich.
Cummins, J. (1980). Psychological assessment of immigrant children: Logic or intuition? *Journal of Multilingual and Multicultural Development, 1,* 97–111.
Cummins, J. (1983a). *Heritage language education: A literature review.* Toronto: Ministry of Education.
Cummins, J. (1983b). Bilingualism and special education: Program and pedagogical issues. *Learning Disability Quarterly, 6,* 373–386.
Cummins, J. (1984). *Bilingualism and special education: Issues in assessment and pedagogy.* San Diego, CA: College Hill Press.
Cummins, J. (1986). Empowering minority students: A framework for intervention. *Harvard Educational Review, 56,* 18–36.
Curran, C.A. (1972). *Counseling-learning in second languages.* Apple River, IL: Apple River Press.
Curran, C.A. (1977). *Counseling-learning: A whole-person model for education.* Apple River, IL: Apple River Press.

Dabney, M. (1980, April). *The gifted Black adolescent: Focus upon the creative positives.* Paper presented at the Annual International Convention of The Council for Exceptional Children, Philadelphia, PA. (ERIC Document Reproduction Service No. ED 189 767)

Dabney, M. (1983, July). *Perspectives and directives in assessment of the Black child.* Paper presented at the meeting of The Council for Exceptional Children, Atlanta, GA.

Darnell, R. (1979). *Reflections on Cree interactional etiquette: Educational implications* (Sociolinguistic Working Paper #57). Austin, TX: Southwest Education Development Laboratory.

Davidson, H.H., & Greenberg, J.W. (1967). *Traits of school achievers from a deprived background.* (Project No. 2805, Contract No. OE-5-10-132). New York: The City College of the City University of New York.

Davidson, J.E., & Sternberg, R.J. (1984). The role of insight in intellectual giftedness. *Gifted Child Quarterly, 28,* 58–64.

Davis, A., Gardner, B.B., & Gardner, M.R. (1941). *Deep South.* Chicago: University of Chicago Press.

Davis, G.B., & Rimm, S.B. (1985). *Education of the gifted and talented.* Englewood Cliffs, NJ: Prentice-Hall.

Davis, P. (1978). *Community-based efforts to increase the identification of the number of gifted minority children.* Ypsilanti, MI: Eastern Michigan College of Education. (ERIC Document Reproduction Service No. ED 176 487)

DBS Corporation. (1982). *1980 elementary and secondary schools civil rights survey: State summaries. Vol. II.* (ERIC Document Reproduction Service No. ED 219 479)

DeAvila, E. (1976, November 17). *Identification of non-mainstreamed gifted.* Presentation made to School District of Philadelphia school psychologists, Philadelphia, PA.

DeAvila, E., & Duncan, S. (1979). Bilingualism and the metaset. *Journal for the National Association for Bilingual Education, 3,* 1.

DeAvila, E.A., & Havassy, B. (1975). Piagetian alternatives to IQ: Mexican-American study. In N. Hobbs (Ed.), *Issues in the classification of exceptional children.* San Francisco, CA: Jossey-Bass.

de Bono, E. (1974). *Thinking course for juniors.* Dorset, UK: Direct Education Services.

Debra P. v. Turlington, No. 78-892 Civ.—T—H (M.D., Fla., *decision* 7/12/79).

deCharms, R. (1984). Motivation enhancement in educational settings. In R.E. Ames & C. Ames, (Eds.), *Research on motivation in education* (pp. 275–312). New York: Academic Press.

DeHaven, E. (1983). *Teaching and learning the language arts.* Boston: Little Brown.

Deiner, D., & Dweck, C. (1978). An analysis of learned helplessness: Continuous changes in performance, strategy, and achievement cognitions following failure. *Journal of Personality and Social Psychology, 36,* 451–462.

Deleon, J. (1983). Cognitive style difference and the underrepresentation of Mexican Americans in programs for the gifted. *Journal for the Education of the Gifted, 6,* 140–153.

Deloria, V., & Lytle, C. (1984). *American Indians, American justice.* Austin, TX: University of Texas Press.

Diana v. California State Board of Education, C-70 37 RFP (N. Dist. Calif. Dist. Ct. 1970).

Dinh, V. (1976). A Vietnamese child in your classroom? Instructor, 85(7), 86.

Douglas, J.H. (1969, April). *Strategies for maximizing the development of talent among the urban disadvantaged.* Paper presented at the annual meeting of The Council for Exceptional Children, Denver, CO.

DuBois, W.E.B. (1961). *The souls of Black folk: Essays and sketches.* Greenwich, CT: Fawcett.

Dyer, H. (1963). *Race and intelligence: An examination of the scientific evidence by four authorities.* Princeton, NJ: Princeton University Press.

Edwards, R.M., Moss, W., & Saletta, P.A. (1983). *A system for talented and gifted education.* Weaverville, CA: Trinity County Office of Education.

Ehrlich, V.Z. (1978). *The Astor program for gifted children.* New York: Teachers College, Columbia University Press.

Eisner, E.W. (1963). Research in creativity: Some findings and conceptions. *Childhood Education,* 371–375.

Elkind, D. (1981). *The hurried child.* Reading, MA: Addison-Wesley.

Encendiendo Una Llama, Bilingual Gifted and Talented Program, Webster School, 5 Cone St., Hartford, CT 06105. (ERIC Document Reproduction Service No. ED 196 197)

Endo, R. (1980). Asian Americans and higher education. *Phylon, 41*(4), 367–378.

Escobar, J.I., & Randolph, E.T. (1982). The Hispanic and social networks. In R.M. Becerra, M. Karno, & J.I. Escobar (Eds.), *Mental health and Hispanic Americans: Clinical perspectives* (pp. 41–57). New York: Grune & Stratton.

Eyster, I. (1980). *Culture through concepts: A teachers guide.* Norman, OK: Southwest Center for Human Relations Studies. (ERIC Document Reproduction Service No. ED 176 928)

Faas, L.A. (1982, June). *Culture and education variables involved in identifying and educating gifted and talented American Indian children.* Paper presented at the Gifted Minorities Conference, Tucson, AZ.

Farley, J., & Farley, S. (1987). Interactive writing and gifted children: Communication through literacy. *Journal for the Education of the Gifted, 10*(2), 99–106.

Felder, R.M. (1986). Identifying and dealing with exceptionally gifted children: The half-blind leading the sighted. *Roeper Review, 8*(3), 174–177.

Feldhusen, J.F., Baska, L.K., & Womble, S. (1981). Using standard scores to synthesize data in identifying the gifted. *Journal for the Education of the Gifted, 4*(3), 177–186.

Feldhusen, J.F., & Hoover, S.M. (1986). A conception of giftedness: Intelligence, self concept and motivation. *Roeper Review, 8*(3), 140–143.

Feldhusen, J., & Kolloff, P.B. (1986). The Purdue three stage enrichment model for gifted education at the elementary level. In J.S. Renzulli (Ed.), *Systems and Models for developing programs for the gifted and talented.* Mansfield Center, CT: Creative Learning Press.

Feldhusen, J., & Robinson, A. (1986). The Purdue secondary model for gifted and talented youth. In J.S. Renzulli (Ed.), *Systems and models for developing programs for the gifted and talented.* Mansfield Center, CT: Creative Learning Press.

Feldman, D.H. (1979). The mysterious case of extreme giftedness. In A.H. Passow (Ed.), *The gifted and the talented: Their education and development* (78th yearbook for the National Society for the Study of Education). Chicago: University of Chicago Press.

Feldman, D.H. (1980). *Beyond universals in cognitive development.* Norwood, NJ: Ablex.

Feldman, D.H. (1982). A developmental framework for research with gifted children. In D.H. Helman (Ed.), *Developmental approaches to giftedness and creativity: new directions for child development* (No. 17, pp. 31–46). San Francisco: Jossey-Bass.

Fersch, S. (1972). Orientals and orientation. *Phi Delta Kappan, 53,* 315–318.

Feuerstein, R. (1979). *The dynamic assessment of retarded performers: The learning potential assessment device, theory, instruments, and techniques.* Baltimore: University Park Press.

Fitzgerald, E.J. (Ed.). (1973). *The First National Conference on the Disadvantaged Gifted.* Los Angeles: National/State Leadership Training Institute.

Fitz-Gibbon, C.T. (1975). The identification of mentally gifted "disadvantaged" students at the eighth grade level. *Journal of Negro Education, 43*(1), 53–66.

Ford, C. (1976). *A study of the family characteristics of selected high achieving upper-elementary age Black children.* Doctoral dissertation, Atlanta University, Atlanta, GA.

Foster, W., & Seltzer, A. (1986). A portrayal of individual excellence in the urban ghetto. *Journal of Counseling and Development, 64*(9), 579–582.

Fox, L. (1981). Identification of the academically gifted. *American Psychologist, 36*(10), 1103–1111.

Frank, M. (1979). *If you're trying to teach kids how to write, you've gotta have this book!* Nashville: Incentive Publications.

Frasier, M.M. (1979). Counseling the culturally diverse gifted. In N. Colangelo & R.T. Zaffran (Eds.), *New voices in counseling the gifted* (pp. 304–311). Dubuque, IA: Kendall/Hunt.

Frasier, M.M. (1980). Programming for the culturally diverse. In J. Jordan & J. Grossi (Eds.), *An administrator's handbook on designing programs for the gifted and talented* (pp. 56–65). Reston, VA: The Council for Exceptional Children.

Frasier, M.M. (1982). Bibliotherapy: Educational and counseling implications for the gifted disadvantaged. In *Identifying and educating the disadvantaged gifted/talented.* Ventura, CA: Office of Ventura County Superintendent of Schools.

Frasier, M.M. (1983). *A comparison of general traits and behaviors attributed to the gifted with traits and behaviors attributed to the gifted disadvantaged.* Unpublished manuscript, University of Georgia, Athens, GA.

Frierson, E.C. (1965). Upper and lower status gifted children: A study of differences. *Exceptional Children, 32*(2), 83–90.

Fuchigami, R.Y. (1978). Summary, analysis, and future directions. In A.Y. Baldwin, G.H. Gear, & L.J. Lucito (Eds.), *Educational planning for the gifted: Overcoming cultural, geographic, and socioeconomic barriers.* Reston, VA: The Council for Exceptional Children.

Fuchs, E., & Havighurst, R.J. (1973). *To live on this earth.* New York: Anchor Books.

Gagne, F. (1985). Giftedness and talent: Reexamining a reexamination of the definitions. *Gifted Child Quarterly, 29*(3), 103–112.

Galbraith, J. (1985). The eight great gripes of gifted kids: Responding to special needs. *Roeper Review, 8,* 15–18.

Gallagher, J. (1975). *Teaching the gifted child* (2nd ed.). Boston: Allyn & Bacon.

Gallagher, J., & Kinney, L. (Eds.). (1974). *Talent delayed—Talent denied: A conference report.* Reston, VA: Foundation for Exceptional Children.

Gallagher, J.J. (1985). *Teaching the gifted child* (3rd ed.). Boston: Allyn & Bacon.

Gallagher, R.M. (1983). Identification of minority gifted. *Illinois Journal for the Gifted, 1,* 3–5.

Gallegos, A.Y., & Flores, J. (1982, June). *The role of the family in the identification and education of gifted minority children.* Paper presented at the Gifted Minorities Conference, Tucson, AZ.

Gardner, H. (1983). *Frames of mind: The theory of multiple intelligences.* New York: Basic Books.

Gay, J.E. (1978). A proposed plan for identifying Black gifted children. *Gifted Child Quarterly, 22*(3), 353–360.

Gear, G.H. (1976). Accuracy of teacher judgement in identifying intellectually gifted children: A review of the literature. *Gifted Child Quarterly, 20,* 478–490.

Gear, G.H. (1978). Within the community and its schools. In A.Y. Baldwin, G.H. Gear, & L.J. Lucito (Eds.), *Educational planning for the gifted: Overcoming cultural, geographic, and socioeconomic barriers.* Reston, VA: The Council for Exceptional Children.

George, K. (1979). *Native American gifted inservice manual, Poulsbo, WA: North Kitsap School District.* Poulsbo, WA: North Kitsap School District.

George, K.R. (Ed.). (1980). *Native American gifted program: Final report.* Olympia, WA: Office of Superintendent of Public Instruction, Gifted/Talented.

Ginott, H. (1972). *Teacher and child.* New York: Avon Books.

Glaser, E.J., & Ross, H.L. (1970). *A study of successful persons from seriously disadvantaged backgrounds: Final report* (Contract No. 82-05-68-03). Washington, DC: Department of Labor, Office of Special Manpower Programs.

Golden, J. (1980). *Como ser apdres de ninos superdotados y talentosos: Manual para los padres (Parenting the gifted and talented: A handbook for parents).* New York: New York City Board of Education. (Available from Community School District Ten, Board of Education of the City of New York, P.S. 95, 3961 Hillman Avenue, Bronx, N.Y. 10463).

Gordon, E.W., & Wilkerson, D.A. (1966). *Compensatory education for the disadvantaged. Programs and practices: Pre-school through college.* New York: College Entrance Board.

Gordon, W.J.J. (1961). *Synectics: The development of creative capacity.* New York: Harper & Row.

Gough, P.B. (1987). The key to improving schools: An interview with William Glasser. *Phi Delta Kappan, 68*(9), 656–662.

Gourley, T.J. (1984). Do we identify or reject the gifted student? *Gifted Child Quarterly, 28*(4), 188–190.

Gowan, J.C. (1975). Identification: Responsibility of both principal and teacher. In W.B. Barbe & J.S. Renzulli (Eds.), *Psychology and education of the gifted* (pp. 280–281). New York: Irvington.

Grant, C.A., & Grant, G.W. (1981). The multicultural evaluation of some second and third grade textbook readers—A survey analysis. *Journal of Negro Education, 50,* 63–74.

Grant, C.A., & Sleeter, C.E. (1986). *After the school bell rings.* Barcombe, England: Falmer Press.

Grant, C.A., & Sleeter, C.E. (1981). *Report to Nicolet High School: Interpersonal/intergroup communication.* Unpublished manuscript. (Available from C. Grant, University of Wisconsin at Madison, Madison, WI.)

Gruber, H.E. (1981). *Darwin on man: A psychological study of creativity.* Chicago: University of Chicago Press.

Guadalupe v. Temple Elementary School District, 71-435, 587 F.2d 1022 (D. Ariz. 1972).

Guilford, J.P. (1967). *The nature of human intelligence.* New York: McGraw-Hill.

Hagen, E. (1980). *Identification of the gifted.* New York: Teachers College Press.

Hakuta, K. (1985). *The causal relationship between the development of bilingualism, cognitive flexibility, and social-cognitive skills in Hispanic elementary school children.* Rosslyn, VA: National Clearinghouse for Bilingual Education.

Hakuta, K. (1986). *Mirror of language: The debate on bilingualism.* New York: Basic Books.

Hall, E.T. (1976). *Beyond culture.* New York: Anchor Press.

Hanson, W.D., & Eisenbise, M.D. (1983). *Human behavior and American Indians.* Rockville, MD: National Institute of Mental Health. (ERIC Document Reproduction Service No. ED 231 589)

Hare, B. (1985). Re-examining the achievement central tendency: Sex differences within race and race differences within sex. In H.P. McAdoo & J.L. McAdoo (Eds.), *Black children.* Beverly Hills, CA: Sage.

Harrington, G.M. (1984). An experimental model of bias in mental testing. In C.R. Reynolds & R.T. Brown (Eds.), *Perspectives of bias in mental testing.* New York: Plenum Press.

Harris, C.R. (1984). Tapping creative potential in the multi-cultural gifted underachiever. In D. Sisk (Ed.), *Gifted International 2*(2). New York: Trillium Press.

Harrison, B. (1981, December). *Informal learning among Yu'pik Eskimos.* Paper presented at the American Anthropological Association Annual Meeting, Los Angeles, CA.

Hatch, T.C., & Gardner, H. (1986). From testing intelligence to assessing competencies: A pluralistic view of intellect. *Roeper Review, 8*(3), 147–150.

Henderson, R.W. (1980). Social and emotional needs of culturally diverse children. *Exceptional Children, 46*(8), 598–605.

High, M.H. (1981). *Closing the gap for disadvantaged gifted: A review of literature and program proposal.* Unpublished manuscript. (Available from M.H. High, Catalina High School, Tucson Unified School District, Tucson, AZ.)

High, M.H., & Udall, A.J. (1983). Teacher rating of studnets in relation to ethnicity of students and school ethnic balance. *Journal for The Education of the Gifted, 6*(3), 154–166.

Hilliard, A.G. (1976, June). *Alternatives to IQ testing: An approach to the identification of gifted "minority" children* (Final report). Sacramento, CA: California State Department of Education, Sacramento Division of Special Education. (ERIC Document Reproduction Service No. ED 147 009)

Hilliard, A. (1984). The emperor's new clothes: A critique of Jensen's bias in mental testing. In C.R. Reynolds & R.T. Brown (Eds.), *Perspectives on bias in mental testing.* New York: Plenum Press.

Hilliard, P. (1976). *Identifying gifted minority children through the use of non-verbal tests.* Unpublished doctoral dissertation, Yeshiva University, New York.

Hirschfelder, O. (1982). *American Indian stereotypes in the world of children.* Metuchen, NJ: Scarecrow Press.

Hoffman, B. (1962). *The tyranny of testing.* New York: Crowell-Collier.

Horn, R.E., & Cleaves, A. (1980). *The guide to simulations/games for education and training.* Beverly Hills, CA: Sage.

Horowitz, F.D., & O'Brien, M. (1985). Perspectives on research and development. In F.D. Horowitz & M. O'Brien (Eds.), *The gifted and talented: Developmental perspectives.* Washington, DC: American Psychological Association.

Hoyt, D.P. (1965). *The relationship between college grades and adult achievement: A review of the literature* (Research Report No. 62). Iowa City, IA: American College Testing Program.

Hsia, J. (1983). Cognitive assessment of Asian-Americans. In M. Chu-Chang (Ed.), *Asian- and Pacific-American perspectives in bilingual education: Comparative research.* New York: Teachers College, Columbia University.

Hsia, J. (1985, March 31–April 4). The silent minority: Asian Americans in education and work. Paper presented at the annual meeting of the American Educational Research Association, Chicago, IL. (ERIC Document Reproduction Service No. ED 261 124)

Institute for Staff Development. (1971). *Hilda Taba teaching strategies program: Unit 1, Unit 2, Unit 3, Unit 4.* Miami, FL: Author.

Irvine, D. (1987). What research doesn't show about gifted dropouts. *Educational Leadership, 44,* 79–80.

Isaksen, S.G., & Treffinger, D.J. (1985). *Creative problem solving: The basic course.* Buffalo, NY: Bearly.

Jacobs, J. (1971). Effectiveness of teacher and parent identification of gifted children as a function of school level. *Psychology in the Schools, 8,* 140–142.

Japanese in U.S. outdo Horatio Alger. (1977, October 17). *Los Angeles Times,* pp. 10–11.

Jaramillo, M.L. (1974). Cultural conflict curriculum and the exceptional child. *Exceptional Children, 40,* 585–587.

Jencks, C. (1972). *Inequality.* New York: Basic Books.

Jenkins-Friedman, R. (1982). Myth: Cosmetic use of multiple selection criteria. *Gifted Child Quarterly, 26,* 24–26.

Jensen, A. (1969). How much can we boost IQ and scholastic achievement? *Harvard Educational Review, 39,* 1–123.

Johnson, B.H. (1968). *Navajo education at Rough Rock.* Rough Rock, AZ: Navajo Curriculum Center.

Johnson, S.T., Starnes, W.T., Gregory, D., & Blaylock, A. (1985). Program of assessment, diagnosis, and instruction (PADI): Identifying and nurturing potentially gifted and talented minority students. *The Journal of Negro Education, 54*(3), 416–430.

Jordan, C. (1981). The selection of culturally-compatible classroom practices. *Educational Perspectives, 20*(1), 16–19.

Joyce, B. & Showers, B. (1980). Improving inservice training: The messages of research. *Educational Leadership, 37,* 379–385.

Joyce, B. & Showers, B. (1981, April). *Teacher training research: Working hypothesis for program design and directions for further study.* Paper presented at the annual meeting of the American Educational Research Association, Los Angeles.

Juntune, J. (1982). Myth: The gifted constitutes a single, homogeneous group! *Gifted Child Quarterly, 26*(1), 9–10.

Kagiwada, G., & Fugimoto, I. (1973). Asian-American studies: Implications for education. *Personnel and Guidance Journal, 51,* 400–405.

Kaneshige, E., (1973). Cultural factors in group counseling and interaction. *Personnel and Guidance Journal, 51*(6), 407–411.

Kaplan, S. (1974). *Providing programs for the gifted and talented: A handbook.* Ventura, CA: Office of Ventura County Superintendent of Schools.

Kaplan, S. (1975). *Providing programs for the gifted and talented.* Reston, VA: The Council for Exceptional Children.

Kaplan, S.N. (1986). Qualitatively differentiated curriculum. In C.J. Maker (Ed.), *Critical issues in gifted education: Defensible programs for the gifted.* Austin, TX: PRO-ED.

Karnes, F.A., & Koch, S.F. (1985). State definitions of the gifted and talented: An update and analysis. *Journal for the Education of the Gifted, 8*(4), 285–306.

Kaufman, A.S. (1984). K-ABC and giftedness. *Roeper Review, 7*(2), 83–88.

Kaufman, A.S., & Harrison, P.L. (1986). Intelligence tests and gifted assessment: What are the positives. *Roeper Review, 8*(3), 154–159.

Kaufman, A.S., & Kaufman, N.L. (1983). *Kaufman Assessment Battery for Children (K-ABC).* Circle Pines, MN: American Guidance Service.

Killialeu & Associates. (1980, February). *Fall 1978 elementary and secondary school civil rights survey: Users guide to the data file.* Prepared for the Office of Civil Rights, U.S. Department of Health and Human Services, Washington, DC.

Kirschenbaum, R.J. (1983). Let's cut out the cut-off score in the identification of the gifted. *Roeper Review, 5,* 6–10.

Kitano, M.K. (1986). Gifted and talented Asian children. In M.K. Kitano & P.C. Chinn (Eds.), *Exceptional Asian children and youth* (pp. 54–60). Reston, VA: The Council for Exceptional Children.

Kitano, M.K., & Kirby, D.F. (1986). *Gifted education: A comprehensive view.* Boston: Little, Brown.

Kleinfeld, J. (1975). Effective teachers of Eskimo and Indian students. *School Review, 83*(2), 301–344.

Kleinfeld, J., & McDiarmid, G.W., & Parrett, W.(1983). Doing research on effective cross-cultural teaching: The teacher tale. In D. McShane (Ed.), *Special issue: The transcultural education of American Indian and Alaska Native children: Teachers and students in transaction. Peabody Journal of Education, 6.*

Kometani, T. (1986, July 4). [Interview with Robert MacNeil on *The MacNeil/Lehrer NewsHour*]. Transcript available from Box 345, New York, NY 10101.

Krashen, S.D. (1982). *Principles and practice in second language acquisition.* Oxford: Pergamon.

Krashen, S.D. (1986, April). Paper presented at the National Association of Bilingual Education Conference, Chicago.

Kravetz, N. (1986). Defining a humanities curriculum for the gifted. *Humanities Journal 1986,* 19–22.

Lajoie, S.P., & Shore, B.M. (1981). Three myths? The over-representation of the gifted among dropouts, delinquents, and suicides. *Gifted Child Quarterly, 25*(3), 138-143.

Lambert, W. (1977). The effects of bilingualism on the individual: Cognitive and sociocultural consequences. In P. Hornby (Ed.), *Bilingualism: Psychological, social and educational implications* (p. 5). New York: Academic Press.

Lang, R., & Ryba, K. (1976). The identification of some creative thinking parameters common to the artistic and musical personality. *British Journal of Educational Psychology, 46*(3), 267–279.

Larry P. v. Riles, No. C71-2270 RFP (N.D. Cal., *decision* 10/16/79).

Lau v. Nichols, 414, U.S. 563 (1974).

Laudenslager, J., & Valdez, A. (1986, November). *Identifying first generation rural Mexican-American gifted.* Paper presented at National Association for Gifted Children, Las Vegas, NV.

Lesser, G.S. (1964). Some effects of segregation and desegregation in the school. *Integrated Education, 2,* 20–26.

Leung, B. (1986). Psychoeducational assessment of Asian students. In M.K. Kitano & P.C. Chinn (Eds.), *Exceptional Asian children and youth* (pp. 29–35). Reston, VA: The Council for Exceptional Children.

Leung, E.K. (1981, February). *The identification and social problems of gifted bilingual-bicultural children.* Paper presented at The Council for Exceptional Children Conference on the Exceptional Bilingual Child. (ERIC Document Reproduction Service No. ED 203 653)

Lindstrom, R.R., & Van Sant, S. (1986). Special issues in working with gifted minority adolescents. *Journal of Counseling and Development, 64*(9), 583–586.

Lipman, M., Sharp, A., & Oscanyan, F. (1980). *Philosophy in the classroom* (2nd ed.). Philadelphia: Temple University Press.

Little Soldier, L. (1985). To soar with the eagles: Enculturation and acculturation of Indian Children. *Childhood Education, 61,* 185–191.

Llanes, J.R. (1980). Bilingualism and the gifted intellect. *Roeper Review, 3,* 11–12.

Locke, P. (1979). *Needs of American Indian gifted children.* Presentation to joint meeting of the U.S. Office of Gifted and Talented and Office of Indian Education, Red Lake, Minnesota, March 1979.

Long, R. (1981, April). *An approach to a defensible non-discriminatory identification model for the gifted.* Paper presented at the meeting of The Council for Exceptional Children, New York, NY.

Low, W.A. & Clift, U.A. (Eds.). (1981). *Encyclopedia of Black America.* New York: McGraw-Hill.

Lynn, J. (1976). In search of fair selection procedures. *Journal of Educational Measurement, 13,* 53–57.

Lyon, H.C. (1979). *The other minority.* Unpublished manuscript, U.S. Office of Education.

Machado, M. (1987). Gifted Hispanics underidentified in classrooms. *Hispanic Link Weekly Report, 5*(7), 1.

MacMillan, D.L. (1982). *Mental retardation in school and society* (2nd ed.). Boston: Little, Brown.

Maehr, M.L. (1984). Meaning and motivation: Toward a theory of personal investment. In R.E. Ames & C. Ames (Eds.), *Research on motivation in education: Vol. 1. Student motivation* (pp. 115–144). New York: Academic Press.

Maker, C.J. (1979a). Developing multiple talents in exceptional children. *Teaching Exceptional Children, 11,* 120–124.

Maker, C.J. (1979b). *Suggested procedures for screening, identification, and diagnosis of the gifted in New Mexico.* Santa Fe, NM: New Mexico State Department of Education.

Maker, C.J. (1980). Personal communication.

Maker, C.J. (1982a). *Curriculum development for the gifted.* Austin, TX: PRO-ED.

Maker, C.J. (1982b). *Teaching models in the education of the gifted.* Austin, TX: PRO-ED.

Maker, C.J. (1983). Quality education for gifted minority students. *Journal for the Education of the Gifted, 6*(13), 140–153.

Maker, C.J. (Ed.). (1986). *Critical issues in gifted education: Defensible programs for the gifted.* Austin, TX: PRO-ED.

Maker, C.J., Morris, E., & James, J.D. (1981). The Eugene Field project: A program for potentially gifted young children. In *Balancing the scale for the disadvantaged gifted: Presentations from the Fourth Biennial National Conference on Disadvantaged Gifted/Talented* (pp. 117–175). Ventura, CA: National/State Leadership Training Institute, Office of Ventura County Superintendent of Schools.

Mar'i, S.K., & Karayanni, M. (1982). Creativity in Arab research: Two decades of research. *Journal of Creative Behavior, 16,* 227–238.

Marland, S.P. (1972). *Education of the gifted and talented. Report to the Congress of the United States* (2 vols.). Washington, DC: U.S. Government Printing Office.

Marland, S.P. (1976). *Education of the gifted and talented: Report to the U.S. Congress by the U.S. Commissioner of Education.* Washington, DC: U.S. Department of Health, Education, and Welfare.

Martinson, R.A. (1974). *The identification of the gifted and talented.* Los Angeles: National/State Leadership Training Institute.

McBeath, M., Blackshear, P., & Smart, L. (1981, August). *Identifying low income, minority gifted and talented youngsters.* Paper presented at the annual meeting of the American Psychological Association, Los Angeles, CA. (ERIC Document Reproduction Service No. ED 214 328)

McClung, M.S. (1979). Competency testing progress: Legal and educational issues. *Fordham Law Review, 47,* 651–712.

McCready, W. (1985). Culture and religion. In P.S.J. Cafferty & W. McCready (Eds.), *Hispanics in the United States: A new social agenda* (pp. 49–61). New Brunswick, NJ: Transaction Books.

McDermott, R.P. (1974). Achieving school failure: An anthropological approach to illiteracy and social stratification. In G.D. Spindler (Ed.), *Education and cultural process: Toward an anthropology of education.* New York: Holt, Rinehart & Winston.

McKenzie, J.A. (1986). The influence of identification practices, race and SES on the identification of gifted students. *Gifted Child Quarterly, 30,* 93–95.

Melendez, D. (1986). Hispanic students: Still not achieving. *Thrust,* 14–16.

Melesky, T.J. (1984). Identifying and providing for the Hispanic gifted child. *NABE Journal, 9,* 43–56.

Mercer, J.R. (1971). Institutionalized Anglocentrism: Labeling mental retardates in the public schools. In P. Orleans & W. Russell (Eds.), *Race, change and urban society,* Urban Affairs Annual Review, Vol. V., Los Angeles: Sage.

Mercer, J.R. (1973). *Labeling the mentally retarded.* Berkeley: University of California Press.

Mercer, J.R. (1981). The system of multicultural pluralistic assessment: SOMPA. In *Balancing the scale for the disadvantaged gifted* (pp. 29–57). Proceedings from the Fourth Biennial National Conference on Disadvantage Gifted/Talented. Ventura, CA: National/State Leadership Training Institute, Office of Ventura County Superintendent of Schools.

Mercer, J.R. (1984). What is a racially and culturally nondiscriminatory test? A sociological and pluralistic perspective. In C.R. Reynolds & R.T. Brown (Eds.), *Perspectives on bias in mental testing.* New York: Plenum Press.

Mercer, J.R., & Lewis, J.F. (1978). Using the system of multicultural pluralistic assessment (SOMPA) to identify the gifted minority child. In A.Y. Baldwin, G.H. Gear, & L.J. Lucito, *Educational planning for the gifted: Overcoming cultural, geographic, and socioeconomic barriers.* (pp. 7–14). Reston, VA: The Council for Exceptional Children.

Miller, D.L., & Garcia, A. (1974, May). *Mental issues among urban Indians: The myth of the savage-child.* Paper presented at American Physiological Association. (ERIC Document Reproduction Service No. 129 485)

Mitchell, B. (1982). Identification of the gifted and talented: A screening process with special emphasis on the culturally different. In *Identifying and educating the disadvantaged gifted and talented* (pp. 109–116). Ventura, CA: National/State Leadership Training Insitute on the Gifted and the Talented, Office of Ventura County Superintendent of Schools.

Mohatt, G., & Erickson, F. (1981). Cultural differences in teaching styles in an Odawa school: A socio-linguistic approach. In H. Trueba, G. Guthrie, & K. Au (Eds.), *Culture and the bilingual classroom: Studies and classroom ethnography.* Rowley, MA: Newberry House.

Momaday, N.S. (1982, December). I Am Alive. *Talking Peace Pipe News*, p. 13;16. Detroit Urban Indian Council, Michigan.

Montgomery, D.M. (1983). *Defining giftedness by examining the self-perceptions of gifted students: A Q-methodological study.* Unpublished doctoral dissertation, University of New Mexico.

Montgomery, D.M. (1986). *1984–1985 AIRD Advisory Board perceptions of giftedness.* Unpublished manuscript. (Available from D. Montgomery, Elmhurst School, Oklahoma City, OK.)

Moore, B.A. (1979). A model career education program for gifted disadvantaged students. *Roeper Review, 2,* 20–23.

Munoz, V. (1983). Family life patterns of Pacific Islanders: The insidious displacement of culture. In G.J. Powell (Ed.), *The psychosocial development of minority group children* (pp. 131–146). New York: Brunner/Mazel.

Mullard, C. (1965). *The social dynamic of migrant groups: From progressive to transformative policy in education.* Paper presented at the OECD Conference on Educational Policies and the Minority Social Groups, Paris.

Naisbitt, J. (1982). *Megatrends: Ten new directions transforming our lives.* New York: Warner Books.

National Advisory and Coordinating Council of Bilingual Education (1985). *New directions in the late 80's.* Ninth annual report, 1984–85. Washington, DC: Author. (ERIC Document Reproduction Service).

Nazzaro, J.N. (1981). Special problems of exceptional minority children. In J. Nazzaro (Ed.), *Culturally diverse exceptional children in school.* Reston, VA: The Council for Exceptional Children.

Nazzaro, J., & Portuondo, M. (1981). Understanding where the students are coming from. In J. Nazzaro (Ed.), *Culturally diverse exceptional children in school.* Reston, VA: The Council for Exceptional Children.

Oakland, T. (1977). Psychological and educational assessment of minority children. New York: Brunner/Mazel.

Ogbu, J. (1978). *Minority education and caste.* New York: Academic Press.

Olszewski, P. (in preparation). The validity of cut-off scores on the SAT for predicting achievement in advanced coursework, College Board research study.

Orange County Unified School District. (1981). *GATE-way to success: Hispanic gifted program. Identification packet and instructional guide.* Orange County, CA: Author. (ERIC Document Reproduction Service No. ED 239 438)

Osterline, S.J. (1983). *Test item bias.* Beverly Hills, CA: Sage University Press.

Padilla, E.R., & Wyatt, G.E. (1983). The effects of intelligence and achievement testing on minority group children. In G.J. Powell (Ed.), *The psychosocial development of minority group children* (pp. 417–437). New York: Brunner/Mazel.

Parnes, S.J. (1966). *Programming creative behavior.* Buffalo, NY: State University of New York at Buffalo.

Parra, E., Baldenegro, S., & Garcia, L. (1986). *The P.B.G. Scale.* (Available from Elena Parra, Tucson Unified School District, 1010 E. 10th, Tucson, AZ 85719).

Parson, T. (1967). *Socialization theory and modern society.* New York: Free Press.

Passow, A.H. (1972). The gifted and the disadvantaged. *National Elementary Principal, 51,* 24–31.

Passow, A.H. (1981). Introduction: There is "gold in them thar hills." In *Balancing the scale for the disadvantaged gifted: Presentations from the Fourth Biennial National Conference on Disadvantaged Gifted/Talented* (pp. 1–26). Ventura, CA: Office of Ventura County Superintendent of Schools.

Passow, A.H. (1986). Curriculum for the gifted and talented at the secondary level. *Gifted Child Quarterly, 30,* 186–191.

Patel, K. (1977, July). *Personal and environmental factors associated with giftedness across cultures.* Paper presented at the World Conference on Giftedness, San Francisco, CA.

Pegnato, C.W., & Birch, J.W. (1959). Locating gifted children in junior high schools: A comparison of methods. *Exceptional Children, 25,* 300–304.

322   Critical Issues in Gifted Education

Peng, S.S. (1985, April). *Enrollment patterns of Asian American students in postsecondary education.* Paper presented at the annual meeting of the American Educational Research Association, Chicago, IL.

Peng, S., Owings, J.A., & Fetters, W.B. (1984, April). School experiences and performance of Asian American high school students. Paper presented at the Annual Meeting of the American Educational Research Association, New Orleans, LA. (ERIC Document Reproduction Service No. ED 252 635)

Perkins, D.N. (1981). *The mind's best work.* Cambridge, MA: Harvard University Press.

Perrone, P., & Aleman, N. (1983). Educating the talented child in a pluralistic society. In D.R. Omark & J.G. Erickson (Eds.), *The bilingual exceptional child* (pp. 269–283). San Diego: College-Hill Press.

Philips, S.U. (1972). Participant structures and communicative competence: Warm Springs children in community and classroom. In C. Cazden (Ed.), *Functions of language in the classroom.* New York: Teachers College Press.

Piaget, J. (1977). *The development of thought: Equilibration of cognitive structures.* New York: The Viking Press (originally published in French, 1975).

Plisko, V.W., & Stern, J.D. (Eds.). (1985). *The condition of education.* Washington, DC: National Center for Educational Statistics.

Pressey, S. (1955). Concerning the nature and nurture of genius. *Science, 31,* 123–129.

Public Law 94-142, The Education for all Handicapped Children Act, November 29, 1975.

Public Law 95-561, Bilingual Education Act, 1976.

Ramirez, B.A. (1984). *Statement of the Council for Exceptional Children to the Subcommittee on Interior of the U.S. House of Representatives Appropriations Committee with Respect to 1985 Appropriations for Bureau of Indian Affairs Education.* Reston, VA: The Council for Exceptional Children.

Ramirez, M., III., & Castaneda, A. (1974). *Cultural democracy, bicognitive development, and education.* New York: Academic Press.

Ramos, G. (1987, April 16). Teachers union comes out one-one in School Board Election. *Los Angeles Times,* Part I, p. 3.

Raven, J.C. (1947). *The Raven's progressive matrices.* Cleveland: The Psychological Corporation.

Raven, J.C. (1956). *Progressive matrices.* London: H.K. Lewis.

Raven, J.C. (1962). *Advanced progressive matrices.* London: H.K. Lewis.

Raven, J.C. (1966). *Manual for Raven's progressive matrices and vocabulary scales: Research Supplement No. 3.* Houston, TX: Psychological Corporation.

Raven, J.C., Court, J.H., & Raven, J. (1985). *Manual for Raven's progressive matrices and vocabulary scales.* London: H.K. Lewis.

Renzulli, J.S. (1973). Talent potential in minority group students. *Exceptional Children, 39,* 437–444.

Renzulli, J.S. (1977). *The enrichment triad model: A guide for developing defensible programs for the gifted and talented.* Mansfield Center, CT: Creative Learning Press.

Renzulli, J.S. (1978). "What makes giftedness?" Reexamining a definition. *Phi Delta Kappan, 60,* 180–184; 261.

Renzulli, J.S. (1979). What makes giftedness? A reexamination of the definition of the gifted and talented. In, *National/State Leadership Training Institute on the Gifted and the Talented,* (NLTI/GT) (Brief Number 6). Ventura, CA: NLTI/GT.

Renzulli, J.S. (1984). The triad/revolving door system: A research based approach to identification and programming for the gifted and talented. *Gifted Child Quarterly, 28*(4), 163–171.

Renzulli, J.S. (Ed.). (1986). *Systems and models for developing programs for the gifted and talented.* Mansfield Center, CT: Creative Learning Press.

Renzulli, J.S. (1986). The three-ring conception of giftedness: A developmental model for creative productivity. In R.S. Sternberg & J.E. Davidson (Eds.), *Conceptions of giftedness.* Cambridge: Cambridge University Press.

Renzulli, J.S., Reis, S.M., & Smith, L.H. (1981). *The revolving door identification model.* Mansfield Center, CT: Creative Learning Press.

Renzulli, J.S., & Smith, L. (1977). Two approaches to identification of gifted students. *Exceptional Children, 43,* 512–518.

Reynolds, C.R. (1983, November). *Changing conceptualizations of race differences in intelligence.* Invited address at the 1983 Minority Assessment Conference, Tucson, AZ.

Richert, E.S. (1985). Identification of gifted students: An update. *Roeper Review, 8,* 68–72.

Richert, E.S., Alvino, J.J., & McDonnel, R.C. (1982). *National report on identification: Assessment and recommendation for comprehensive identification of gifted and talented youth.* Sewell, NJ: Educational Improvement Center-South.

Riles, W., et al. (1987). Conflicting ideas on the banning of intelligence tests. *Education Week, 6*(20), Washington, DC.

Rimm, S. (1984). Underachievement. *G/C/T, 27.*

Rimm, S.B. (1986). Gifted programs and instrument development: A compatible marriage. *Journal for the Education of the Gifted, 9,* 277–289.

Rivera-Martinez, C. (1985). Hispanics and the social service system. In P.S.J. Cafferty & W. McCready (Eds.), *Hispanics in the United States: A new social agenda* (pp. 195–213). New Brunswick, NJ: Transaction Books.

Roberts, C.H. (1981). *Equilibration and intelligence: Individual variation in cognitive development as a function of CA, MA and IQ.* Unpublished doctoral dissertation, Bryn Mawr.

Rodriguez, R.F., Prieto, A.G., & Rueda, R.S. (1984). Issues in bilingual multicultural special education. *NABE Journal, 8,* 55–65.

Robinson, N.M., & Chamrad, D.L. (1986). Appropriate uses of intelligence test with gifted children. *Roeper Review, 8*(3), 160–163.

Roedell, W.C. (1984). Vulnerabilities of highly gifted children. *Roeper Review, 6*(3), 40–41.

Rogers, K.B. (1986). Do the gifted think and learn differently? A review of recent research and its implications for instruction. *Journal for the Education of the Gifted, 10,* 17–39.

Rokeach, M. (1973). *The nature of human values.* New York: Free Press.

Rosier, P., & Holm, W. (1980). *The Rock Point experience: A longitudinal study of a Navajo school.* Washington, DC: Center for Applied Linguistics.

Rowan, C.T. (1987). Peer pressures can be destructive. *The Register Guard,* Eugene, OR: Tuesday, May 28th, 1987, North American Syndicate, Inc.

Samuda, R.J. (1975). *Psychological testing of American minorities: Issues and consequences.* New York: Harper & Row.

San Bernandino City Schools. (1964). *A minority of one. The story of the Franklin Junior High School Training Natural Talent Project, 1959–1963.* San Bernardino, CA: Author. (ERIC Document Reproduction Service No. ED 032 350)

Sanborn, M.P. (1981). Clinical observations and assertions about guidance of gifted children. In W.R. Miles (Ed.), *Research and issues in gifted and talented: Implications for teacher education.* Washington, DC: ERIC Clearinghouse. (ERIC Document Reproduction Service No. ED 200 517)

Santos, R.A. (1983). The social and emotional development of Filipino-American children. In G.J. Powell, (Ed.), *The psychosocial development of minority group children* (pp. 131–146). New York: Brunner/Mazel.

Sato, I.S. (1974). The culturally different child: The dawning of his day? *Exceptional Children, 40*(8), 572–576.

Schierbeck, H.M. (1982–83). Confronting the continuing dilemma. *Integrateducation, 19–20,* 2–6.

Schiever, S.W. (1986). The effect of two teaching/learning models on the higher cognitive processes of students in classes for the gifted. Unpublished doctoral dissertation, University of Arizona, Tucson.

Schulkind, C.R. (1982). Creative programming for the multilingual, culturally-conflicted gifted. In *Identifying and educating the disadvantaged gifted/talented.* Ventura, CA: Office of Ventura County Superintendent of Schools.

Schwartz, J. (1977). The illogic of IQ tests. In P. Houts (Ed.), *The myth of measurability.* New York: Harcourt Brace.

Scollon, R., & Scollon, S.B.K. (1980). *Interethnic communication.* Fairbanks, AK: University of Alaska.

Scott, K.P. (1981). Whatever happened to Dick and Jane? Sexism in texts reexamined. *Peabody Journal of Education, 58,* 135–140.

Scruggs, T.E. (1986). Learning characteristics research: A personal perspective. *Journal for the Education of the Gifted, 9,* 291–301.

Scruggs, T.E., & Cohn, S.J. (1983). A university-based summer program for a highly able but poorly achieving Indian child. *Gifted Child Quarterly, 27,* 90–93.

Scruggs, T.E., & Mastropieri, M.A. (1985). Spontaneous verbal elaboration in gifted and non-gifted youths. *Journal for the Education of the Gifted, 9,* 1–10.

Shade, B.J. (1978). Social-psychological traits of achieving Black children. *The Negro Educational Review, 29,* 80–86.

Shuy, R.W. (1978). Problems in assessing language ability in bilingual education programs. In H. Lafonatine, H. Persky, & L. Golubchick (Eds.), *Bilingual education.* Wayne, NJ: Avery.

Shuy, R.W. (1981). Conditions affecting language learning and maintenance among Hispanics in the United States. *National Association of Bilingual Educators Journal, 6,* 1–18.

Siegler, R.S., & Kotovsky, K. (1986). Two levels of giftedness: Shall ever the twain meet? In R.S. Sternberg & J.E. Davidson (Eds.), *Conceptions of giftedness.* Cambridge: Cambridge University Press.

Silverman, L. (1986). What happens to the gifted girl? In C.J. Maker (Ed.), *Critical issues in gifted education: Defensible programs for the gifted* (pp. 43–89). Austin, TX: PRO-ED.

Simon, S., Howe, L., & Kirschenbaum, H. (1972). *Values clarification: A handbook of practical strategies.* New York: Hart.

Sisk, D. (1987). *Creative teaching of the gifted.* New York: McGraw-Hill.

Skinner, D.C. (1981). *Bi-modal learning and teaching: Concepts and methods.* Unpublished manuscript, Hispanic Training Institute.

Skupaka, B.M. (Ed.). (1972). *The "holding power" workshop.* Santa Fe: New Mexico State Department of Education. (ERIC Document Reproduction Service No. ED 194 284)

Skutnabb-Kangas, T., & Toukomas, P. (1976). *Teaching migrant children's mother tongue and learning the language of the host country in the context of the sociocultural situation of the migrant family.* Helsinki: The Finnish National Commission for UNESCO.

Solomon, I.D. (1985). Minority status, pluralistic education and the Asian-American: A teacher's perspective and agenda. *Education, 106*(1), 88–93.

Sparling, S.S. (1984). *J.P. Torrance and the U.S. public school movement to include minority and low socioeconomic status students in gifted programs, 1975–77.* Unpublished manuscript. (Available from S. Sparling and Associates, Los Angeles, CA.)

Sparling, S.S. (1985). *The shared responsibility model.* Unpublished manuscript. (Available from S. Sparling and Associates, Los Angeles, CA.)

Sparling, S.S. (1986). The shared responsibility model. In B. Clark, *Optimizing learning* (pp. 137–145). Columbus, OH: Charles E. Merrill.

Spearman, C. (1904). "General Intelligence," objectively determined and measured. *American Journal of Psychology, 15,* 201–293.

Spindler, G.D. (1963). *Education and culture: Anthropological approaches.* New York: Holt, Rinehart & Winston.

Stallings, C.J. (1972). *Gifted disadvantaged children.* National Leadership Institute Teacher Education/ Early Childhood. Storrs, CT: University of Connecticut.

Stallings, C.J. (1975). *Stallings' environmentally based screen (SEBS)* (3rd rev.). San Diego, CA: U.S. Naval Personnel Research and Development Center.

Stalnaker, J.M. (1969). Recognizing and encouraging talent. In D. Wolfe (Ed.), *The Discovery of Talent.* Cambridge, MA: Harvard University Press.

Stanford, B., & Stanford, C. (1969). *Learning discussion skills through games.* New York: Citation Press.

Start, K.B. (1985). *The education of gifted and talented children:* Paper submitted to the Senate Standing Committee on Education and the Arts, Parliament House, Canberra, Australia.

Stedman, R. (1984). *Shadows of the Indians.* Norman, OK: University of Oklahoma Press.

Stephenson, W. (1953). *The study of behavior: Q-technique and its methodology.* Chicago: University of Chicago Press.

Sternberg, R.J. (1977). *Intelligence, information processing, and analogical reasoning: The componential analysis of human abilities.* Hillsdale, NJ: Erlbaum.

Sternberg, R.J. (1981). A componential theory of intellectual giftedness. *Gifted Child Quarterly, 25,* 86–93.

Sternberg, R.J. (1982a). Nonentrenchment in the assessment of intellectual giftedness. *Gifted Child Quarterly, 26*(2), 63–67.

Sternberg, R.J. (1982b). Lies we live by: Misapplication of tests in identifying the gifted. *Gifted Child Quarterly, 26*(4), 157–161.

Sternberg, R.J. (1986). Identifying the gifted through IQ: Why a little bit of knowledge is a dangerous thing. *Roeper Review, 8*(3), 143–147.

Stevenson, G., Seghini, J.B., Timothy, K., Brown, K., Lloyd, B.C., Zimmerman, M.A., Maxfield, S., & Buchanan, J. (1971). *Project implode: Igniting creative potential.* Salt Lake City, UT: Bella-Vista-Institute for Behavioral Research in Creativity.

Stodolsky, S.S., & Lesser, G.S. (1967). Learning patterns in the disadvantaged. *Harvard Educational Review, 37,* 546–593.

Success story: Outwhiting the Whites. (1971, July 21). *Newsweek.*

Sue, D., Sue, D.W., & Sue, D.M. (1983). Psychological development of Chinese-American children. In G.J. Powell (Ed.), *The psychosocial development of minority group children* (pp. 159–166). New York: Brunner/Mazel.

Sue, D.W., & Sue, D. (1973). Self-expression and the Asian-American experience. *Personnel and Guidance Journal, 51,* 390–396.

Sue, S., & Morishima, J.K. (1982). *The mental health of Asian Americans.* San Francisco: Jossey-Bass.

Sullivan, A.R. (1973). The identification of gifted and academically talented Black students: A hidden exceptionality. *Journal of Special Education, 7,* 373–379.

Suzuki, B.H. (1977). Education and the socialization of Asian Americans: A revisionist analysis of the "model minority" thesis.

Szasz, M.C. (1977). *Education and the American Indian* (2nd ed.). Albuquerque: University of New Mexico Press.

Taba, H., & Elkins, D. (1964). *Teaching strategies for the culturally disadvantaged.* Chicago: Rand McNally.

Tachibana, J. (1986). California's Asians, power from a growing population. *California Journal, 535–543.*

Tannenbaum, A.J. (1983). *Gifted children: Psychological and educational perspectives.* New York: Macmillan.

Taylor, C. (1986). Cultivating simultaneous student growth in both multiple creative talents and knowledge. In J.S. Renzulli (Ed.), *Systems and models for developing programs for the gifted and talented* (pp. 306–350). Mansfield, CT: Creative Learning Press.

Taylor, C.N., & Ellison, R.L. (1983). Searching for student talent resources relevant to all USDE types of giftedness. *Gifted Child Quarterly, 27*(3), 99–106.

Taylor, C.W. (1968). The multiple talent approach. *The Instructor, 77,* 27;142;144;146.

Terman, L. (1925). Mental and physical traits of a thousand gifted children. In L. Terman (Ed.), *Genetic studies of genius* (Vol. I). Palo Alto, CA: Stanford University Press.

Thompson, S.H. (1984, January–February). Refining the children of gold—social aspects of the gifted child. *G/C/T,* 5–7.

Tidwell, R. (1979). *A psychoeducational profile of gifted minority group students identified without reliance on aptitude tests.* (ERIC Document Reproduction Service No. ED 177 231)

Tizard, J., Schofield, W.N., & Hewison, J. (1982). Collaboration between teachers and parents in assisting children's reading. *British Journal of Educational Psychology, 52,* 1–15.

Tonemah, S. (1985). *Tribal-cultural perspectives of gifted and talentedness.* Unpublished manuscript. (Available from D. Montgomery, Elmhurst School, Oklahoma City, OK.)

Tonemah, S. (1986). *Procedures in developing a tribal-cultural checklist to assess Indian students' gifts and talents.* Unpublished manuscript. (Available from D. Montgomery, Elmhurst School, Oklahoma City, OK.)

Tonemah, S. (1987). Assessing American Indian gifted and talented students' abilities. *Journal for the Education of the Gifted, 10*(3), 181–194.

Tonemah, S.A., & Brittan, M.A. (1985). *American Indian gifted and talented assessment model.* Unpublished manuscript, American Indian Research & Developoment, Inc., Norman, OK.

Tonkin, H., & Edwards, J. (1983). A world of interconnections. In G. Hass, *Curriculum planning: A new approach* (4th ed.) (p. 54). Boston: Allyn & Bacon.

Torrance, E.P. (1987a). *Using tests of creative thinking to guide the teaching of creative behavior.* Bensenville, IL: Scholastic Testing Service.

Torrance, E.P. (1987b). *Why fly?* Buffalo, NY: Bearly Ltd.

Torrance, E.P. (1984). The role of creativity in identification of the gifted and talented. *Gifted Child Quarterly, 28*(4), 153–156.

Torrance, E.P. (1979a). *The search for satori and creativity.* Buffalo, NY: Bearly Ltd.

Torrance, E.P. (1979b). An instructional model for enhancing incubation. *Journal of Creative Behavior, 13,* 23–35.

Torrance, E.P. (1978). Ways of discovering gifted Black children. In A.Y. Baldwin, G.H. Gear, & L.J. Lucito (Eds.), *Educational planning for the gifted: Overcoming cultural, geographic and socioeconomic barriers.* Reston, VA: The Council for Exceptional Children.

Torrance, E.P. (1977). *Discovery and nurturance of giftedness in the culturally different.* Reston, VA: The Council for Exceptional Children.

Torrance, E.P. (1974a). Differences are not deficits. *Teachers College Record, 75,* 471–488.

Torrance, E.P. (1974b). *Torrance tests of creative thinking: Norms-technical manual.* Bensenville, IL: Scholastic Testing Service.

Torrance, E.P. (1973). Non-test indicators of creative talent among disadvantaged children. *Gifted Child Quarterly, 17,* 3–9.

Torrance, E.P. (1972). Training teachers and leaders to recognize and acknowledge creative behavior among disadvantaged children. *Gifted Child Quarterly, 16,* 3–10.

Torrance, E.P. (1971). Are the Torrance tests of creative thinking biased against or in favor of "disadvantaged groups?" *Gifted Child Quarterly, 15,* 75–80.

Torrance, E.P. (1970a). *Encouraging creativity in the classroom.* Dubuque, IA: William Brown.

Torrance, E.P. (1970b). Non-test indicators of creative talents among disadvantaged children. *Gifted Child Quarterly, 14,* 139–147.

Torrance, E.P. (1969a). Creative positives of disadvantaged children and youth. *Gifted Child Quarterly, 13*(2), 71–81.

Torrance, E.P. (1969b). Motivating and guiding creative reading. In Clymer, T. (Ed.), *Teacher's edition: Reading 360 program* (pp. 15–17). Boston: Ginn.

Torrance, E.P. (1969c). *Teaching skills for creative ways of learning.* Chicago: Science Research Associates.

Torrance, E.P. (1969d). What is honored: Comparative studies of creative achievement and motivation. *Journal of Creative Behavior, 3,* 375–389.

Torrance, E.P. (1965a). *Mental health and constructive behavior.* Belmont, CA: Wadsworth.

Torrance, E.P. (1965b). Motivating the creatively gifted among economically disadvantaged children. *Gifted Child Quarterly, 9,* 9–12.

Torrance, E.P. (1965c). *Rewarding creative behavior.* Englewood Cliffs, NJ: Prentice-Hall.

Torrance, E.P. (1964). Identifying the creatively gifted among economically and culturally diverse children. *Gifted Child Quarterly, 8,* 171–176.

Torrance, E.P. (1962). *Guiding creative talent.* Englewood Cliffs, NJ: Prentice-Hall.

Torrance, E.P. (1958). *Mastery of stress.* Wright-Patterson Air Force Base, OH: USAF Orientation Group.

Torrance, E.P., Gowan, J.C., Wu, J-J, & Aliotti, N.C. (1970). Creative functioning of monolingual and bilingual children in Singapore. *Journal of Educational Psychology, 61,* 72–75.

Torrance, E.P., & Myers, R.E. (1970). *Creative learning and teaching.* New York: Harper & Row.

Treffinger, D.J. (1975). Teaching for self-directed learning: A priority for the gifted and talented. *Gifted Child Quarterly, 19,* 46–59.

Treffinger, D.J. (1984). Editorial: In search of identification. *Gifted Child Quarterly, 28*(4), 147–148.

Treffinger, D.J., & Renzulli, J.S. (1986). Giftedness as potential for creative productivity: Transcending IQ scores. *Roeper Review, 8*(3), 150–154.

Troike, R. (1978). Research evidence for the effectiveness of bilingual education. *National Association of Bilingual Educators, 3,* 13–24.

Tsang, S.L., & Wing, L.C. (1985, Winter). Beyond Angel Island: The education of Asian Americans. *ERIC/CUE Urban Diversity Series, 90.* (ERIC Document Reproduction Service No. ED 253 612)

Udall, A. (1987). *Peer referral as a process for locating unidentified gifted Hispanic students.* Unpublished manuscript. (Available from C.J. Maker, University of Arizona.)

Urban Associates (1974). *A study of selected socioeconomic characteristics based on the 1970 census. Asian Americans, 2.* Washington, DC: U.S. Government Printing Office.

U.S. Commission on Civil Rights. (1979). *Civil rights issues of Asian and Pacific Americans: Myths and realities.* Washington, DC: U.S. Government Printing Office.

U.S. Department of Commerce, Bureau of the Census (1986). *Statistical abstract of the United States 1986* (106th ed.). Washington, DC: Author.

Van Tassel-Baska, J. (1986). The use of aptitude tests for identifying the gifted: The talent search concept. *Roeper Review, 8*(3), 185–189.

Van Tassel-Baska, J. (in press). The effects of low income on SAT scores among the academically able, NAGC special monograph.

Vogel, E.F. (1963). *Japan's new middle class* (2nd ed.). Berkeley: University of California Press.

Wallach, M.A. (1976). Tests tell us little about talent. *American Scientist, 64.*

Ward, V. (1980). *Differential education for the gifted.* Ventura, CA: Office of the Ventura County Superintendent of Schools.

Watanabe, C. (1973). Self-expression and the Asian American experience. *Personnel and Guidance Journal, 51,* 390–396.

Webb, J.T., Meckstroth, E.A., & Tolan, S.S. (1982). *Guiding the gifted child.* Columbus, OH: Psychology.

Wechsler, D. (1974). *Wechsler intelligence scale for children—Revised.* New York: Psychological Corporation.

Weiner, B. (1984). Principles for a theory of student motivation and their applications within an attributional framework. In R. Ames & C. Ames (Eds.), *Student Motivation,* Vol. 1, (pp. 15–38). New York: Academic Press.

Weisz, J.R., Rothbaum, F.M., & Blackburn, T.C. (1984). Standing out and standing in: The psychology of control in America and Japan. *American Psychologist, 39*(9), 955–968.

Welch, G.S. (1967). Verbal interests and intelligence: Comparison of strong VIB, Terman, cmt, and d-48 scores of gifted adolescents. *Educational Psychological Measures, 27*(2), 349–352.

Williams, B.P. (1983). *A process for deriving elements of definition.* Unpublished manuscript.

Williams, F.E. (1970). *Classroom ideas for encouraging thinking and feeling* (2nd ed.). Buffalo, NY: DOK.

Williams, F.E. (1972). *A total creativity program for individualizing and humanizing the learning process.* Englewood Cliffs, NJ: Educational Technology.

Williams, J.H., & Addison, L. (1980). Training teachers to work with gifted minority students. In *Balancing the scale for the disadvantaged gifted: Presentation from the Fourth Biennial National Conference on Disadvantaged Gifted/Talented.* Ventura, CA: Office of Ventura County Superintendent of Schools.

Williams, R.L. (1974). The problem of match and mismatch in testing Black children. In L.P. Miller (Ed.), *The testing of Black students* (pp. 17–30). Englewood Cliffs, NJ: Prentice-Hall.

Witt, G. (1971). The Life Enrichment Activity Program Inc.: A continuing program for creative disadvantaged children. *Journal of Research and Developing in Education, 4*(3), 67–73.

Witty, P.A., & Jenkins, M.D. (1934). The educational achievement of a group of gifted Negro children. *The Journal of Educational Psychology, 24,* 585–597.

Wolf, M.H. (1981). Talent search and development in visual and performing arts. In *Balancing the scale for the disadvantaged gifted* (pp. 103–115). Ventura, CA: The National/State Leadership Training Institute on the Gifted and the Talented.

Wong, O.K. (1985, February 20). *Language assessment of Asian students: Problems and implications.* (ERIC Document Reproduction Service No. ED 253 563)

Wong-Fillmore, L. (1983). The language learner as an individual: Implications of research on individual differences for the ESL teacher. In M.A. Clark & J. Handscombe (Eds.), *On TESOL '82: Pacific perspectives on language learning and teaching* (pp. 157–171). Washington, DC: TESOL.

Wood, T.C. (1983). *Final report of the evaluation of the gifted and talented education program* (RMC Report No. UR-497). Mountain View, CA: RMC Research Corporation.

Yamamoto, J., & Iga, M. (1983). Emotional growth of Japanese-American children. In G.J. Powell (Ed.), *The psychosocial development of minority group children* (pp. 167–178). New York: Brunner/Mazel.

Young, J. (1977). *Discrimination, income, human capital investment and Asian Americans.* San Francisco: R & E Research Associates.

Yu, K.H., & Kim, L.I.C. (1983). The growth and development of Korean-American children. In G.J. Powell (Ed.), *The psychosocial development of minority group children* (pp. 147–158). New York: Brunner/Mazel.

INDEX

A

Abbott, J. A., 94, 95, 98
ABDA. See Abbreviated Binet for Disadvantaged Children.
Abilities
  Black, 291–292
  Hispanic, 28–33
Abstract concepts, 44, 53
Academic development, 29–30
Academic underachievement, 198
Access, in service delivery, 60
Acculturation. *See also* Biculturalism.
  of American Indians, 120–121, 142–143
  of Asian-Americans, 201–202
Achievement testing
  of Asian-Americans, 157–159
  of Hispanics, 64–65
Acknowledgement component, 268
Activities, cognitive function and, 264
Adaptive creative behaviors, 252–253
Addison, L., 47
Administration
  of American Indian programs, 138–141
  of Asian-American programs, 197–200
  of Black programs, 281–284
  of Hispanic programs, 66–68
  implications of, 303–306
Advanced Progressive Matrices (AdvPM), 217, 218
Affective development
  of American Indians, 147
  of Blacks, 290
  of Hispanics, 30, 38
Affective function, 260
Affective needs, 47, 55, 73
Alcoholism, 77
Aleman, N., 62

Aliotti, N. C., 35
Alvino, J. J., 215
American Indian Research and Development Inc., 81
American Indians
  characteristics of, 128–129
  conflicting values of, 133–137
  cultural characteristics of
    competitive role, 119–120
    cultural sharing, 125
    ethnic identity, 120–121
    group vs. individual concept, 120
    language use, 117–118
    time concepts, 121–122, 125
  defining, 75–76
  education of
    curriculum for, 110, 126, 129, 131–132
    early, 129–130
    open-ended approaches to, 127
    special, on reservation, 77–78
    teaching strategies for, 122–125
    teaching styles in, 103–104, 119
  ethnic identity of, 137
  family involvement among, 130–131, 146–147
  history of, 76–77
  identifying. *See* Identification, of American Indians.
  leadership development among, 129
  less verbal, 123–124
  model attributes for, 125–127
  needs of, 133–137
  programming for, 116–127
    administration of, 138–141
  self concept of, 107–112
Applebome, 20
Appropriateness, of definitions, 307

Argulewicz, E. N., 2
Articulation, of programs, 307
Asian-Americans
  assessment of, 165-167
  behaviors of, 152-153
  Cantonese, 182-188
  characteristics of, 155-156
  cultural identities of, 194
  defining, 149-150, 163-164
  discrimination against, 192-193
  education of
    needs of, 169-170
    programs for, 170-173
    recommendations for, 195-196
    special, 179-181, 194
    teaching strategies for, 175-177, 199
  evaluating, 157-160, 165-167
  family involvement of, 206
  first-generation immigrant, 193
  identifying. See Identification, of
    Asian-Americans.
  in mathematics, 195
  native-born, 193-194
  population of, 151-152
  in science, 195
  U.S. experience of, 150
Assessment procedures, 295-296
Astor Program, 231
Authority, Chinese concept of, 184-185

B

Baldwin, Alexinia Y., 28, 44, 45, 86, 171,
  210, 215, 216, 224, 237-258, 260, 282,
  283, 285, 286, 287, 289, 290, 291, 292
Baldwin Identification Matrix (BIM), 219-220
Banda, Clarissa, 27-40, 69, 70-71, 72, 73, 298
Banks, J. A., 31, 103
Barik, H., 29
Barnhardt, C., 122
Barron, F., 2
Baska, Leland K., 219, 226-236, 285-286,
  287, 289, 291, 297
Behavior
  adaptive creative, 252-253
  empowering, 266
Bennett, John, 17
Benson, S. S., 260, 261
Bergman, 104
Bernal, E. M., 2, 24, 26, 27, 29, 34-36, 42,
  43, 46, 69, 70, 71, 73, 82, 302
Beuf, 130
Bias, 82-83
Biculturalism. See also Acculturation.
  Asian-American, 204-205
  Black, 291
  development of, 299
Bilingual Identification Project (BIP), 175
Bilingualism
  curriculum for, 171-173

as program purpose, 138-139
  skill development in, 35-36, 299, 302
  social development and, 62-63, 70-71
BIM. See Baldwin Identification Matrix.
BIP. See Bilingual Identification Project.
Black, 217
Blackburn, T. C., 150
Blacks
  biculturalism of, 291
  counseling of, 290
  dealing with giftedness, 250-251
  defined, 209-210
  differential treatment of, 235-236
  distinctiveness of, 210-211
  education of
    curriculum for, 259-274, 282-283
    programming for, 237-259, 281-284
    strategies for, 271-274, 283
    testing in, 226-236, 286-287
  identifying. See Identification, of Blacks.
  mainstream participation of, 278-279,
    287-288
  motivation of, 276-277
  perceptions of, 286
  role models for, 229, 251-254
  socioeconomic differences among, 285-286
  special strengths of, 270-271
  traits of gifted, 223
Blackshear, P., 215, 219
Blaylock, A., 220
Bloom, 232
Bloomer Learning Test, 158
Boston, B. O., 27, 30, 198
Botkin, J. W., 273
Bracken, B., 231
Bradley, Charmaine, 133-137, 142, 144, 145,
  146, 298, 302, 304, 305
Brittan, M. A., 77, 79, 92, 94, 96-97, 98
Brooks, Deena Lyn, 138-141, 142, 146, 148,
  298, 305-306
Brown, S. R., 85
Bruch, C. B., 82, 217, 218
Bureau of Indian Affairs (U.S.), 75, 76, 77
Burns, M., 50
Bushman, J. H., 51
Butterfield, F., 149
Butterfield, R. A., 276

C

Calfee, R. C., 118, 119, 125
California Achievement Tests (CAT), 217
California Tests of Mental Maturity (CTMM),
  217
Campos, S., 23
Cantonese students, 182-188
Cantu, R., 46
Career counseling, 173
Case study, 25, 296-297
Castaneda, A., 1, 2-3, 42, 48, 61

CAT. See California Achievement Tests.
Center for Excellence in Education, 35
Cesa, T. A., 170
Chambers, J., 2
Chan, K. S., 150, 165, 167, 193, 194
Channeling abilities, 291–292
Charlesworth, W. R., 83–84
Chavers, D., 76
Checklist of Creative Positives, 87, 216
Checklists, in screening, 215–216
Chen, Jocelyn, 154–168, 198, 201, 202, 203, 204, 206, 294
Chin, Frank, 180
Chinn, P. C., 165
Choice making, 267
Chomsky, N., 89
Clarity, of definitions, 307
Clarizo, H. F., 2
Clark, B., 3, 24, 27, 30, 31, 32, 42, 57–59, 70, 74, 170-171, 175, 213, 215, 224, 232, 259, 260, 261, 263, 264, 269
Classrooms, self-contained, 247–248
C-L/CLL. *See* Counseling-Learning Approach to Community Language Learning.
Cleaves, A., 251
Clift, U. A., 210
Clustering, 186–187
Clymer, T., 273
Coaching, student, 187
Cognition, 157, 260, 264
Cognitive Abilities Test, 234
Cohen, Leonora M., 210, 246–254, 285, 287, 288, 289, 290, 291, 298
Colangelo, N., 251
Coleman, L. J., 104
Coloured and Standard Matrices, 234
Columbia Mental Maturity Scale, 159
Commission on Civil Rights (U.S.), 192–193
Commonalities, among students, 190
Communication, in service delivery, 60–61
Community involvement, 45, 53
Compensatory education, 31, 35
Comprehensible input, 35, 72
Comprehensiveness, 308
Computers, 235
Conceptual approach
  to American Indians, 147
  to Hispanics, 44, 53
Conferences, 28
Consistency, of program elements, 291, 308
Cooper, H., 259
Cooper, J., 259
Cooperative learning
  by American Indians, 147
  by Asian-Americans, 207
  by Blacks, 291
  by Cantonese students, 185–186, 207
  by Hispanics, 73
Coping skills, 31–32

Cordova, R. H., 52
Counseling
  of American Indians, 147
  of Asian-Americans, 172–173, 198, 206
  of Blacks, 290
  of Hispanics, 73
Counseling-Learning Approach to Community Language Learning (C-L/CLL), 172–173
Court, J. H., 97
Cox, J., 27, 30, 198
CPS. *See* Creative Problem Solving.
Crawford, T., 81, 122
Creative Problem Solving (CPS)
  for American Indians, 131
  for Blacks, 221
  for Hispanics, 46
Creativity
  of Asian-Americans, 199
  of Blacks, 251–254, 261
Cronbach, L. J., 210
CTMM. See California Tests of Mental Maturity.
Cultural bias, 83
Cultural comfort zone, 122–123
Cultural identities
  American Indian, 120–121, 142–143
  Asian-American, 173, 194
  Cantonese, 182–185
  diversity of, 189
  Hispanic, 44–45, 53
  survival of, 144–145
Culture-specific identification model, 219
Cummins, J., 21–25, 35, 61
Curran, C. A., 172
Curriculum
  for American Indians
    content of, 129
    differentiated, 131–132
    design of, 110
    social studies, 126
  for Asian-Americans, 171–173
  for Blacks
    administration of, 282–283
    theory of, 260–263
  for Hispanics
    administration of, 66–68
    design of, 72
    implementation of, 48
    student needs in, 43–44

D

Dabney, M., 47, 219, 244, 245
Dade County (FLA.) Public Schools, 66–68
Daniel, N., 27, 30, 198
Darnell, F., 117, 119, 122
Davidson, H. H., 94
Davis, A., 217
Davis, G. B., 28, 29, 30, 213, 215, 220
Davis, P., 215

DeAvila Cartoon Conservation Scales, 249
DeAvila, E., 29, 42, 249
de Bono, E., 274
deCharms, R., 261, 264
Decisionmaking, 267
Defensible Programs for the Gifted (Maker),
    306–307
Deferring judgment, on achievement, 221–222
DeHaven, E., 251
Deiner, D., 264
Deleon, J., 41
Deloria, V., 129
Demos, E. S., 276
Department of Commerce (U.S.), 210
Department of Education (U.S.,), 64
Descriptors, for disadvantaged children,
    240–242
Diagnostic testing, 88
Differences, among students, 190
Dinh, V., 167
Discrimination, 192–193
Dreaming, 266
Dropout prevention, for American Indians, 129
DuBois, W. E. B., 65
Duncan, S., 29
Dweck, C., 264

E

East Los Angeles, 5–6
Educating Able Learners (Cox et al.), 198
Education Department (U.S.), 64, 80
Education Week, 230
Edwards, R. M., 103
Ehrlich, V. Z., 231
Eisenbise, M. D., 134
Elkins, D., 47
Ellison, R. L., 215
Elmandjra, M., 273
Emerson, Ralph Waldo, 213, 225
Encoding, physical, 264
Endo, R., 150
English as a Second Language, 35
Erickson, F., 121, 122
Escalante, Jaime, 14
Escobar, J. I., 61
Ethic, work, 183–184
Ethnic identity, 83–84, 139
Eyster, I., 134

F

Faas, L. A., 84, 85, 89
Families
    American Indian, 130–131, 146–147
    Black, 232, 288
    Cantonese, 182–185
    Hispanic, 32, 39, 71–72
Farley, J., 250
Farley, S., 250
Feeling function, 260

Feldhusen, J. F., 213, 219
Females, Hispanic, 47, 73
Fersch, S., 154
Fetters, W. B., 149, 169, 172
Feuerstein, R., 26, 227
Fitz-Gibbon, C. T., 216–217
Fixed outcomes, 190
Flexibility, of identification, 95–96
Flores, J., 29, 30, 31, 32
Flugelman, A., 51
Ford, Doris Jefferies, 255–258, 287, 290, 298
Foster, W., 251
Franklin, Aretha, 255
Frasier, Mary M., 28, 30, 31, 32, 210,
    213–225, 226, 227, 232, 282, 285, 287,
    288, 289, 297
Frierson, E. C., 215
Fuchigami, R. Y., 45, 59
Fuchs, E., 76
Fugimoto, I., 154
Future Leaders of America, 35

G

Gagne, F., 213
GAIN. See Gifted Attitudes Inventory for
    Navajos.
Galbraith, J., 94–95
Gallagher, J. J., 45, 177, 178, 223
Gallagher, Rosina, 149, 169–178, 171, 179,
    180–181, 198, 201, 202, 205, 213, 215
Gallegos, A. Y., 29, 30, 31, 32
Games, singing, 234
Garcia, A., 134
Gardner, B. B., 217
Gardner, H., 3, 139, 223
Gardner, M. R., 217
Garrison, Leslie, 116–132, 139, 142, 144, 145,
    146, 147, 148, 301
Gay, J. E., 215–216, 224
Gear, G., 24, 28, 45, 216, 224
George, Karlene R., 81, 107–112, 122, 142,
    143, 144, 145, 146, 148, 297, 302
Gifted Attitudes Inventory for Navajos (GAIN),
    98
Gifted girls
    Asian-American, 207
    Black, 291
    Hispanic, 73
Gifted Program Planning Committee, 108–111
Ginott, H., 262
Glaser, E. J., 223
Glasser, W., 271
Goal setting, 266
Goodenough-Harris Human Figure Drawing
    Test, 159
Goon, S., 154, 155–156
Gordon, W. J. J., 100
Gough, P. B., 271
Gowan, J. C., 35, 100, 170

Grant, Carl A., 275–280, 282, 283, 285, 286, 287, 288, 290, 298, 304
Grant, G. W., 276
Gregory, D., 220
Gross, Stanley, 170
Group role, among American Indians, 120
Guidance, in two tribes project, 110–111
Guilford, J. F., 126

H

Hagen, E., 223, 224
Hakuta, K., 35, 172
Hanson, W. D., 134
Hare, B., 259
Harrison, B., 117, 120, 124, 125
Hasegawa, Chris, 149, 192–196, 201, 202, 203, 204, 206, 298, 304, 305
Havassy, B., 42
Havighurst, R. J., 76
Henderson, R. W., 30
Hewison, J., 23
High, M. H., 24, 41
Hilda Taba Teaching Strategies, 126, 127, 131
Hilliard, A. G., 42, 43, 58, 216
Hirschfelder, O., 132
Hispanics
  abilities of, 28–33
  characteristics of, 2–4, 42–43
  curriculum for, 41–59
  defined, 1–2
  emotional development of, 62–63
  family dynamics of, 14–16
  female, 47, 73
  general statements about, 69–74
  identifying, 19–26
  profiles of, 28
  program goals for, 27–32
  social development of, 62–63
  teacher expectations of, 64–65
  teaching strategies for, 44–48
Holm, W., 23
Home teaching, of American Indians, 119
Hoover, S. M., 213
Horn, R. E., 251
Horowitz, F. D., 249
How Do You Really Feel About Yourself? Inventory, 98
Howe, L., 31
Hsia, J., 169, 170, 172
Huang, David, 180

I

Identification
  of American Indians
    administration of, 139–140
    differential, 80–82
    flexibility of, 95–96
    multi-option procedure for, 96–99
    in nonreservation schools, 99–100
    philosophical approaches to, 82–84
    procedure for, 96–99
    research in, 88–89
    screening in, 84–88
    specificity of, 95–96
  of Asian-Americans
    assumptions about, 160–161
    criteria for, 166
    methods of, 166–167
    need for, 154–155, 164–165
    programs for, 170–175
    rationale for, 164–165
    screening in, 155–156
  of Blacks
    administrative reactions to, 281–282
    consistency in, 291
    factors hindering, 215
    future of, 221–225
    instruments for, 217–218
    models in, 218–220
    as program purpose, 249
    screening in, 215–217
    standards in, 220
  of Hispanics
    current practices in, 24–25
    multidimensional, 19–26
    recommendations in, 25–26
    situational, 5–18
  of special populations, 294–307
IEM. *See* Integrative Education Model.
Iga, M., 165
Immigrant students, 193
Implementation, curriculum, 48
Indians, American. *See* American Indians.
Indian Student Biographical Data Questionnaire, 97
Individual, role of, among American Indians, 120
Input, comprehensible, 35, 72
Inservice training, 199
Insightful function, 261
Instruction phase, 12–13
Integrative Education Model (IEM), 260–265, 270, 283
Interviewing, of Hispanic students, 25
Intuition, 261, 264, 265
Involvement, community, 45, 53
Isaksen, S. G., 221, 223

J

James, J., 45, 86–87
Jaramillo, M. L., 32
Jefferson, Thomas, 200
Jencks, C., 228
Jenkins, M. D., 217
Jensen, A., 231
Johnson, B. H., 76
Johnson, S. T., 220
Jones, S. K., 51

Jordan, C., 166
Joyce, B., 140

K

K-ABC. *See Kaufman Assessment Battery for Children.*
Kagiwada, G., 154
Kamehameha Early Education Project, 166
Kaneshige, E., 177
Kaplan, Sandra N., 131, 189–191, 204, 205, 206, 238, 300
Karnes, F. A., 85
Kaufman, A. S., 158, 218, 231
Kaufman Assessment Battery for Children (K-ABC), 158, 218, 231
Kaufman, N. L., 158, 218, 231
Keatings, B., 23
Kim, L. I. C., 165
Kinney, L., 223
Kirby, D. F., 24, 213, 215, 219, 222, 282
Kirschenbaum, Robert J., 31, 91–101, 142, 143, 144, 145, 146, 147, 294, 298
Kitano, Margie K., 24, 149, 150, 165, 193, 194, 195, 201, 202, 203, 204, 206, 207, 213, 215, 219, 222, 282, 294
Kleinfeld, J., 117, 119
Koch, S. F., 85
Kometani, T., 192
Krashen, S. D., 35
Kravetz, N., 29
Kush, J. C., 2

L

Lambert, W., 29
Lang, R., 243
Language
  empowering, 266
  native skills of, 35–36
  patterns of
    American Indian, 117–118
    Hispanic, 62–63
  proactive use of, 16–18, 73
  second, 20–24
Larry P. v. Riles (case), 230–231
Larson, Paul D., 197–200, 203, 205, 305, 306
Leadership training, 45–46, 54
Learning
  cooperative. *See* Cooperative learning.
  environment of, 263
  models of, for American Indian students, 131
  peer, 127
  self-paced, 186
Leiter International Performance Scale, 175
Lesser, G. S. 170
Leung, B., 3, 27, 30, 42, 166, 167
Lewis, J. F., 67, 219
Lindstrom, R. R., 254
Lipman, M., 251
Llanes, J. R., 35

Long, R., 219
Los Angeles Unified School District, 67
Low, W. A., 210
Lucito, L., 28, 216, 224
Lynn, J., 83
Lyon, H. C., 237
Lytle, C., 129

M

MacMillan, D. L. 215
Maehr, M. L., 261, 262
Mainstreaming, 278–279, 287–288, 300–301
Maker, C. June, 41, 45, 69–74, 86–87, 88, 125, 131, 142–148, 201–208, 215, 224, 238, 249, 285–309
Malitza, M., 273
Marland, S. P., 24, 80, 213
Mastropieri, M. A., 94
Matrix model
  for Blacks, 218–219
  for Hispanics, 24
McBeath, M., 219
McCready, W., 64
McDonnel, R. C., 215
McGreevey, P., 248
McKenzie, J. A., 41
Meeker, Mary, 126–127, 149
Melesky, T. J., 46
Mendoza, Elizabeth, 13–14
Mentors, 46, 54, 73
Mercer, J. R., 24, 67, 219
Mexican-Americans. *See* Hispanics.
Microcomputers, 235
Migrant and Gifted Impact Center, 35
Miller, D. L., 134
Mitchell, B., 219, 282
Models. *See also* Role models; Shared Responsibility Model.
  for American Indian students, 125–127
  for Blacks, 216–220
  for identification, as adjuncts, 218–220
  integrative education, 260–265, 270, 283
  learning, 126, 131
  matrix
    for Blacks, 218–219
    for Hispanics, 24
  quota system, 219–220
  revolving door, 24, 166
  structure of intellect, 126, 131
Mohatt, G., 121, 122
Momaday, N. S., 107
Monitoring, self, 268
Montebello (CA) Unified School District, 174–177
Montgomery, Diane, 79–101, 140, 142, 143, 144, 145, 146, 294, 298
Morishima, J. K., 169
Morris, E., 45, 86–87
Motivation, of Blacks, 276–277

Movement, 264
Moy, P. S., 276
Multicultural education, 31
Munoz, V., 166
Myers, R. E., 270, 273

N

Naisbitt, J., 2
National Advisory and Coordinating Council of
  Bilingual Education, 28
National Association for Gifted Children, 133
Native Americans. *See* American Indians.
Native-born Asian-Americans, 193–194
Naturalistic observation, 86–87
Navajo Indians, 98
Nazzaro, J., 45
Needs, affective, 47, 55, 73
Nominations, in screening, 215
Nonreservation public schools, 99–100
Northern Arizona University, 35
Nurturance, 6, 13–18

O

O'Brien, M., 249
Observation
  of Hispanic students, 25
  in screening, 86–87
Office for the Gifted and Talented (U.S.), 128,
  145
Office of Civil Rights (U.S.), 209
Office of Education (U.S.), 20
Office of Indian Education (U.S.), 145
Ogbu, J., 62
Okura, K. Patrick, 192–193
Olszewski, P., 226
Orange County Unified School District, 1, 42
Order, Chinese concept of, 184–185
Oscanyan, F., 251
Otis-Lennon School Abilities Test, 171
Otis-Lennon School Ability Index, 234
Outcomes, 190
Owings, J. A., 149, 169, 172

P

PADI. *See* Program of Assessment, Diagnosis
  and Instruction.
Padilla, E. R., 166
Parent-teacher dialogue, 187–188
Parnes Creative Problem Solving model, 126,
  127, 131
Parnes, S. J., 46
Parson, T., 106
Passow, A. H., 27, 31, 32, 82, 215
Patel, K., 89
Peabody Language Development Kit, 87
Peer learning, 127
Pei, I. M., 180
Peng, S. S., 149, 169, 172

Perez, A. L., 276
Perrine, J., 5–18, 19, 69, 70, 71, 72, 73, 294,
  302
Perrone, P., 62
Pfeiffer, Anita Bradley, 102–115, 142, 143,
  144, 145, 146, 147, 148, 297, 298, 300
Philips, S. W., 117, 119, 120, 125
Physical encoding, 264
Physical function, 260
Plata, M., 165
Plisko, V. W., 75, 77
The Plum Plum Pickers (Barrio), 63
Portuondo, M., 45
Potential, creative, 254
Preschool Talent Checklist, 159
Prieto, A. S., 64
Proactive language, 16–18, 73
Problem-solving skills, 46–47, 55
Profiles
  gifted, 110
  student, 28
Program of Assessment, Diagnosis and
  Instruction (PADI), 220
Programs
  for American Indians
    administrative implications of, 138–141
    assumptions about, 108–109
    cultural characteristics and, 117–122
    goals of, 116
    in meeting needs, 113–115
    obstacles to, 92–93
    population served, 140–141
    purposes of, 138–140
    social context of, 94–95
    social forces and, 104–106
    special, 77–78
  for Asian-Americans, 170–173, 197–200
  for Blacks
    administrative reactions to, 281–284
    consistency in, 291
    design of, 238–245
    elements of, 306–309
    for minority groups, 297–301
    modifications of, 301–303
PSAT-NMSQT, 231
Psychometric identification, 82–83
Public Law 95–561, 20
Public schools, nonreservation, 99–100

Q

Q-study, 85–86
Quota system model, 219–220

R

Ramirez, M., 1, 42, 48, 61
Randolph, E. T., 61
Rating scales, 215–216
Raven, J., 97, 218, 234
Raven, J. C., 97, 218

Ravens Progressive Matrices, 97
Ravens Standard Progressive Matrices (SPM),
   217, 218, 234
Reading 360 Programs, 273
Reading 720 Programs, 273
Records, of Hispanic students, 26
Referral, in screening, 86
Relaxation, 264
Remedial education, 286
Renewal experiences, 267
Renzulli, J. S., 20, 25, 82, 126–127, 155, 163,
   166, 199, 213, 225, 238
Research and Guidance Laboratory for Superior
   Students, 112
Responsibility, Chinese concept of, 184. See
   also Shared Responsibility Model.
Responsiveness, of learning environment, 263,
   308
Revol, S. K., 248
Revolving door model, 24, 166
Reyna, 42
Reynolds, C. R., 97
Richert, E. S., 159, 215
Riles, W., 230–231
Rimm, S. B. 28, 29, 30, 98, 213, 215, 220
Rivera-Martinez, C., 60, 61
Rocco, Hilary de, 17
Rodriguez, L. S., 37–40, 64, 69, 70–71, 73,
   298
Roedell, W. C., 30
Rogers, K. B., 94
Rogers, Will, 79
Rokeach, M., 210–211
Role models. See also Models.
   American Indian, 130, 147
   Asian-American, 180, 207
   Black, 229, 251–254
   Hispanic, 63–64, 71, 73
Ronvik, Richard W., 281–284, 286, 287, 288,
   289, 290, 291, 300, 305, 306
Rosier, F., 23
Ross, H. L., 223
Rothbaum, F. M., 150
Rough Rock, AZ., 76
Rowan, C. T., 251
Rueda, R. S., 64
Ruiz, Richard, 60–65, 68, 69, 70, 71, 72, 73,
   298, 304, 305
Ryba, K., 243

S

St. Marie, Buffy, 79
Sanborn, M. P., 112
Santos, R. A., 165
SAT. See Scholastic Aptitude Test.
Sato, I. S., 30
Schierbeck, H. M., 76
Schiever, Shirley W., 285–292
Schofield, W. N., 23

Scholastic Aptitude Test (SAT), 169, 177, 217,
   231
Schulkind, C. R., 52
Scollion, R., 117
Scollion, S. E. K., 117
Scott, K. P., 276
Screening and Instructional Program, 5, 6–13
Screening
   of American Indians, 86–88
   of Asian-Americans, 155–156
   of Blacks, 215–217, 232–234
Scruggs, T. E., 94
Search phase, 6–12
SEBS. See Stallings' Environmentally Based
   Screen.
Self-concept and Motivation Inventory, 159
Self-concept
   of American Indians, 107–112
   of Blacks, 248
Self-contained classrooms, 247–248
Self-Determination and Education Assistance
   Act, 76
Self-Directed Learning model, 126, 131
Self-monitoring, 268
Self-paced instruction, 186
Seltzer, A., 251
Sensory function, 260
Sequoya, 79
Set criteria, in identification, 24
Shade, B. J., 223
Shared Responsibility Model
   for Blacks, 261–268, 270, 283, 289, 290
   for Hispanics, 30
Sharp, A., 251
Sheldon Jackson Boarding School, 121
Shorter, E., 248
Showers, B., 140
Shuy, R. N., 21
Simon, S., 31
Singing games, 234
Sisk, Dorothy A., 128–132, 144, 145,
   146–147, 148, 251
Skills
   assessment of, 126
   basic, 46, 54–55
   coping, 31–32
   development of, 267–268
Skupaka, B. M., 134
Skutknabb-Kangas, T., 21
Sleeter, C. E., 277, 278
Smart, L., 219
Smith, L., 25
Sociograms, 235
Sociometric evaluation, 156
Solomon, I. D., 195–196
SOMPA. See System of Multicultural Pluralistic
   Assessment.
Sparling, S. S., 30, 259–274, 282, 288, 289,
   290

Special education
  for Asian-Americans, 179–181, 194
  on Indian reservation, 77–78
Specificity, of identification, 95–96
Spencer, J., 2
SPM. See Ravens Standard Progressive Matrices.
Staffing
  in American Indian programs, 139–140
  in Hispanic programs, 32
Stallings, C. J., 218
Stallings' Environmentally Based Screen (SEBS), 218
Standardized testing. *See* Testing.
Stanford, B., 51
Stanford-Binet, 175, 218, 234
Stanford, C., 51
Starnes, W. T., 220
Start, K. B., 237
Stedman, R., 129, 131–132
Stephenson, W., 85, 110
Stereotyping, 202–203
Stern, J. D., 75, 77
Sternberg, R. J. 94, 223, 224
Stodolsky, S. S., 170
Structure of Intellect model, 126, 131
Students. *See special groups, e.g.,* Asian-Americans.
Success, for Blacks, 229
Sue, D., 154, 165
Sue, D. M., 165
Sue, D. W., 154, 165
Sue, S., 169
Sullivan, A. R., 24
Summer Career Institute, 35
Suzuki, B. H., 169
Swain, M., 29
System of Multicultural Pluralistic Assessment (SOMPA), 67, 219
Szasz, M. C., 76

T

Taba, Hilda, 47, 126, 127
Talent
  defined, 93–94
  recognition of, 87–88
Tanaka, Kazuko, 149, 174–178, 201, 202, 203, 204, 205, 206, 207
Tannenbaum, A. J., 213, 218
Tao, Terrence, 170
Task involving context, 265–266
Taylor, C. N., 215
Taylor, Calvin, 131
Teachers
  selection of, 122
  students knowing, 279–280
Teaching
  of American Indians
    at home, 122

  modalities of, 126–127
  models of, 131
  multisensory approach of, 124
  role of, 111,
  strategies of, 122–125
  of Asian-Americans
    programs for, 170–173
    recommendations for, 195–196
    strategies for, 175–177, 185–187
  of Blacks, strategies for, 271–274
  of Cantonese, 182–188
  expectations of, 64–65, 302–303
  of Hispanics
    role of, 48–51
    strategies of, 44–48
  role models in
    American Indian, 130, 147
    Hispanic, 63–64, 71, 73
Teaching Models in Education of the Gifted (Maker), 125
Tension reduction, 264
Terman, L., 213
Testing
  of American Indians, 144
  of Asian-Americans, 157–160, 165–167
  bias in, 82–83
  of Blacks, 226–236, 286–287
  diagnostic, 88
  of Hispanics, 25–26, 70
  instruments for, 296
  overreliance on, 203–204
  procedures in, 295–296
  validity of, 309
Thinking Course for Juniors (de Bono), 274
Thinking function, 260
Thompson, S. H., 30
Thoreau, Henry David, 128
Thorpe, Jim, 79
Throssell, Stanley G., 113–115, 298, 299
Tidwell, R., 42
Time, Indian concept of, 121–122
Tizard, J., 23
Tom, Y. H., 259
Tonemah, S., 75, 77, 79, 80, 81, 92, 94, 96–97, 98
Tonkin, H., 103
Torrance, E. Paul, 35, 87, 95, 98, 177, 207, 215, 224, 259, 270–274, 286, 287, 288, 289, 290, 301
Torrance Tests of Creative Thinking (TTCT), 98, 159, 167, 217–218
Toukomas, B., 21
Toys, educational, 234
Training
  basic skill, 46, 54–55
  inservice, 199
  institutional, for Blacks, 229
  leadership, 45–46, 54
Treffinger, D. J., 126–127, 221, 223, 225

Trevino, D., 46
Tribal survival, 144–145
Tsang, S. L., 169
TTCT. See Torrance Tests of Creative Thinking.
Tucson Unified School District, 2, 42
Two Tribes Project, 108–111

U

Udall, Anne J., 24, 41–59, 68, 69, 70, 72, 73, 302
Underachievement, academic, 198
Uniqueness, of programs, 308–309
Urban Associates, 170

V

Validity, 309
Values
  awareness of, 187
  cultural, 133–135
Valuing experiences, 267
Van Sant, S., 254
Van Tassel-Baska, J., 217, 226

W

Walther, K. P., 46
War Department (U.S.), 76
Ward, V., 170, 238
Watanabe, C., 151
Weaknesses
  Asian-American, 205–206
  Black, 289
Webb, J. T., 20
Wechler, D., 66, 97
Wechsler Intelligence Scale for Children—Revised (WISC-R)
  for American Indians, 97
  for Asian-Americans, 167, 175
  for Blacks, 216–217, 234, 249
  for Hispanics, 66
Weiner, G., 262
Weiss, 305, 306
Weisz, J. R., 150
Welch, G. E., 117
Williams, B. P., 85
Williams, F. E., 98
Wing, L. C., 169
WISC-R. See Wechsler Intelligence Scale for Children—Revised.
Witty, P. A., 217
Womble, S., 219
Wong, O. K., 198, 202, 205, 206, 207, 300
Wong, Sally Young, 182–188, 205, 206, 207, 300
Wong-Fillmore, L., 23, 198
Woo, Elaine, 179–181, 201, 202, 203, 204, 205, 206, 298
Wood, T. C., 259, 260
Wooster, J., 218
Word, C. O., 259
Work ethic, 183–184
Wright, Frank Lloyd, 180
Wu, J.-J., 35
Wyatt, G. E., 166

Y

Yamamoto, J., 165
Young, J., 170
Yu, K. H., 165

Z

Zaffron, R., 251
Zanna, M. P., 259
Zappia, Irene Antonia, 19, 69, 70, 72, 73, 294

THE EDITORS
AND CONTRIBUTORS

C. June Maker, Ph.D.

Dr. Maker is Associate Professor of Special Education at The University of Arizona in Tucson. She is responsible for the development and coordination of graduate degree concentrations in education of the gifted and advises students at the masters, specialist, and doctoral levels. She has been active in the National Association for Gifted Children (NAGC), The Association for the Gifted (TAG), and the World Council for the Gifted and Talented (WCGT), serving as chair of various committees, an officer in TAG and NAGC, and on the board of directors of NAGC.

Her publications include books on the topics of gifted handicapped, curriculum development, and teaching models in education of the gifted. She is series editor for *Critical Issues in Gifted Education* and has authored numerous chapters and articles. She currently serves on editorial boards for three journals in education of the gifted.

International cross-cultural experience and recognition include development of a summer program for educators and researchers from the United States and Mexico interested in giftedness in Hispanic students. She has received a Fulbright scholarship enabling study and advisement to universities and public schools in Mexico and currently is principal investigator in a study of the problem-solving process of bilingual and limited English proficient Hispanic children and adults. She has assisted the Navajo Nation in development of a school for gifted students.

In the past, she has been a teacher, a regional supervisor for a state department of education, an administrative intern in the federal office for the gifted, and an assistant professor at the University of New Mexico. She has consulted with numerous local school districts, state departments of education, and other public and private agencies, both in the United States and in other countries. Her educational background consists of degrees in education of the gifted and related areas from the University of Virginia (Ph.D.), Southern Illinois University (M.S.), and Western Kentucky University (B.S.)

Shirley W. Schiever, Ph.D.

Dr. Schiever is currently coordinating a research project at The University of Arizona, which has the long-term goal of developing an observational tool to help identify students who are gifted in one or more intelligences, regardless of ethnic or cultural background. Dr. Schiever has taught in the regular classroom and a resource room for gifted students, as well as coordinating a district-wide program for gifted students and being a curriculum specialist. The school districts in which she has been employed have multi-ethnic populations, and serving these students has long been of special interest to her. Shirley is a past president of the Arizona Association for Gifted and Talented and a member of the curriculum committee of the National Association for Gifted Children. Other professional affiliations include the Council for Exceptional Children, The Association for the Gifted Division; the World Council for Gifted and Talented Children; the Arizona Alliance for Math, Science and Technology in Education; and the Association for Supervision and Curriculum Development. Her publications include journal articles, chapters in edited books, and curriculum materials.

Alexinia Young Baldwin, Ph.D.

Dr. Baldwin has taught gifted elementary school students. She is the author of the *Baldwin Identification Matrix* and several publications on gifted students from minority populations. Dr. Baldwin is past president of The Association for the Gifted (TAG), and she has served as associate editor of the *Exceptional Child*. Presently, she is an Associate Professor at State University of New York at Albany.

Clarissa Banda, M.A.

Ms. Banda is coordinator of the gifted program at Schurr High School in Montebello, California. She has taught English, humanities, and bilingual classes for gifted as well as other students, and she is active in professional organizations concerned with the gifted and gifted Hispanics.

Leland Baska, M.M.Ed., M.Sci.Ed.

Mr. Baska has varied professional experiences in music and education. He has been a band director, counselor, school psychologist, and psychologist exclusively for programs for gifted students. After 27 years with the Chicago Public Schools, Mr. Baska is now with the Williamsburg, Virginia, Public School system.

Ernesto M. Bernal, Ph.D.

Dr. Bernal is a former classroom teacher of the gifted, school administrator, and director of service projects and development programs for bilingual and gifted students. His areas of expertise include bilingual education, bilingual special education, education of the gifted, psychometrics, and program evaluation. Dr. Bernal currently serves as Director of Research at the Center for Excellence in Education at Northern Arizona University, Flagstaff, Arizona.

Charmaine Bradley, M.A.

Ms. Bradley is an Acoma Pueblo/Navajo who is pursuing a doctoral degree in education of the gifted and talented at Texas A&M University. She has taught language arts and has been a counselor at a community school and for a tribal project. Ms. Bradley presently is co-director of a mentorship project for minority students.

Deena Lyn Brooks, M.A.

Ms. Brooks is an educator who presently is principal of Willow Creek Elementary School in the Cherry Creek School District, Colorado.

Jocelyn Chen, Ph.D.

Dr. Chen has been a teacher, learning consultant, and psychologist for educational institutions and private industry. She is currently a psychologist in Bethlehem, Connecticut.

Barbara Clark, Ed.D.

Dr. Clark is a professor in the Division of Special Education at California State University, Los Angeles, where she coordinates graduate programs in the area of education of the gifted. She has taught preschool children on television and both regular and gifted students at the elementary level. Dr. Clark is a prolific author and is active in local, state, national, and three international organizations that support and advocate for gifted and talented individuals.

Leonora (Nora) M. Cohen, Ed.D.

Dr. Cohen has taught gifted children and coordinated the Mentally Gifted Program in Philadelphia. She is currently an assistant professor at the University of Oregon's Talented and Gifted (TAG) Institute, where she teaches a wide variety of courses related to education of the gifted.

Doris Jefferies Ford, Ph.D.

Dr. Ford is the Assistant Vice-President of Academic Affairs and Affirmative Action at The University of Arizona, Tucson. She has held faculty positions at several universities and been a juvenile court psychologist. Dr. Ford is a successful adult by any standards, and as a successful Black adult she has made a unique contribution to this volume.

Mary M. Frasier, Ph.D.

Dr. Frasier has worked closely with Dr. Paul Torrance, and she is developer and director of the Torrance Center for Creative Studies. Additionally, Dr. Frasier is an associate professor and coordinator of the graduate program for education of the gifted and talented at the University of Georgia. Her research interests are the identification of gifted children from minority populations and counseling for the gifted. She is active in national organizations for the gifted and serves on the editorial boards of several professional journals.

Rosina M. Gallagher, Ph.D.

Dr. Gallagher was born and raised in Mexico. She is on the faculty of St. Augustine College in Chicago, Illinois, an institution founded to serve Hispanics. She has been an evaluator of bilingual educational programs and has worked with gifted students from a variety of minority populations in the Chicago Public Schools. Dr. Gallagher is also involved in developing the Community Language Learning Approach to second language acquisition.

Leslie Garrison, M.S.

Ms. Garrison teaches in the Anchorage Multicultural Gifted Program, and her responsibilities include testing, developing curriculum for, and teaching students from more than ten different cultures. She also has worked as a lecturer and consultant in the fields of education of the gifted and culturally different students.

Karlene R. George, M.Ed.

Karlene George is a professional trainer and consultant in education of the gifted, who lives on the Port Madison Reservation in Suquamish, Washington. She and her husband, who is chairman of the Three Bands of the Klallam Tribe, are active in local and national projects that contribute to education of American Indians. Ms. George became committed to improving educational opportunities for American Indian students at the age of 18 when she served as a summer school teacher's assistant. She has been a teacher of gifted students, a curriculum coordinator, supervisor of teachers, and director of several federally funded projects for American Indian students, including a project focused on special services for gifted students. She has presented at local, state, national, and international conferences on the subjects of education for gifted students and related areas of education.

Carl A. Grant, Ph.D.

Dr. Grant is a professor in the Department of Curriculum and Instruction and Chair of the Afro-American Studies Department at the University of Wisconsin at Madison. His research interests include school life and race, class, and gender for teachers, students, and administrators.

Chris Hasegawa, M.A.

Mr. Hasegawa has taught science and math at the middle and high school levels. He is a doctoral candidate at the University of Oregon, where he teaches courses and works on a grant concerned with drug education for beginning teachers.

Sandra N. Kaplan, Ed.D.

Dr. Kaplan is Associate Director of the National/State Leadership Training Institute on the Gifted and Talented. She has served as an international and national consultant to state departments of education, regional centers, and local school districts and as an adjunct instructor to universities throughout the country. Dr. Kaplan has authored and co-authored articles and books in general education as well as education of the gifted. Her background in curriculum development, instruction, and programs for the gifted results from the knowledge and experience gained as a classroom teacher of the gifted and as an administrator of programs for the gifted in the public schools.

Robert J. Kirschenbaum, Ph.D.

Dr. Kirschenbaum has worked with emotionally disturbed American Indian youth and directed a special education program for a school district on the Navajo Reservation in Arizona. He also has taught and conducted research on migrant, Chapter I, and special education students. Dr. Kirschenbaum is currently a school psychologist for the Tolleson School District in Tolleson, Arizona.

Margie K. Kitano, Ph.D.

Dr. Kitano is currently Associate Dean for Research and Faculty Development in the College of Education at San Diego State University. Formerly, she was department head of Special Education/Communication Disorders at New Mexico State University, where she directed the university's preschool for gifted children since its inception in 1982.

Paul D. Larson, Ph.D.

Dr. Larson is the Assistant Superintendent for the Steamboat Springs Public Schools in Colorado. He has taught and has been an administrative assistant and a principal at the elementary school level. In addition, Dr. Larson has been a K–12 director of student programs and a college instructor.

Diane Montgomery, Ph.D.

Dr. Montgomery is principal of a private school for gifted children in Oklahoma City and consultant and evaluator of Explorations in Creativity for the American Indian Research and Development. She is past president of the Oklahoma Association for Gifted, Creative, & Talented, Inc. Dr. Montgomery has been a teacher of the gifted, the director of research for Oklahoma State University Medical School, and served as a consultant for the development and evaluation of programs for gifted American Indian students.

Judd Perrine, M.A.

Currently, Mr. Perrine is District Advisor for programs for the gifted in the Los Angeles Unified School District. In this capacity, he supervises 112 schools in East Los Angeles. In addition, he is Director of the Conservatory of Fine Arts, a Saturday instructional program operated by the Los Angeles School District. In the conservatory, approximately 300 children identified as gifted in the areas of voice, drama, dance, and the visual arts receive instruction from master teachers and professionals in the arts. Mr. Perrine also has been a teacher of the gifted in East Los Angeles and is bilingual in English and Spanish. He serves on the board of directors of the California Association for the Gifted (CAG) and is chairperson of the CAG Inquiry Committee on the Hispanic Gifted Child.

Anita Bradley Pfeiffer, M.Ed.

Anita Pfeiffer is a Navajo educator from Kayenta, Arizona, and an associate professor in multicultural teacher education in the Department of Curriculum and Instruction at the University of New Mexico in Albuquerque. She also is working on her doctorate in education of the gifted. Because of her interest in gifted, talented, and highly motivated students, she was co-founder of the Navajo Academy, a contract school operated by the Navajo nation for its gifted students. Currently, she serves as an officer of the board of trustees for the Navajo Academy. Prior to joining the faculty at the University of New Mexico, she served as principal of Rough Rock Demonstration School, the first contract school, and as director of teacher education for the Dine bi Olta Association. In 1986, she received an award for her outstanding contributions to Navajo education, and in 1987 she received the Tanner Award presented by The University of Arizona for her outstanding contributions to American Indian education.

Honorable Lina S. Rodriguez, J.D.

Judge Rodriguez is one of the few female Hispanic judges in the country. She is a judge to the Pima County Superior Court and an active leader in the Tucson, Arizona, community. She has served on boards of directors for several community and professional associations and has made numerous speeches and presentations. Former experiences include being a teacher of writing and language arts, a law clerk for the public defender's office, and an attorney/shareholder with a law firm in Tucson. She has received several awards and scholarships and was nominated for the 1982 YMCA Woman of the Year Award.

Richard W. Ronvik, M.A.

Mr. Ronvik has been the Director of Programs for gifted and talented for the Chicago Public Schools for the past 20 years. He was a student of Paul Witty's at Northwestern University where he received his undergraduate and graduate degrees. Mr. Ronvik served as an English consultant to the Chicago Public Schools and taught a one-year television course in English literature for the school system in cooperation with CBS. He currently serves on the Talent Search Advisory Board for the Center for Talent Development at Northwestern University.

Richard Ruiz, Ph.D.

Dr. Ruiz received degrees from Harvard College (language and literature) and from Stanford University (anthropology and philosophy of education). He was a faculty member at the University of Wisconsin at Madison from 1976 to 1985 and is currently a member of the faculty of the College of Education at The University of Arizona. His major teaching and research interests are in the areas of language policy and language planning and in the education of minority groups. Publications on these topics are numerous.

Dorothy A. Sisk, Ed.D.

Dr. Sisk is an internationally known educator who currently serves as executive director of the World Council on the Gifted and Talented and as editor of Gifted International. As professor of education at the University of South Florida, she coordinates degree programs in education of the gifted and directs the Center for Creativity, Innovation, and Leadership. Formerly a teacher of the gifted, and more recently, director of the Federal Office for the Gifted and Talented, her experiences and interests are varied but focus on the development of better programs for the gifted in all parts of the world. She has been an invited speaker and consultant in many countries, including Bulgaria, Portugal, South Africa, Mexico, and Brazil. She is the author or co-author of several books as well as articles on many topics related to education of gifted students.

Saundra Scott Sparling, Ph.D.

Dr. Sparling holds a masters and a doctorate in special education for the gifted. She is Assistant Professor of Elementary Education at California State University–Bakersfield; in addition, she owns and directs Saundra Sparling and Associates, a consulting firm. She is a researcher, author, teacher-trainer, counselor, workshop leader, and the parent of two gifted children. Dr. Sparling is one of the very few Black researchers in the field of education for the gifted.

Kazuko Tanaka, M.A.

For the past nine years, Ms. Tanaka has been coordinator of the program for gifted students in the Montebello Unified School District, a suburb of Los Angeles, California. Prior experiences include teaching in a regular elementary classroom in the Los Angeles Public Schools and teaching in the Montebello program for the gifted. The responses of her two sons (who were attending college at the time the chapter was written) to the educational system have reinforced her views of the importance of special programs for gifted students.

Stanley G. Throssell, B.A.

Mr. Throssell is President of The Quijotoa Company, the publishing company for two American Indian community newspapers, *The Papago Runner* and *The Gila River Indian News*. He is a tribal member of the Tohono O'Odham Nation in Arizona. He has a degree in journalism from The University of Arizona. Additionally, he serves as president of the Indian Management Association, a nonprofit organization that provides business education and business seminars for American Indians, particularly those with business interests on Indian reservations.

E. Paul Torrance, Ph.D.

Dr. Torrance is Alumni Foundation Distinguished Professor Emeritus at the University of Georgia. He founded the Future Problem Solving Program and the International Network of Gifted Children and Their Teachers. He also started the Torrance Creative Scholars and Mentors Program. He is author of *The Torrance Tests of Creative Thinking*, more than 30 books, and over 1,500 articles. His articles, books, and tests have caused many significant changes in the identification and education of gifted and creative learners of all ages. He is known particularly for his emphasis on finding giftedness and creativity in people of all economic and ethnic backgrounds.

Anne J. Udall, Ph.D.

Dr. Udall teaches gifted students with learning disabilities in a program she developed and had refined during the past seven years. In addition to this program, which is located in an inner city magnet school in Tucson, Arizona, she has developed an enrichment program for Hispanic students with high potential. Her research and writing have been focused on the development of metacognitive thinking skills, teacher and peer referral of Anglo and minority students, and programs for learning disabled gifted students. Dr. Udall's leadership activities also include consulting, presenting at a variety of conferences, and serving as an officer in state and national organizations.

Alan M. Weiss, M.S.

Currently, Mr. Weiss is principal of the New World School of the Arts in Miami, Florida, a unique school (grade 10 through the fourth year of college) resulting from the cooperation of the Dade County Public Schools, Florida International University, and the Miami-Dade Community College, which serves students gifted in the arts. Prior to this appointment, Alan supervised the program for gifted students in the Dade County Public Schools. Past experiences include teaching in and administering a variety of educational programs, primarily at the secondary level.

Pauline Renee Wong, M.A.

Ms. Wong taught 28 years in the Los Angeles Unified School District and two years in the Department of Defense Dependents Schools in Japan. As coordinator of bilingual programs, she implemented a language proficiency program. As advisor and resource teacher she researched, developed, and implemented multicultural and linguistic materials for Asian students. Presently, she is an assistant principal at Gates Elementary School in the Los Angeles Unified School District, a school of approximately 1,200 students, 60% Hispanic and 32% Asian. Gifted students are clustered in grades 3–6.

Sally Young Wong, B.A.

A teacher of sixth grade bilingual Cantonese students, Ms. Wong is coordinator for science and programs for the gifted for the Los Angeles Unified School District. She has taught gifted students for approximately five years, after her graduation from the University of California–Berkeley. Other experiences include District Literature Cadre, CORE Literature Cadre, Nuclear Age Issues Cadre, Multicultural Education Cadre, and Title VII Demonstration Teacher. She was Teacher of the Year in 1988.

Elaine Woo, B.A.

Ms. Woo is a native Californian who attended the Los Angeles Public Schools and Occidental College. She is Chinese-American, born in Los Angeles. She graduated magna cum laude with a degree in women's studies. In 1977, she became a feature writer for the *Los Angeles Herald Examiner*, and in 1986, she joined the staff of the *Los Angeles Times*. Since 1986, she has covered educational programs from kindergarten through community college. She has received awards from the National Association of Secondary School Principals and the California School Boards Association for articles about education. Elaine Woo also is a founding member of the Asian American Journalists Association.

Irene Antonia Zappia, Ph.D.

Dr. Zappia is a school psychologist with the Tucson, Arizona, Unified School District. She is part of a bilingual diagnostic team, whose focus is on assessing the achievement, abilities, and other characteristics of students with limited proficiency in English. She is bilingual in English and Spanish and has recently completed a doctorate in educational psychology with an emphasis on assessment of minority students.